THE RISEN PHOENIX

THE AMERICAN SOUTH SERIES

Elizabeth R. Varon and Orville Vernon Burton

EDITORS

THE RISEN PHOENIX

Black Politics in the Post–Civil War South

Luis-Alejandro Dinnella-Borrego

UNIVERSITY OF VIRGINIA PRESS

CHARLOTTESVILLE & LONDON

University of Virginia Press
© 2016 by the Rector and Visitors of the University of Virginia
All rights reserved
Printed in the United States of America on acid-free paper

First published 2016

1 3 5 7 9 8 6 4 2

Library of Congress Cataloging-in-Publication Data

Names: Dinnella-Borrego, Luis-Alejandro, author.
Title: The risen phoenix : Black politics in the post–Civil War South /
  Luis-Alejandro Dinnella-Borrego.
Description: Charlottesville : University of Virginia Press, 2016. |
  Series: The American South series | Includes bibliographical
  references and index.
Identifiers: LCCN 2016001877| ISBN 9780813938745 (cloth : alk. paper) |
  ISBN 9780813938738 (e-book)
Subjects: LCSH: African Americans—Southern States—Politics and
  government—19th century. | Southern States—Politics and
  government—1865–1950. | Southern States—Race relations—
  History—19th century.
Classification: LCC E185.6 .D56 2016 | DDC 323.1196/07307509034—dc23
LC record available at http://lccn.loc.gov/2016001877

Cover art: "Making His First Speech in the House of Representatives,
January 16, 1891," C. H. Warren, 1894. Illustration from John Mercer
Langston's autobiography, *From the Virginia Plantation to the National Capitol.*
(E185.97 .L27 1894, Special Collections, University of Virginia)

To the memory of my grandparents,
who taught me the real meaning of history

José Aníbal Borrego (March 19, 1927–November 29, 2012)
Irma Alicia Gordillo (October 28, 1928–November 6, 2013)

Luciano Dinnella (August 9, 1917–August 31, 2014)
Giuseppina Anna Brusca (October 8, 1918–January 6, 1993)

And to my parents,
Louis John Dinnella and Maria Grisell Borrego,
who have supported me in all my endeavors
and taught me never to lose faith

Hold onto dreams,
For if dreams die,
Life is like a broken-winged bird
That cannot fly.

Hold fast to dreams,
For when dreams go,
Life is a barren field
Frozen with snow.

—Langston Hughes, "Dreams"

CONTENTS

Acknowledgments xi

Introduction 1

PART I

The Crucible of War and Emancipation

1. Democracy of the Dead:
The Roots of Black Politics in the Aftermath of the Civil War 17

2. Ballots, Bullets, and Blood:
Celebration and Militancy in the Postwar South 43

PART II

The Struggle for Interracial Democracy

3. Dark Days: Black Congressmen Confront
the Culture of the Postwar Congress 65

4. The Emancipatory Vision of Civil Rights in America:
Black Policy during Reconstruction 79

5. "Color-Line Politics" and the
Coming of Redemption 113

PART III

The Changing of the Guard

6. The Politics of Uncertainty:
Emigration and Fusion in the New South 139

7. The Last Hurrah: The Demise of Black Politics
and the Rise of the New Order 175

Conclusion 209

Notes 219

Bibliography 257

Index 275

ACKNOWLEDGMENTS

I HAVE ACCUMULATED many debts over the years, and I appreciate the chance to repay some of them here. My adviser, Sheila Culbert, and her wonderful husband, Richard Wright, supported me during my time at Dartmouth College, as did many teachers in the history and theater departments: Craig Wilder, Edward Miller, David Lagomarsino, Walter Simons, Tanalís Padilla, Marysa Navarro, Annalise Orleck, Amy Holzapfel, James Rice, Peter Hackett, Mara Sabinson, and Laura Edmondson. My growth as a historian accelerated at the University of Virginia. Along these lines, I must thank my adviser, Michael F. Holt, and my teachers at the Corcoran Department of History: Peter Onuf, Gary Gallagher, Olivier Zunz, and Mark Thomas. My teachers in the Department of History at Rutgers University were inspiring and helped expand my intellectual horizons. I feel a great sense of gratitude to Seth Koven, Paul Clemens, Peter Silver, Virginia Yans, Donna Murch, David Foglesong, Minkah Makalani, Jennifer Mittlestadt, and Deborah Gray White. My doctoral advisers, Ann Fabian and Mia Bay, read drafts with patience. I also wish to thank my other committee members: David Greenberg, Jackson Lears, and Eric Foner of Columbia University. The department's staff—Dawn Ruskai and Candace Wolcott-Shepherd—helped make my stay at Rutgers enjoyable and incredibly productive.

I must thank the staffs and archivists whom I met in person as I traveled across the South on a whirlwind tour ahead of the aptly named Hurricane Isaac, especially the good folks at the Mississippi Department of Archives and History in Jackson; the Alabama Department of Archives and History in Montgomery; the National Archives and Records Administration–Southeast Region at Morrow, Georgia; the State Records Center and the State Archives of North Carolina (both in Raleigh); and the Virginia Historical Society in Richmond. I'd like to single out Anne L. Webster at the Mississippi Department of Archives and History and LeRae Sikes Umfleet at the State Archives of North Carolina for pulling out all the stops and helping make my research easier than it otherwise would have been.

My research required repeated trips to Washington, D.C., and to New York City. The librarians at the Schomburg Center for Research in Black

Culture at the New York Public Library were incredibly helpful. I also want to thank the librarians at the Manuscripts Division and at the Newspapers and Current Periodicals Reading Room of the Library of Congress in Washington, D.C. At Howard University, I greatly appreciated help from Ida E. Jones and Joellen ElBashir of the Manuscript Division of the Moorland-Spingarn Research Center. Finally, Tab Lewis at Archives II in College Park, Maryland, suffered through what must have seemed to be mind-numbingly vague citations of Treasury Department records. At the National Archives and Records Administration Center for Legislative Archives, Richard McCulley, Richard Hunt, Christine Blackerby, and Allison Noyes put up with me as an undergraduate intern and provided insightful research opportunities. Richard McCulley has remained a steadfast friend and advocate, always willing to talk shop with me over coffee or lunch during several of my visits to Washington. Christine Blackerby generously gave me access to her invaluable research on black congressional policy.

Funding for this project was made possible by a fellowship from the Rutgers University History Department, as well as generous Summer Research Grants provided by the department via the Andrew W. Mellon Foundation. The Jacob K. Javits Fellowship Program of the U.S. Department of Education provided much financial support, and I wish to thank Sara Stark, Carmen Gordon, Harvey Waterman, and especially Simona Turcu. I also thank the Social Science Research Council Mellon Mays Graduate Initiatives program for its small grants that helped keep me afloat during my research; specifically, I am grateful to program director Cally Waite and especially Adam Radwan. I would not have benefited from this support had it not been for the Mellon Mays Undergraduate Fellowship Program.

I must thank an amazing group of mentors, historians, and old friends, including: Louis Moore, John Domville, Elizabeth Terry, Kiran Parkhe, Matt Maccani, Iden Sinai, Will Kurtz, Peter Cruz, Stacy Sewell, Anthony Troncone, Stephanie Jones-Rogers, Pat McGrath, Ben Resnick-Day, Christina Chiknas, Adrienne Harrison, Gretchen Heaton, Adam Wolkoff, Matt Loprieno, Paul Hartung, Steve Olszowy, Tom Hazlett, Frank Seuffert, Thomas (Jong-Hun) Nah, and Bobby Davies. Brian W. Johnson was always willing to drop whatever he was doing to take me and my family to Kennedy Airport. I also thank my brothers and sisters in the Neocatechumenal Way—the Third Community of Our Lady of Mount Carmel in Ridgewood, New Jersey.

Special thanks are reserved here for my second family—Mark and Tara Hart and company (Joseph, Sarah, John Paul, Catherine, Patrick,

Simon, and Monica). As always, I must thank my catechists from back home—Mike, Ann, Bob, Joan, Stefano, Elizabeth, and Fr. Kevin Waymel. I must also thank a few others: Faith (Brancale) Jablonsky; Emma Seuffert; Josephine Perez; Ken Quintilian; Marianne Titus; Joan Clifford; Bob and Mary Allison; Avilio and Yamilka Genao; Jack, Joan, and John Craig; Auxiliary Bishop Peter Baldachinno of Miami; Fr. Ivan Sciberras; Fr. Sean Manson; Fr. Raul Silva; and the pastor of Mount Carmel, Fr. Ronald J. Rozniak. Finally, Fr. Tony Medeiros's patience was legendary, and I am deeply thankful for his support throughout the process. Several seminarians at the Redemptoris Mater Seminary of Boston put up with this project in various ways; I single out here Leonardo Moreira, Mauricio Acosta, Kevin Pleitez, Vincenzo "Vinnie C" Caruso, Mateus Oliveira Martin, and *el revolucionario*—my good friend Fernando Vivas.

An earlier version of my work on John Mercer Langston appeared in the *Virginia Magazine of History and Biography*. I thank Graham T. Dozier and Nelson D. Lankford for granting me permission to use material from this article in the book. My previous work on Josiah Walls was originally published as Chapter 3, "Manhood and Freedom in the Sunshine State: Josiah Thomas Walls and Reconstruction Florida," in Matthew Lynch, ed., *Before Obama: A Reappraisal of Black Reconstruction Era Politicians*, Vol. 1, *The Life and Times of John R. Lynch and His Political Contemporaries* (Santa Barbara, Calif.: Praeger, 2012), 65–98. I must also thank Matthew D. Lynch and ABC-CLIO (Praeger Publishers), especially Suzanne Paris and Jeff Clerk, for allowing me to use material from my chapter.

My editors at the University of Virginia Press—Elizabeth Varon, Richard Holway, Anna Kariel, Morgan Myers, and Mark Mones—were excellent and professional in shepherding this project forward. I'd like to thank the two anonymous reviewers for their wonderful comments and suggestions, which helped to make the manuscript substantially better and clarify many of my ideas. I have also benefited from an extraordinary personal editor, Bruce Barron, who has looked at multiple drafts of this project, pushed me to strengthen my prose and tighten my ideas, and offered invaluable advice, encouragement, and sound editorial suggestions that have made this a better book. Robert Burchfield put the finishing touches on this book in the final stages of editing. Finally, I cannot overlook José Lopez-Isa, who bears significant responsibility for this mess—he gave me my first history book when I was eight.

I dedicate this book to my grandparents and my parents. On the Cuban side, José Aníbal Borrego and Irma Alicia Gordillo did much to raise me as I grew up in Ridgefield Park, New Jersey. They, along with my Italian American grandparents, Luciano Dinnella and Josephine Brusca, sparked my first true love of history by regaling me with stories of little towns in Sicily, Mussolini's Italy, the famous sword from Pepe Botellas's Napoleonic army, José Martí, and fleeing from Castro's revolution in Cuba. All four of them taught me to appreciate the most important moments in our families' history. I must thank my uncle Humberto Borrego, who housed us on several occasions during trips to Georgia, and my cousins Humbertico and Maria Borrego (and their daughter, Marcela), as well as Carlos Borrego, Sebastian Borrego, Nayla Borrego, my tía Chacho and my late tío Allan, and my cousins from Newark—Allancito and Yudit Machado and their children, Allan and Alina.

My parents have been the two most important supporters in my life. My father, Louis John Dinnella, read more versions of this book than he cares to admit. His editorial prowess, good humor, and interest in the success of this project made it enjoyable and saved me from many costly mistakes. My mother, Maria Grisell Borrego, has patiently listened to my ideas and offered several crucial insights that have made this a better work. My parents' love and support for me and my work has served as a model for the kind of life that I hope to lead. They raised me with an appreciation for literature and stories, which form the basis of any historian's task. My father generously prodded me by exposing me to his form of "classical education," having me read the classics of literature and art, and I am thankful for the many stories he shared with me from his vivacious life, most of which began with the stirring words, "When I was in Colombia, South America . . . " My mother exerted a different sort of force, providing me with books to nourish my soul as well as my mind and exposing me, ever so gently, to the Bible, which equally contributed to my growth as a historian.

Finally, all thanks go to Jesus Christ, who puts into perspective, in so many different ways, what life is really all about. Through his death and resurrection, Christ has saved me from my sins and given me a new life in him. That fact has enabled me to endure the ups and downs of this process and is more important than any historical endeavor I could ever undertake.

THE RISEN PHOENIX

INTRODUCTION

B Y DECIDING to run for reelection in November 1878, black South Carolina congressman Robert Smalls took his life in his hands. Laura M. Towne, a white Northern teacher, former agent of the Freedman's Bureau, and a close friend of Smalls, described the situation in her diary: "Political times are simply frightful. Men are shot at, hounded down, trapped, and held till certain meetings are over, and intimidated in every possible way. It gets worse and worse as election approaches." She quoted the words of a local newspaper: "In order to prevent our county falling into [Republican] hands, *any* measures that will accomplish this end will be justifiable, *however wicked* they might be in other communities."[1]

When Smalls attended a Republican rally in the small town of Gillisonville, South Carolina, no sooner had he arrived at the meeting with forty men than "eight hundred red-shirt men, led by colonels, generals, and many leading men of the state, came dashing into the town, giving the 'real rebel yell.' . . . Every few minutes a squad of three or four would scour down street on their horses, and reaching out would 'lick off the hats' of the colored men or slap the faces of the colored women coming to the meeting. . . . This made the colored men so mad that they wanted to pitch right into a fight with the eight hundred, but Robert Smalls restrained them, telling them what folly it was."[2]

The red-shirted men demanded equal speaking time with Smalls at the event. When he refused, their leaders gave him ten minutes to think about his decision. He went into a local store with his forty men "and drew them all behind its counters. They had guns. [Smalls] told them to aim at the door, and stand with finger on trigger, but on no account to shoot unless the red-shirts broke in. Meantime, when the ten minutes were over, the outsiders began to try to break down the door." The armed whites called to Smalls and threatened to set fire to the building with him inside it. They began to shoot repeatedly through the windows and walls.[3]

But Smalls had reinforcements on the way. Upon seeing that Smalls's life was threatened, those blacks who had come to the meeting raised "the alarm in every direction, and in an incredibly short time the most distant parts of the county heard that their truly beloved leader was trapped in a house surrounded by red-shirts, and that his life was in danger. Every colored man and woman seized whatever was at hand—guns, axes, hoes, etc., and ran to the rescue." Within a short time "a thousand negroes were approaching the town, and the red-shirts thought it best to gallop away." As Smalls stealthily took a train back to his political base in Beaufort, at every station "they met troops of negroes, one and two hundred together, all on their way to Gillisonville to the rescue." Towne concluded that it was unlikely that Smalls would be harmed "unless he is elected . . . when I do not think his life would be worth a button."[4]

The sheer outpouring of support and bravery that Smalls received from his constituents testifies to the electrifying effect that high-ranking black politicians could have on their communities. In an era characterized by a largely one-sided campaign of white violence and intimidation against African Americans, this episode, showing an unusual reversal of roles as blacks sent whites fleeing, suggests that the black community had not been shattered and vividly illuminates the significance of black political leadership in the post–Civil War South. Despite innumerable challenges and dangers, black congressmen who represented districts in Southern states from 1870 to 1900 bravely articulated the desires not only of black constituents in their own districts but of blacks across the nation. In so doing, they foreshadowed future civil rights struggles that would culminate in the election of America's first black president in 2008.

Black Congressmen: Bold, Determined, and Effective

On one level, *The Risen Phoenix* is a book with six black Southern congressmen, from various social and regional backgrounds, at its heart. But this book is more than a combination of six biographies. It is also a study of black politics that draws on those biographies to illuminate broader themes. In other words, while there is a set of main characters, these congressmen's activities and ways of defending black equality cannot be divorced from the electoral campaigns, regional developments, violence, and events that are interwoven with their life stories. The focus on these six men does more than simply describe their *individual* struggles on behalf of their constituents; it also highlights an important piece of the *collective* struggles of all African Americans to gain meaningful freedom in the wake of emancipation.

By focusing on six congressmen, their careers in Washington, and how they interacted with their constituents in the South, I take a substantially different approach from Philip Dray's pioneering work, *Capitol Men* (2008). Dray covers all twenty black congressmen and two black senators who served between 1865 and 1900 (though the bulk of his interest is in the Reconstruction period). Although he effectively examines the contours of black political achievements, his Washington-centered focus keeps him from digging deeply into the policy motivations of black congressmen, nor does he provide much context regarding the grassroots nature of black political motivations. Meanwhile, Douglas R. Egerton's stimulating *The Wars of Reconstruction* (2014) examines some of the same congressmen as I feature here, but his account encompasses a wider range of figures in the black community (especially veterans and activists); I too consider the wider black community, but primarily to explain how individual black congressmen interacted with and responded to the concerns of their constituents. In effect, I am merging the individualistic approach favored by Dray with the broader collective view that Egerton sets forth.

I selected six congressmen from across the South on whom enough documentary evidence was available to permit me to examine their careers and policies thoroughly and assess how their efforts related to the desires of their constituents. The backgrounds of these black congressmen varied considerably, reflecting a broad spectrum of their community. Four of them were born into slavery. Three gained access to formal education: Virginia's John Mercer Langston and Alabama's James Thomas Rapier (both born free), and George Henry White of North Carolina. Two were veterans of the Civil War: Robert Smalls of South Carolina and Josiah Thomas Walls of Florida. Mississippi's John Roy Lynch was a self-made man who showed great political skill in taking advantage of the opportunities afforded to blacks following the defeat of the Confederacy. All were committed to the Republican Party and represented a rural and formerly enslaved constituency. These six individuals belonged to various Christian denominations, and most were connected to black fraternal orders, especially the Prince Hall Freemasons.[5]

These men consistently defined the black struggle for freedom in terms of blacks' service and sacrifice during the Civil War, viewing this wartime service as the basis for their equal rights as American citizens; for most of them, their Civil War experience played a critical, formative role in their rhetoric and political stances.[6] They used their positions to protest against the widespread anti-black violence and intimidation that were hallmarks of the postbellum political era. Black congressional leaders also believed that they represented not only their districts but all blacks across the country. In their speeches they articulated their constituents' desire for desegregation, access to education, and federal protection of their civil and political rights.[7] They echoed the larger black political culture prevalent across the South by embracing a language and political imagery that engaged in sarcasm, farce, and manipulation. They also emphasized American nationalism while championing a broad view of American citizenship and black equality.

Moreover, these leaders linked black citizenship with a distinctly black vision of manhood. As the historian Craig Thompson Friend noted, the Civil War shifted traditional ways of viewing gender. Reconstruction brought about "a new purposefulness" that "characterized definitions of manliness." Along these lines, blacks could also participate in what had once been a traditional white male political world. Like their white counterparts, black congressmen embraced a balance between the image of the restrained "Christian gentleman" and the masculine martial ideal. Though these images emerged among white men in the South, black leaders engaged in much the same sort of discourse on manhood, but for different purposes. In arguing for Charles Sumner's 1875 Civil Rights Bill, black congressmen called upon the Christian sentiments of their white Democratic counterparts while emphasizing that they should be treated as "men" and not as "brutes." Likewise, black leaders and their constituents continually linked black military participation in the Civil War with their participation in civil government. These sentiments permeate the rhetoric of black congressmen throughout the nineteenth century, reflecting many of the strategies employed by the black community to survive and thrive in the wake of the dislocations wrought by the Civil War.[8]

Nor did black congressmen or their Southern constituents operate in a vacuum. As the historian Stephen Kantrowitz illustrates, the Northern black community spent much of the antebellum period honing its strategies in the abolitionist movement and articulating the vision of black citizenship that would find its fullest expression in the postbellum South. Moreover, several black congressmen, particularly Langston and Rapier, spent significant time in the North. They (along with their constituents) adopted many of the tactics and goals that their Northern black counterparts had long articulated, but they did so on their own terms and contributed their own unique experiences to this older black political culture. This should not be understood as a one-sided process. As Reconstruction unfolded, considerable exchange of ideas and tactics took place between black activists across the Mason-Dixon Line.[9]

Domestic developments were not the only concerns on the minds of black political leaders. These congressmen also looked abroad, either by traveling to foreign locales (as Rapier did, in his capacity as Alabama's state commissioner to the 1873 Fifth World's Fair in Vienna) or by speaking out on behalf of embattled peoples seeking freedom from tyranny (like Walls, who openly supported Cuban insurgents' struggle for independence during the Ten Years' War, 1868–78). This consciousness of a world beyond the Union parallels long-standing concerns for countries that offered counterexamples to the slave regime in the American South, such as Haiti and the British West Indies.[10]

Several critical points are relevant to understanding the rhetoric and imagery of black congressmen.[11] These men were brutally frank in discussing the perpetuation of violence, which they blamed on their white Democratic opponents. Though they cited specific examples of disfranchisement, intimidation, and violence, they were less likely to share their own personal experience of such practices. This reticence seems to have reflected their awareness that such descriptions provided ammunition and even joy to their white opponents, who often reveled in instances of black humiliation and intimidation.[12]

Certainly, African American congressmen knew that they were performing for a larger audience, one that transcended white and black Southerners and often encompassed the nation as a whole. Indeed, African Americans were scrutinized not only by their opponents in the South but also by their white allies in the North, who paid close attention to such developments as allegations of black political corruption in South Carolina. Northern perceptions of the Palmetto State's government significantly influenced support for Reconstruction governments across the South; in fact, as the historian Heather Cox Richardson pointed out, South Carolina "became the stage on which Northerners examined an America controlled by workers."[13] In order to safeguard the gains made during Reconstruction, black politicians had to find ways to articulate the goals of their constituents without unduly alienating their white counterparts. To do so, they often emphasized "colorblind" issues that benefited both black and white Southerners. For example, Langston urged white Southerners to establish literacy tests that would be

implemented equally among all citizens in order to avoid disfranchising
white voters, and Lynch downplayed the belief that African Americans
desired social equality with whites.[14]

The rhetoric and policy agendas of black congressmen form one piece of
the intricate puzzle of postbellum black political life. Another key piece are
the strong ties between black congressmen and their formerly enslaved constituents. Smalls's frightening experience during the 1878 elections provided
only one example of these connections. In 1888, when Langston faced a divisive independent campaign that pitted him against the white Republican
establishment and national black leaders such as Frederick Douglass, his
followers did not withdraw their support. Black pastors urged their congregants to support Langston and threatened to expel any man who thought
of voting against him. Of course there were occasions when black constituents disagreed with and opposed their elected leaders, but examples such
as Langston's 1888 campaign illustrate the strength of the bonds between
black congressmen and the communities they represented.

These six congressmen, along with their black colleagues in the House
and Senate, articulated the dreams and desires of newly freed slaves. They
also strove to serve the needs of their districts by fighting for patronage
and other government improvements. They influenced national debates
on policy initiatives regarding race relations and black civil and political
equality, taking on the mantle of national black political leadership while
simultaneously listening to and embracing the aspirations of the local black
electorate. They were definitely effective in articulating their constituents' interests, although they were certainly less effective in implementing
those interests.[15] They were often unable to preserve the civil and political
rights gained during the era of Reconstruction. The forces arrayed against
them—Northern indifference, bisectional racism, Southern violence and
intimidation—were too great even for the most able of them to overcome.

Some critics contend that these black leaders were out of touch with
the fundamental concerns of their constituents. Charging them with class
interest, elitism, and blind loyalty to the Republican Party, these critics
argue that black politicians failed to address the economic plight of black
constituents and that some were willing to sacrifice black civil and political
equality in favor of preserving their own positions of power.[16] This critique
is largely unjustified. While black congressmen could not stave off the demise of Reconstruction or the erosion of civil rights by the century's end,
they did represent the political and economic concerns of their constituents. In fact, they could work within the new political arena made possible

by emancipation and civil war precisely because they connected with and responded to the black community. Black leaders represented their constituents not only on race-specific issues like civil rights but also by working to provide valuable internal improvements to their states, addressing the personal concerns of individuals, and dutifully presenting petitions written by both their white and black constituents.

Along these lines, *The Risen Phoenix* attempts to bridge the gap between two ways of viewing black politics: Eric Foner's assertion that blacks saw themselves as American citizens and the "proto–black nationalist" perspective championed by Steven Hahn. While Foner emphasizes that blacks desired to form part of the American body politic, Hahn focuses on grassroots perspectives and argues that many blacks considered themselves more as a "a new political nation." He provides an excellent analysis of grassroots transformations among newly freed slaves, demonstrating the fundamental awareness and political acumen present within the black community as early as the antebellum period and especially at the moment of emancipation.[17]

But Hahn's perspective may understate the extent to which the vast majority of African Americans embraced their role as American citizens. Certainly, long before the Civil War, black slaves were aware of the major issues of their day. However, it is perhaps overreaching to label slaves as a "genuine political people" who engaged in "pre-political" acts of "resistance" and "accommodation." Fundamental differences exist between individual or collective acts of resistance and more formal political involvement. Black life in antebellum Northern cities, though certainly circumscribed by a system of "Jim Crow" racism in the North, provided much broader avenues for blacks to organize, meet as a community, and protest against white racism in ways that would have been unthinkable throughout the antebellum South. While the free black community in the North engaged in more formal political struggles against slavery and racism, black slaves in the South engaged in a struggle for their basic human rights against the control and indignities visited upon them by white planters. In the wake of emancipation, however, African Americans transformed their previous struggle for human rights (the right to be treated as human beings rather than as chattel property) into struggles for economic autonomy, civil and political equality, and education—all of which entailed formal political involvement and participation. With emancipation, blacks across the South exercised their right to vote, to serve in various political offices, and to participate openly in the body politic of the American nation.[18]

Black leaders were deeply immersed in local concerns in rural areas as well as in the towns and cities. They were not constrained by their region and engaged in a push-and-pull with their Northern and Southern counterparts, white as well as black. For this reason, it is impossible to tell the story of these black congressmen without delving into developments that may initially seem unrelated to their lives and careers—accounts of black politics at the grassroots level, developments in the larger national political arena, and the perspectives of black men and women who braved violence and intimidation to assert their rights to civil and political equality. The story of black congressmen's drive for reform is also a story of how they differed from unelected black activists like Frederick Douglass and Ida B. Wells—how they made their way from centers of reform to the center of national political life as representatives in Congress. Therefore this is a story as much about black activism in general as about the larger claims, embraced by black congressmen, to full citizenship in a newly interracial American republic.

All the officeholders featured in this book, at one point or another, broke ranks with the Republican Party and supported political alternatives, from fusion voting deals with Democrats to strategic alliances with agrarian parties such as the Readjusters, the Greenback Party, and the Populist Party. Several embraced emigrationism (that is, encouraging blacks to leave the South) and challenged the views of prominent black leaders such as Frederick Douglass, Timothy Thomas Fortune, and Ida B. Wells. Black congressmen knew that, to be effective, they needed to consider the views of both their white allies and their opponents, and they were willing to cooperate with whites in order to achieve their goals of civil and political equality. The evidence suggests that black congressmen navigated the tumultuous political climate in the South and fought for the rights and freedoms of their black constituents by embracing a balancing act between forces demanding immediate equality (the overwhelming majority of freedmen) and those who favored patience and accommodation with whites (mostly white Southern Republicans and transplanted Northern Republicans). These strategies should not be viewed as evidence of the ineffectiveness of black leaders or of their inability to connect with and respond to the desires of their constituents. Rather, they reflect black congressmen's understanding of the necessity of compromise and their prudence in abandoning an all-or-nothing approach in favor of negotiating the best result possible for their constituents.

Black Political Leadership: Informal and Formal Activists

The best-known nineteenth-century black leaders were a group of informal political activists: the towering figure of Frederick Douglass, fiery journalists like editor Timothy Thomas Fortune of the *New York Age* and antilynching activist Ida B. Wells, and the turn-of-the-century leaders who tried to fill the void left by Douglass's passing, namely Booker T. Washington and, later, W. E. B. Du Bois. While scholarship on black leaders emphasizes the importance of national figures like Douglass, Wells, and Du Bois, it fails to take into consideration the complexity and fluid nature of black political leadership that emerged after 1865. Indeed, a generational divide emerged as older black elected officeholders such as Langston, Lynch, and Walls came into conflict with rising younger black leaders like Wells and Fortune by the close of the century.

While black elected officials were responsive to their own state's concerns, in numerous instances their influence far transcended their role in their own congressional districts. For example, Langston was considered second only to Frederick Douglass in influence among blacks long before he became a congressman. He spoke and traveled widely, often sharing the stage with Douglass. Both Smalls and White were well known outside their respective states and published in national periodicals like the *North American Review* and the *Independent*. White, Smalls, Langston, and Lynch were often the subject of news stories in the national black press. Rapier, though he had a less prominent national profile, was called to testify before a congressional committee as an expert on black migration in the early 1880s. Walls was mentioned in the black press until his political demise obliterated any influence that he had enjoyed beyond Florida. In any case, all black congressmen emphasized in their speeches that they represented not only their own district's constituents but all African Americans throughout the United States, thus explicitly positioning themselves as national spokesmen for their race.

National black political leaders did not seek to exclude informal political actors, journalists, and unelected activists like Douglass or Wells. In fact, all six black congressmen featured in this study relied heavily on networks of informal political activists and journalists. For example, Rapier and Walls attended a national convention on black civil rights on December 9, 1873, where they listened to delegates from twenty-five states. The memorial produced from this convention directly influenced black congressmen's attempts to secure passage of Sumner's 1875 Civil Rights Bill. Likewise, at the height of resurgent violence across the South around the mid-1870s, outgoing Alabama congressman James Rapier held a strategy meeting at his rooming house in Washington, D.C., with a wide assortment of national and local leaders including Douglass, Langston, former acting governor P. B. S. Pinchback of Louisiana, Arkansas judge Mifflin Wistar Gibbs, labor organizer George Thomas Downing, Alabama editor Philip Joseph, and North Carolina's George W. Price Jr., a Union naval veteran and local state politician.[19]

This pattern continued through the remainder of the century. North Carolina's George White met with Ida B. Wells to discuss the subject of compensation for the family of a recently lynched federal officeholder. White also provided asylum to Alexander Manly, beleaguered editor of the *Wilmington Daily Record*, employing him as his secretary.[20] When White came to the conclusion that migration was the only solution for his people, he worked with a company, backed by Booker T. Washington, to create an all-black town in Cape May, New Jersey, for displaced black refugees of Southern violence.

In all these instances, black congressmen were at the center of black political power and served as important mediators for their community. This observation does not minimize the importance or influence of unelected national leaders like Douglass, Wells, or Washington. But formal political power provided black congressional leaders with access to some of the levers of power, the public square, and a large measure of influence on the national stage that they otherwise might not have attained by remaining informal activists. The defining characteristic of national leadership for these black congressmen lies in their early careers, which paralleled those of better-known informal leaders like Douglass and Wells but distinguished them from white congressmen and senators. Smalls escaped from slavery by delivering himself and his crew to a Union naval blockade, thus setting up his meteoric rise as a Union naval war hero and a politician. Langston became a major voice for abolitionism in Ohio and later traveled throughout the South as a general inspector for the Freedmen's Bureau, helping to establish branches of the Union League. The varied experiences, generally marked by considerable suffering, of Smalls, Langston, and their black colleagues enabled them to speak for all African Americans in a language that emphasized emancipation, the Civil War, and economic and political equality—all messages that resonated with the majority of blacks across the nation.

The story of post–Civil War American politics remains incomplete without an understanding of how these black politicians behaved under extremely trying circumstances and reacted to situations facing the black community. *The Risen Phoenix* illuminates the strategies employed by black congressmen and how they meshed with the motives and desires of their newly freed constituents. Black congressmen embraced their role as citizens rather than thinking of themselves and of their constituents as a nation apart. They viewed themselves as national leaders and were viewed as such by large portions of the black electorate. Finally, in order to achieve their goals and defend the interests of their constituents, black congressmen practiced a balancing act, attempting to tiptoe between forces encouraging measured, gradual reform and black demands for immediate civil and political equality.

Stories of Celebration, Struggle, and Sorrow

The Risen Phoenix charts the rise and fall of national black political leadership between the Civil War and the turn of the century in seven chapters across three parts. Part One introduces the emergence of black politics after the momentous passage of the Thirteenth Amendment and the conclusion of the Civil War. Chapter 1 begins with black troops' participation in the Union war effort and the shift toward emancipation, both factors that were central to the formation of a dynamic African American political community in the opening years of Reconstruction. Five of the six congressmen featured in this study (Langston, Smalls, Walls, Rapier, and Lynch) rose to prominence in this period, seeking to find their place in the postwar world as politicians, newly freed citizens, or spokesmen for the desires of their race. Chapter 1 focuses on their wartime careers, their early struggles and observations among the freedmen, and the emergence of a political culture defined by a "democracy of the dead"—that is, rooting the black political experience in the fires of black patriotism and military service in the Civil War. It also begins to explore the rise of anti-black violence throughout the South.

Chapter 2 shifts the focus to ground-level struggles between 1867 and 1871, looking primarily at the impact of anti-black violence in the early years of Reconstruction. It juxtaposes celebratory scenes following the passage of the Fifteenth Amendment with the initial, often violent struggles between white Southerners and newly freed black men and women. Descriptions of a series of riots and outbreaks of violence during these years, especially the "Meridian Riot" in Mississippi, set the stage for a discussion of black congressmen's responses and their participation in intense debates over political strategy and whether African Americans should remain committed to the party of Lincoln.

Part Two examines the various ways in which black congressmen fought to establish a truly interracial democracy in the United States. Chapter 3 describes the culture of Congress that newly elected black leaders confronted upon their arrival in Washington. After reviewing the corruption and inefficiency that pervaded the post–Civil War Congress, it analyzes how black congressmen functioned in that context and the issues they chose to pursue.

Chapter 4 reviews how violence at the local level affected black congressmen's advocacy for the Ku Klux Klan Act, adopted on April 20, 1871, and their engagement in debates over the Amnesty Act of 1872. It then shows how the strands of violence, amnesty, and civil rights came together by the mid-1870s in debates over Sumner's Civil Rights Bill. Here the focus is squarely on the rhetorical strategies embraced by Walls, Langston, Rapier, and Lynch in their struggle to secure stronger guarantees of civil rights for their embattled constituents.

Chapter 5 considers the shifting currents of black policy as Reconstruction gave way to Redemption. In the wake of the passage of the Civil Rights Act of 1875, renewed white violence overtook the South, and Northerners increasingly began to turn their backs on the freedmen's plight. I trace how black congressmen responded to this violence, advocated educational opportunities, and (beginning with a major black convention in 1876) became open to innovative and independent political strategies. This openness to new alternatives other than loyalty to the Republican Party set the stage for engagement in fusion voting (that is, alliances with renegade Democrats) and the black embrace of emigration. The chapter concludes with a look at the Redemption-era spike in violence in Southern states like Mississippi and South Carolina and at black congressional opposition to the Federal Electoral Commission, which was appointed to decide the victor of the disputed 1876 presidential election.

Part Three features the substantial changes in black political leaders' tactics in the aftermath of Redemption. Chapter 6 follows two emerging alternative political routes, fusion voting and emigration, and how these approaches began to split apart the cadre of black leaders, informal activists, and politicos who had formed a relatively united front since the Civil War. By 1879, blacks were clashing in heated intraracial rhetoric and policy disagreements. Within this context, major black political actors reevaluated their priorities. Some, like Rapier, moved fully into the emigrationist camp. Others, like Lynch and Walls, embraced fusion and biracial alliances with mixed results. This chapter also introduces North Carolina congressman George Henry White and discusses several electoral campaigns, especially Langston's tumultuous run for the Fourth Congressional District seat in Virginia.

Chapter 7 examines the final attempts by the remaining black congress-men to preserve some degree of autonomy for their constituents. The narra-tive recounts the rise of lynching and the responses of leaders like Langston and White to these atrocities. Both Langston and Smalls attempted to put forward their own responses to disfranchisement in Congress and at the local level, but unsuccessfully. I then feature tragic and decisive develop-ments in North Carolina, including the violent overthrow of the interra-cial Fusionist government there and the Wilmington Riot of 1898. The resourceful White's ever-changing strategies failed to stave off the inevitable destruction of black political autonomy, leading him — the last remaining black member of Congress — not to seek reelection in 1900.

The book's epilogue jumps forward to three much later incidents that provide a retrospective on the struggles and the significance of nineteenth-century black congressmen in the South. The most recent of these is an address by President Barack Obama to black elected officeholders, in which he reflected on the progress of black politicians and referred directly to Congressman George Henry White. I also recount the tense correspon-dence between Lynch and the prominent white historian James Ford Rhodes over the legacy of Reconstruction, and I conclude with a story that Harlem Renaissance poet Langston Hughes told about an event in the life of his great-grand-uncle, John Mercer Langston. These anecdotes capture the unyielding resilience displayed by black political leaders in the late nine-teenth century as they blazed a trail for the civil rights activists who would come after them.

The Unknown World of Black Politics

The Risen Phoenix argues that many late nineteenth-century African Ameri-can leaders embraced a careful balancing act between accommodation and demands for immediate civil and political equality. This middle ground was often characterized by duplicity, dissembling, and skilled manipulation. As such, it is critical to read between the lines of what specific congressmen were arguing at particular moments in time.[21] What black congressmen could do during Reconstruction was different from what they could do in the latter part of the century. Black leaders were constrained as much by the changing situations they confronted as they were by generational and policy differences among their own ranks. Although this emphasis on flexible strategies alone does not account for the nature of black political involvement after the Civil War, it illuminates how black politicians represented their constituents.

Other scholars have generally just scratched the surface of a complex political world. They have not yet taken what the historian Simon Schama called "the broken, mutilated remains" of the past and restored them "to life in our own time and place."[22] This study attempts to do that by examining the activities of black congressmen to determine how they related to black constituents in the late nineteenth century. Freedmen and freedwomen played a critical role in maintaining and furthering the struggle for civil and political equality in the wake of emancipation.[23] But how black political leaders responded to the needs of the active and vibrant communities that helped to elect them has been largely overlooked.

Black congressmen successfully articulated and represented the interests of the black community, even if they were unable (due to forces beyond their control) to implement the policy concerns of their constituents. Only by examining the behavior and strategies of black politicians can one hope to grasp the political culture and the distinctive political consciousness that emerged among African Americans in the postwar period. This study, by placing six black congressmen within the context of their communities, illuminates the intimate connections between the black community and its political leadership in the American South. It shows that, far from being out of touch or unrepresentative of their constituents, African American politicians were fundamentally committed to defending and securing the rights and aspirations of all their constituents, especially the newly freed slaves.

PART I

*The Crucible of War
and Emancipation*

1

Democracy of the Dead

The Roots of Black Politics in the Aftermath of the Civil War

THE COMING OF THE Civil War brought the hope of liberation to thousands of African Americans enslaved across the South. However, for a daring young slave named Robert Smalls, it became much more: it was his pathway to heroism and to prominence as a black leader.

Smalls was born in Beaufort, South Carolina, on April 5, 1839, the son of Lydia (a slave) and an unknown white man, quite possibly his mother's master, John K. McKee. He grew up in a region where 83 percent of the population consisted of slaves, and he witnessed the atrocities of the system personally. When John McKee died, his son Henry inherited Smalls and his mother, subsequently hiring out the twelve-year-old Smalls to his sister-in-law in 1851. Smalls worked many different jobs, ranging from hotel waiter to lamplighter. He met and fell in love with another slave, Hannah Jones, a hotel maid, and the two married on December 24, 1858, when Smalls was seventeen years old.

The young Smalls earned money on the side in hope of eventually purchasing his family's freedom. He did this in spite of the South Carolina law, passed in 1820, that flatly banned private manumission and self-purchase. Smalls made a contract with his wife's owner to purchase his wife and child for $800.[1] When the Civil War began, one of his jobs was as a pilot on a Confederate transport, the *Planter*. After hostilities broke out, Smalls saw an opportunity for freedom. Increasingly, federal forces had begun to see the untapped potential in attacking the institution of slavery directly and creating black regiments. On May 9, 1862, Union general David Hunter declared as free all slaves throughout Florida, Georgia, and South Carolina to encourage black enlistments. This pronouncement moved Smalls to act decisively. On the morning of May 13, 1862, Smalls, along with other enslaved deckhands, boldly navigated the *Planter* into the Union naval blockade outside the port of Charleston and handed the boat over to Union forces.[2]

In addition to delivering him from slavery, Smalls's heroic act made him famous in the Northern press and in the black community. Indeed, members of the Fifty-Fourth Massachusetts Colored Regiment were well aware of Smalls's pluck and courage and were concerned about his welfare. Writing from Morris Island, South Carolina, on November 28, 1863, Corporal James Henry Gooding of the Fifty-Fourth Massachusetts Colored Regiment recounted rumors of the capture of a former Confederate warship and its crew: "It is reported that the steamer Planter, the same [Confederate ship] which was run out of Charleston harbor by Robert Smalls and turned over to the blockade fleet [the Union navy], has been captured by the rebels. The pecuniary loss will not be very great, as the vessel was an old cotton dragger; but the fate of her crew may be a rather serious matter, for all except the captain and engineers are contrabands [former slaves], and some of them formed a part of the crew who ran away with her. It is believed that Smalls was piloting her on the occasion." The rumors of the capture of the *Planter* proved to be false. Nevertheless, it is notable that Gooding and his counterparts were aware of Smalls's heroism and particularly concerned about his fate.[3]

Less than a week after Gooding wrote his letter, on December 1, 1863, Smalls was still piloting the *Planter* (now part of the Union navy) under the command of Captain James Nickerson. Their assigned task was to traverse the Light House Inlet, near Secessionville, South Carolina, to take rations from Folly Island and resupply troops stationed in Morris Island. But when the Confederate batteries at Secessionville recognized their former ship, they began to shell the *Planter*, attempting to prevent its escape. The fierce shelling left the upper decks of the *Planter* badly damaged, but the ship remained stable.

Out of fear, Nickerson ordered Smalls to beach the ship and surrender to the Confederates. Smalls would have none of that order. He shouted back at Nickerson: "If we surrender, you—a white man and an officer—will be treated as such. But the rest of the crew are all runaway slaves. If the Confederates catch us, they will give us no quarter!" After stressing his own confidence in piloting the ship to safety, Smalls shouted again, "Not by a damn sight will I beach this boat."

Nickerson became so frightened by the intensity of the shelling that he fled to the ship's coal bunker to hide from the noise of the Confederate assault. Smalls wasted no time in taking command. Calling another crewman to take the wheel briefly, he raced to the coal bunker to latch the door shut so that Nickerson could not get out. He then returned to the wheel and guided the ship safely back to Morris Island, where he explained to his superiors all that had occurred. Nickerson was immediately dismissed by Admiral Samuel DuPont, and Smalls was promoted to the rank of captain.[4]

Smalls's fame opened the door for him to embark, after the Civil War, on a political career that would take him all the way to the U.S. Congress. Nor was he the only future black congressman to demonstrate wartime valor in South Carolina. When the Third Infantry Regiment, United States Colored Troops (USCT), participated in the capture of Fort Wagner and Fort Gregg in August and September 1863, among them was a twenty-year-old ex-slave named Josiah Thomas Walls. He was born on December 30, 1842, near Winchester, Virginia; his prewar status remains a mystery, but much of the evidence suggests that he was born in slavery.[5] He may have been impressed into Confederate military service for a time, but there is no doubt that he was a private in the USCT's Third Infantry Regiment by July 1863. His unit was poorly trained and did not see much action; nevertheless, he participated in the assaults that ultimately captured Fort Wagner. By 1864, Walls was transferred to the Thirty-Fifth USCT, positioned in Picolata near St. Augustine, Florida. When the war concluded in 1865 he was still stationed in Florida, where he would settle and launch his political career.

Smalls and Walls represented one segment of an emerging group of black leaders who seized the opportunities afforded to them during the Civil War. As they rose to prominence in the postwar years, they would be joined by others who came from different walks of life, had attained a high level of education, and had participated in the abolitionist movement—men like John Mercer Langston of Virginia.

Langston was a peculiar representative of black Americans. Born free on December 14, 1829, in Louisa County, Virginia, he was the youngest son of Captain Ralph Quarles, a Virginia planter, and Lucy Jane Langston, Quarles's half-Indian and half-black former slave mistress. Langston went to great lengths to emphasize that the views of his white father, "with regard to slavery and the management of slaves upon a plantation by overseers, were peculiar and unusual."[6] In fact, Quarles freed Lucy Langston, and the former master and the former bondswoman had a genuine love for each other. When Lucy died she "was borne thence to her grave by his side."[7] Though Langston's parents died when he was a young boy, their legacy to him was immense. Indeed, his inheritance from Ralph Quarles eventually aided him in his efforts to secure a seat in Congress.

Langston was well educated and accomplished. Leaving Virginia at an early age, he settled in Ohio, graduating from Oberlin College in 1849 and receiving a master's degree in theology there in 1853. In 1854, following the completion of his schooling, Langston was admitted to the bar. While in Ohio he became one of the first African Americans to hold elected office, winning an 1855 election to serve as a township clerk. He married Caroline Matilda Wall on October 25, 1854, and the couple had five children.[8]

Langston quickly became a major black figure in the abolitionist movement and in Ohio's nascent Republican Party. His speeches encapsulated "his own hard earned definition of liberty and the responsibilities his guardians and teachers on both sides of the color line had taught him to associate with it." Self-reliance formed a crucial part of his ideological framework. Oberlin inculcated several crucial traditions into Langston, among them evangelical Christianity, republicanism, abolitionism, and self-restraint—all of which permeate his later political rhetoric. Within the larger abolitionist movement, Langston worked without the help of white abolitionists with whom he little contact and less communication. This was due in part to the racism of some of his white abolitionist counterparts. Having a long-standing commitment to the abolitionist movement, Langston worked diligently to help the Union free the slaves, recruiting men for the Fifty-Fourth and Fifty-Fifth Massachusetts Colored Regiments and the Fifth Ohio Colored Regiment.[9]

In November 1864, Langston, along with other black activists, traveled to the Brooklyn Navy Yard to tour a recently commandeered Confederate vessel. When they arrived, Captain Robert Smalls welcomed them aboard and personally gave them a tour of the *Planter*, which he had delivered to Union forces two years earlier. Langston was so taken by Smalls that he formally congratulated him, "in behalf of the Colored of the United States," for his services to the cause of black freedom and equality. Two days later, Langston accepted an invitation by Smalls to join him and thirteen other black activists for Sunday dinner.[10]

This interaction between an uneducated ex-slave and a cultured free black abolitionist on board a stolen Confederate steamship illustrates the two strains of black leadership that would emerge during and after the Civil War. Ex-slaves of modest means and polished, college-educated black leaders could join together in the struggle against racism and for political equality. In so doing, leaders like Smalls and Langston could not help but look back to their own particular experiences, and to those of their forebears, for guidance in the struggle for interracial democracy and black equality.

Manhood and Citizenship Rights

Once the Civil War began, a shared discourse of black citizenship rights that emphasized martial valor and manhood quickly took shape. This understanding of black masculinity had to contend with the dominant white discourse on blacks. As the historian Kirk Savage asserts, for American men, "to be a soldier in battle was the ultimate test of manhood, because men battled men and battled to the death," but the test endured by the male slave "was even more profound since his masculinity has been denied from the outset. To become a Union soldier, then, was not only to acquire the conventional trappings of masculinity, but to resist the very institution that suppressed [the slaves'] masculinity in the first place."[11]

This emphasis on black manhood is clearly visible in the careers of major political leaders like Smalls and Walls. Considering Smalls's valiant service in the Union navy and Walls's participation in subsequent assaults on Fort Wagner and Fort Gregg in South Carolina, it is not surprising that these former veterans would describe blacks' wartime exploits as evidence of their masculinity. Their focus on black manhood as displayed in battle was consistent with a tradition that dated back to the American Revolution and that would flourish again in the late 1890s as African Americans moved to join the military during the Spanish-American War. This tradition, in the version espoused by Smalls and Walls, reflected blacks' deep sense that they had proven themselves worthy of civil rights through their sacrifices on the battlefields of the Civil War.[12]

Prominent black leaders such as Douglass and Langston, along with black veterans like Smalls and Walls, regularly emphasized an emancipationist discourse of manhood. Whether connected with freeing oneself from the chains of bondage or with destroying slavery through military service, this discourse served as a powerful rallying cry for the black community. One well-known example appears in Douglass's 1845 autobiography, in which he noted that his battle with the slave driver Edward Covey "rekindled the few expiring embers of freedom, and revived within me a sense of my own manhood."[13] Indeed, two of Douglass's sons went on to serve in the Massachusetts Fifty-Fourth Regiment (one of them transferred to the Fifth Cavalry). Many other activists had sons and sons-in-law who served in the army, and they endlessly emphasized the connections between emancipation and manhood.

Langston's antebellum experiences also highlight the close ties between black manhood and citizenship rights; in fact, his use of physical force in opposition to prejudice and racism began well before the Civil War. Langston's legal practice initially consisted primarily of representing white Democrats, but he also had black clients. While defending a black man whose daughter had been removed from his custody, Langston got wind of a comment made by a white attorney who asked the black man "whether he had really employed the '*nigger* lawyer' to attend to his case and warned, 'If you have, he will sell you out'; meaning thereby that the colored lawyer would prove treacherous." Langston, unwilling to have his honor slighted by this white attorney, confronted him and, "deeply moved by indignation and anger, administered to him not only a sound slapping of the face, but a round and thorough kicking as he ran crying for help." In another instance, a white attorney insulted Langston during a trial by affirming that he was "talking to a *white* man"; in response, Langston "immediately struck him with his fist, felling him to the floor."[14]

As black leaders entered public office, they continued to emphasize their manhood as part of their wider political rhetoric. This discourse embodied the grounding of African American equality and dignity in their physical prowess, whether displayed on the battlefield or in their willingness to physically challenge their oppressors. For the bulk of emerging black leaders, then, manhood and citizenship were two intertwined claims that undergirded their policy agendas.

Emancipatory Democracy:
Slavery and War in Emergent Black Political Culture

The wartime careers of Smalls and Langston, different as they might be, illuminate the formative experiences that were central to the emergence of black politics in the wake of the Civil War and emancipation. African Americans developed a particular kind of political culture—a "democracy of the dead" that recalled and glorified two stages of black suffering, as slaves and as warriors.[15] In this way, then, African Americans embraced the martial ideal of manhood and incorporated it into their politics as they made their way in the postemancipation American nation.

For most white Northerners, the Civil War was fought primarily to save and preserve the Union.[16] For them, emancipation was largely a military necessity, secondary to the overriding aim of preserving the United States. By contrast, African Americans across the nation understood, from the beginning, that any war waged between the North and the South would inevitably have to confront the thorny issue of institutionalized slavery. Thus the outbreak of hostilities that followed the firing on Fort Sumter in 1861 served as a powerful political catalyst for African Americans. Two distinguishing features marked the emergent black political sensibilities that would soon take center stage in the postbellum Southern political arena.

First, African Americans' understanding of democracy and citizenship highlighted the enlistment of black soldiers, asserting that blacks had earned the right to be free citizens by fighting and dying on the battlefields of the Civil War. During the conflict, blacks proved their manhood in such locations as Fort Wagner on the coast of South Carolina; the trenches of Petersburg, Virginia; and Milliken's Bend in Louisiana. These experiences not only served to shift and, in some cases, challenge prevailing Northern prejudices against African Americans but also provided blacks with a powerful legacy that they could hand down to their descendants. This participation by African Americans in the Union war effort remained a great source of pride for the black community and inspired future political endeavors, from the moment when the first black regiments were mustered through the close of the nineteenth century.

Second, African Americans, especially those who had themselves lived under slavery, could not forget those who lived and died enslaved before them. The newly freed slaves who confronted a war-ravaged Southern landscape in 1865 were not blank slates; rather, their collective experiences under slavery and those of their forebears informed their emerging political sensibilities.[17] African Americans had experienced personally the violence of white men and women; they had seen insurgencies and rebellions crushed and families torn apart by sale at the auction block. These travesties of justice formed lasting bonds within the black community. One result was that resistance against white masters, even if in small forms, became a common part of the slave experience. Nor were these thoughts confined to Southern blacks; they also resonated with free blacks in the North. As Douglass noted in the first issue of the *North Star* on December 3, 1847: "What you suffer, we suffer; what you endure, we endure. We are indissolubly united, and must fall or flourish together." Many free blacks emphasized the shared suffering of African Americans across sectional lines, invoking their experience of slavery or that of their families.[18]

Individual acts of resistance (breaking a plow, deliberately slowing down the pace of work, feigning sickness, or running away) were embraced by the black community throughout the South. Likewise, collective actions (secret assemblies or hidden church meetings on plantations) were important to the health and unity of African American communities. These experiences were etched into the memories of newly freed slaves. They found expression through a wide range of government institutions and in more overt and formal political organizations including the Freedmen's Bureau, the Union League, the postbellum Black Convention Movement, and the first Republican campaigns for elected office in which aspiring black leaders participated.[19]

Antebellum acts of black resistance, both collective and individual, merited the same degree of honor and pride as black military service within the nascent political culture that developed after emancipation. But these acts of resistance could never become explicitly political in a world where white masters held all the cards. Only with the dislocations wrought by the Civil War—only with the death of slavery through the Emancipation Proclamation and the Thirteenth Amendment to the U.S. Constitution—could such experiences transcend their limited influence and be transformed into viable forms of African American politics.

Langston's understanding of these varied political currents within the black community would influence his subsequent articulations of black desires in the wake of emancipation. Shortly after his meeting with Smalls, on December 3, 1864, when a group of African Americans met in the Bethel African Methodist Episcopal (A.M.E.) Church in Philadelphia to "raise subscribers and solicit donations" for an African American newspaper called the *Christian Recorder,* the most noteworthy speaker was "the well-known lawyer of Oberlin," Langston. He made some revealing extemporaneous remarks at the event, stating that "the three things mostly needed by colored men in this land are, first, money—second, cultivation of intellect—third, political power."[20]

With these words a future black congressman set forth a concrete and straightforward vision of what African Americans would need in the aftermath of emancipation. Soon after this event, on January 13, 1865, the U.S. House approved the Thirteenth Amendment. Although the amendment's ratification, formally abolishing institutionalized slavery across the United States, would not occur until December 18, 1865, Abraham Lincoln's reelection in November 1864 had sealed the fate of the Confederacy and the nation's "peculiar institution." As a result, Langston and other blacks, free and enslaved alike, could begin to envision joining the American body politic.[21] Although they might differ as to the best way to gain equal rights as citizens, the majority of African Americans shared a desire for all the privileges then held exclusively by white males.[22]

That new world excluded women of all races from the formal political process. Like many of his counterparts in the abolitionist movement, Langston favored women's rights. Indeed, he had been educated at Oberlin, which was racially integrated, coeducational, and a hotbed of abolitionist and protofeminist sentiments. Early on, however, Langston had to choose between supporting black civil rights and women's rights. As early as 1854, he had presented a petition to the Ohio state legislature demanding rights for "colored people." The legislature refused to hear him, but, as he explained, it spent most of the next morning "listening to a lengthy and elaborate address on woman's rights. It was fit and proper that the Senate should hear this address in regard to woman, and her rights. Against their procedure in this case I have not a single word to offer. I do say, however, that it was equally fit and proper that I should be heard in behalf of the colored people of Ohio, and their rights."[23]

His decision to emphasize black rights and leave women's rights aside manifested itself even more clearly in remarks delivered at the Cooper Institute in New York on February 28, 1865. Drawing on the wellspring of martial imagery that had become a hallmark of emergent black political culture, Langston "demanded the franchise because the colored people were men. They had been overpowered by brute force; but, similar to the Roman slave in chains, they rush out into the arena, and demand before all the people their rights as native born inhabitants and men. They had not called women to the battle field, they had not called boys to the battle field—and the negro had fully proved his manhood there before God and before the nation."

Langston's militaristic rhetoric soared further as he recalled the example of Crispus Attucks (a black victim of the Boston Massacre) to make a larger point about black citizenship claims. "In the Valley of the Mississippi," he said, "are the monuments of the heroism of colored men, and may the last man who sheds his blood in this war—may the last man who falls before the walls of Richmond—be, to the honor and glory of America, a black man." Langston made it clear to his audience that once the war was over, Northerners would need the help of loyal blacks. There would be traitors across the South, he asserted. "You will need the black man with the ballot box as you have with the bayonet, and when you want him you know he is ready to cry, 'Here I am.'"[24] Black women, as the historian Martha S. Jones has illustrated, contributed to this rhetoric by affirming that black military prowess had earned black men the rights of citizenship. Nevertheless, despite his theoretical support for women's rights, Langston believed that, in the wake of the war, he had to privilege black male citizenship over and above the rights of women. Although black military service also enabled women to take on a greater role in the black community, the connection between military service and citizenship rights reinforced sexual differences and weakened women's claims to the franchise.[25]

His sense of the significance of black military contributions may have led him not only to emphasize traditional gender roles but also to actively pursue a place for himself in the armed conflict so that he too could display his manhood. Following his successes as a recruiter, and with the support of Congressman James A. Garfield, Langston sought to be commissioned as a colonel in the Union army. Garfield wrote, on March 28, 1865, that Langston "is an exceedingly fine speaker & has taken an active part in recruiting colored men—He has probably done much more in that way than any Colored Man in the U.S."[26] In making his own case for an army commission, Langston highlighted his service to the Union cause: "Since the outbreak of our terrible Rebellion I have been as actively ingaged [*sic*] in the Recruitment of Colored Troops for the service as a colored man could be. I desire, Sir, to make myself more useful to the Government. I think if I had a respectable rank, in the service, I could make myself of special use in the Recruitment and Organization of colored Troops. I therefore ask to be commissioned as a Colonel, if compatable [*sic*] with the rules and regulations of the service." Perhaps Langston saw service as a common soldier as beneath his status as an educated lawyer and recruiter, hence why he emphasizes himself as "special" and "more useful to the Government."

Regardless of his motivations, Langston did not receive the commission he desired. For several reasons, including racism on the part of government officials who were unwilling to commission more African Americans in the ranks than necessary, Langston received from Assistant Adjutant General C. W. Foster a response stating, "I am directed to say that the recruitment has ceased, and there is no vacancy to which you can be appointed."[27] This rejection did not stymie Langston's desire to serve his newly freed brothers in the South; on the contrary, it may have inspired him to head to the

South and help directly in efforts to better the condition of freedmen and freedwomen.

Langston's subsequent experiences in the South, particularly his work with the Freedmen's Bureau in establishing schools for newly freed blacks, illuminate the emergence of African American politics in the immediate post–Civil War era. In his memoir, *From the Virginia Plantation to the National Capitol* (1894), Langston provided an insightful, third-person account of his journey to the South a quarter-century earlier: "The colored American had hardly been made free, the War of the Rebellion had not been closed, when Mr. Langston commenced his travels among the freed people. Thus he gained broad and minute observation at once of their actual condition and probable future." He also took pains to document his impressions.

As early as 1864 Langston journeyed to Nashville, Tennessee, and then on to Louisville, Kentucky. His observations from Louisville encapsulate the hopes of freedmen in the aftermath of emancipation: "Their condition was not promising, and yet, they moved at once and promptly, in intelligent, earnest and considerate activity, as if impelled and directed by an Allwise Supreme Power." This religious tone pervades his entire description of these Kentucky freedmen. Langston describes a people who were oppressed, but who entrusted themselves completely to God.

In Langston's view, these freedmen and women were nothing less than the embodiment of a holy remnant, a chosen people, guided by absolute faith in God and anchored to the deepest spiritual and moral virtues. With respect to the freedwomen, Langston commented: "No history can be written of those early days of American freedom . . . without large place and truthful mention of the women of the freed classes. They have in their conduct and labors, so far as their race is concerned, emulated largely, the 'virtuous woman' of the Scriptures."[28]

He took great pains to emphasize the central role played by black women in emancipation. Indeed, he stresses that they emulated the model of the "virtuous woman" found in the Bible (perhaps referring to Proverbs 31). The explicit link between black women and virtue cannot be understated. White resistance to black political power often rested on a devious dichotomy that depicted black men as illiterate, unworthy beasts (thus subverting their claims to manhood) while simultaneously painting black women either as angry or as seductive temptresses with loose morals. Langston was well aware of the need both to emphasize black manhood and to defend the moral character of "the women of the freed classes."[29]

Langston's observations are also crucial in understanding his views on the place of religion in the project of racial uplift. Langston made no distinction between the political future of blacks and their spiritual development. The historian Glenda Gilmore helps to explain Langston's views, writing that blacks "saw electoral politics as an aspect of spiritual striving, not as a secular profane activity. Ballots were tools for building an ideal community on earth. The church was a political structure, and politics was a practical means to a religious end. To fail in one was to fail the other."[30] Returning home to Virginia, Langston made use of all the "practical means" at his disposal to unite newly freed slaves with their former white masters. He increasingly viewed education as the key in creating a new biracial polity in the South.

Upon his arrival at Louisa Court House, Virginia, on June 15, 1867, Langston emphasized his potential place as a bridge unifying blacks and whites. He noted how "the whole county had come out, so far as the whites were concerned, to see and hear 'Quarles' boy'; and so far as the colored people were concerned, they had all come to see and hear 'Lucy's son.'" Addressing his fellow Virginians, Langston said he desired "nothing for the negro because he was black, but because he was a man, he would ask everything for him that other men had." Langston's definition of liberty inspired him to emphasize continually that blacks had to "secure character and influence" and employ "these moral levers to elevate [themselves] to the dignity of manhood and womanhood."[31]

Although he did not obtain a commission in the Union army, Langston was undeterred in his desire to support former slaves. Two days after his speech at Louisa Court House, Major General Oliver Otis Howard appointed Langston as general inspector of schools in the Bureau of Refugees, Freedmen, and Abandoned Lands.[32] This post enabled Langston to get a sense of the condition of newly freed African Americans across the South. Drawing on his observations, he helped to form schools, established local Union Leagues, and emphasized that blacks should embrace their status as free citizens by abandoning what he saw as negative behaviors from their time as slaves (such as excessive drinking and smoking).

Writing to Howard from Huntsville, Alabama, on July 30, 1867, Langston could take solace in the overall progress of freedmen. He noted, "I find here no opposition on the part of the former Slaveholders to the Education of the Freedmen. And I find a reasonable amount of determination on the part of the Freedmen, to avail themselves of every opportunity for improvement." Langston continued: "Yesterday I had the opportunity of addressing a very large and attentive audience, of white and colored persons, in this city, and I did not fail to impress upon both classes, and especially the Freedmen, the importance and the necessity of throwing off at once, all the bad practices of slave life and the [inculcation] of sobriety, modulation, and good order in their new relations of Freedom."[33]

These views paralleled those expressed in another letter to Howard four days later, on August 3, describing the conditions of the freedmen in Vicksburg, Mississippi. Langston noted that "the parents of the scholars are not only well disposed towards the teachers now in their schools, and those who formerly conducted them; but I find a settled purpose on their part to educate their children, even if they must make sacrifice and endure hardships to do it. This spirit promises well."[34] Education was rapidly becoming the cornerstone of black life in Mississippi, and blacks throughout the state were doing what they could "to buy sites and to build or aid in building Schoolhouses thereon," displaying "a growing appreciation of education."[35] Young students received instruction in arithmetic, geography, grammar, reading, and writing. Langston was pleased to report that "many of the children are making commendable progress."[36]

In spite of these positive observations among blacks in Mississippi, Langston also expressed his sense of what was and was not acceptable for the development of a virtuous African American character. He wrote that the "expensive, filthy, and blighting habits of using Tobacco and drinking liquor, so common among the Freedmen, as well as all other classes of the people, in the Southern part of the country, prevails [*sic*] to an alarming extent in Mississippi." Langston added emphatically that the state's "poor Freedmen" were spending "thousands of dollars more . . . for these poisonous articles, than for books, or School Houses, or Churches. On this subject however . . . the people are willing to hear, and are teachable; therefore, they are not in a hopeless condition." Langston believed that the solution to these challenges could only stem from divine providence: "Their salvation, in this as in other respects, can be made sure under God."[37]

This mix of genuine concern and elitism in Langston's reports was common among influential black leaders during this period. Indeed, this perspective was central to the kind of black manhood Langston and other leaders envisioned. As Phillip Brian Harper asserts in his study of black masculinity in the twentieth century, the "subscription of black identity itself bespeaks a masculine status because the courage thus to claim social autonomy is precisely what constitutes conventional manhood, no matter what the racial context." In other words, black men linked their own fortunes with ideas regarding civilization and social autonomy, all of which played a significant role in how they articulated conceptions of black manhood. Martial prowess demonstrated on the field of battle was not enough—one also had to combat any weakness within the black community that might leave an opening for attacks by white Southern men, whether they be direct physical attacks, obnoxious provocations contesting the integrity of black men and women, or assaults on the moral character of African Americans.[38]

In spite of this elitism, Langston's reports also illuminate the freedmen's strong desire to secure education and uplift, an aspiration that would play a significant role in the black political culture that emerged in the aftermath of the Civil War.[39] Though Langston claimed that whites seemed amenable to working together with blacks to forge a new order, this was by no means consistently the case, particularly in areas of the Deep South (like Mississippi and Alabama) where slavery had permeated much of society.

"We'se *Made* the White People": Competing Visions of Postwar Citizenship Rights

As early as the close of hostilities in 1865, freedmen's vision of the postwar United States stood in stark contrast to that of their former masters. Writing from Vicksburg, Mississippi, on July 4, 1865, Chaplain James A. Hawley of the Sixty-Third United States Colored Infantry (USCI) shared his observations of the interactions between freedmen and white Southerners with the Mississippi Freedmen's Bureau assistant commissioner: "It might have been supposed that between this place & Jackson nearly every white man would be tolerably well posted as to the relations subsisting between the Freedmen & their former masters, But this seems not to be the fact concerning many of them. & this ignorance not only of the relations of the people but also of current events increases with each remove from these head Quarters."[40] Commenting on the divergent understandings of politics between whites and blacks, Hawley believed that the "sun of freedom [and] intelligence" could not be found among the whites in Vicksburg, but rather among the blacks who "were in advance of their old time masters, in knowledge of their real political situation, which shows how much the prejudices & wishes of the people have to do with their opinions."[41]

Hawley indicated that the vast majority of white planters acknowledged the end of slavery but also wanted their former slaves to "remain '*as they always had done*'"—that is, always laboring on plantations with as little change in their prewar status as possible. He also described the machinations in which whites were willing to engage so as to minimize social change: "Many of the people are taking the amnesty oath, simply to acquire political power to be used, in again reducing the people as nearly to Slavery as possible." Indeed, these white Southerners believed that by controlling the state government, "they hope to use it in the interest of the Planters, as against the free labor of the State. They swear—many of them—to support the government & *the emancipation proclamation,* & then seek to destroy the efficacy of the proclamation, by cruel endeavors to destroy the people for whose benefit it was made."[42]

Especially revealing in Hawley's extended report were his observations regarding the character of emerging political sensibilities among newly freed slaves, particularly in the midst of virulent racism and prejudice on the part of former slaveholders. "In doing justice to the freed people," he wrote, "we have to encounter the prejudices also of Southern people who are set in the notion that negroes will not work, that they cannot take care of them selves, & of course are in the way to temporal destruction." Hawley praised a counterexample to the prejudices of whites, citing the words of an anonymous freedman, a "very bright darkie" from Tennessee, who declared that "we'se *made* the white people." He thought that it would be a pity "if they [blacks] could not support themselves without the white folks to take care of too. He was himself amused at his former groundless fears of the Yankees, & asked many interesting questions concerning the condition & rights of the Freedmen."[43]

The perspective expressed by the anonymous freedman whom Hawley quoted demonstrates that former slaves understood very well the political changes wrought by the Civil War, as well as their place in the new Southern order. Black labor had made white Southern society possible, and, given the restrictions and oppression that had characterized that world, many blacks mistrusted the words and motives of their former owners. The experiences of countless ex-slaves were bound up in a shared understanding of the meaning of the war, one that led many freedmen into sharp disagreement with Southern whites. In fact, the prescient comments of this anonymous "darkie" from Tennessee closely parallel the challenging political environment faced by a future black congressman from Mississippi, John Roy Lynch.

Lynch's experiences as a slave and his service after gaining freedom, as a cook and waiter for both the Union army and navy in the South during the Civil War, contributed to his later political development. Born on September 10, 1847, on Tacony Plantation, Concordia Parish, Louisiana (three miles from the town of Vidalia), he was the son of an Irish-born plantation manager named Patrick Lynch and Catherine White, a slave woman.[44] Lynch's father purchased his "wife" and children, becoming their owner. At his father's death in 1849, ownership of Catherine's family passed to a friend who, rather than honor Lynch's father's desire to free the family, kept them as slaves. This formative experience would have a profound impact on Lynch's future as a politician. His experiences as a slave influenced his future political maneuvering; he knew the limits that existed but was willing to push hard when he thought that he could achieve his legislative goals.

Lynch saw firsthand the ravages of the Civil War as the Union army invaded the Lower Mississippi River Valley. "This was, for him, a war of deliverance," wrote the historian John Hope Franklin, "and when the Union forces approached that area, he joined other slaves in the 'general strike' and in the enjoyment of freedom long before the cessation of hostilities." Lynch would acquire a sporadic and largely informal education. With respect to his occupation as a photographer in Natchez, Lynch wrote, "This employment proved to be the opportunity of my life. It marked the beginning of a somewhat eventful career." Lynch attended a night school established by Northern whites for four months; at the end of that time, he recalled, "I could compose and write a pretty good letter. Composition, grammar, and spelling might have been very imperfect, still it was a letter that could be read and understood." The lack of formal education was not a hindrance for the young Lynch. Indeed, his "occupation happened to be favorable for private study," and Lynch was able to dedicate two to three hours daily to reading and educating himself at his place of business.[45]

The nature and content of this private education were already nurturing Lynch's nascent interest in politics: "Among the books that I carefully read and studied was one on parliamentary law, which I found to be of great advantage to me in after life. I also kept myself posted on the current events of the day by reading newspapers and magazines. I was especially interested in the proceedings of Congress, for it was just about that time that the bitter fight was going on between Congress and President Johnson."[46]

Lynch also benefited "indirectly" from the white public school in Natchez. His office was located close to the public school, and he "could easily hear the recitations that were going on in the school across the way." Eager to receive the same sort of education, he "would sometimes sit in the back of the room for hours and listen with close attention to what was going on in the school. . . . I could clearly and distinctly hear the questions asked by the teacher and the responses given by the class or the individual pupil."

His interest in the material was so profound that Lynch would often lose himself in the lessons, imagining that he was "a member of the class . . . eager to answer some of the questions." From his studio he could see "problems that were on the blackboard that was directly in front of where I was sitting." He concluded that this informal education greatly assisted him. Lynch shared the concerns of many of his newly freed brothers and sisters. He knew their desire to learn, and he shared their desire to obtain independence and autonomy in the new world created by the blood of civil war. Involving himself in the local Natchez Republican club, he was selected to present the club's slate of candidates for county and municipal offices to the military governor, General Adelbert Ames, who was staying in the capital city of Jackson.[47]

Lynch put his education to good use when he met with Ames, who paid close attention as the young photographer "presented as forcibly as I could the merits and qualifications of the different persons whose names appeared on the slate that I placed in his hands." Ames thanked Lynch and said he would consider the candidates. When the nominees' names were released several weeks later, Lynch discovered to his great surprise that his own name was on it, as a prospective justice of the peace. Lynch initially desired to turn down the post but was "reliably informed that I had not been recommended or suggested by any one, but that the governor's action was the result of the favorable impression I had made upon him when I presented the slate referred to."[48] Thus, in 1869 and at age twenty-two, Lynch was nominated for his first political office, giving him a powerful stepping stone from which to launch his future political career. But he would face powerful, sometimes life-threatening resistance along the way. Nor was his experience unique, as the nation came to terms with the revolutionary changes that accompanied the Civil War and emancipation.

Embers of Interracial Violence, Seeds of Black Voting Rights

It was no surprise that former masters diverged from the views of those they had formerly enslaved. But they were not alone. The brave new world inaugurated by the close of the Civil War was also a highly contested and divisive political arena. Lincoln's successor to the presidency, Tennessee Democrat Andrew Johnson, though he seemed interested in punishing former Confederates, rapidly proved himself to be no friend to African Americans. With Congress out of session at the close of the Civil War, Johnson moved to pursue Reconstruction as he saw fit. This amounted to a program of general amnesty for most ex-Confederates, with the unintended consequence of restoring much of the conservative white elite to positions of power. States across the board generally ratified the Thirteenth Amendment, but they passed Black Codes throughout the summer of 1865, effectively replicating the old slave codes and replacing the word "slave" with "freedman" as if the war had altered nothing.

When the Republican-controlled Congress returned, the situation that it confronted was appalling. As scholars such as Hannah Rosen and Elizabeth Varon have demonstrated, most white Southerners did not accept defeat in the aftermath of Appomattox. Rather, they drew strikingly different conclusions from their defeat than did many of their Northern counterparts. Members of Congress were not unaware of these sentiments, and their growing concern with Johnson's approach led Congress to take control of Reconstruction away from the president. Rapidly, Republicans moved to bar newly elected Southerners from presenting their credentials to be seated in Congress. Over the president's veto, Congress passed the Civil Rights Act on April 9, 1866, to protect the embattled rights of blacks in the South. This law recognized all who were born in the United States as citizens, allowing them to enter contracts, file lawsuits, and give testimony in a court of law, but it did not enshrine the right to vote. In June, Congress passed a strong definition of national citizenship rights in the form of the Fourteenth Amendment, but this measure was also silent about suffrage. At this point black citizenship was not defined in terms that included voting.

That mindset was radically altered in the wake of two violent episodes that rocked the nation. On May 1, 1866, in the city of Memphis, a riot broke out between the Memphis police, supported by local white businessmen, and black Union soldiers stationed in and around the city. At least forty-eight African Americans were killed in the riots, and another seventy or eighty were wounded. In addition, whites set fire to ninety-one houses and cabins, four black churches, and all twelve schools that served the African American community. Only a few months later, on July 30, riotous whites confronted a convention of white Republicans and African American supporters who had gathered at the Mechanics' Institute in New Orleans. Local police helped to perpetrate the attack, and by the time federal soldiers arrived, thirty-four blacks and four white radicals had been killed. These riots collectively moved Republicans to accept the necessity of granting blacks the right to vote in order to protect their rights.

Given the inability of Johnsonian amnesty to quell the violence spreading throughout the South, Congress moved swiftly to pass a series of

Reconstruction Acts in 1867. These measures provided for black suffrage, disfranchised former Confederate soldiers and officeholders, and divided the South into five military districts to be supervised by the army. By 1868, the Fourteenth Amendment was finally ratified, protecting guarantees to national citizenship for all. Under the congressional Reconstruction Acts, newly freed slaves registered and voted by the thousands, selecting delegates to attend constitutional conventions across the South that would redraw the contours of Southern social and political life.[49] Many former Confederates were still barred from participating in the political process, but this fact did not guarantee stability or political comity between various white leaders and their newly freed counterparts.

Florida represents an example of the kind of intraparty factionalism and strife that permeated the entire region. Alliances were complex and shifting, and blacks in Florida were not a monolithic unit. Black Republicans regularly clashed with each other. At the outset of Reconstruction in Florida, three separate factions emerged within the Republican Party, and all of them would play a significant role in the future direction of the state's government.

On April 14, 1867, the Union-Republican Club met in the offices of former Confederate soldier and slaveholder Ossian Bingley Hart in Jacksonville, where it drew up and summarily ratified a constitution.[50] This was thus the first meeting of Florida's Republican Party, attended by a wide assortment of members who would go on to cooperate but also to challenge each other in future political contests. Future white governors Harrison Reed and Ossian Hart as well as prominent blacks, including future secretary of state and secretary of public instruction Jonathan Clarkson Gibbs, were among the original signatories.[51] By the time the Republicans came together to draw up a platform, two other factions emerged: the Lincoln Brotherhood (the rank-and-file of which was black but which was led by moderate whites) and the radical Loyal League of America (also known as the Mule Team), which consisted primarily of ex-slaves.[52]

In Florida, as in other parts of the South, political power among black leaders often rested on ministers and military veterans. Allegiances were ambiguous at best, and even within large blocs (particularly religious ones such as the A.M.E. Church) intense and divisive rivalries could emerge. The Lincoln Brotherhood, backers of the head of the state's Freedmen's Bureau, Thomas W. Osborn, drew its support from black Baptists and their congregants.[53] Osborn also relied heavily on some men, such as Harrison Reed, who maintained uncomfortably close ties to Florida's white conservatives.

The faction controlled by the national Republican committee, the Loyal League of America, was led by two whites (Daniel Richards and Liberty Billings) and a black Northerner (William U. Saunders). They relied upon black Methodists for support.[54] Veteran Josiah Walls and Presbyterian minister Jonathan Clarkson Gibbs were also aligned with this faction.

Even whites could shift their allegiances in rapid succession. Florida Loyalists (Unionists), such as Ossian Bingley Hart, were a case in point. Hart demanded black enfranchisement as early as September 1866, but he would also attempt, in February 1868, to undermine efforts by the Mule Team to dominate the writing of the state's constitution.[55] Unlike the planter elite who defended the status quo in Tallahassee, Hart represented the segment of Florida's white population (centered in the northeastern portion of the state, especially around the city of Jacksonville) that had tried to remain loyal to the Union during the Civil War.[56] Thus, from the very beginning of Reconstruction, Florida's nascent Republican Party was rife with factionalism.

The first test between competing factions emerged early in 1868 when delegates met at the state's constitutional convention. Out of forty-six delegates, eighteen (including Walls and Gibbs) were black.[57] Many of these delegates were affiliated with the A.M.E. Church, and most were former slaves. Leaders of the Mule Team quickly seized an opportunity and, on January 20, successfully took control of the convention. The Mule Team promptly adopted rules designed to preserve its power and began the difficult task of drawing up a new state constitution.[58]

Frightened by the increasingly heated rhetoric of their more radical black colleagues, some white delegates concluded that the Mule Team aimed at nothing less than "the positive supremacy of the Colored people throughout the state." These fears prompted whites like Reed and Osborn to reach out to Hart for advice.[59] The two more moderate factions (the Union-Republican Club and the Lincoln Brotherhood) merged and teamed with conservatives in order to blunt the Mule Team by denying black radicals a quorum. When Hart and his associates returned to the constitutional convention in early February, they were joined by several other black delegates. This group successfully wrote a liberal but significantly more reserved constitution for the state.[60] The Mule Team initially refused to give up the struggle against the constitution, nominating its own slate of candidates in case the constitution was adopted. It soon became apparent that the constitution would pass and that it was futile to run against the regular Republican nominees. It appeared, for the moment, that the Osborn faction had carried the day as Harrison Reed won the gubernatorial election and Osborn became one of the state's U.S. senators. Shortly thereafter, Reed appointed Gibbs as secretary of state, and the military veteran Walls took a seat in the Florida state legislature, which would provide the stepping stone for his future career in Congress.

Violent opposition and rampant factionalism were hallmarks of postwar life. Though it seemed that men like Walls and Lynch could make their way through normal political channels, sometimes white opposition took the form of threats of murder and assassination. This would be the experience of a future black congressman from Alabama.

Not a Safe Occupation: James Rapier's Early Political Life

James Thomas Rapier was born free in Florence, Alabama, on November 13, 1837, the son of prosperous free black parents. His father ran a successful barbershop and owned several hundred acres of property. Rapier attended school in Nashville, Tennessee, while staying with his grandmother between 1844 and 1850. Between 1854 and 1857 he drank heavily and lived the life of a gambler on riverboats. Eventually he resumed his education, attending the King School in Buxton, Ontario. He attended a Toronto normal school from 1860 to 1864, gaining a teaching certificate and then teaching at Buxton.[61]

Buxton was a successful black utopian community. Founded by the Scottish Presbyterian minister William King in 1848, it began with only King and his sixteen emancipated slaves but grew rapidly into a large and interracial community. Blacks and whites learned and played together in the school, offering a rare illustration of the potential for a truly egalitarian society. Rapier continued his dissolute lifestyle when he first arrived at Buxton, flaunting the rules by gambling and entertaining "women in the business." He had also stopped attending church at this point in his life. However, in April 1857 he experienced a profound religious conversion, renouncing his earlier ways and committing himself to his studies; for a while he even considered preparing for the ministry. This life transformation would set him on a course to become a major political leader in his native state of Alabama.[62]

Between 1864 and 1865 Rapier returned to the South, where he worked as a correspondent for a northern newspaper. Around this time he also delivered a keynote address at the Tennessee Negro Suffrage Convention in Nashville. By 1866, he had returned to Florence, Alabama, where he rented

Congressman James Thomas Rapier.
(Moorland-Spingarn Research Center, Howard University,
Washington, D.C.)

several hundred acres of land and became a prosperous cotton planter. In 1867, he organized newly freed blacks under the auspices of the congressional Reconstruction Acts, attended the first state Republican convention, and gained election to the Alabama Constitutional Convention.[63]

However, Rapier's early involvement in black politics in Alabama was not an easy task. With the onset of emancipation came the rising tide of white vigilante violence against newly freed blacks and their spokesmen. One illustration of the severity of these hostilities appears in a commentary published on October 20, 1870, in the *Mobile Daily Republican*, a black newspaper. The writer railed against both Ku Klux Klan violence and white Democratic skepticism, attacking the white *Mobile Weekly Tribune* for its portrayal of white vigilantism in Tuskegee, Alabama. The *Tribune* had published a letter from Rev. J. M. Butler to Rev. E. D. Taylor of Mobile discussing a recent violent racial incident in nearby Tuskegee. In response, the *Daily Republican* decried the *Tribune*'s refusal to inform its readers that Rev. Butler, the one man killed, and the four wounded were all black, or that "the 'two churches burned to the ground' were places where *colored people* met to worship the Creator." The *Daily Republican*'s black editors wondered why their white counterparts could "not confess that the Tuskegee outrage is but the type of innumerable similar acts by Democrats formed into bands called Ku Klux." Moreover, the paper was outraged by the *Tribune*'s insinuations that Democrats were not responsible at all: "The *Tribune* certainly does not expect its readers to believe the last part of its article wherein it intimates that these men were employed by Republicans to murder for political capital. The outrage was perpetrated by Democrats, for the purpose of intimidating Republican voters, as the *Tribune* well knows. . . . And yet, when U.S. troops are sent to protect these helpless people from the repetition of such outrages as the one at Tuskegee, the Democratic press cry out against it."[64]

One sobering telegram sent on March 1, 1870, revealed the tenuous situation confronting many Republicans across the state. A teacher named R. Starkweather wrote a terse message to the commanding general of U.S. troops in Alabama, General Samuel W. Crawford: "Guard needed— Civil guard overpowered and prisoner taken out by Ku Klux, our lives in danger—Officer in charge refused to stay."[65] Not surprisingly, Klan violence increased when state elections were in full swing. In the same issue of the *Daily Republican* that covered the Tuskegee Outrage one could find the "Republican State Ticket," including the GOP's candidate for secretary of state, James Rapier (an election that Rapier ultimately lost).

Following the conclusion of the Civil War, Rapier returned to his birthplace in northwestern Alabama. There he participated in politics and campaigned actively for Ulysses S. Grant in 1868. His activism ultimately put his life in danger. When the Tuscumbia Female Academy (not far from Rapier's hometown of Florence) was destroyed by fire, suspicion fell on several blacks, including the future congressman. Writing to President Chester A. Arthur on May 31, 1882, Rapier explained the "proposition" put forward by the Democrats as rumors of revenge against him and other blacks filled the air: "The Democracy made a proposition to me to this effect that if I would publish a card stating that I would have nothing to do with politics no harm should befall me." He rejected this attempt to stop his activism through intimidation: "I spurned the proposition and rallied the colored voters in my county as best I could. The result was, I lost my steamboat woodyard and my entire crop, and barely saved my life. One night four of us had been selected for hanging. By merest chance, I escaped."[66] Having been warned by another freedman, Rapier fled for Montgomery. The other three men targeted that night were not so lucky. They were arrested, and following that Sunday's church services a mob of one hundred disguised men took the three from their cell and hanged them from a nearby bridge. Their bodies remained there for almost a week with cards pinned on them, warning other blacks of the cost of political involvement.[67]

Ten years later, in testimony before a congressional committee investigating the exodus of Southern blacks, Rapier made an explicit reference to the "bulldozing" tactics of whites that drove him from his home. He described how in 1868 an organization "known as the Kuklux" threatened his life. After threatening to hang another activist, going so far as to put a rope around his neck, 400 or 500 of these men "came and paid their respects" to Rapier. He continued, noting that "I was a very popular colored man at the time, and they wanted to give me a dose of their regulation tactics, but I ran faster than they did. I fought some and ran a good deal; and now, as answer to why the negroes do not fight more down there, I desire to say that when they heard I was armed and ready to fight, the Federal soldiers came there to hunt me down and see if I was armed."[68] Thus, at an early point in Alabama's experiment with Reconstruction, violence and intimidation were a crucial part of the white establishment's tactics in weakening and neutralizing black voters.

The violent circumstances that drove Rapier to flee his hometown led him toward his future political base in the Second Congressional District. His experience mirrored broader changes in the black community in Alabama as many freedmen began to migrate away from plantations, relocating by the thousands into cities like Mobile and Montgomery.[69] Some were impelled by a desire to liberate themselves from the hateful and watchful eyes of their former masters, while others, like Rapier, fled white violence and intimidation.

It was easy to see why Rapier became a target of violence, especially considering his prominence as a leader. Indeed, he had clearly gained the confidence of the white Republican establishment. Writing to Secretary of the Treasury George S. Boutwell on March 14, 1871, Alabama Republican congressman Charles Hays recommended Rapier for the post of assessor of internal revenue. Hays called Rapier "the leading colored man of our State, a gentleman of the highest priority, character and capacity, who justly receives the unbounded confidence and respect of all our citizens. He has performed great service for the Republican party, not only in Alabama, but throughout the South, and in education and ability, is considered the peer of either Mr. Douglass or Mr. Langston."[70]

Rapier's campaign for secretary of state again put his life in jeopardy. At a series of congressional hearings held in Montgomery, Alabama, on October 19, 1871, white postmaster John M. Ward delivered testimony on the intimidation of African American voters by the Ku Klux Klan. Ward's testimony highlighted disturbances that took place during a political meeting in La Fayette, Chambers County, where Rapier was campaigning. According to Ward, Rapier began to address the audience in earnest, but he was "frequently interrupted" at the beginning of his speech by a black man in the audience. The local marshal for the county attempted to arrest the unknown black man, who "broke and run" away from Ward's sight and into the woods. The marshal pursued him, firing his pistol and fatally shooting the black man, an act that effectively "broke up the meeting." Many prominent Republicans were on hand to speak, but as a result of "the excitement" they were not able to address the meeting.

It is hard to make sense of Ward's account. According to the postmaster, local blacks were not sure about the political affiliations of the dead black man who had run from the meeting. Ward said the marshal who shot him was a Democrat, but added that "it was the opinion of the colored men generally" that the entire scene was set up "to disrupt the meeting." If this had been the intention, it worked well. As a result "of the excitement that grew out of the killing of the negro," the meeting was canceled. Lest blacks forget their place, local whites took pains to remind them of the consequences of holding future meetings. Ward explained, "A great many whites from La Fayette came there to the crowd, and remarked that if any such meeting was ever gotten up again they would kill the leaders of it."[71]

African Americans were not simply passive victims; Klan atrocities provoked retaliation. An unidentified Democratic newspaper in Alabama published an intriguing article on August 11, 1870, titled "Difficulty between Negroes and Mean White Men," which revealed class fissures within the white community as well as fundamental challenges to Klan depredations on the part of the black community. The paper wrote of a "controversy about a sheep . . . between a low white man and a negro . . . and it was settled by a Justice of the Peace in favor of the Negro." After threats by the disgruntled white man and his friends, the paper reported a harrowing fight on the black man's plantation. Around thirty or forty black men took the threats seriously and "prepared for self-defense." They armed themselves, and that night about a dozen white men "disguised as Ku Klux" arrived on horseback near the cabin of the black man who had won the suit. Two of the men were left to care for the horses, while the rest made their way to the stable. Immediately the blacks opened fire, mortally wounding one of the men, who held on to life for about half an hour. After wounding another and driving off the rest of the night riders, the blacks returned to the cabin with the body of the dead Klansman. The newspaper added that other white Democrats and former Confederates had vowed to pursue the "lawless 'white trash'" and assist blacks "whenever they were assailed by such men, who were known to be among the meanest in the country."[72] It was impressive that a white Democratic newspaper admitted the existence of the Klan and described blacks as men who were equipped to defend their homes, using lethal force if necessary. Despite the perils of interracial confrontations and anti-black violence, African Americans increased their militancy and gained a political foothold.

A Fearless Foray into the Political Arena

In the aftermath of the Civil War, emergent black political leaders shared with their newly freed constituents a deeply rooted desire for education and a strong awareness of the injustices and racism faced by freedmen and women throughout the South. For Walls and Smalls, black veterans who had confronted Confederate forces on several occasions, the struggle against slavery was heightened by their awareness of black sacrifices for the Union war effort. Langston confronted the racism of the federal government while also closely observing events among whites and blacks in Mississippi and Alabama. Indeed, on one of his speaking tours in Natchez, he directly inspired Lynch to enter politics. Lynch recalled, later on in his career, how Langston's rhetoric showed him what an ambitious and articulate black man could become.[73] He had seen firsthand how devious the institution of slavery could be, and through his own yearning to educate himself he would eventually carve out a space in Mississippi politics. Rapier's entry into politics was marked by direct threats to his life, typical of the emerging anti-black vigilante violence that took root in the Deep South shortly after the conclusion of hostilities. In this highly dangerous environment, early black political leaders found inspiration by embracing a "democracy of the dead," remembering the suffering of the slaves and black veterans who had come before them, and especially finding inspiration from those who had risked their lives for the hope of black civil and political equality during the Civil War. Collectively, these five men's formative experiences prepared them well for their future service in another difficult role, as some of America's first black congressmen.

2

Ballots, Bullets, and Blood

Celebration and Militancy in the Postwar South

URING THE DECADE following the Civil War, no event merited greater celebration and commemoration among African Americans than the adoption on February 3, 1870, of the Fifteenth Amendment to the U.S. Constitution, protecting black men's voting rights. In the wake of the passage of this amendment, massive celebrations took place throughout the South. On April 30, 1870, Republicans in Macon County, Alabama, gathered together to celebrate passage of the new law. In the town of Tuskegee, at around nine o'clock in the morning, "the sound of music was heard, as a band of colored men marched through our streets, bearing aloft the stars and stripes. Men and women were seen gathering from every direction. Our town presented a lively appearance. After promenading the streets for half an hour, the procession, now swelled to hundreds, marched over to the headquarters of the club—'Over on Zion'—where others had met." Led by the local congressman, the procession continued to a stand prepared for speakers near the white Baptist church. After several speeches were made, James Rapier stood and addressed the crowd for a half an hour. According to an account published by a national black newspaper, "His address was suited to the occasion, and was calculated to win for him the respect of his enemies and to strengthen the cords which bind his many friends. He clearly described the nature of the fifteenth amendment, also the character of the political party with which it originated."[1]

On May 19, 1870, a similar rally took place in Baltimore to celebrate passage of the amendment and African Americans' full entrance into the nation's political culture. Present at this large gathering were Frederick Douglass, William Lloyd Garrison, and law professor John Mercer Langston of Howard University. As the "orator of the day" Langston was greeted with immense applause by the many who thronged to hear his words. In "a loud, clear voice that reached even to the outskirts of the assemblage" he spoke words laced with deep meaning for the black audience in front of him: "FELLOW CITIZENS: In the presence of this occasion and the fact it honors, eloquence itself stands abashed. We celebrate to-day the triumph of genuine democracy, that democracy which asks nothing but what it concedes, and concedes nothing but what it demands; destructive of despotism, it is the sole conservator of liberty, labor, and property. It is the law of nature pervading the law of the land."[2]

After discussing the events that had made the Fifteenth Amendment possible, Langston explained why it was so important. Slavery had "chattelized" African Americans, but it also had a pernicious effect on white Americans by stripping them of "their freedom of thought, freedom of speech, freedom of locomotion, thus showing itself the enemy of all." It was thus appropriate for his audience, "forgetting now our complexion, our former condition, and our nationality, to join in the celebration of triumph upon the field of battle as well as in the field of politics and morals, which presages and promises us *all* a free home, and a Government which is indeed, a democracy, and rejoice together as citizens of a common country, to whose welfare and destiny we make a cordial pledge of 'our lives, our property, and our sacred honor.'"[3] These sentiments connecting Union victory, the promise of a true democracy, and emancipation were clearly in evidence in the lithographs depicting this particular celebration, which showed just how far black understandings of politics had come since the conclusion of the Civil War.

"The Result of the Fifteenth Amendment, and the Rise and Progress of the African Race in America and Its Final Accomplishment, and Celebration on May 19th, A.D., 1870," published in Baltimore by Metcalf and Clark, presents a familiar array of political images, including major white figures (Lincoln, Grant, John Brown, Thaddeus Stevens) and black leaders (Douglass, Senator Hiram Revels, and Martin Delaney). The fundamental relevance of this lithograph, however, is less in the political message that it contains than in its depiction of African American political rallies. The sides of the piece show well-dressed members of black fraternal orders and Masonic groups leading the parade and holding up banners with white politicians (among other figures) on them. Likewise, the central image depicts well-dressed black civilians and soldiers marching with banners and flags in a massive parade on the street, with thousands of mostly black spectators gathered on the sides. Some of these black men are clearly part of Masonic

"The Result of the Fifteenth Amendment, and the Rise and Progress of
the African Race in America and Its Final Accomplishment, and Celebration
on May 19th, A.D., 1870" (Baltimore: Metcalf and Clark, c. 1870).
(Library of Congress, Prints and Photographs Division, LC-DIG-pig-02178)

groups and black fraternal orders. Participation in such orders served as a
major proving ground for emergent ideologies of black manhood and created a space in which rising black leaders forged ideas concerning the uplift
of their newly freed constituents.[4]

This sort of imagery is displayed in even greater detail in another lithograph of the same parade, "The Fifteenth Amendment and Its Results,"
published by E. Sachse & Co. in 1870. It features black men dressed in
sashes and mounted on horseback at the head of a parade with banners and
American flags, and it also has strong political overtones. Words emphasizing black uplift and desires for self-improvement—"Education" and "Science"—express the fundamental role of these factors in the success of the
newly emancipated and enfranchised black electorate.

Both images reveal much about the concerns of the black community,
the role played by community leaders, and the nature of black political
rallies and celebrations in the postbellum period. African Americans from

"The Fifteenth Amendment and Its Results"
(Baltimore: E. Sachse & Co., c. 1870). (Library of Congress,
Prints and Photographs Division, LC-DIG-pga-02587)

all walks of life participated in or attended these parades. Indeed, the Washington *New Era* (published by Douglass) highlighted the presence of various black fraternal orders and mutual aid societies at these events. Newly freed African Americans affirmed their integration as national citizens, not only by participating in such rallies and political hoopla (which were reminiscent of antebellum white political rallies and spectacles) but also by marching under the nationalistic banner of the Stars and Stripes, carrying images of national political leaders. At least one group of marchers displayed a "Banner with picture of Senator Revels shaking hands with the Goddess of Liberty."[5] These images also contain early examples of postwar projects for racial uplift. Paralleling the rhetoric and policy agendas that black political leaders were embracing, the images extol the future promise of the race and assert that black success rested on autonomy, education, and free labor—

concepts that would have resonated powerfully with newly enfranchised constituents.

Not everyone, however, was pleased with the passage of the Fifteenth Amendment or the ways in which black men's right to vote was privileged over the rights of white women. Indeed, the passage of the Fifteenth Amendment in 1870 divided two groups of former allies—black abolitionists and white women's rights activists. Even though most black activists supported women's rights, for most of their struggle (both before and after the war) they always gave priority to black civil and political equality over and above women's rights. We can see this prioritization in black congressmen's subsequent advocacy for stronger civil rights legislation during the mid-1870s. Only two black congressmen—Robert Smalls and Richard Harvey Cain—put forward petitions for a constitutional amendment in favor of female suffrage. With the exception of Alonzo Ransier, no black congressman ever delivered a speech in favor of women's rights, nor did any of them explicitly link their pursuit of stronger guarantees of civil and political equality with calls for equal treatment for men and women. Rather than connecting the causes of racial and gender equality, black congressmen made their claims on the basis of their shared manhood with white men, or they grounded their claims against segregation on the familiar rhetoric of protecting the respectability of black women from denigrating conditions. As indicated by Langston's martial imagery and the decidedly male images in the lithographs, the Fifteenth Amendment was conceived in terms of the rights of black males. Black women are present in the crowds, but they remained, in many ways, excluded from the promised citizenship rights that Langston was claiming for black men who had served and bled on the battlefields of the Civil War.[6]

Regardless of who benefited most from the passage of the Fifteenth Amendment, it certainly signaled a profound sense of possibility and a brighter future for African Americans. That future, however, was repeatedly challenged by events like the Tuskegee Outrage, as well as by more ominous scenes of violence that occurred in Mississippi in early 1871.

The Meridian Riot:
White Violence Takes Shape in the South

As soon as Mississippi's first Republican governor, James L. Alcorn, took office in March 1870, he and his Republican counterparts faced an unprecedented surge in violence. By 1871, this violence had evolved into a tidal wave of Ku Klux Klan activity, much of it centered in Mississippi's eastern counties.[7] One of the bloodiest episodes of this violence was the Meridian Riot of March 1871.

African Americans in the town of Meridian were subjected to cross-border raids by Alabama night riders seeking to apprehend blacks who had reneged on labor contracts. The local black response in Meridian involved armed militias of African Americans parading through the streets in a show of force against the Klan. This conflict was magnified when a fire broke out in the business district on March 4, leading to rumors that blacks intended to burn down the town. Three major black leaders were rounded up and brought to trial. On March 6, as these men were brought before the court, shots broke out; when the smoke had cleared, the white Republican judge and two blacks lay dead. In the ensuing riot, armed whites went through the town, murdering as many as thirty African Americans.[8] Conflicting accounts and sentiments as to who perpetrated the worst atrocities during the riot illustrate the confusing nature of violence in Reconstruction-era Mississippi.

Writing from Meridian on March 11, 1871, B. F. Moore, clerk of the circuit court of Lauderdale County, Mississippi, addressed Governor Alcorn: "I see you have sent troops *at last*—Please *Keep* them here. . . . The negroes have acted badly; the whites *far worse*. I have been living here thirteen years, born in North-Carolina. My grandfathers were slave owners. We *need peace*, and *the strong* arm to protect us—The whites have *committed* [and] *applauded outrages committed;* which History must hand down as only equaled by the most uncivilized of the Human Race—Half is not told in the papers." Moore concluded by illustrating his fears, his frustrations, and his determination to support the use of force in Meridian: "*This is Confidential;* I would not *have its contents Known for the World* Put your *foot down*, and *Keep* it *there* I'm tired of living in a county, in which I cannot express a *moderate* sentiment in favor of the *Government*, the *Flag*."[9]

The part of the story that Moore described as "not told in the papers" was omitted in Democratic coverage of the Meridian Riot. A special correspondent for the *Vicksburg Herald* wired a telegram dated March 6, 1871, noting that "a terrible tragedy occurred in Meridian this afternoon." While the case of a black man "charged with riotous conduct" was being investigated, the writer explained, "a difficulty occurred in which Warren Tyler (negro) shot and killed Judge Bramlette, the presiding magistrate. The excitement was intense and the melee became general. Tyler and two other negroes were killed. Several whites and blacks were wounded. The town is in arms, and the greatest excitement prevails, though everything is now quiet." Building on white fears of black violence, the correspondent contended that "the difficulty is caused by the riotous conduct of the negroes on Saturday, and threats to burn the town."[10]

By contrast, the Republican Speaker of the Mississippi House of Representatives, Henry W. Warren, in later memoirs portrayed the riot quite differently from contemporary Democratic newspaper coverage. He noted, "The riot seemed to be the result of preconcerted arrangements of Alabamians and white men in Meridian to overthrow the Republican city government of that town."[11] Democrats predictably cast blame for the violence on militant blacks, saying that they should never have paraded in the first place. But it was striking that both a former slaveowner and a transplanted white Northerner could agree that, irrespective of how badly blacks may have behaved, the Meridian Riot's worst violence was perpetrated by whites. Scenes like those in Meridian were not isolated, and they did much to encourage Ulysses S. Grant and Congress to pass legislation to curb the violence afflicting large swaths of the South. Thanks in part to the passage of the Ku Klux Klan Act (signed into law by President Grant on April 20, 1871), a vigorous and successful prosecution of white vigilantism helped to decrease violence across the region. But many African Americans in the state, though appreciative of the increased prosecution of organizations like the Klan, remained wary that the violence might rise up again.

Racially motivated political violence coexisted with the emergence and growth of increasingly militant black communities. Indeed, the birth of Union Leagues in Mississippi and Alabama was linked with increasing white violence. The more blacks displayed militancy or independence, the more their white counterparts responded with violence. Nor was this ugly aspect of early interracial politics limited to those two states. One of the most defining experiences for African American political communities was the emergence of Union Leagues across the South in the late 1860s and early 1870s. These leagues were, in some respects, offshoots of the Freedmen's Bureau, in that many of their white and some black leaders initially served in the bureau. Langston, for example, represented the close ties between the Freedmen's Bureau and the Union League movement in the South. In his capacity as general inspector for schools for the Freedmen's Bureau, Langston spread and organized Union Leagues throughout his travels in the Deep South.

These organizations were originally crafted to pave the way for the creation of Southern Republican coalitions by bringing white Unionists and freedmen together. However, in the late 1860s and early 1870s they became training grounds for aspiring black leaders and hotbeds for radical demands from the black electorate. Ultimately, the success and increasing militancy of Union Leagues provided forums in which blacks could articulate their desire for economic autonomy and political power. These developments did not go unnoticed by the white establishment or the planter class. Initially, whites across the Deep South tried to blunt the growth and effectiveness of Union Leagues through stiff economic coercion. When this method failed, thanks to freedmen's strong support for the leagues, whites turned to physical coercion, including the formation of white terrorist and paramilitary organizations such as the Ku Klux Klan. The Klan had infinitely more success than economic coercion did in decimating the growth and strength of Union Leagues and, for that matter, many other kinds of black political organizations across Mississippi and Alabama.

Not all African American leaders supported the Union League. While Langston actively organized leagues and John Roy Lynch supported them, Rapier opposed them. Having already begun to form radical organizations in his hometown of Florence, he was not pleased to see white Northerners undertaking similar efforts in the form of local Union Leagues. Indeed, Rapier attended some of the earliest Union League meetings and denounced the organizers as frauds.[12] Nevertheless, leaders like Lynch and Rapier could not ignore the black community's increasing militancy and its demands for greater political participation and economic autonomy. These priorities would inform their attempts to secure economic rights and to combat increasing white violence and coercion at the state level.

The Black Convention Movement Becomes Political

By the late 1860s and early 1870s, several major black political leaders began to make their presence felt in the postwar Southern political arena. While Langston served in the Freedmen's Bureau, Josiah Walls, followed by Lynch and Rapier, began to take bolder steps into national politics.

Reconstruction Florida was characterized by an intense factionalism within the Republican Party that unfolded as early as the meeting of the 1868 Constitutional Convention. The demographic composition of the state also did not seem to bode well for an aspiring black military veteran like Walls. In 1860, Florida had 77,746 whites and 62,677 blacks, but by 1870 the balance was more even, with 96,057 whites and 91,689 blacks.[13] This virtually even distribution of the races should have positioned Florida's blacks

Congressman Josiah Thomas Walls.
(Library of Congress, Prints and Photographs Division,
LC-DIG-cwpbh-00552)

to pose an effective challenge to their white neighbors. But appearances were deceptive. One biographer of Walls concluded that, in contrast to the numerical superiority wielded by blacks in states like Louisiana, Florida's freedmen were not as able to assert themselves against whites because, although they were almost evenly matched in terms of population, white and black Floridians were not evenly distributed across the state.[14] Whites were spread out, while the bulk of the African American population remained in the state's plantation belt, where they lived alongside a hostile white population exposing the blacks to greater amounts of violence and intimidation than they otherwise might have faced. Relevant information on the eligible pool of voters is also quite revealing. According to the 1870 census, 38,854 male citizens in Florida were twenty-one years of age or older. Out of this group, 16,809 black males and 3,876 white males could not write. Thus a total of 20,685 eligible voters (53.2 percent) were unable to write. This number parallels the overall level of education among all Floridians, especially in the Black Belt.

The total number of those who could not write stood at 71,803, and 66,238 individuals ten years or older could not read.[15] African Americans were not only at a geographic disadvantage, but, as in so many other states, they were also at an educational disadvantage relative to their white counterparts.

Nevertheless, in spite of the political and educational barriers that confronted the newly freed population, black Floridians successfully elected Josiah Walls to an at-large congressional seat (representing the entire state). Walls won 51.3 percent of the vote. When he began his term on March 4, 1871, Walls was among the first African Americans to take a seat in Congress during Reconstruction, joining South Carolina's Joseph Hayne Rainey, Robert Brown Elliott, and Robert Carlos De Large.

Barely through the first year of his term, Walls (along with several of his congressional colleagues) decided to attend a national political convention of African American leaders in South Carolina. In the midst of frequently contentious state political contests and revolutionary constitutional conventions across the South, emergent black political leaders had maintained the tradition, established during the Black Convention Movement of the 1850s and 1860s, of holding major gatherings as a means of seeking consensus on coherent regional and national policies for the post–Civil War political world. One of the first such events to confront the political environment of Reconstruction was the Southern States Convention of Colored Men, which met in Columbia, South Carolina, on October 18–25, 1871.[16] A wide range of current and future elected officials attended the convention, including Walls, Elliott, Rainey, former Georgia congressman Jefferson Franklin Long, future congressmen Richard Harvey Cain of South Carolina and Rapier of Alabama, and the Palmetto State's lieutenant governor, Alonzo Jacob Ransier.

The presence of such a wide assortment of leaders, from the cultured and freeborn Rapier to the Union veteran and ex-slave Walls, at major conventions indicates that, despite divisions within the black community, strong unifying forces were at work. The Southern States Convention of Colored Men covered a wide range of issues, from education to civil rights, and attempted to solidify and coordinate black political activity across the South.

It appointed a drafting committee of nine members who unanimously adopted an "Address to the People of the United States" that identified and promoted nationwide the major concerns and desires of African Americans from the South. Among the members who affixed their names to this document were two congressmen, Elliott of South Carolina and Walls of Florida. The committee sought to speak for the mass of newly freed slaves and, to express a sense of unity among the convention's delegates, declared that blacks from thirteen Southern states and the District of Columbia "have delegated to us, their representatives . . . authority to give expression to their purposes, desires and feelings, in view of the relation they sustain to the Government and the people of the United States, under the course of events that has arisen since, and as a consequence of, the war of rebellion."[17]

Even at this relatively late date of 1871, the "war of rebellion" retained its central place in the minds of the assembled delegates; indeed, it would remain an important component of the formative years of postemancipation black politics. While most African Americans certainly agreed with the emphasis on the Civil War, they might not have necessarily agreed with the delegates' claims to represent all African Americans across the South. The address purported to speak for all blacks, but several major leaders and delegates were unable to attend the convention. Furthermore, despite the long list of Southern states named, not all of them were represented at the convention. These realities were undoubtedly mitigated by the presence of several prominent state political leaders (lieutenant governors) and a handful of newly elected and former black congressmen, enabling the delegates in attendance to claim the mantle of state and national black leadership.

Beyond this strong claim to broad representation, the address made familiar calls for protecting black civil and political equality, expanding and strengthening educational opportunities, and granting African Americans their place in the American body politic. Yet it is remarkable for several reasons. It was the product of one of the first efforts to bring together a majority of Southern black leaders in one convention. The committee felt the need to explain why it chose the medium of an address to communicate effectively with white Americans. Indeed, its explanation acknowledges the difficulties that confronted the black community in the early years of Reconstruction: "We have not at command the all-important instrument of a local public press as the medium of communicating with you; the press of the South, with few exceptions, being in the hands of those interested to lower us in your esteem. We have deemed a Convention of our representatives as the most efficient means of laying before you the true state of our condition and feeling."[18] As early as October 1871, African American leaders thought that producing such an address was necessary to circumvent the Southern press and present their views in an unbiased and unadulterated fashion to white Northerners.

Several paragraphs later, the delegates confronted racial discrimination more explicitly as they spoke of repeated attempts by Southern whites to confine them to conditions as close to their previous condition of servitude as possible. If Black Codes did not work, then white Southerners would turn toward other means of countering the revolutionary impulses of newly freed slaves. In pointing out that the Southern press was out of their control and bent on distorting the truth, the nine committee members who drafted this address were more prescient than they could have imagined.[19] The fact that these delegates perceived the danger of a biased Southern press, so early in the experiment with Reconstruction, provides compelling evidence that only strong support from the government (and the North) could guarantee the preservation of black civil and political equality. Indeed, this realization may have played an instrumental role in prompting some black leaders in attendance to run for political office.

The black convention delegates' address attempted to gain and strengthen Northern sympathy through the use of moderate and nationalistic language —a rhetorical strategy that black congressional leaders would use for the rest of the century. For example, when asking for increased educational opportunities, they wrote: "We ask that your Representatives in Congress; may be instructed to afford such aid in extending education to the un-educated classes in the States we represent as may be consistent with the financial interests of the nation. Although we urge our unrequited labors in the past as the ground for this appeal, yet we do not seek these benefits for ourselves alone, but for the white portion of the laboring class in our States, whose need is as great as ours."[20] The concluding sentence of this passage represents a remarkable feat of rhetorical acrobatics. On one hand, African Americans demanded expanded educational opportunities on the basis of their long service as unpaid slaves. On the other hand, they claimed these benefits not only for themselves but also on behalf of all laborers, including whites. This interracial approach would appear frequently in subsequent speeches and interviews given by a wide range of black congressmen.

Indeed, the text of this address contains the blueprint for the political and rhetorical strategies embraced by congressmen as diverse as Walls, Langston, and Lynch. No matter how strongly committed they were to the political fortunes of the Republican Party, the delegates who met at

Columbia were not naive enough to believe that suddenly, with the conclusion of the Civil War, white prejudice had been completely exterminated from the United States. They may have occasionally claimed this to be the case, but only in statements crafted for public consumption. African American political leaders knew, just as their constituents did, that forceful and racially exclusive demands for redress would likely go unheeded and might even engender opposition among many segments of Northern white society. Furthermore, they were also aware that they could not afford to be seen as serving only the interests of their black constituents. Such insights are especially visible in the case of Congressman Walls of Florida, since he was initially elected as Florida's sole at-large congressman. In this capacity he had to campaign across the whole state, and, once elected, he had a duty and an obligation to serve as the congressman for all Floridians, not simply those in the narrow Black Belt that existed in northern Florida. In almost every congressional district where African Americans gained election, they had to balance the desires of newly freed slaves and those of their white counterparts. While these strategic considerations do not negate the sincerity of the convention address's appeal to expand educational opportunities for both blacks and whites across the South, they do put in context the specific ways in which most black politicians crafted their appeals for civil and political equality. If they desired white Northern support, they would need to stake their claims on the basis of equality for all Southerners.

Toward the end of their address, the convention delegates selected another intriguing use of language to make their case before white Americans: "It is our privilege, in addressing you, to offer the voice of four millions of citizens of this great country. That voice is addressed to those whose humane feelings rendered practicable that consummate act that elevated so vast a body at once to the enjoyment of civil and political manhood." Since most of the legal protections for African Americans owed their completion to the efforts of white Northerners, black delegates hoped that this reality would influence Northerners to "watch carefully the development of its practical results; that no perversion from the purposes of your bounty shall prevent the full fruition of the great principles of justice that actuated you."[21]

The images and political metaphors contained here and their implications are critically important for understanding the mindset of African Americans by the early 1870s. Once again, the black convention participants sought to establish themselves as the (unelected) representatives of four million African Americans. But the writers went further and reminded white Northerners of their crucial role in liberating the slaves and elevating them to a position where they could enjoy full civil and political equality as men. The emphasis on the connections between manhood and citizenship as a product of the Civil War is the central focus of this passage. Interestingly enough, the delegates concluded this paragraph with a plea as well as a warning to the white Northerners. They contended that it was in the North's interest, given its fundamental role in securing emancipation and equality, not to lose focus or abandon African Americans, but to see the process all the way through. Emancipation may have been a fact, but the full implementation of the process set in motion by the Civil War and the Thirteenth Amendment was far from over. The North had to keep a steady watch over Southern affairs, lest the promise and possibilities brought about by the defeat of the Confederacy come to naught.

The address produced by the convention on October 21, 1871, was a political milestone in the life of the black community. In addition to setting out the major concerns and desires of the black electorate, it correctly predicted the future of the nation's tenuous experiment with Reconstruction. Within this milieu one can make sense of another major event that occurred at this convention: substantial division over whether to support President Ulysses S. Grant's bid for a second term.

For a few days, several prominent black political leaders sparred over how strongly to come out in support of Grant and the Republican Party itself. Congressman Walls consistently supported the Northern Republicans and the party as a whole. On the second day of the convention, October 19, future Alabama congressman James Rapier put forward a resolution endorsing President Grant. On the same day, Walls introduced a resolution explicitly supporting the Republicans as the only viable party advocating for the rights of African Americans and expressing confidence and trust in Northern Republican politicians. Walls also backed another strongly worded pro-Republican and pro-Grant resolution, by John H. Johnson of Arkansas, which stated that "this Convention hereby affirms an unswerving devotion to the great principles of the Republican Party," and that "we heartily endorse the successful Administration of President Grant, viewing with no less satisfaction his victories in peace than his victories in war."[22]

However, tension was in the air throughout the convention. At several points, delegates expressed exasperation with the infighting over how thoroughly they supported the Republican Party or the Grant administration. Initially, Grant had been popular among the majority of African Americans, who believed that his administration was quite willing to defend black civil rights. After all, his attorney general, Amos T. Akerman, had moved swiftly against the Ku Klux Klan in the South.[23] However, Grant's leadership in enforcing Reconstruction was inconsistent at best, and by 1870 the political tide seemed to be going against Republicans. In November of that year, the state legislatures of Virginia, Tennessee, North Carolina, and Georgia fell to Democratic control. Soon other states joined their ranks as the border states of West Virginia and Missouri also joined the Democratic fold.[24] It is thus understandable that doubt and suspicion hung in the air among the black delegates assembled at Columbia. Perhaps black men were wisely hedging their bets, since they didn't care to endorse Grant well in advance of the Republican convention. African Americans had also learned to be cautious from their years as slaves.

On October 21, the fourth day of the convention, Louisiana's P. B. S. Pinchback introduced a strongly worded resolution supporting Grant's administration. He called Grant "the greatest military chieftain of the age," lauded his extensive "recognition of the colored people in the distribution of Federal patronage," and saw him as the "crowning act in our elevation to American citizenship." Pinchback's resolution affirmed "that we heartily endorse his administration, and believe that, under his leadership, with judicious management, the Republican party can be led to a glorious victory in 1872." Not everyone in attendance, however, shared Pinchback's view. Two days later, when the convention took up the question of endorsing President Grant, some delegates argued against endorsing him so far in advance of the election. Indeed, one resolution stated that it was "impolitic at this time to appear even to dictate or anticipate the action of the great Republican party, of which we form but a fraction."[25]

As the convention dragged on toward its evening session, whether the assembled delegates would support Grant's bid for reelection remained unresolved. Walls moved to continue his support for the Republicans and Grant. In response to a pending resolution (a substitution for Pinchback's effusive resolution backing Grant) that tepidly supported the Republican president, Walls rose to address his colleagues and offered a bold alternative: "that this Convention recommends to the next nominating Convention of the Republican party, the name of John Mercer Langston, as a candidate for the Vice Presidency of the United States." Although not able to make the convention, Langston was at the time the second most prominent black man in America, after Douglass. Interestingly, Walls presented this unconventional resolution in the face of increasing white violence in South Carolina. Even for this convention of black delegates, the idea of nominating an African American as Grant's running mate was seen as going too far. Ultimately, however, Walls's resolution may have had the necessary effect of breaking the deadlock. Immediately after the tabling of this controversial alternative, a vote was called on the substitute resolution that watered down Pinchback's endorsement of Grant. Of the forty-eight delegates present, only eighteen supported it and thirty (including Walls) voted against it. Following this vote, "The question recurred on agreeing to the resolution of Mr. Pinchback, and was decided in the affirmative."[26] The convention signaled the powerful birth of formal black politics, and soon other leaders like Lynch and Rapier moved to enter the political arena.

Black Inroads in Mississippi and Alabama

Lynch moved quickly up the political ranks following his election as justice of the peace in 1869. He earned popularity and respect as a member of the Mississippi state legislature and rose to the position of Speaker of the House. Though he claimed that his "friends" decided it was the right time for him to go to Congress, most likely Lynch himself aspired to higher political office by 1872. He recalled later: "The sitting member, Hon. L. W. Perce, was a strong and able man and had made a creditable and satisfactory representative. He was a candidate for renomination. He and I not only lived in the same county, Adams, but in the same town, Natchez. Adams County not only had the largest population of any county in the [Sixth Congressional] district, but it also had the largest Republican majority. It was conceded by all that an Adams County man should be nominated, and since the two opposing candidates lived in that county, the one that would win the primary therein would receive the nomination. This made Adams County the battleground of the campaign for the nomination."[27] Lynch described the race as "warm and exciting" and also "free from bitterness."

In the end, Lynch won a "sweeping" victory in the Sixth Congressional District, reaching the constitutional age of eligibility (age twenty-five) in September 1872 and winning the election in November with 64 percent of the vote (15,000 votes).[28] Republicans, as a whole, captured a statewide majority of over 5,000 votes and took every congressional seat except the First Congressional District, which sent Democrat L. Q. C. Lamar to the House of Representatives.[29] The sizable Republican victory in the 1872 election is not surprising when one considers certain demographic realities. According to the 1870 census, 444,201 blacks lived in Mississippi, outnumbering its 382,896 whites by 53.7 to 46.3 percent. In the Sixth Congressional District (which Lynch represented), 29,264 citizens were twenty-one

Congressman John Roy Lynch. (Thomas H. and Joan Gandy
Photographic Collection, Mss. 3778, Louisiana and Lower Mississippi
Valley Collection, Louisiana State University Libraries)

years of age and older and thus able to vote. Once again there was a vast
education disparity across racial lines throughout the district. Almost half
of these eligible voters (14,365) were African American men who could not
write, compared to 1,956 eligible white male voters who could not write.[30]

Unlike in Mississippi, blacks were not in the majority in postwar Alabama, which as of 1870 had 521,384 whites and 475,510 blacks. In the Second Congressional District (which elected Rapier), 41,006 males were eligible to vote. Much as in Mississippi, almost half of the electorate (19,475)
consisted of black men twenty-one years of age and older who could not
write. By contrast, only 3,290 white males twenty-one years of age and
older were unable to write.[31] Though most black officeholders and political
leaders from Alabama were born in slavery, reflecting regional patterns,

several major leaders were of mixed race and had been freed prior to the outbreak of hostilities in 1861. Rapier represented this mixed-race and free-born class of leaders; after the failure of his candidacy for secretary of state, he ran for Congress, winning 54.5 percent of the vote. Thus by 1872 several black leaders had gained election to Congress, hoping to put into practice the policies and ideas that they had hashed out in conventions like the one held at Columbia.

Life and Death at the Ballot Box

By the beginning of the 1870s, a new generation of African American leaders had emerged from Southern plantations and from Northern abolitionist struggles in urban cities. These leaders shared a common set of strategies through which they sought to connect with the hopes and desires of their newly enfranchised constituents. African Americans wanted the rights and privileges that white Americans took for granted. Having proved themselves as loyal men in the service of the Union cause, they reasoned that their sacrifices on the battlefield had earned them the right to be political citizens. Nor could they or their leaders forget the individual and collective acts of resistance by which they and their forebears had combated the unimaginable sufferings of slavery.

This new sense of pride, engendered by the sight of hundreds of thousands of black men taking up arms, combined with informal strategies of resistance to forge a new and distinctive political consciousness for the black community in the postbellum South. African Americans knew well that the silencing of the guns at Appomattox signaled only the end of one phase of a much larger conflict. The world that would replace the old slave order was as yet undetermined. The formative political decade for black America would soon give way to the realities of interracial political strife and increased factionalism during Reconstruction.

As the assembled delegates at the Southern States Convention of Colored Men thoroughly understood, the specter of white coercion, violence, and intimidation was never far away. The Civil War liberated the slaves and gave them a sense of pride, manhood, and citizenship that they had never felt before. The conflict provided the necessary catalyst for the emergence of a political culture undergirding African Americans' claim to civil and political equality across the South. Northerners, and Republicans in particular, needed to understand the gravity of the situation. Preservation of the Union may have been the overriding factor motivating thousands of white Northerners to fight the Confederacy. Nevertheless, the war had also resulted in the emancipation of slaves, and now four million loyal black citizens needed their country's aid and protection.

As the delegates at Columbia concluded their meeting, already there were signs of how much remained unsettled both in Southern society and in the nation as a whole. Former slaves and aspiring leaders continued to embrace a "democracy of the dead," recalling the legacies of enslaved ancestors and Union veterans in support of their political organizing within the black community. But as the war faded from memory and the task of Reconstruction came to the fore, African Americans were confronted with the realities of putting their political consciousness into action. Their blood had been drawn by the lash of their masters and spilled on the battlefield; now blacks would be called upon to sacrifice their blood once more, this time at the ballot box.

PART II

The Struggle for
Interracial Democracy

3

Dark Days

Black Congressmen Confront the Culture of the Postwar Congress

U PON THEIR arrival in Washington, newly elected black congressmen had a remarkable opportunity to participate fully in
the arena of national politics. However, they had to learn to
navigate a well-established congressional culture that excluded nonwhites.[1]
They also had to find their political footing in an increasingly powerful
postwar Congress that was both inefficient and blighted with corruption.

As the historian Morton Keller notes, Congress was the most important
branch of the postbellum government. President Grant made a point of
highlighting the supremacy of the legislature in the realm of policymaking
when he labeled the president as a "purely administrative officer." In this
environment, congressmen held the reins of power in state and national
party organizations. Furthermore, if they belonged to the Republican majority they also controlled access to federal patronage.[2] Though President
Grant may have exaggerated, he was not too far off the mark. The postwar Congress wielded control over federal finances, and it formalized its
institutions and practices by creating a host of new committees and setting
specific parameters for how individuals could gain election to office. In the
ten years between 1865 and 1875, the number of bills and resolutions introduced in each Congress shot up to an astounding 4,800, with an average of
824 being passed. By contrast, between 1855 and 1865, an average of 1,700
bills and resolutions had been introduced in each Congress, with only 430
becoming law.[3]

The importance of Congress in the second half of the nineteenth century
was further bolstered by a succession of relatively weak presidential admin-
istrations. Even Lincoln's administration did not approach the strength of
the "Imperial Presidency" that emerged in the early and mid-twentieth

century. Lincoln knew how to work constructively alongside Congress, sharing power with the legislative branch while doing his best to retain control over Civil War strategy and over the question of slavery.[4] Following his assassination, and due to the missteps of Andrew Johnson, Congress took over control of federal policy for the reconstructed states. Between 1865 and 1901, no presidential administration was able to assert the same degree of influence over Congress as Lincoln did during the Civil War.

Post–Civil War congressmen were dominant figures in state and national party organizations, and, since Republicans maintained majorities in both houses for much of the 1870s, Republican congressmen exerted control over federal patronage.[5] Ostensibly, this patronage, in the form of appointment of political officeholders to various local and state positions, was supposed to serve the needs of a particular congressional district; in reality, it was often one of the most thoroughly corrupt areas of the postwar Congress.[6] For example, the *Daily Cleveland Herald* highlighted a congressional committee's investigation into the number of government employees (and their total salaries) working in the District of Columbia; the committee "recommended . . . that most of those positions be vacated in order that members of Congress from the various States may fill them with their friends, who have done service to the party or to the particular members who make recommendation."

Nor was dispensing patronage the only way in which Congress proved itself to be a den of corruption. Outright buying of votes and abuse of money during campaigns were also fixtures of this era. On March 4, 1873, Denver's *Daily Rocky Mountain News* noted that one U.S. senator (senators were still elected by their state legislatures at this time) had "purchased his seat by an expenditure of 60,000 dollars or thereabouts." Thus corruption was a vibrant part of the culture that black congressmen confronted as they took their seats in the House. Describing the character of the postwar House of Representatives, the historian Margaret Thompson notes that the House of Representatives "was a fundamentally antebellum institution, endeavoring, with limited success, to cope with the enlarged federal purview of postwar America."[7] The complex rules governing legislation, the incredibly high turnover rates among representatives (leading to large numbers of relatively inexperienced congressmen), and the unbalanced distribution of political power and expertise served to weaken the ability of the House, its committees, and its overall legislative activities in the aftermath of the Civil War.

In addition, Congress had no effective seniority system, particularly when it came to committee appointments. Between the Forty-Third and

Forty-Sixth Congresses (1873–81), out of a total number of 190 committees with 1,824 slots available in them, only 923 slots (50.7 percent) were held by members who had previous experience in the House of Representatives, and just 302 slots (16.6 percent) were held by members with previous experience serving on the same committees. Committee assignments either broadened or limited the potential legislative power wielded by specific congressmen. Both the relative inexperience and inefficiency of Congress and the ways in which committee assignments were distributed played a role in the power wielded by black congressmen, many of whom were considered ineffective because of the relatively few pieces of legislation that they were able to pass during their tenures.

Most congressmen in this period, regardless of their party affiliation or their race, found it difficult to get much legislation considered or passed due to confusing rules and large numbers of committees. Thus one must be cautious in criticizing black congressmen for their performance. Indeed, most blacks were assigned to committees (like War Claims and Invalid Pensions) that dealt with the bulk of private legislation considered by the House. Though such committees were important, they paled in significance relative to those committees that were the focus of major policy formulation, such as Ways and Means, Appropriations, Naval Affairs, and Commerce.[8] Black congressmen (like the overwhelming majority of their white counterparts) could not access the high-ranking and powerful committees that would have enabled them to put forward and perhaps implement more robust policy agendas. More than anything else, however, Northern racism played a decisive role in limiting the scope of black congressional power.

National black political leaders made the best of this trying situation. Unable to pass much legislation, most black congressmen were a "symbolic generation" of officeholders; nevertheless, they were more than just sources of pride for their race.[9] Their effectiveness should be judged not in terms of what they were able to pass, but by what they proposed during their tenures in Congress. Black congressmen voted, participated in debates, delivered speeches, and proposed substantive bills, petitions, and resolutions aimed at addressing concerns of black civil and political equality, economic and educational opportunities, and economic modernization in the former Confederacy. They were effective in articulating the concerns and desires of their constituents, in spite of bisectional racism and violent instability across the South.

With this understanding of the Gilded Age Congress in mind, it is possible to place black policymaking within the context of Washington's tangled political culture and to connect it with the desires and concerns of the black electorate. A survey of the *Congressional Globe* and the *Congressional Record* reveals a breakdown of the issues that took up black congressmen's attention. These issues fall into four distinct categories: personal issues and private legislation; internal improvements and state issues; racial issues and civil rights; and national issues.[10]

The Legislative Business of Black Congressmen

Most of the legislative activity that black congressmen pursued centered on personal issues and private legislation. These activities often involved seeking payment or relief for individuals (or groups) for damages sustained during the Civil War, pensions for discharged soldiers, addressing the needs of local businesses, fighting for invalid pensions, and asking for relief for former political officeholders. The overwhelming number of petitions and private bills related to invalid pensions and war claims reveals a palpable legacy of the Civil War: long after the fighting ended, many whites and blacks throughout the South and across the country continued suffering from its physical and economic effects.

Private legislation was not limited to issues arising from the Civil War. For example, Josiah Walls introduced H.R. 1315, which called for "the relief of enlisted men who served for thirty days in the war against the Seminole Indians in the State of Florida."[11] Likewise, Congressman James Rapier of Alabama introduced a bill (H.R. 1544) seeking relief for the estate of Alabaman J. M. Micow.[12]

Considering Congress's power over the federal purse strings and patronage, it is not surprising that black congressmen devoted a considerable amount of attention to personal issues or private legislation. Their embrace of patronage and private legislation shows that they understood and made extensive use of the levers of power and influence available to them. More important, the attention and energy with which black congressmen fought to represent individuals and groups of citizens (mostly those from their districts and home states) illustrates that they were very much attuned to and responsive to the needs and desires of their electorate.

The second-largest segment of policy engagement for black congressmen dealt with internal improvements and state issues. This legislative activity often entailed petitions or bills requesting the construction of new buildings, the establishment of ports, repairs to rivers and roads, setting aside public money for erecting colleges, moving federal courts to different locations, or aiding the construction of railroads. These policy initiatives were fundamentally important ways in which black congressmen responded to the needs and desires of black (and white) constituents, although, again just like their white Southern counterparts, blacks may have engaged in pushing proactive railroad legislation due to self-interest as well as more altruistic concerns.

The South had suffered tremendous wartime loss of life and property, and its economy was in disarray. Black congressmen were very interested in responding to demands for economic opportunities for their formerly enslaved constituents. The legislative initiatives that they embraced included measures that linked internal improvements with expanding economic opportunities for their home states. For example, Mississippi congressman John Roy Lynch proposed a bill (H.R. 4148) "authorizing the Harrison Harbor Company to excavate a channel and harbor in the Mississippi Sound, and to construct docks and breakwaters in connection therewith."[13] Congressman Walls, especially attuned to the prospect of international relations as well as economic growth, introduced H.R. 130 "making a grant of lands to aid in the construction of a railroad in the State of Florida, and to secure railroad connections with the nearest available harbor to Cuba and other West India islands."[14]

Policymaking with respect to state issues and internal improvements provided black congressmen with a chance to secure tangible benefits and services for their constituents. Support for such legislation was racially neutral and could be framed in such a way as to provide economic benefits for both black and white constituents. In pursuing such policies, black congressmen followed the lead of many of their white Republican counterparts.[15]

These strategies reflect the desire for economic opportunity and autonomy expressed by African American constituents across the South. National black political leaders reflected the increasing militancy of the communities that had elected them. This strain of thought was present from the moment of emancipation and was manifested in different ways—from the establishment of independent black communities in the Sea Islands in Georgia and South Carolina in 1865, to the increasingly radical desires of formerly enslaved members of the Union League in Alabama and Mississippi, to a series of tumultuous strikes in the late 1870s carried out by disaffected black rice cultivators in the South Carolina Low Country. This last episode directly involved Robert Smalls, who intervened to quell the tensions between white planters and striking laborers.[16] Considering the increasing stridency of black demands for greater economic opportunity and autonomy, it is fitting that black congressmen moved to champion legislation that would have modernized and expanded the Southern economy.

In sharp contrast to the attention that black congressmen lavished on private legislation and internal improvements, they spent comparatively less time speaking out on racial issues or on matters of civil rights, even though these issues were among the most important of their concerns. Ultimately, less time was spent on these issues not because of lack of interest but because of the overwhelming amount of bills on private legislation, economic issues, and internal improvements. The black approach toward civil rights policy was varied. Much initial legislation came in the form of petitions advocating political amnesty for disfranchised white Southerners (which reflected a strategy embraced by black leaders in order to obtain support for black civil rights legislation). Other pieces of legislation were more subtle and reflected the violence that afflicted states like Mississippi and Alabama. The black push for general amnesty (for ex-Confederates) was complemented by a desire for more proactive civil rights legislation and greater use of district courts to defend against white violence. While events like the Meridian Riot or the Tuskegee Outrage galvanized congressional Republicans to pass the Ku Klux Klan Act of April 1871, some black leaders saw the need for district courts far earlier than their white counterparts. As early as the Second Session of the Forty-First Congress, Mississippi senator Hiram Revels put forward at least three petitions from his constituents requesting that the U.S. District Court for the Northern District be moved from Oxford to Corinth and one petition requesting that the court be moved from Oxford to Aberdeen. Similar petitions or proposals relating to district courts or the Southern legal system were repeatedly brought up by all three black congressmen from Alabama (Rapier, Benjamin S. Turner, Jeremiah Haralson) and by Mississippi congressman Lynch between the Forty-Second and Forty-Fourth Congresses.

As a fourth main category of legislative activity, black congressmen were also interested in a broad array of national issues. They presented petitions from their constituents opposing the franking privilege (which allowed congressmen to send mail without paying postage), as it represented another area of congressional corruption in the postwar era. They proposed a wide range of legislative initiatives dealing with the District of Columbia (which is under the purview of Congress); bills calling for aid to companies like the West India Mail Steamship Company (to establish an American line of ocean steamships to open up trade between Haiti and the United States and transport mail from America); and memorials "in relation to the condition of agricultural laborers of the South and West." National black political leaders also participated in debates on federal appropriations, currency, taxation, and more mundane matters relating to proper congressional procedure.[17]

Several black congressmen showed strong interest in matters of American diplomacy and foreign affairs. For example, one of the major events in American foreign relations during the period of Reconstruction was the Ten Years' War in Cuba. South Carolina congressmen Joseph Hayne Rainey and Robert Brown Elliott presented petitions and resolutions in support of Cubans who were revolting against Spanish rule. Florida's Josiah Walls introduced H.R. 23, a joint resolution "for the recognition of belligerent rights on the part of the island of Cuba, in their civil war against the Kingdom of Spain," and also delivered a lengthy speech outlining his support of the Cuban rebels and urging the United States, having emancipated its own slaves, to support antislavery Cuban freedom fighters as well.[18]

One national issue absent from the concerns of black congressmen was the question of women's rights. The almost total silence on this issue begs for some explanation, especially considering how closely connected the struggles for female and black equality were during the antebellum and Civil War years. As noted previously, South Carolina's Robert Smalls and Richard Harvey Cain were the only black congressmen during or after Reconstruction to put forward petitions supporting the right of women to vote. In fact, South Carolina's black delegation tended to be the most forthright in supporting women's rights (locally Elliott, De Large, and Ransier were active in their support for these issues). No black congressman or senator between 1870 and 1900 ever made the subject of women's rights a central issue when they spoke before Congress. One major exception to this trend may be found in Alonzo Ransier's speech in defense of Sumner's Civil Rights Bill, where he hoped that the "day be not far distant when American citizenship in civil and political rights and public privileges shall cover not only those of our sex, but those of the opposite also; until which time the Government of the United States cannot be said to rest upon the 'consent of the governed,' or to adequately protect them in 'life, liberty, and the pursuit of happiness.'"[19]

Nevertheless, there was a remarkable silence at the congressional level regarding the subject of women's rights, particularly vis-à-vis the black struggle for civil rights. This fact is even more outstanding when one considers how men like John Mercer Langston supported women's rights and even fought for women to be included in black conventions (especially in the antebellum period). The record here is also mixed, since there is little evidence to indicate that black women were present at several of the major postemancipation black political conventions (like those that met at Columbia or at Nashville).

The historian Martha S. Jones shows convincingly, however, that one should not romanticize the alliance of women and African Americans in the antebellum period. There had been divisions between the two groups from the very beginning. Even such a relatively ardent women's rights supporter as Frederick Douglass concluded, in an 1855 speech to the Rochester Ladies' Antislavery Society, that "while I see no objection to my occupying a place on your committee, I can for the slave's sake forego that privilege. The battle of Woman's Rights should be fought on its own ground; as it is, the slave's cause, already too heavy laden, had to bear up under this new addition; but, I will not go further on that subject, except to characterize it as a sad mistake." Nor was he alone. These were precisely the same feelings that Langston experienced after he was rebuffed by the Ohio State Senate, which then agreed to listen to pleas from female activists the next day. The result was the emergence of two different movements, one race-oriented and the other gender-oriented, that increasingly worked at cross purposes to each other and even, at times, competed directly for support. Antebellum black political conventions began to move away from openly endorsing the issue or even mentioning women at all. Jones concludes that, in most cases, these conventions "fell nearly silent" on the issue of women's rights.[20]

Indeed, as the historian Faye E. Dudden notes, this tension would continue to occupy a prominent place in reform debates before, during, and after the Civil War. Langston sided with Wendell Phillips in insisting that black men's voting rights had to come first. Dudden also emphasized that the debate over who got voting rights first often obscured the fact that black women too wanted the vote. While Langston (and others, including Douglass) talked of prioritizing black men, Elizabeth Cady Stanton and Susan B. Anthony responded by discussing the claims of middle-class white women. Nowhere in this discussion were the voting rights of black women mentioned. Freedwomen were effectively excluded from these policy debates. In fact, very few activists spoke on behalf of black women. Frances Ellen Watkins Harper outlined her treatment as a widow while juxtaposing this with sharp criticisms against white middle-class women (who, she believed, needed to be educated above their "selfishness" and vapidity). At a later convention, Sojourner Truth stood virtually alone in her demands for black female suffrage, claiming that if only black men got the right to vote, they would oppress their wives in ways that paralleled the treatment of slaves by their masters.[21]

Given this perspective in the 1850s and the martial rhetoric embraced by so many black political leaders in the form of "democracy of the dead," it is not surprising that black congressmen chose to fight for black civil equality and remain relatively silent on issues of women's rights. Nevertheless, when they fought for the rights of blacks, they were fighting to protect black men and women alike, and both genders played vibrant roles in the emerging black political culture. Indeed, when Smalls's life was in danger, it was notable that "every colored man and woman" came to the rescue. Thus national black political leaders could and did make use of black women in campaigns and in grassroots-level political mobilizations, even though they were unwilling to openly endorse women's rights at the potential expense of gains toward black civil and political equality.

Though issues of internal improvements or private legislation seem to have occupied most of their time, African American congressmen engaged with crucial national issues on both the domestic and foreign policy fronts. Participating in domestic policy debates enabled African American congressmen both to address issues of broader concern to the national Republican Party and to respond to the petitions and desires of constituents in their home districts. National black political leaders were most reflective of their black constituents when they could speak out in such a way as to call attention to the gulf between America's professed ideals and the increasingly oppressive political realities confronted by blacks across the South.

Black Congressmen's Advocacy during Reconstruction

The legislative record of the first seven black congressmen, who served in the Forty-First and Forty-Second Congresses (December 20, 1870, through March 3, 1873), reveals much about their policy interests. The heavy emphasis on internal improvements should not be surprising, given the high level of Republican support for free labor and industrialization. African American congressmen reflected the broader Republican consensus that free labor and rapid modernization held the key to the rebuilding and economic transformation of the South. The most ambitious agenda was put forward by Walls, who, in his first term, served as the only congressman for the entire state of Florida.[22]

Walls established a reputation as one of the foremost black champions for internal improvements and expanded economic opportunities across the

South. Though he built up a reputation as a potent leader, initial descriptions of this veteran-turned-politician were far from flattering. Reporting on the earliest African Americans in the U.S. Congress, on May 25, 1872, the *Christian Recorder* gave a rather snide assessment of Walls's stature: "He has rather the airs and manners of a legislator, and he has not been in his seat since the early days of the session. The only thing known to *The [Congressional] Globe* from him is a long speech, which he read with the manner of a rustic schoolteacher."[23] Walls soon proved his critics wrong. Only a few days after the *Christian Recorder* leveled criticisms against him, Walls presented petitions in favor of establishing new postal routes and a memorial related to the creation of a "southern trans-continental interior line of water communication through the Gulf States between the Great Western and the Atlantic Ocean." His legislative agenda was ambitious and embraced modernization for the South. He proposed bills for the construction of public buildings (such as customhouses), improving harbors in Cedar Woods and Pensacola, and providing lands and the right-of-way for railroads. He also fought for land grants for public schools and local universities.[24] Only with greater educational opportunities and with the expansion and improvement of communication and transportation systems, Walls believed, could the conditions for a prosperous and independent African American citizenry be fostered. His various petitions and bills thus reflected the central concerns of the black electorate—economic autonomy and independence.

Not all black congressmen could engage in such energetic legislative activity as Walls. Georgia's Jefferson Franklin Long gained the local Republican establishment's support only to run for the remainder of an expiring term in the House. He served during the Third Session of the Forty-First Congress (January 16, 1871, through March 3, 1871), was not appointed to any committees, and presented no petitions or bills for consideration. Indeed, his only major act was to deliver a speech in opposition to the removal of political disabilities from former Confederates. Some black congressmen also faced the problem of contested electoral contests, which limited their ability to propose substantive legislation.

It is remarkable, given such challenges, not that black congressmen lacked major legislative accomplishments but that some of them were able to continue proposing legislation and serving their constituents in the face of dire political circumstances. In their first years of service, black congressmen tended to propose bills on various topics and spoke out on a wide range of issues. By the middle of the 1870s, however, they tended to propose mostly private legislation and internal improvements. The diverse circumstances and political constraints under which these first black congressmen served must be considered when one assesses their legislative accomplishments and policy initiatives. Taken as a whole, the data on black legislative actions in the Forty-First and Forty-Second Congresses reveals much about ideological and tactical differences among black politicians. Most of their lawmaking attention was focused on bills and petitions seeking amnesty for ex-Confederates, along with speeches in support of stronger civil rights legislation. Black congressmen defy easy classification in terms of their politics, as they diverged somewhat on matters of race and civil rights. Knowing that they had to address a national audience, they did not want to be regarded as single-issue congressmen. Nor did this multifaceted approach to congressional policy weaken their cause. Though black constituents clearly cared more about civil rights and economic autonomy, they could relate to broad demands for racial equality (relating to European and Asian immigration and the treatment of Native Americans) and calls for a policy of emancipatory diplomacy. Tensions between more privileged and mixed-race officeholders, on one hand, and those who came from different economic backgrounds and were of darker complexion reflected long-standing class and racial divisions within the larger black community. These divisions have often been cited (particularly in localized state studies of the period) as a cause of factionalism and of black political leaders' failure to address their constituents' needs.[25] But the shifting nature of black congressional policy may have had more to do with the fortunes of the Republican Party than with these intraracial tensions.

The Forty-Third Congress (1873–75) witnessed a large spike in black legislative activity across all four key issue categories (the most pronounced one being in the area of private legislation). When the next Congress convened, however, only legislative activity concerned with private legislation continued to rise, while the frequency of attention given to all other issues dropped significantly. Two fundamental conclusions emerge from these changes. First, support for high levels of black legislative activity in the Forty-Third Congress may be related to the fact that Republicans still dominated both houses of Congress. In the 1874 elections, Republicans would lose control of the House for the first time in the postbellum period.

With majority control of the House of Representatives in the hands of unfriendly Democrats, black Republicans had less opportunity to put forward an ambitious policy agenda. However, shifting partisan control of Congress does not fully explain why blacks overwhelmingly engaged in private legislation far more than all other issues. A more revealing conclusion may be drawn from the collective thrust of black policymaking when one considers the concerns of white and black constituents at the state level.

Second, even though black constituents desired full civil and political equality, they were more fundamentally concerned with obtaining greater autonomy and economic independence. Southern whites, regardless of their political affiliation, similarly favored any legislation that would modernize the Southern economy and provide relief and appropriations for damages or losses sustained during the war.[26] The two races' shared (albeit somewhat divergent) economic interests largely explain why black congressmen supported both high levels of private legislation and internal improvements. In these areas of activity they could work to increase the autonomy of their black constituents while also responding pragmatically to the pressing economic needs of white constituents not necessarily enamored with the presence of black representatives in the political arena.

This focus on private legislation and internal improvements fits nicely with the primary concerns motivating blacks and whites at the local level. However, one cannot so easily divorce black policy considerations from the politics of Reconstruction. National black political leaders embraced a varied agenda not only to reach out to white constituents but also as a means of advancing the well-being of their black constituents. Embracing color-blind or race-neutral pieces of legislation could provide subtle and more acceptable avenues to establish concrete gains for black constituents without antagonizing white Democrats.

Were Black Congressmen Successful?

As the 1870s witnessed the birth and greatest concentration of national black political strength, the question of how successfully black congressmen represented their constituents' interests during this period is of fundamental importance. In the immediate postwar period, Southern Republicans (including black congressmen) did not differ significantly from their white colleagues from other regions or from their Southern Democratic counterparts.[27] In terms of implementing their policy agendas, black congressmen were no more or less successful than their white counterparts, since the vast majority of legislation proposed by individual congressmen (irrespective of partisan affiliation or racial composition) did not pass. Power in the postwar Congress was concentrated in a very small number of committees and an even smaller number of individuals. Indeed, Southern congressmen (particularly Southern Republicans) as a whole rarely received assignments to the most important committees. However, when the Democrats regained power during the Forty-Fourth Congress, Southern Democrats were considered for influential committees.[28]

Given these legislative realities, black congressmen's success and representativeness must be judged in accordance with the strategies and proposed legislation that they put forward and how well these policy proposals squared with the concerns of their constituents. In a little more than eight years, sixteen black congressmen collectively put forward around 657 legislative actions, including major speeches, proposed bills and resolutions, and petitions on a wide variety of issues. They were imaginative, dynamic, and pragmatic representatives of their constituents (white as well as black). They demanded strong federal protections for black civil rights and applied intricate political strategies that revealed the high level of sophistication with which black politicians engaged their opponents. They focused their attention on issues that could bridge the gap between white and black Southerners. Due to the damage suffered during the Civil War, for much of the 1870s Southerners of all political stripes and races demanded the expansion of commerce through postal routes, homesteading, and appropriations for railroads, so that they could enjoy the accompanying modernization and economic benefits that would emerge from such legislation. Black and white Southerners also demanded relief and redress from the federal government through private legislation. For African Americans, this often meant submitting petitions for pensions and pay for black veterans as well as appropriations for communal and fraternal institutions fundamental to the black community. White Southerners who had sustained personal damages as a result of the Civil War could seek compensation for their losses as well as support for Southern publishing houses and crucial segments of Southern public institutional life that were desperately strapped for cash.

Given the high amount of interest convergence between white and black Southerners on internal improvements and private legislation, it should not be surprising that black politicians devoted much of their legislative activity to these types of issues.[29] Pragmatic and sophisticated African American congressmen recognized the potential to create a biracial coalition by embracing these shared issues. Their rhetoric reveals black political attempts to tie the fate of whites (especially poor whites) to the strivings of blacks, particularly with respect to increased public educational opportunities.

Regardless of how much the South's black congressmen could achieve, blacks across the nation took great pride in having members of their race in Congress. The culmination of emergent black political imagery may be found in one of the most powerful political images of the Reconstruction period: "The First Colored Senator and Representatives, in the 41st and 42nd Congress of the United States," published in 1872 by Currier & Ives. This lithograph, a group portrait of the first African Americans to serve in Congress (with Florida's Walls prominently in the center), presents an image that would have been inconceivable to most Americans only a few years earlier. Whereas the previous celebratory images of black parades provide a glimpse into nascent black political consciousness, this image highlights the emergent leadership class that stepped forward to represent the black electorate. The optimism and pride engendered by this triumphant portrait of the first black congressmen illustrate the concrete results wrought by emancipation and black enfranchisement. The institution of slavery, which had tormented generations of African Americans, was now replaced by the first fruits of citizenship and emancipation—black political representation on the national stage.

The growth of explicitly black political imagery fits in well with the dominant threads of postbellum black political culture. These early images were made for consumption by a politically cognizant black culture, composed of people who could never forget the travails of slavery and who clung tightly to the proud memory of their race's participation in the American Civil War. Former slaves drew upon their experiences of both slavery and war as sources of political strength in the aftermath of emancipation as they confronted hostile whites in their efforts to claim their full rights as free citizens.

4

The Emancipatory Vision of Civil Rights in America

Black Policy during Reconstruction

ON NOVEMBER 11, 1871, Frank Myers, a white Democratic former county commissioner from Florida, testified before a congressional committee regarding Ku Klux Klan activities. He had been invited to join the Klan but refused. His comments provided a stark reminder of why Northern vigilance over Reconstruction remained a top priority. When asked if he knew anything about the "hanging of a negro" in Columbia County the previous winter, he replied no. Then he added that a black man had been hung in Alachua County, which happened to be the home of Josiah Walls. He did not know the man's name, but when asked if the man had been put to death by the Klan, he said yes. Then he was asked, "You have said that, according to your understanding, this organization is what is commonly known in the community as the Ku-Klux?" His answer was as terse as it was chilling: "I so regard it."[1]

Florida had not escaped the violence that plagued Mississippi and Alabama in 1870 and 1871. Throughout the state, Young Men's Democratic Clubs (the equivalent of the Klan) formed, embodying the connections between white violence and state politics. The white men in these clubs were linked by their desire to regain control of the state government (for Democrats in 1870) and often by their willingness to use violence to achieve those ends. Roving bands rode across the state to strike fear into the hearts of those who refused to vote their way. Intimidation included whipping, burning homes, and even murder. Whites in Florida wielded violence as a powerful tool to eliminate blacks—and white Republicans—from the political equation. Between 1868 and 1871 in Alachua County, Walls's home base, nineteen people were murdered, and there were many more violent confrontations. In the same period, in Jackson County, according to Secretary of State Jonathan Clarkson Gibbs (a close political ally of Walls), 153 black Floridians were slaughtered.[2]

Some of the most disturbing testimony came from average blacks, many of whom drew connections between their desire for independence and economic autonomy and the assaults and intimidation by night riders. The case of Samuel Tutson of Clay County illustrates the tactics employed by local white agitators. Testifying on an attack against his family, Tutson recounted how nine men invaded his house in the early morning hours. Five of the intruders tackled him, and four went to his wife.

One member of the committee asked him if the intruders were disguised. Tutson replied that "one came in his shirt-sleeves, but all the rest had on their coats." He was then asked, "Tell us what they did when they came, and all that was done." Tutson answered, "They came to my house, and my dog barked a time or two, and I went out and could not see nobody; my wife went out and could see nobody at all; we had not more than got into the house and got into bed, when they came and flung themselves against the door, and it broke loose on both sides, and fell right into the middle of the floor, my wife said, 'Who's that?'" George McCrea, whom Samuel Tutson recognized, "made to her," and as Samuel went to help her "some one standing by the door caught me by my right arm, and I could not get to her; they pulled and pulled, and tried to pull me away, but they could not, and then they dragged my feet from under me and flung me down across a cellar-door and near broke my back; they dragged me over the fence, and broke down five or six panels, and took me away down the hill on the side of a hammock, and tied me to a pine and whipped me." When pressed further about how many lashes he received, Samuel replied, "It is out of my power to tell you."

According to Hannah Tutson, Samuel's wife, it was clear why the "Ku-Klux" had paid a visit to her house. Three weeks prior to the attack that Samuel described, many of the same people who participated in the raid had come to "dispossess" her of her property. One member of the committee asked her, "They came to tell you that you had better give up the land?" Hannah's response was telling: "Yes, sir; they told me it was not my land; that it was another man's; that is all; so they told me the night they whipped me."[3]

The *Tallahassee Sentinel* published excerpts of other testimony given before the committee that corroborated the accounts put forward by Samuel and Hannah Tutson. These excerpts appeared on the front page, on October 19,

1872, under the byline "The Ku-Klux in Florida. They Won't Allow 'D—d Niggers to Live on Land of Their Own.'" The byline referred to testimony delivered by Doc Rountree, a black man who, in testimony on November 14, 1871, explained how, three years earlier, he had experienced brutal treatment at the hands of the Klan: "They beat us . . . they took me up hand and foot and dragged me out, and they flung my children out of doors," then whipping Rountree, his wife, and four children. When asked why he and his family had been subject to such treatment, Rountree replied, "They said to me, didn't I know they didn't allow damned niggers to live on land of their own? They gave me orders to go the next morning to my master, John Sellers, and go to work." Sellers had not owned Rountree before the war, and Rountree was living on government land. Nor was the violence confined only to poor blacks and former slaves. During his first campaign for the House of Representatives in 1870, Walls barely escaped an assassin's bullet at a rally in Gainesville, Florida.[4]

Walls thus arrived in Congress quite aware of the scale of violence aimed at his black constituents. He also understood their desire for economic autonomy and access to land and education, which were just as important to black Floridians as the right to vote. Walls proposed policies favoring homesteading, the construction of railroads, the expansion of postal routes, and the bolstering of his state's educational institutions. The large-scale violence, motivated by a desire to curb black economic advancement, required Walls to fight back with his own version of Southern "boosterism."[5] Like Walls, the other members of the postemancipation generation of black congressmen would make it their mission to put protecting and empowering Southern blacks at the forefront of their policy agendas in Congress.

White Amnesty and Black Civil Rights

Newly elected black congressmen were confronted with still-unsettled issues relating to the Civil War and Reconstruction. Chief among these varied issues was the question of amnesty for disfranchised whites across the South. To many white Southerners, the newly formed Reconstruction governments were illegitimate and lacked constitutional authority. Whites did not hold this view simply because Republican regimes had turned the South's accepted racial and political order upside down, although that was an enduring complaint as cries of "Africanization" were often used as justifications for violence. Rather, they saw these governments as oppressing the mass of white Southerners. As the historian George C. Rable noted, "Such a situation in which rulers are or seem to be unresponsive to the aspirations of a large group encourages civil violence."[6]

Congressional Republicans' commitment to safeguarding black civil and political rights across the South was strongest between 1865 and 1873. With the passage of the Fifteenth Amendment to the Constitution (which guaranteed the right of black men to vote) in 1870 and the adoption of the Enforcement Acts in 1870 and 1871, congressional Republicans reached the high-water mark of their follow-through on this commitment.

The Enforcement Acts were passed in response to anti-black violence across the South, which had obviously become a pressing concern for black politicians and their allies. In the midst of Klan violence, and after the failure of anti-Klan legislation put forward by Massachusetts's Benjamin Butler, Ohio Republican Samuel Shellabarger proposed another civil rights bill modeled on Butler's earlier legislation. After much debate, the House of Representatives passed this bill on April 7, 1871, by 118 to 91. All five black congressmen voted in favor of the bill.[7] The Third Enforcement Act (better known as the Ku Klux Klan Act) was signed into law by Ulysses S. Grant on April 20, 1871, and U.S. Attorney General Akerman used the bill's provisions to undermine Klan activity.

But during the 1870s, Northern support for black political rights began to fade. Indeed, after 1871 the situation facing congressmen, and African American congressmen in particular, was delicate. Early black electoral successes in many areas of the South were made possible by the disfranchisement of large numbers of former Confederate officeholders and soldiers. Keeping ex-Confederates from the polls helped Republicans to implement their plans for Reconstruction at the local level. Although congressional Republicans and most Northerners opposed the lax pardon policy embraced by President Andrew Johnson, it was clear by the early 1870s that Northern and Republican interest in Reconstruction was waning.[8] White violence in the South spurred Congress to act against the Ku Klux Klan, but it also brought about a national shift away from civil rights legislation toward general amnesty by 1872.

Congressional debates over granting amnesty to former Confederates occupied many in the Forty-First Congress until the passage of the Amnesty Act of 1872, which enfranchised about 10,000 to 15,000 former Confederates. The bill passed without a roll call vote.[9] African American congressmen could not escape these debates over Reconstruction policy. Most white congressional radicals, including many radical members of Southern congressional delegations, hesitated to remove white political disabilities. At least one black congressman voiced his opposition to amnesty: Georgia representative Jefferson Franklin Long devoted his one major speech while in Congress to the topic.[10] However, other black congressmen took a different tack. In a changing political climate, most national black political leaders attempted to link calls for leniency for ex-Confederates with the passage of stronger civil rights protections for black constituents back home.

Of the six congressmen and one black senator who served between the Second Session of the Forty-First Congress and the Second Session of the Forty-Second Congress (December 20, 1870, to June 10, 1872), six favored amnesty. This group included Mississippi senator Hiram Rhodes Revels, Walls of Florida, Alabama's Benjamin Turner, and three South Carolinians—Robert Carlos De Large, Joseph Hayne Rainey, and Robert Brown Elliott. De Large, Rainey, and Elliott delivered remarks favoring amnesty; all except De Large (who was preoccupied with a contested election case that ultimately cost him his seat) put forward petitions and resolutions favoring amnesty for individuals and, in some cases, for all disfranchised individuals in their home states.

Elliott and Rainey emphasized a similar logic in their support for amnesty, stating that it was meant as a quid pro quo in exchange for the passage of civil rights legislation protecting colored citizens. Elliott's words captured the prevailing sentiment among black congressmen: "I desired that the magnanimous action of the Government on behalf of those who were untrue to the Government in the past should go hand in hand with the righteousness of the Government in protecting its own citizens."[11] Black congressmen were not naive. They saw how stubbornly white Democratic opponents had stalled and attempted to prevent voting on strong civil rights legislation and how stridently they demanded general amnesty. Thus black congressmen were willing to vote for amnesty only if doing so facilitated the passage of a civil rights bill.

Walls went further than his black colleagues. On December 18, 1871, he introduced H.R. 734, a supplementary bill to the Civil Rights Act of 1866. Its purpose was "to remove all legal and political disabilities imposed by the third section of the Fourteenth Amendment to the Constitution of the United States for participation in the late rebellion."[12] In calling for full amnesty for ex-Confederates, Walls was following the general drift of Republican policy in this period; President Grant had already broached the subject of amnesty in his annual message to Congress in 1871.[13]

Whatever his motives may have been, the black press was pleased with

Walls's activities. On December 21, 1871, the Washington *New National Era* praised Walls for "coupling therein amnesty as proposed by President Grant . . . with provisions securing to the outraged colored man the advantages and securities contained in Senator Sumner's bill supplementary to the Civil Rights Bill." The paper thanked Walls "for this happy suggestion. He deserves the thanks and support not only of his colored constituents in Florida, but of every colored man of the nation; nor does it stop here; he deserves consideration at the hands of every lover of justice." The *New National Era* thus concurred with the general drift of Grant and the Republicans toward amnesty, but it added the explicit stipulation that legislation guaranteeing black civil rights must be passed at the same time. *"This must be the terms of our assent to amnesty,"* the newspaper emphasized. "The colored people virtually say, through Mr. Walls (who speaks their sentiments), 'We want to be generous, you must afford to be just.'"[14]

Several factors may have led Walls to propose this piece of legislation. Most likely the culture of violence in Florida affected his decision. He may also have been consciously joining in a strategy that Elliott had devised.[15] Many Southern Republicans embraced general amnesty, agreeing with North Carolina Republican congressman Oliver Dockery that "we have had quite enough of the peddling process" concerning individual cases of pardon. As the historian Terry L. Seip has noted, Southern Republicans hoped that the "olive branch" of amnesty would "cool the political warfare in the South."[16] Unfortunately for both black congressmen and Southern Republicans, this strategy backfired.

Immediately following the vote that passed the amnesty bill in the House, Elliott moved for a suspension of the rules so that a vote could be taken to speed up the consideration of strong legislation favoring civil rights. Elliott, Rainey, Turner, and Walls were among the 112 members of the House who voted to suspend the rules. Seventy-six congressmen voted against the measure (including some notable Republicans like Speaker of the House James G. Blaine), and fifty-two (including Robert De Large) did not vote. As a two-thirds majority was required for passage, the rules were not suspended.[17]

Black congressmen impressed members of the political establishment by their willingness to compromise on the issue of amnesty. As Blaine noted in his memoirs, "Coals of fire were heaped on the heads of all their enemies when the colored men in Congress joined in removing the disabilities of those who had before been their oppressors, and who . . . have continued to treat them with injustice and ignominy." Blaine believed that, in spite of "lingering prejudice" among Southerners, it was to "the credit of the colored man that he gave his vote for amnesty to his former master when his demand for delay would have obstructed passage of the measure." While praising all black congressmen who served during his tenure, he singled out Rapier and Lynch as "studious, earnest, and ambitious men, whose public conduct . . . would be honorable to any race."[18]

As the debate over amnesty for whites illustrated, compromise was a major factor in black policy considerations. Additional sophisticated maneuverings and rhetorical strategies would accompany their later advocacy for stronger civil rights legislation. Their calls for civil protections would echo the use of color-blind language and references to black martial valor that were the double-edged sword of the black political establishment throughout the Reconstruction years. This protracted struggle for civil rights marked a turning point for national black politicians as well as for their constituents. By the mid-1870s, that struggle would expose the limits of white Northern support for newly freed blacks and would set the stage for the emergence of new strategies.

The Cornerstone of Black Citizenship Rights: Public Education and Racial Uplift

Along with civil rights debates, black congressmen also engaged heavily in battles for improved educational opportunities. One of Walls's first major speeches in Congress, on February 3, 1872, dealt with expanding public education. The subject of the proposed funding was the expansion of public schools.[19] Nor was Walls alone in this advocacy. At the state level, free and integrated public schooling had been Robert Smalls's chief issue. Freedmen had long desired education. For some, this was a way to read the Bible, while others saw education as the key to bettering their economic status. In all cases the former slaves' yearning for education was rooted in their overriding desire for autonomy, independence, and self-improvement.[20]

In this regard Walls could empathize with his constituents. He was born a slave and had little formal education. Serving in the Union army and acquiring some education helped Walls to achieve self-reliance; entering the charged and divisive arena of Reconstruction politics was the culmination of his journey toward becoming a fully independent citizen. He understood clearly that education was crucial to black progress, and no Democratic tactic would blunt his insistence on securing educational opportunities for his constituents.

Walls's speech in support of H.R. 1043 — "to establish an education fund, and to apply the proceeds of the public lands to the education of the people" — provided a powerful answer to objections raised by Congressman Archibald Thompson MacIntyre (D-Ga.).[21] Originally proposed by the chairman of the House Committee on Education and Labor, Legrande Winfield Perce (R-Miss.), the bill provoked an outcry from MacIntyre, who opposed it on the grounds of states' rights and offered a substitute that would have given the states discretion and control over the use of proceeds from public lands. Labeling Perce's bill as federal overreach, MacIntyre called attention to the fact that Georgia had just appropriated $800,000 for education, adding, "That educational system is not confined to the whites alone. The colored people of that State are entitled, under that law, to the same rights that the whites will enjoy."[22]

In remarks on February 2, 1872, MacIntyre revealed his true motivation by mentioning how Georgia had "grievously suffered from that sort of State administration—I mean the administration of a 'carpet-bag' government." He was proud that his state was now "under the control of the good, true, and patriotic men of that State, under the control of men born within her limits. All Georgia wants is to let her alone, and in a few years she will get back to the proud position she occupied in former times."[23]

Walls directly countered MacIntyre by stating, "We know what the cry about State rights means and more especially when we hear it produced as an argument against the establishment of a fund for the education of the people."[24] Walls identified the white establishment as the enemy of both newly freed blacks and poor whites, noting that he was "somewhat suspicious" of these rights because of the consequences for African Americans. He asserted that the Democrats in Georgia and the rest of the South "have been opposed to the education of the Negro and poor white children." Walls's fury was aimed not at all whites, but at the power of the Southern Democrats. He continued, "We know that the Democratic party used to argue that to educate the Negro was to set him free. . . . Their argument against educating the poor whites was that the Negro more directly associated with poor whites than with that class who controlled the destinies of slavery." Walls made his plea based on equal rights for all Americans, but the surprising part of his argument was how central the experience of poor whites had been. Blacks were mistreated by Democrats, but poor whites also had received a raw deal when it came to public education.

Rebuffing MacIntyre's attempt to interrupt, Walls demolished the

Georgia congressman's statistics and assertions of color-blindness and challenged him, "Will the colored people have an opportunity or be permitted to enjoy the same rights that the whites enjoy?" Considering past experiences, Walls was not optimistic about this prospect. Not while the "Ku Klux Democracy" was allowed to run rampant burning down blacks schools and churches throughout Georgia, not "while they shut the doors of the schoolhouses against the colored children." He then laid out his sweeping vision of equality in education. Walls favored a national system of education because he believed that the federal government was "the guardian of the liberties of all its subjects." Blacks could not defend their rights without education. And they could not "be educated under the present condition of society . . . without the aid, assistance, and supervision of the General Government." Southern prejudice had denied slaves the right to be educated, and it now denied freedmen their rights as citizens to receive an education.

Walls charged that the Democratic Party opposed expanding access to education because "they know that no educated people can be enslaved. They well know that no educated people can be kept in a helpless and degraded condition, but will arise with a united voice and assert their manhood." He emphasized the general societal benefits of expanded education: "An educated people possess more skill, and manifest more interest and fidelity in the affairs of the Government, because of their chance to obtain more general information, which tends to eradicate the prejudices and superstitions so prevalent among an ignorant people."[25]

Walls thought that prejudice and ignorance led Southerners to perpetrate the violence and intimidation that he and his colleagues had witnessed. To both obtain civil equality for newly freed blacks and protect the mass of poor whites, his solution was to give ex-Confederates the right to vote and educate all people out of their ignorance. Letting blacks and whites embrace their manhood and their dignity would inaugurate a new chapter in Southern politics and race relations. This was Walls's fundamental understanding of the legacy of the Civil War, rooted in his status as a veteran and in his distasteful experience of violence and factionalism in Florida.

When an amended version of Perce's bill (with provisions that would remove federal funds if they were misused or misapplied by state or territorial governments) came up for a vote on February 8, 1872, it passed with 117 votes in favor. Black congressmen Walls, Rainey, and Turner supported the bill; De Large and Elliott did not vote.[26] Passage of this bill could not, however, overcome the ever-present fears of anti-black violence. In the wake of debates over amnesty and the failure to secure a stronger civil rights bill, local blacks were justly concerned about the possibility of a resurgence of the violence that they endured in the late 1860s and early 1870s.

The Urgency of Civil Rights Legislation

Echoes of the Meridian Riot resounded in a "Letter from Mississippi," published on March 14, 1872, in Frederick Douglass's *New National Era*, that made the ramifications of racialized violence perfectly clear. Writing from DeKalb, Mississippi, the unnamed author (identifying himself only as "Loyal") wrote of the trial of "those parties who have been identified as being accessories to that terrible massacre that occurred at Meridian about a year ago . . . to satisfy the sanguinary desire of Ku Kluxism."[27] While commending U.S. District Judge Robert A. Hill and District Attorney E. P. Jacobson for their rigorous prosecution of the cases, "Loyal" also spoke out against those who thought that the Klan did not exist: "We would like for some of those credulous-minded beings who doubt the existence of that hell-born Klan to visit the court-room and listen to the tales of horror, bloodshed, and crime as recounted by those who still bear the marks of its cruel inflictions." Even though Grant and his "boys" had successfully halted "the open perpetration of those crimes," "Loyal" warned his readers that threats of violence and intimidation had not abated: "Like the smothered fires they but wait an opportunity to recommence their work of destruction and death. Do not be deceived, Ku-Kluxism is not dead, it but sleepeth; it is ready to wake at the first call of the 'Grand Cyclop.' I write thus because as a colored man and living in the South I am fully acquainted with the rebellious spirit of a majority of the people in the midst of whom we live." "Loyal" feared what would happen if the current efforts to prosecute Klan violence abated: "Unless we have the full protection of the Government . . . you will hear of a great many more loyal citizens being forced to make their exit from these regions."[28] Nevertheless, the Ku Klux Klan Act had mixed results and unintended consequences. What made later white vigilantism so hard to combat was its decentralized nature. The Ku Klux Klan Act taught Southern whites that organizing into larger units was dangerous, and that engaging in acts of violence brought unwanted attention from the newspapers and drew the wrath of Grant. It was far easier for one or two men to simply assassinate a lone activist in the dead of night than for whites to instigate a larger riot like the ones in Memphis and Meridian. So while the Ku Klux Klan Act stifled white violence for a time, in some ways it just drove white violence underground.

If Klan deniers abounded among certain segments of white society, African American congressmen would step forward to call out white violence wherever they saw it. In the case of the Deep South (especially Mississippi and Alabama), black congressmen would put forward various petitions and bills favoring the establishment of district and circuit courts for the express purpose of curbing Klan violence and other forms of racialized white violence that engulfed much of the South in the early 1870s.[29] Thus the expressions of unnamed blacks like "Loyal" resonated with national black politicians and informed their political and rhetorical strategies once they took their seats in Congress, especially as black leaders renewed their calls for stronger and more effective civil rights protections.

After winning election from Alabama's Second Congressional District, Rapier entered Congress on March 4, 1873. There he joined six other black congressmen, including Walls and Lynch, among 189 House Republicans, the largest party majority in the nation's history.[30] The day after Rapier's arrival in Congress, Senator Charles Sumner once again put forward strong civil rights legislation.[31] Sumner had first proposed his bill (as a supplement to the Civil Rights Act of 1866) on May 13, 1870; the original version was most likely drafted with the help of Langston. The language of the bill reflected Sumner's long-standing concern with black equality, but it also specifically emphasized the importance of integrated public schools for the black community. Education had long been a fundamental concern for Langston since his days in the immediate postwar period as general inspector of schools for the Freedman's Bureau.[32]

In its original form, the bill protected black civil rights in public accommodations, allowed for service on juries, and mandated public expenditures on schooling. It also made it clear that racism was anathema to the American republic by declaring "that every law, statute, ordinance, regulation or custom, whether national or State, inconsistent with this act, or making any discriminations against any person on account of color, by the use of the word 'white,' is hereby repealed and annulled."[33]

African Americans would make use of traditional means, such as holding a national convention and contacting members of Congress, in support of this legislation. The task was anything but easy. While Walls and Langston drew upon the emancipatory experience of the Civil War to urge Americans to support civil rights at home and abroad, Rapier and Lynch defended black claims to civil rights in other ways. They focused on American hypocrisy at home and emphasized distinctions between public and social rights in defending Sumner's legislation. The debates over the Civil Rights Bill were, in many ways, a direct result of anti-black violence in the early years of Reconstruction.

Nine months after entering Congress, Rapier and Walls (along with fellow black congressmen Alonzo Ransier, Joseph Rainey, and Robert Elliott) attended a national convention on black civil rights held on December 9, 1873, in Washington, D.C. There they heard delegates from twenty-five states discuss the issue of civil rights for African Americans.[34] The delegates demanded protections for black civil and political equality, and they presented a memorial to the Forty-Third Congress.[35] All the delegates signed the memorial, thanks to efforts by the acting president of the convention, the activist and entrepreneur George Thomas Downing. Downing had been active in the Underground Railroad and the abolitionist movement, and he counted both Frederick Douglass and Senator Sumner among his friends. Until 1878, Downing ran the dining room of the U.S. House of Representatives, giving him opportunities to influence congressional policymakers. He was also a founder of the Colored National Labor Union. In the short run, the memorial that he helped to craft had significant influence on the strategies used by black congressmen to argue in favor of Sumner's civil rights legislation.

Many of the arguments made in this memorial, which Elliott referred to the House Committee on the Judiciary on December 18, 1873, anticipate later arguments by several black congressmen in favor of Sumner's bill.[36] The memorial also echoed Walls's debate with MacIntyre in challenging the legitimacy of the "State-Rights theory" as a justification for denying expanded civil rights or color-blind schooling opportunities. Linking the discredited theory of states' rights with slavery, it declared: "The interest of slavery, a State institution, was so great and overshadowing as to subjugate church as well as state, morality as well as the laws of the land; decisions were rendered in its interests; it was ever keen, active, resolute, extremely suspicious. The State-Rights theory, one essential to slavery, was persistently argued. How it was adhered to may be seen in its producing the late rebellion, its grave-yard." The memorial argued that, given the Union's victory in the Civil War, any arguments based on states' rights had no bearing on congressional considerations regarding civil rights legislation. It went on to charge "objecting Senators" with hypocrisy concerning civil rights protections. It questioned how politicians could affirm the constitutional right of

Congress to "go as far as it had gone in protecting the civil rights of citizens in the several States . . . [but not] far enough to effectually protect the civil rights of a citizen wherever the stars and stripes have sway."[37]

The memorial forcefully asserted that the federal government could and should defend the rights of African Americans: "If Congress may throw the protecting arm of the law around any citizen of the United States, in every State, so as to forbid any denial or discrimination in hotels and public conveyances, on account of race and color, it certainly may do so in protecting him from invidious rules impairing the right of property." The government should not permit public schools "to serve to the degradation and humiliation of any class"; rather, it should not allow schools to train pupils "in opposition to the Government's fundamental principles."[38] The black understanding of the role of government was in evidence here, one that emanated from the formative years of the Civil War.

Delegates at the convention also drew sharp distinctions between "the private school maintained at the private expense of individuals, and . . . public schools maintained by moneys taken from the pockets of all." If interracial public education was not "agreeable" to some, then those parents who felt uncomfortable should enroll their own children in private schools rather than "outraging the rights of others."[39] African Americans made clear distinctions between the public and private spheres, or what Mississippi congressman Lynch would subsequently describe as public and "social" rights. Overall, the memorial encapsulated major themes and armed black congressmen with a diverse set of rhetorical strategies aimed at one goal—protecting the civil rights of their black constituents.

Blacks recognized Sumner's Civil Rights Bill as vital to the political fortunes of their community. The issue was so critical that Elliott's defense of it was enshrined in a spectacular piece of political imagery in the mid-1870s. "The Shackle Broken—by the Genius of Freedom," published in 1874 by the Baltimore-based lithographers E. Sachse & Co., depicts Elliott debating Alexander H. Stephens, the former Confederate vice president who had recently been elected to Congress. Delivered on January 6, 1874, the day after Stephens had voiced his opposition to Sumner's pending bill, Elliott's impassioned defense of the legislation made him a national icon among African Americans.[40]

Elliott denounced Stephens as a dangerous relic of a bygone era who represented a palpable threat to the stability of the American Republic: "It is scarcely twelve years since that gentleman shocked the civilized world by announcing the birth of a government which rested on human slavery as

Detail from "The Shackle Broken—by the Genius of Freedom"
(Baltimore: E. Sachse & Co., c. 1874). (Library of Congress,
Prints and Photographs Division, LC-DIG-pga-02592)

its corner-stone." The speech also afforded Elliott the opportunity to make broad political claims for his race: "The progress of events has swept away that *pseudo-government* which rested on greed, pride, and tyranny; and the race whom he then ruthlessly spurned and trampled on are here to meet him in debate, and to demand that the rights which are enjoyed by their former oppressors . . . shall be accorded to those who even in the darkness of slavery kept their allegiance true to freedom and the Union."[41]

Elliott linked his approach to a unique interpretation of the recent Supreme Court ruling in the *Slaughter-House Cases* (1873). There the Court ruled that the Fourteenth Amendment protected the privileges and immunities of American citizens but did not protect the privileges and immunities of citizens of a particular state (in other words, if federal law was broken, that required government intervention, but not if state laws were at stake).

Nevertheless, Elliott viewed the decision in a more positive light than did his white Democratic counterparts.[42] Elliott articulated the general consensus of all black congressional leaders that the Reconstruction amendments established federal obligations to all citizens. This part of his speech is so memorable that an excerpt of it is embossed above the American flag hanging over the House of Representatives in the lithograph. Using the *Slaughter-House Cases* as support for his contentions, Elliott declared that the Reconstruction amendments were designed to ensure for blacks "not only their nominal freedom, but their complete protection from those who had formerly exercised unlimited dominion over them." He believed that in "this broad light," the Reconstruction amendments had to be interpreted as intending complete equality for all American citizens: "What you give to one class you must give to all; what you deny to one class you shall deny to all, unless in the exercise of the common and universal police power of the State you find it needful to confer exclusive privileges on certain citizens, to be held and exercised still for the common good of all."[43] He saw these principles as the "doctrines of the *Slaughter-House Cases*" and denied that these rulings (which limited the protections of the Fourteenth Amendment) left Congress impotent to pass strong legislation against "plain discrimination" by the states.

At the center of the lithograph memorializing this speech is the imposing figure of Elliott, speaking in defense of Sumner's Civil Rights Bill. He inhabits a biracial House of Representatives in which other white and black congressmen conduct business and look on as Elliott speaks with his arm raised. Surrounding this central image are excerpts from Elliott's message, along with images of Abraham Lincoln, Senator Sumner, and several scenes depicting African American service in the Union army and navy.

Juxtaposed with these images is the passing of the old order of plantation slavery, symbolized by the depiction of a black family surveying their own land. Beneath this image is a caption: "American Slave Labour is of the Past—Free Labour is of the Present," followed by words that surely would have startled most Southern whites: "We toil for our own children and not for those of others." The lithograph encapsulated the emancipatory message by highlighting four major themes that captured the desire of former slaves in the mid-1870s: equality, liberty, jury, and ballot.

The lithograph taps into a familiar set of themes in the black community. The "democracy of the dead" tradition, with its emphasis on emancipation, the Civil War, black military service, and racial uplift, was in full bloom in this image. The image presents a transformative moment in the political life of black Americans. Leaders like Elliott, Walls, Rapier, Lynch, and Langston were no longer merely regional spokesmen, but national political leaders whose views increasingly transcended congressional districts and embodied the hopes of all African Americans. The image of a biracial Congress crystallized the idea that blacks were no longer an oppressed minority, but American citizens. The lithograph thus encapsulated the words of John Mercer Langston, who, while addressing an African American audience on August 1, 1866, linked black pride with American nationalism: "We want to understand that we are no longer colored people, but Americans. We have been called all manner of names. I have always called our people negroes. Perhaps you don't like it—I do. I want it to become synonymous with character. We are no longer negroes simply—no longer colored people simply, but a part of the great whole of the mighty American nation."[44] The arrival of black men in Congress, serving as national politicians, made Langston's vision a reality.

As the image of a biracial Congress illustrated, Elliott was not alone in the House but had many colleagues, black and white, on his side. The visibility of black politicians on the national stage served as a source of pride for the black community. Also, by depicting Elliott in midspeech, the lithograph illustrates the role that rhetoric played in the formation of policies to defend black civil and political equality.

Civil Rights, Reconciliation, and Emancipatory Diplomacy

Other black congressmen built on Downing's memorial and Elliott's powerful rhetoric to put forward far-reaching civil rights proposals. Despite some broad similarities, the approaches of these congressmen diverged significantly. Walls made bold assertions regarding the government's right to legislate behavior, while Langston crafted a sophisticated legal brief supporting Sumner's bill and also calling for the liberation of Cuba from Spanish rule. Rapier highlighted the incongruity experienced by immigrants to America once they discovered that not all citizens were free and equal members of society. Lynch, meanwhile, emphasized the distinction between public rights (or political equality) and social rights. As the historian Hannah Rosen deftly illustrates, the fight over black civil rights was just as much about gendered understandings of race as it was about black inferiority and white supremacy. Nor were black politicians unaware of the extremes to which their white opponents would go to undermine their demands for political equality. Whites denigrated blacks as men but also used sexual violence as a tool to undermine black communities (by raping women) while painting black men as beasts who were undeserving of equality.[45] The distinction between public and social rights, also raised by Downing's memorial, was the most prevalent theme used by national black political leaders fighting for Sumner's bill. Although they used this argument to make the legislation more palatable to Democrats, the embrace of this strategy marked the limits of black gregariousness. Walls made it especially clear that political niceties and conciliation with whites were included in black congressmen's rhetorical arsenal but were not their most preferred weapons.

On January 6, 1874, Walls spoke up in defense of the Civil Rights Bill. In brief but revealing comments, he supported Elliott and Rainey's political strategy. Walls recalled black support for general amnesty and then analyzed the roots of racism in American society: "Men may concede that public sentiment, and not law, is the cause of the discrimination of which we justly complain and the resultant disabilities under which we labor. If this be so, then such public sentiment needs penal correction and should be regulated by law." He concluded, "It is the duty of the men of to-day . . . to remove from the path of [the Republic's] upward progress every obstacle which may impede its advance in the future." Walls asserted that civil rights legislation was the only way to curtail ignorant and racist behavior—a fairly radical sentiment in 1874. Given these radical beliefs, one can appreciate how sophisticated and restrained his political strategies usually were.

Walls's vision of emancipatory reconciliation directly challenged the emergent "Lost Cause" ideology embraced by many white Southerners. Whereas some whites still contended that national reconciliation required the subordination of blacks as second-class citizens, Walls suggested that true reconciliation consisted in all sides coming together to eliminate racism and ignorant behavior in order to create a new, just society. He scoffed at claims that social equality would follow "the concession of equal public rights," calling this result about "as likely as that danger will come to the Republic because of general amnesty." The familiar white Southern fears of anarchy and racial turmoil were emerging once again, and Walls moved swiftly to counter them. He argued that the only people putting forward such arguments were "those whose political life depends upon the existence of a baseless prejudice wholly unworthy of a civilized country and disgraceful to the American people." On the other hand, he also denounced the idea that race relations would be radically changed by giving "simple justice" to African Americans. He described this line of reasoning as a "clap-trap addressed to the ignorant and vicious, and [one that] finds no response in the American heart, which in its best impulses rises superior to all groveling prejudices." Walls insisted that his constituents' demands were reasonable, since without such legislation African Americans would not have "a fair opportunity to demonstrate their fitness for American citizenship," and would see "the channels of advancement in the legitimate pursuits of life . . . forever closed."[46]

Shortly after delivering this speech, Walls would begin to set forth a still more ambitious vision of black civil and political equality—one that transcended national borders—by arguing that the United States needed to apply the results of the Civil War to its international diplomacy. By venturing into a discussion of American foreign relations, Walls tapped into long-standing black desires to oppose slavery outside the United States. In doing so, he also helped to craft a new strategy for defending Sumner's legislation, one that Rapier and Langston would later adopt.

Walls's ideal of emancipatory diplomacy was a natural counterpart to his sweeping vision of emancipatory reconciliation at home. Blacks' concern with the fate of colonial subjects and enslaved peoples abroad was not new; black abolitionists had paid close attention to emancipation in the British West Indies and the black republic of Haiti. Indeed, prior to the Civil War, a young Langston was captivated by Haiti's experience with emancipation and briefly embraced emigration and black nationalism as possible solutions to his race's plight. These concerns were intensified with the 1868 outbreak of the Ten Years' War in Cuba, which galvanized black politicians and their constituents. *La Guerra de los Diez Años* highlighted the connections that Walls saw between black emancipation in the South and demands for black freedom in the Caribbean.[47]

The Ten Years' War was, in many respects, a rehearsal for Cuba's later struggle for freedom from Spanish colonialism. Some of the key figures who would lead the struggle for Cuban independence in 1895 appeared for the first time in 1868. The conflict began as a war both against black slavery and for Cuban independence; on October 10, 1868, the prominent sugar planter and insurgent leader Carlos Manuel de Céspedes staged *el Grito de Yara* (the Cry of Yara), freeing his slaves and urging them to join him in the struggle against Spanish colonialism.[48] Though this action did not put an end to interracial tensions, it profoundly impacted the future course of Cuban struggles for independence. Indeed, when the ultimately successful war for independence commenced, the brilliant poet-revolutionary José Martí framed the battle as an interracial affair. The similarities between black emancipation and the struggle for Cuban independence struck a chord with Walls.

More practical concerns may have influenced Walls's support for the Cuban rebels. The small but growing population of Cubans in Florida strongly backed the Republican Party, prolonging Republican competitiveness in Monroe County (which included the city of Key West) as Reconstruction suffered elsewhere in the state. Reconstruction politicians were not immune to matters of diplomacy or international affairs. An antislavery and anticolonial struggle for independence occurring just ninety miles away from Florida could not be easily ignored, even as domestic issues of race relations, economics, and political corruption took center stage. Indeed, as Morton Keller notes, "it is not surprising that in the wake of a war fought to end slavery and sustain Union, American diplomacy displayed an active concern for the rights of citizenship."[49] In the aftermath of emancipation, the postwar American government actively criticized the continued existence of slavery throughout the New World; newly freed slaves joined in, expressing deep interest in the plight of blacks in Cuba.

On October 31, 1873, Spanish forces intercepted the *Virginius*, a ship smuggling guns to Cuban revolutionaries under the American flag. Fifty-three crew members, including some American citizens, were executed as pirates. Secretary of State Hamilton Fish smoothed over relations between the two nations as best as he could by convincing the Spanish to pay an indemnity to the families of the executed Americans. Even so, the Spanish actions incensed many Americans, particularly the Cuban population in Florida.[50]

On January 24, 1874, Walls urged the adoption of a joint resolution supporting the Cuban revolutionaries. He also demanded that his colleagues recognize the connections between American emancipation and the Cuban patriots' commitment to the antislavery cause. Walls proceeded to recall numerous struggles against oppression throughout history, from the revolt in Haiti to the Greek struggle against Turkey. He chastised the United States for its failure to act at home or abroad, stating that the American government's ability to act decisively was hampered by "conditions of neutrality." A century had passed since independence, and Walls lamented that already the "struggle of the fathers for liberty, and the heroism and sacrifices of our own patriots" was being forgotten. These developments were leading the United States into a paralysis of sorts, hindering "the strong arm that was ever ready to protect the weak and assist the oppressed to a

"Arrival of the surviving prisoners of the *Virginius* crew at
New York; demonstrations of welcome by their friends and sympathizers
at Trujillo's restaurant on Pine Street" (*Frank Leslie's Illustrated Newspaper,*
January 17, 1874, 312–13). (Library of Congress, Prints and
Photographs Division, LC-USZ62-121645)

higher plane of manhood." Not only had Americans forgotten their history, but
worse still, Walls believed, "we have forgotten the grand principle which
underlies our institutions; ceased to have a 'manifest destiny'; have given
the 'Monroe Doctrine' to the winds of heaven; while upon our own soil
continued atrocities are committed to violation of every principle we have
enunciated in the past."[51]

Walls's appeals and the very phrasing of his arguments reflect the rhetoric of manhood and manliness that emerged in the 1880s and 1890s. Male
dominance was tied to a particular vision of what constituted civilization.
Increasingly, white middle-class males viewed race as a factor integral to
their understandings of gender. As the cultural historian Gail Bederman
notes, "whiteness was both a palpable fact and a manly ideal for these
men."[52] In public spaces such as the 1893 World's Columbian Exposition in

Chicago, the connections between race and gender were made explicit. The exposition "demonstrated . . . that 'nonwhite' and 'uncivilized' denoted 'unmanly' and, conversely, that whiteness and civilization denoted powerful manhood."[53] In many instances, how minorities were treated in the exposition communicated their inferiority and their relative lack of civilization and masculinity. In some ways, then, Walls's invocation of manhood in this context could be seen as an early iteration of the discourse of manliness and civilization that would emerge at a later point in American history. For Walls, this message could serve the purpose of racial uplift, encouraging his hearers to take the unfortunate nonwhite races and raise them to a higher level of civilization.

Walls's perspective also highlighted another aspect of how gender and race intersected in the late nineteenth century. The historian Kristin L. Hoganson argues that gendered rhetoric and a desire among politicians to assert their manhood influenced the U.S. initiation of the Spanish-American War in 1898. She notes that as the Civil War faded from memory, "the manly ideal of politics became ever more elusive. As the number of Civil War veterans dwindled, the argument that military service had proven the right of all men to participate in politics lost credibility, for the vast majority of men who had matured since the war could not demand political rights based on such service."[54] This new generation of postwar Americans had lost the tangible connection to the ideology and worldview described by Kirk Savage—that manhood and citizenship were linked with courage on the battlefield. Hoganson concludes that "rather than reflecting on the shared experiences of combat, political commentators paid an increasing amount of attention to the differences that divided immigrant and native-born men, working-class and wealthier men, and black and white men."[55] Indeed, the breakdown of the "fraternal character of politics," as a result of these shifts and of voter disfranchisement (along both racial and class lines), set the stage for the combative rhetoric that would briefly sweep Americans into colonial wars of occupation.[56]

In this respect, Walls's bold defense of the Cuban struggle for independence is instructive. He articulated an emancipatory discourse of manhood in his plea for American intervention. In this way, his call for American support of Cuban independence illuminates two distinctions between two forms of imperialism: an emancipationist vision and a white supremacist vision. Walls believed that American intervention was required because Cubans were equal to Americans (and to African Americans in particular).

Their cause merited the support of the United States, which had recently abolished slavery. Therefore Walls supported intervention on the grounds that it was the United States' duty to help other countries liberate themselves from oppression. This was distinct from the motivations of latter-day Yankee imperialists from Alfred Thayer Mahan to Theodore Roosevelt, who largely espoused a white supremacist vision of imperialism (intimately linked with their own views on the necessity of economic and territorial expansion for the well-being of the United States), viewing potential colonies from the perspective that the nonwhite peoples were inferior (either racially or culturally) to Americans and, as such, needed to be placed under the guardianship of a more civilized nation.[57]

Walls's advocacy is especially interesting in view of the spectacular failure of President Grant's earlier attempt to annex the Dominican Republic, which was defeated by the U.S. Senate on June 30, 1870. Indeed, in addition to the material benefits of taking the island, Grant cited "humanitarian and abolitionist motives" along with racial considerations, in ways that were strikingly similar to Walls's subsequent rhetorical defense of American intervention in the Ten Years' War. According to the diplomatic historian Eric T. L. Love, Grant believed that, by taking the Dominican Republic, he might be able to contribute substantially to the erosion of slavery elsewhere (particularly in Cuba and Brazil), a goal shared by Walls and later articulated by Langston. The president thought that the Dominicans shared an admiration for and a desire to possess America's democratic institutions. Grant spoke positively of their character in a private memorandum in 1869, stating that they were "anxious to join their fortunes with ours; industrious, if made to feel that the products of their industry is [sic] to be protected; tollrent [sic] as to the religious, or political views of their neighbors." Furthermore, Grant saw the Dominican Republic as providing (in Love's words) "a safety valve for the country and a safe haven for African Americans." Acknowledging the existence of racism and its injustice, Grant nonetheless believed that giving African Americans an island where they could find respite might enable them to prove their worthiness to white Americans, and that this result would create a more just society at home as well. Moreover, acquiring the Dominican Republic would create other alternatives. Should the problem of American racism not be resolved, African Americans would be able to emigrate and "find a home in the Antillas."[58] Nevertheless, publicly Grant hid his explicitly racial concerns as he attempted to court powerful leaders (like abolitionist senator Charles Sumner) and the American public, which was not enamored with the idea of acquiring a nonwhite population.[59] Ironically, it was precisely the racism of the American public and even of such allies of the black community as Sumner that doomed the treaty to annex the Dominican Republic. Indeed, Sumner declared that the island, "situated in tropical waters, and occupied by another race, of another color . . . never can become a permanent possession of the United States. . . . Already by a higher statute is that island set apart to the colored race. It is theirs by right of possession, by their sweat and blood mingling with the soil, by tropical position, its burning sun, and by unalterable laws of climate. Such is the ordinance of Nature . . . which I am not the first to recognize."[60] Walls may not have been aware of Grant's particular intentions, but he must have recognized the nearly impossible position in which he was placing himself by demanding American intervention in Cuba when prior attempts to intervene in the Caribbean had failed.

Nevertheless, Walls drew upon the traditional nineteenth-century understanding of manhood to make his case for American intervention in the Cuban Ten Years' War. He drew upon the sacrifices of the Civil War, which were still fresh in the minds of many Americans. For Walls, manhood was rooted in physical prowess, courage, and the ability to affirm one's rights through distinguished service on the battlefield, but it also incorporated emergent notions of racial uplift and liberation of nonwhite populations — ideas that would ultimately be rejected in favor of the white supremacist notions of imperialism that motivated American colonial projects of the early twentieth century. Though critical of American inaction, Walls believed that in the end the Cubans would receive American support.[61] By advocating support for the Cuban revolutionaries, he sought to lead the American people to a different kind of manhood, one rooted in a language of equal rights rather than domination.

Walls's vision of emancipatory diplomacy almost certainly influenced how Langston and Rapier articulated their support for Sumner's bill. As we shall see, Langston believed that his vision of an interracial America necessitated a commitment to supporting Cuban independence. Rapier, meanwhile, called attention to the hypocrisy of American society by comparing his treatment abroad with what he experienced at home. He challenged Americans to live consistently with their ideals, so that newly arriving immigrants would not see a racial double standard in American society. Both Langston and Rapier drew upon Walls's language of manhood and emancipatory diplomacy. In so doing, they made Sumner's legislation into something more than just a guarantee for black citizenship; they also saw it as the key to revolutionizing America's domestic and diplomatic priorities.

Marshaling the Law against Racial Hypocrisy

Returning to his alma mater of Oberlin College (where he had studied as an undergraduate and received a master's degree in theology) on May 17, 1874, the anniversary of the adoption of the Fifteenth Amendment, Langston spoke on "Equality before the Law." Fondly recalling his college days, Langston said Oberlin had treated him as it would have treated any other American. Though a poor black man, Langston found himself treated as an equal whether he stayed in a local hotel, attended classes in college, or spent time with different families. Langston knew he was addressing a national audience, even as he spoke in an Oberlin auditorium. While his congressional colleagues sought to advance Sumner's civil rights agenda in the face of Democratic and Southern white opposition, Langston was working outside Congress to secure the support of historically abolitionist allies in Ohio.

Warming to his main argument, he described the progress of the cause of racial equality and emphasized his vision of an emergent biracial polity: "Within the last fifteen years, the colored American has been raised from the condition of four-footed beasts and creeping things to the level of en-franchised manhood."[62] Langston affirmed the theme, common in post–Civil War black political culture, that blacks were not only free but politically equal as American citizens.[63] "Indeed," Langston declared, "two nations have been born in a day. For in the death of slavery . . . the colored American has been spoken into the new life of liberty and law; while new and better purposes, aspirations, and feelings, have possessed and moved the soul of his fellow-countrymen." Langston stressed that emancipation "fixed by law that the place where we are born is *ipso facto* our country; and this gives us a domicile, a home."

He reviewed the evolution of American thinking regarding citizenship rights, starting with the 1821 opinion of James Monroe's attorney general, William Wirt, who accepted the possibility that free blacks and mulattoes could satisfy some of the requirements of citizenship but could not view them as full citizens. Langston recalled the statements of Attorney General Hugh S. Legare, who in 1843 classified blacks as "denizens," and then turned to the broadly conceived comments in favor of black citizenship made by Lincoln's attorney general, Edward Bates, in 1862. Bates's opinion undermined the 1859 *Dred Scott* decision in which the Supreme Court had ruled that blacks could never be American citizens.[64]

Drawing on this history, Langston crafted a legal argument in favor of Sumner's bill. Though great changes had taken place concerning the "legal

Professor John Mercer Langston of Howard University.
(Library of Congress, Prints and Photographs Division,
LC-DIG-cwpbh-00690)

status" of African Americans, Langston believed that blacks had not yet been "given the full exercise and enjoyment of all the rights which appertain by law to American citizenship." Those rights were being denied to blacks on the assertion that "their recognition would result in social equality. . . . Such reasoning is no more destitute of logic than law." Langston then added two other arguments for his vision of civil rights that merit closer attention: one dealing with common schooling and the other with the influence of "emancipatory legislation" at home on American policy abroad.

Like Walls, who supported the government's right to legislate against ignorant or racist behaviors, Langston argued against segregation and unequal educational opportunities. "Equal in freedom, sustained by law; equal in citizenship defined and supported by the law; equal in the exercise of political powers, regulated and sanctioned by law; by what refinement of reasoning, or tenet of law, can the denial of common school and other educational advantages be justified?" If the Civil War, emancipation, and the long series of Reconstruction acts and constitutional amendments had enshrined African Americans as equal citizens, Langston argued, then surely there could be no legitimate basis for opposing equal schools. He understood why whites opposed such advances—prejudice and racism were to blame. But the solution was not to acquiesce to the demands of opponents of Sumner's legislation. The consequences of such actions would be detrimental to both races.

Segregated schools would not resolve the problems facing white and black Southerners, Langston argued, but would only exacerbate existing tensions: "Schools which tend to separate the children of the country . . . which foster and perpetuate sentiments of caste, hatred, and ill-will . . . are contrary to the spirit of our laws and institutions. Two separate school systems . . . tolerating such a state of feeling and sentiment on the part of the classes . . . cannot educate these classes to live harmoniously together." Therefore it was not sufficient for the government to guarantee blacks voting and citizenship rights. The government had to expand its conception of civil rights beyond enfranchisement into public spaces and guarantee blacks equal and desegregated educational opportunities. Without these steps, the lingering prejudices and racism that bred white contempt would never be conquered.

Langston concluded by considering how passage of Sumner's legislation would affect U.S. relations with other nations in the Americas. With the dawning of freedom in the United States, Langston believed that Americans needed to consider their duty to help to abolish slavery elsewhere, particularly in areas "where [it] is maintained by despotic Spanish rule, and where the people declaring slavery abolished, and appealing to the civilized world for sympathy and justification of their course, have staked all upon 'the dread arbitrament of war.'" Like Walls, Langston believed that the legacy of the Civil War had bequeathed Americans a duty to undertake the course of emancipatory diplomacy, and he thus linked support of the pending Civil Rights Bill with justification of American intervention in Cuba. Going beyond Walls's earlier arguments, Langston exhorted his audience that there could be "no peace on our continent" until slavery was abolished completely and freedom guaranteed by the law. Every nation had the right to experience a "new birth of freedom," and a "government of the people, by the people, and for the people." Langston concluded that "where battle is made against despotism and oppression, wherever humanity struggles for national existence and recognition, there his sympathies should be felt, his word and succor inspiriting, encouraging and supporting."[65]

In presenting an inspiring vision of an interracial American republic, Langston captured the optimism of national black political leaders and their constituents. His policy agenda was far-reaching: Americans needed to pass Sumner's Civil Rights Bill and secure truly equal and desegregated public accommodations, modes of transportation, and educational institutions for the benefit of all races. In addition, he contended, the United States should build on its revolutionary legacy and work actively to topple slavery throughout the Americas. This commitment to liberty was the cornerstone upon which American society now rested.

Where Walls and Langston emphasized broad conceptions of the reach of the federal government and the liberating potential of embracing strong civil rights legislation, Rapier took a different approach. Rather than extolling the virtues of American society or arguing in favor of legislating behavior, he sought to shame his colleagues into action by depicting American hypocrisy. Echoing the transnational focus of Walls and Langston, Rapier illustrated the inconsistencies between the idealized version of America held by immigrants and the black experience at home and abroad.

On June 9, 1874, speaking in support of Sumner's bill, Rapier drew attention to incongruities in the arguments put forward by Democratic opponents, particularly Tennessee's John Morgan Bright and James Beck of Kentucky. In measured tones, he acknowledged the awkwardness of his position as an African American serving in the U.S. Congress. "I must confess it is somewhat embarrassing for a colored man to urge the passage of this bill," Rapier stated, because in advocating for it he risked being "charged with a desire for social equality." But he added that "it is just as embarrassing for him not to do so, for if he remains silent while the struggle is being carried on around . . . he is liable to be charged with a want of interest in a matter that concerns him more than anyone else."[66]

Rapier explained that the law recognized his right to serve as a congressman, yet no laws guaranteed him the right to equal accommodations while he sought to serve his constituents in Washington. "Here I am the peer of the proudest, but on a steamboat or car I am not equal to the most degraded. Is not this most anomalous and ridiculous?" Rapier contended that the United States was not a shining beacon of hope for immigrants. He hoped that there were no foreigners present in his audience. They had been "lured to our shores by the popular but untruthful declaration that this land is the asylum for the oppressed," but the reality was far from the truth. How could America be that asylum if a member of Congress had "no civil rights that another class is bound to respect"? Foreigners could learn a terrible lesson in the United States, one that they could not find in any other country. Here "it is possible for a man to be half free and half slave . . . for a man to enjoy political rights while he is denied civil ones; here he will see a man legislating for a free people, while his own chains of civil slavery hang about him."[67] Much of Rapier's speech exposed the divergence between the image of the United States as a land for immigrants and the ugly reality of prejudice experienced by African Americans of all classes.

Rapier buttressed his discussion of what he termed "American hypocrisy" by drawing on his own experience as Alabama's state commissioner to the Fifth World's Fair in Vienna. He repeated, somewhat sarcastically, the familiar theme of black claims to manhood and citizenship: "I left home last year and traveled six months in foreign lands, and the moment I put my foot upon the deck of a ship that unfurled a foreign flag from its mast-head, distinctions on account of my color ceased. I am not aware that my presence aboard the steamer put her off course. I believe that we made the trip in the usual time." In other countries Rapier could go to a hotel without fear that someone would slam the door in his face. Returning to such treatment in his native country left him with deep scars: "I feel this humiliation very keenly; it dwarfs my manhood, and certainly it impairs my usefulness as a citizen."[68]

In words reminiscent of Frederick Douglass's famous 1852 speech, "What to the Slave Is the Fourth of July?," Rapier noted his lack of enthusiasm about commemorating the centennial of American independence: "How would I appear at the centennial celebration of our national freedom, with my own galling chains of slavery hanging about me? I could no more rejoice on that occasion . . . than the Jews could sing in their wonted style as they sat as captives beside the Babylonish streams. . . . After all, this question resolves itself to this: either I am a man or I am not a man."[69]

Rapier saw the debate over the Civil Rights Bill as something other than a normal debate over policy. Policy "has nothing to do with it; . . . in this case justice is the only standard to be used, and you can no more divide justice than you can divide Deity."[70] In other words, it was possible to have constructive disagreements over internal improvements or private legislation, but basic civil rights and political equality should not be matters of debate. Of course, many whites did not see the issue in the same way; in fact, the thought of providing blacks with civil rights or greater access to education incensed them as few other policy debates did. Rapier, however, rejected white Democrats' insistence that further civil rights legislation would lead to disaster. No disasters had occurred once blacks received the vote or were allowed to attend schools. Why should expanded protections or increased educational opportunities produce a different result? Rapier believed that the drumbeat of Democratic opposition to any expansion of civil rights protections or educational benefits rested on intransigent racism. His impassioned plea, however, did not change the minds of his white opponents, nor did it bolster his chances for reelection as whites turned to violence and intimidation. He would lose his seat in 1874.

Returning to the lame-duck session of the Forty-Third Congress after his defeat, Rapier called a meeting of black national and state political leaders at his rooming house on 1619 K Street N.W. to craft a response to the civil disorder afflicting the Deep South. Those at the meeting included Douglass, Langston, Pinchback, Downing, South Carolina's Robert Purvis, Judge Mifflin Wistar Gibbs, Alabama editor Philip Joseph, Dr. Charles Burleigh Purvis of Howard University, and North Carolinian George W. Price Jr.[71] After several hours of discussion, the men drafted a declaration on behalf of all African Americans throughout the United States. Their statement placed the blame for violent depredations on Democrats. Any victory that the Democratic Party gained, whether in "a northern state or upon the floor of Congress, tends directly to increase the audacity and lawlessness of the enemies of constitutional freedom and the Union as now established," they stated. They also decried the "timid assertion of rights by our friends" and urged Congress not to adjourn "without enacting and providing for the enforcement of appropriate laws for the better protection of persons, property, and political rights" in the South. The black leaders floated the possibility that if Congress failed to act despite the strong Republican majority in both houses, blacks could either choose neutrality or align themselves with "their old oppressors" in the Democratic Party.

Rapier, Douglass, and Langston feared another possible scenario— namely, that should Southern blacks be "stung to madness and desperation by continued and unceasing outrages, and seeing no means of escape, a spirit of retaliation and revenge may be aroused which will fill the south with scenes of rapine, blood and fire." To avoid this calamity, they urged Congress to pass strong protections of civil rights.[72] Throughout the Forty-Third Congress, and especially in the days and hours before a vote on Sumner's bill, all seven black members of the House of Representatives spoke in its favor and detailed the violence aimed at black Southerners.[73] Not until this moment had any black politician seriously raised the possibility that blacks might turn on their white oppressors and initiate a violent race war in the South.

A Diplomatic Distinction: Public and Social Rights

Mississippi's John Roy Lynch took a markedly different approach. Speaking on February 3, 1875, two days after the meeting in Rapier's boardinghouse,

Lynch outlined his reasons for supporting the bill, expressing the hope that his remarks would not further intensify the partisan feelings in Congress.[74] Building upon arguments made by his congressional colleagues, he explained why public and social rights (that is, civil rights and social equality) were separate issues that should not be linked in the debate on this bill.

Lynch challenged the idea that social equality was the bill's objective: "I have never believed for a moment that social equality could be brought about even between persons of the same race. But those who contend that the passage of this bill will have a tendency to bring about social equality between the races . . . admit that [that is, act as if] there are no social distinctions among white people whatever." His Democratic colleagues, Lynch asserted, did not really believe that "the immoral, the ignorant and the degraded of their own race are the social equals of themselves, and their families." If they seriously believed that, then they obviously did not put "as high an estimate upon their own social standing as respectable and intelligent colored people place upon theirs." Furthermore, he knew that thousands of white people were socially inferior to many "respectable" and "intelligent" African Americans.[75]

Lynch was not trying to insult his white colleagues. Rather, he crafted his arguments in order to expose the inconsistencies of opposing arguments and to make clear exactly what rights African Americans sought through Sumner's legislation. Using sarcasm to make his point, Lynch referred to his "Democratic friends" as his "social inferiors," promising them a seat at the same table with him but saying that this gesture did not mean that he accepted them as his social equals. While (satirically) denying them social equality, Lynch promised that if anyone attempted to discriminate against these Democrats, Lynch would favor protecting their rights "by suitable and appropriate legislation."[76]

He went on to clarify the relationship between public rights and social rights: "It is not social rights that we desire. We have enough of that already. What we ask for is the protection in the enjoyment of public rights—rights that are or should be accorded to every citizen alike." As Rapier had done previously, Lynch described the inconsistencies in America's "present system of race distinctions." An immoral white woman could go to any public space or use public transportation and receive the same treatment given to the best members of society. But if "an intelligent, modest, refined colored lady presents herself" and asks for the same privileges that have been given to "her social inferior of the white race . . . in nine cases out of ten . . . she will not only be refused, but insulted for making the request." Though

Lynch placated white Southerners and Democrats by denying that blacks had any desire for social equality, he also made it obvious that social standing had nothing to do with civil rights. He implored his white colleagues to see the injustice of this state of affairs: "I appeal to your sensitive feelings as husbands, fathers, and brothers, is this just? You who have affectionate companions, attractive daughters, and loving sisters, is this just? If you have any of the ingredients of manhood in your composition, you will answer the question most emphatically, No!"[77]

In his effort to win support for Sumner's Civil Rights Bill, Lynch abandoned black claims to social equality with whites but also played along with traditional Southern conceptions of gender roles. As Phillip Brian Harper and others have pointed out, black masculinity has largely been dominated by a desire to affirm black males' manhood in opposition to femininity. Though Harper focuses largely on the twentieth century in his analysis, such thinking was present in the nineteenth century as well. Lynch was defending the rights of black women by relying on traditional white Southern understandings of a man's role in society. Men (and Southern men in particular) were supposed to protect their women, who were defenseless but also pure ladies. Lynch operated from the same framework. In affirming black manhood and equality, he relied on the assumption that black women (like their white counterparts) needed to be defended by strong black men because they too were pure ladies. Thus, in seeking to confront segregated transportation, Lynch affirmed traditional Southern gender roles.[78]

Again like Rapier, Lynch then turned to his personal experience: "Here I am, a member of your honorable body . . . and yet, when I leave my home to come to the capital of the nation . . . in coming through the God-forsaken States of Kentucky and Tennessee . . . I am treated, not as an American citizen, but as a brute. Forced to occupy a filthy smoking car both night and day, with drunkards, gamblers, and criminals; and for what?" Lynch could pay his own way and was not disrespectful, yet he suffered this treatment solely because of his complexion.[79]

This sort of treatment might have been tolerable had it been limited only to black men, but black women faced the "same insults" and the "same uncivilized treatment." Lynch mocked the suggestion that these issues should be resolved by court cases rather than legislation. "What a farce!" he exclaimed. "Talk about instituting a civil-rights suit in the State courts of Kentucky . . . where the decision of the judge is virtually rendered before he enters the courthouse, and the verdict of the jury substantially rendered before it is impaneled."[80]

Lynch concluded, "The only moments of my life when I am necessarily compelled to question my loyalty to my Government or my devotion to the flag of my country are when I read of outrages having been committed upon innocent colored people and the perpetrators go unpunished." As long as this situation of "unjust discrimination" is tolerated, he said, "our boasted civilization is a fraud, our republican institutions a failure; our social system a disgrace; and our religion a complete hypocrisy." Though he expressed confidence that Americans would not continue to tolerate this state of affairs, Lynch's open revulsion to the continued violation of his constituents' rights is striking, especially since he understood that a forceful defense of the federal government's role in legislating behavior would likely enhance white opposition to Sumner's bill.[81]

To rally support for his position, Lynch quoted from an editorial by the leading conservative Democratic newspaper in Mississippi, the *Jackson Clarion,* that minimized the bill's likely impact on segregated public education. The editorial stated, "The provisions of the bill do not necessarily break up the separate school system, unless the people interested choose that they shall do so; and there is no reason to believe that the colored people of this State are dissatisfied with the system as it is or that they are not content to let well enough alone."[82] Implicitly accepting this viewpoint, Lynch stated that blacks wanted the school clause included in civil rights legislation not because they believed "that their children can be better educated in white than in colored schools . . . but they recognize the fact that the distinction when made and tolerated by law is an unjust and odious proscription; that you make their color a ground of objection, and consequently a crime. This is what we most earnestly protest against." Lynch acknowledged that mixed-race schools would emerge only in small localities and that for "years to come" segregated educational institutions would persist throughout the South. Thus he did not call for immediate desegregation, but agreed with Langston's earlier proposals opposing the establishment of any system of education that would transmit and reinforce damaging distinctions between the two races. He concluded that once equal citizenship rights were conferred, blacks and whites could choose to separate their children lawfully since the "separation is their own voluntary act, and not legislative compulsion."[83] Though Lynch tried to use this more moderate strategy to gain support for the school clause of Sumner's Civil Rights Bill, ultimately that provision was dropped before final passage.

The 1875 Civil Rights Act and the Downfall of Reconstruction

Walls, Langston, Rapier, and Lynch played their part at the national level to put into practice the black electorate's desire for strong civil rights legislation. Though the lame-duck Republican majority succeeded in passing a watered-down version of Sumner's original bill, this act would prove to be one of the last major pieces of civil rights legislation enacted during Reconstruction. Nor would the final bill be satisfactory to all black congressmen. When the final vote took place on February 4, 1875, the lack of a school clause proved too much for Walls to stomach. Four black congressmen, including Lynch and Rapier, joined with the majority of 162 members to pass the Civil Rights Act, but Walls and South Carolina's Alonzo Ransier abstained.[84]

The bold attempts by national black political leaders to link black civil rights with expanded educational opportunities may have helped to damage the Republicans' chances of electoral success by the mid-1870s. At the same time, the limits of Northern willingness to fight for black civil and political equality were clearly evident. Indeed, the historian Ward M. McAfee asserts that Republican support for racially integrated schools nationwide cost the party its majority in the House of Representatives. As long as Republican support for black civil rights focused on making changes only in the South, it was able to press forward. But the issue of racial integration in the nation's public schools brought Reconstruction "to an insurmountable stone wall."[85]

The efforts by black congressmen to deny that they were pursuing social equality or mandatory integrated schooling did not convince the majority of Southerners or whites across the nation. The lack of white Northern support for continued civil rights legislation (particularly on the subject of mixed schools) did not help either black Republicans or their white congressional allies; rather, it almost certainly contributed to the Democratic resurgence in the House of Representatives in 1874, which in turn set the stage for a potential Democratic comeback in the presidential race of 1876. Despite the political backlash against stronger federal civil rights protections for freedmen, black congressional support for the Civil Rights Act of 1875 displayed creativity and unwavering tenacity.

This determined support must be understood within the context of the rampant violence across the South and the broader policy agendas put forward by the generation of black congressmen who served in the decade after the adoption of the Fifteenth Amendment. National black politicians' considerable experience of racial violence, contested elections, and political instability in their respective states and congressional districts necessitated a vision of civil rights and political equality that moved beyond the electoral franchise. When black congressmen arrived in Washington, they brought with them the optimism and terror they had experienced at home and confronted the limitations of practical politics in the House of Representatives. But they also went beyond their local experience. In all their rhetoric they emphasized that the promise of the Republic had yet to be fulfilled. They transformed black "democracy of the dead" rhetoric and tapped into a wellspring of sentiment regarding the Union. Rather than celebrating the triumph of American democracy, black congressmen highlighted the "unfulfilled Union"—one that needed to incorporate all citizens regardless of race. The limits of the nation's commitment to fulfilling its promises illuminated the tenuous nature of black political power as Reconstruction gave way to Redemption by the close of the decade.[86]

5

"Color-Line Politics" and the Coming of Redemption

ON MARCH 2, 1875, one day after President Grant signed the Civil Rights Act of 1875 into law, Josiah Walls delivered a searing address in Congress on the condition of affairs in the South, decrying the increasing violence that accompanied the decline of Reconstruction. Unfortunately, there are no indications he was able to give the speech directly to the assembled House, as a colleague of his requested that the remarks be printed in the *Appendix to the Congressional Record*. In response to remarks by Senator John Brown Gordon of Georgia, Walls reluctantly admitted "that unless partisan and sectional feeling shall lose more of its rancor . . . unless we shall ere long reach that point in our history when a full comprehension of the true mission of the result of the [Civil War] will be plain to all public men regardless of party affiliation, Arkansas, Louisiana, Alabama, and Mississippi will not be the only States in this Union in which fundamental law will be disregarded, over thrown [*sic*], and trampled underfoot, and in which a complete reign of terror and anarchy will rule supreme."[1]

Terror and violence were becoming more rampant as Reconstruction was challenged and as state after state was bloodily "redeemed." Walls declared that what Southerners had "lost by the bayonet . . . they now expect to gain by what they call the ballot."[2] He sarcastically questioned if it was the intention of white Southerners, after regaining power, to vote for compensated emancipation, to have the federal government pay the Confederate debt, and call for the repeal of the three Reconstruction amendments.[3] His indignation not yet spent, Walls went on to discuss the political realities of the South. Intraparty factionalism had been tearing at Florida's Republican political establishment since its inception, but that was a minor issue compared to the disfranchisement, intimidation, and outright violence that unfriendly white Democrats were carrying out against blacks and their white allies: "All the appeals to race, color, and the daily teachings on one class of people to hate the other have invariably come from Democratic orators and their friends. Here in my place I ask, is there any place in the history of our country where it can be found that the colored people of this land have banded themselves together by such pledges into black leagues to overthrow legislative, judicial, and ministerial offices? The answer is emphatically No!"[4]

Walls's summary of history ignored vast slave conspiracies whose goals did indeed include overthrowing the government, such as Gabriel's slave rebellion in 1800, Nat Turner's unsuccessful rebellion in 1831, or the aggressive calls for slave rebellion found in David Walker's *Appeal to the Coloured Citizens of the World* (1829), which advocated the use of violence to destroy slavery. Nevertheless, though eschewing the violence advocated by Walker, he drew upon the same intellectual tradition as did these earlier activists, emphasizing what the historian Mia Bay has described as the theme of the "Redeemer Race." Blacks defended themselves as equal members of the United States in terms that highlighted their moral superiority to their white opponents. But whereas Walker's belief in the moral superiority of blacks over whites led him to openly advocate violence, Walls chose to emphasize black moral superiority by highlighting instances of black loyalty to slaveowners in wartime as they pursued their dream of an independent slaveholding republic.[5]

Walls emphasized that "when I say that we cherish no animosity toward those who were once our masters, I speak for all the colored people of this broad land." In fact, he shifted swiftly from strident condemnations and demands for immediate equality to claiming that blacks wished only to live side by side with whites. As evidence for this claim Walls asserted that the slaves could have rebelled en masse during the Civil War, when most able-bodied whites were off fighting for the Confederacy, but did not. Walls's rhetoric appears calculated to convince his white colleagues on both sides of the aisle that blacks not only merited equal treatment but were largely innocent victims of the machinations of resentful whites and the Democratic Party.[6]

For Walls, the Civil War had been fought to preserve the Union and to emancipate the slaves. However, white Southerners had not acquiesced in defeat, nor had they accepted African Americans as equal citizens and participants in the body politic. Walls questioned the continual representation of Reconstruction in the South as a failure, countering that "the white-leaguers banded together for the very purpose of overthrowing regularly established State governments by force and fraud." He demanded of his counterparts that Congress intervene in Arkansas, and that it guarantee education for blacks and the preservation of legitimate government and peace. Walls compared the crisis that was undoing Reconstruction with the Confederate secession, saying that people across the country wanted to see this "new rebellion . . . nipped in the bud and the country saved." Ultimately, however, such rhetoric could neither sway his counterparts nor save the bold experiment of Reconstruction.[7]

Racial Uplift and the Importance of Vocational Education

While Walls was denouncing white violence, John Mercer Langston, not yet a congressman, accepted an invitation to deliver a speech to Baltimore's Colored Men's Progressive and Co-operative Union on November 25, 1875. This organization's mission included advocating for African Americans' educational opportunities, as well as for their civil rights and moral and social elevation. In close alignment with these goals, Langston titled his lecture "Future of the Colored American, His Civil Rights and Equal Privileges—Mental and Physical Qualities—Adaptation to Skilled Labor." In it, he touched on the virtues of industrial labor and the relationship between industrial schooling and academic education, noting, "We often feel, very erroneously, however, that through what are termed the learned professions, the legal, the medical, and the theological, alone do we, or can we, rise to distinction." Those who aspired to "future greatness" could also rise through "obscure and humble industrial pursuits," which Langston believed would advance them "in those more conspicuous and influential paths of reform, legislation and politics."[8]

Langston was not counseling his audience to abandon the "more conspicuous and influential paths" of law, theology, and medicine in favor of industrial and mechanical labor. Rather, he insisted that industrial education could not be divorced from academic pursuits, and that both paths were crucial for black progress in American society. Langston stressed this point by comparing the freedmen's situation with that of English peasants. He emphasized, "Industrial effort inspired and sustained intellectual and moral endeavor, and those reacting upon each other not only led the people to value, assert and maintain their freedom and independence, but to make the progress and accomplish the results which their history records."[9]

Langston urged that blacks should embrace the highest achievements possible: "No child, the children of no class of our people, should be taught, or in any wise impressed, that anything less than the most perfect educational accomplishment will suffice."[10] Langston insisted that blacks must focus on attaining "the moral plane of the truth" and put all their energies into educating themselves. In his view, black education and the development of a virtuous character would ensure the prosperity and progress of the race while simultaneously undermining white racism. But no one in the South, or in the nation, was listening to Walls or Langston. The nation's turn away from Reconstruction increasingly forced African Americans to consider their place in the political arena and whether they should remain in the Republican fold or go their own way.

A "New Departure" for Blacks?

The shifting political currents that reverberated throughout the nation were illustrated in the new and challenging environment that confronted John Roy Lynch in Mississippi. After a bruising series of state elections, Lynch tried to get the federal government to intervene. In late November 1875, he met privately with President Grant at the White House. Lynch came on the pretext of arguing in favor of dismissing a local postmaster, but he had more pressing concerns. The recent elections in Mississippi had concluded amid troubling anti-black and anti-Republican violence. Lynch wanted to know why Grant had not intervened with federal troops. Grant explained that he wanted to send troops into Mississippi but thought that by doing so he would alienate the Ohio Republican Party; obviously, in his political calculations, success in Ohio trumped Republican victory in Mississippi. Keeping troops stationed in the South to protect black civil rights was no longer popular among the Northern electorate, and it caused electoral difficulties for Northern Republicans. Grant had to keep his party's fortunes front and center almost as much as his concern to secure justice for African Americans. Republicans needed to win in the Midwest; if they lost too many of these states, it would damage their ability to secure the White House and protect Republican Reconstruction in the South. According to his autobiography, Lynch answered Grant: "Can it be possible . . . that there is such a prevailing sentiment in any state at the North, East, or West, as renders it necessary for a Republican president to virtually give his sanction to what is equivalent to a suspension of the Constitution and the laws of the land to insure Republican success in such a state [Ohio]? What surprises me more, Mr. President, is that you yielded and granted this remarkable request. That is not like you. It is the first time I have ever known you to show the white feather."[11]

Lynch recalled Grant's response: "I admit that you are right. I should not have yielded. I believed at the time that I was making a grave mistake. But the way it was presented, it was duty on one side and party obligation on the other. Between the two, I hesitated, but finally yielded to what was believed to be party obligation. If a mistake was made, it was one of the head and not of the heart." Clearly, Northern commitment to black civil rights had reached its lowest point, and even Grant (who generally supported black equality) was more willing to follow political expediency than risk angering prospective Republican voters.[12]

Lynch's serious concerns about the growing violence are quite evident in his later reflections on the composition of Southern voters: "The Republican vote consisted of about ninety-five percent of the colored men and about twenty-five percent of the white men. The other seventy-five percent of the whites, or most of them, formerly constituted a part of the flower of the Confederate Army. They were not only tried and experienced soldiers, but they were fully armed and equipped for the work before them." Although some black Republicans had been Union soldiers, they were not as well organized as whites, nor did they have sufficient arms. "In such a contest, therefore," Lynch concluded, "they and their white allies were entirely at the mercy of their political adversaries." For white Democrats, meanwhile, "It was a case in which the ends justified the means and the means had to be supplied."[13] Within the context of these rapid changes in Northern sentiment, black leaders began to reconsider their options. Once again they met as a group to determine the future course of their political agenda.

In April 1876, the National Convention of Colored Men met in Nashville, Tennessee. The downfall of Reconstruction weighed heavily on delegates' minds. They were not optimistic about their political future, nor were they firmly committed to the Republican Party.[14] Several delegates had participated (either directly or indirectly) in earlier conventions, including Arkansas judge Mifflin Wistar Gibbs (the convention president), former acting governor Pinchback of Louisiana, and Langston of Howard University. Though the convention affirmed its loyalty to Republicans, black delegates increasingly sounded independent notes. Indeed, the 1876 convention set the stage for the building of fusion political alliances as well as illustrating the ways in which black political leaders responded to emigration when that movement among blacks crested in the early 1880s. Only when black voters looked beyond the Republican Party to other alternatives could the black political establishment begin to contemplate fusion voting schemes or imagine the possibility of leaving the South permanently. Writing in 1902, retired judge Gibbs described the motivations of the assembled delegates, saying that they had learned through bitter experiences "that politics was not the panacea," but that black support for Republicans was "the main offense." Many delegates were willing to work with white Southerners "for race protection and opportunity." Prominent leaders like Pinchback, "while preferring to maintain their fealty to the Republican party, were willing to sacrifice that allegiance if they could secure protection and improve conditions for the race."[15]

Gibbs's comments make sense in the context of a changing political environment in the South and across the nation. This convention met while the North's retreat from Reconstruction was in full swing, and discussions at the convention reflected decisions on the part of black politicians to downplay the most divisive racial issues. Black politicians may also have been influenced by the failure of the "New Departure," a conscious decision to abandon racial appeals when waging political campaigns, adopted by Southern Democrats in the early 1870s. The strategy failed to achieve Democratic hegemony over Southern political life, and the party abandoned this approach in favor of renewed campaigns of violence and intimidation that secured Redemption across the South.[16] Though by this time Democrats had abandoned the New Departure, nevertheless many whites in both the North and the South desired to put sectional and racial issues behind them.

Newspapers covered the Nashville convention's proceedings within this context. Some correspondents believed that black political leaders would embrace the nation's move away from the divisive issues of Reconstruction. Other reporters thought otherwise, and their coverage reflected the sentiments of certain delegates who denounced the violence and intimidation in which white Democrats engaged.

Highlighting this latter theme, the *New York Times* reported that the delegates condemned the "deplorable state of affairs in many parts of the South" that was due "to the partisan frenzy of Democratic leaders." Though the tone of the assembled delegates was in line with Republicanism, they "had just reasons of complaint . . . against those who had proved recreant to the trust reposed in them."[17] Langston sought to keep his colleagues focused on the larger threat to black civil and political equality. The *Times* summarized his comments: "No step had been taken by Democratic leaders in behalf of the negroes. As a Christian people they could no more be asked to support the Democratic Party, in view of the manner in which it had treated them, than to support the devil against God. Outrages were severely denounced and ascribed to the Democratic party. The negro could not be driven out of the States, but would stay with the whites, whether in the cornfield or Senate."[18]

Other coverage, however, noted that black confidence in the Republican Party was wearing thin. The principal spokesman for this view was Pinchback. According to the *Daily Arkansas Gazette,* while Pinchback "did not take the new departure anticipated . . . his speech had a strong flavor of independence." He emphasized that blacks were "beginning to think for themselves" and should not be counted on as solid Republican voters. "He wanted no more color-line party politics, but the division of parties on other than race lines."[19] *Frank Leslie's Illustrated Newspaper* provided further coverage of Pinchback's position. Republicans had not turned away from African Americans, Pinchback said, but they had given black voters a clear message—"Halt!" Black political leaders had made mistakes, Pinchback noted: "We organized our Republican Party upon the basis of race rather than of principle, and out of that mistake has followed a long train of evils and outrages. We are not only impoverished, not only bankrupt, but worse—immeasurably worse—the black people have lost all their manhood."[20]

Convention speeches revealed the fissures that began to emerge among black leaders. Pinchback's derisive comments show how the confident affirmation of black manhood, so prominent in the Civil War era, had faded in the wake of losses in recent political contests. The Southern press saw such comments as signs that black leaders were beginning to fall in line with a new political order. But many black politicians (including Langston) disagreed with some of Pinchback's ideas. Pinchback may have felt the sting of Republican betrayal because he had suffered the simultaneous loss of contested election cases in both the U.S. House and the Senate.[21] Nevertheless, his comments expressed tensions and political misgivings shared by other black leaders. Why had they failed? Had they focused too much on securing passage of civil rights legislation? Now that Redemption was taking its bloody toll, would they need to break free of the Republican establishment in order to secure a viable political future for themselves and their constituents? These were pressing questions, especially as the situation across the South was taking a dire turn for the worse.

Red Shirts, Striking Workers, and Hemp Necklaces

As Reconstruction began to be torn apart little by little, the former captain of the *Planter* made his entry into American politics, but naval hero Robert

Smalls would find it difficult to navigate the thicket of postwar politics in black-majority South Carolina. The existence of a large and assertive black population actually increased the threat of violence from whites who disliked being outnumbered. Most whites were unwilling to accept the radical changes to society imposed by the Civil War and emancipation, and blacks would no longer tolerate the conditions under which they had lived prior to the Civil War.[22] Much like their counterparts across the region, African Americans in South Carolina grew increasingly militant in their demands for economic autonomy, political rights, and access to land.[23]

Entering the Forty-Fourth Congress in March 1875, Smalls served alongside incumbent black congressmen Lynch (Mississippi), Joseph Rainey (South Carolina), and Walls (Florida), as well as fellow freshmen Charles Nash (Louisiana), Jeremiah Haralson (Alabama), and John Adams Hyman (North Carolina). In addition, Blanche Kelso Bruce of Mississippi was the sole black member of the U.S. Senate. Despite the larger contingent of blacks in Congress, Smalls arrived at a time when Republican supremacy was waning: the 1874 congressional elections had produced a Democratic majority in the House of Representatives for the first time in eighteen years. Incoming Democrats would hold 169 seats to the Republicans' 109.[24] Thus the election of 1874 signaled the beginning of the end for Radical Reconstruction. The signs of these remarkable changes confronted Smalls on the campaign trail as he accompanied the Republican governor of his state.

On August 12, 1876, in the white Democratic stronghold of Edgefield, South Carolina, Republican governor Daniel Chamberlain attempted to address a party rally attended by hundreds of armed Red Shirts (paramilitary supporters of the Democratic Party). Congressman Robert Smalls was there with Chamberlain and other Republican officials. But the armed Red Shirts' persistent demand for "divided time" (that is, splitting time evenly between representatives of both parties) won the day. The angry Red Shirts, who began to shout down Chamberlain, also threatened Smalls's life.

According to Smalls's later testimony before Congress, the leaders of the Red Shirts, specifically former Confederate generals Martin W. Gary and Matthew C. Butler, were vicious in their attacks. Butler asked the crowd if they were "White Liners" and "Ku-Klux," and they shouted "No." "Well," Butler continued, "there is a man, Robert Smalls, who has used my name in the halls of Congress as being the leader of the Ku Klux. I dare him to open his lips on this stand today." Smalls testified that the crowd shouted loudly and that Gary followed up by making the same challenge. The assembled audience shouted, "Kill the damn son of a bitch! Kill the nigger!"

Congressman Robert Smalls of South Carolina.
(Library of Congress, Prints and Photographs Division,
LC-DIG-cwpbh-03683)

Gary then took the stage, excoriating Governor Chamberlain: "You damn bald-headed renegade and bummer of Sherman's Army, and now so-called governor of South Carolina!"[25] Smalls was supposed to speak after Gary, but was shouted down. When another Republican official attempted to get Smalls a chance to speak, the furious crowd reportedly responded: "No, that God damn nigger shall not speak here today. If he opens his mouth here today, we will take his life."[26] Ultimately, Smalls left without speaking; the fact that he stayed as long as he did is a testament to his bravery. Indeed, he would attend similarly disruptive rallies later on during the campaign despite threats to his life.[27]

On August 18, 1876, two days after Wade Hampton received the Democratic nomination for governor and almost a week after the disruptive Republican rally at Edgefield, black laborers in the South Carolina Low Country (including Smalls's hometown of Beaufort) went on strike. As the work stoppage began spreading to other plantations, members of the local judiciary (which was all white) called upon a local rifle club to restore order. Members of this group arrested five of the strike's ringleaders at the Clay Hall Plantation, owned by trial justice Henry H. Fuller, in Sheldon, South Carolina. A crowd of blacks arrived, released their compatriots, and drove the whites (members of the rifle club, the sheriff, and the constables) to hide in the plantation threshing mill. State attorney general William Stone con-tacted Smalls, who was attending a rally with Lieutenant Governor Robert Gleaves, an African American, at Walterboro. Smalls was a major general in the state militia, and Stone ordered him to muster the troops and put down the striking workers.[28]

According to H. D. Elliott, a twenty-eight-year-old white superintendent of a local plantation, the striking laborers wanted their wages for cutting rice increased from $1 to $1.50 per acre. Strikers were attacking laborers still willing to work for the old price and forcing them to leave their fields.[29] Elliott reported seeing a crowd of 150 black strikers drive out thirty who refused to fight for higher wages and beat many of them. Three of the most badly beaten came to where Elliott and others were standing and "desired to take out warrants against those parties for beating them." When the trial justice (presumably Henry Fuller) signed warrants, the deputy sheriff, accompanied by another man, attempted to arrest some of the perpetrators but met some resistance, forcing him to return to a local store. As he made his return, Elliott claimed, a large crowd of blacks followed and surrounded the deputy sheriff in the store. Elliott could speak as an eyewitness to these events because he joined a thirty-five-man posse that met in the store the following day "in case the sheriff needed our services." He explained: "We sta[ye]d in that store the whole night, the lives of these men being threat-ened if they would come out, and the negroes threatening not only to burn the store, but all the houses on the river, if those men could not be had to satisfy their revenge."

When asked how he had been rescued, Elliott stated that after being trapped in the store for twenty-four hours "we were finally released by the influence of Congressman Robert Smalls, who had gone up to Walterbor-ough to a political meeting." Smalls averted the bloodshed by "persuad[ing] the crowd that they were acting entirely illegally, and that they had better disperse and go to their homes." When asked if the strikers were "quite violent during the night," Elliott replied that "they were violent at all times, even after Smalls arrived. Some of them did not want to respect him."[30]

Smalls's own account of the "Combahee Riot" (named for the Combahee

River that formed part of the South Carolina Low Country), written to Governor Chamberlain on August 24, 1876, differed significantly from Elliott's: "I proceeded yesterday to the disturbed rice districts and found no rioters, nor had there been a riot, but I did find a large body of men numbering about three hundred who had refused to work for checks." Smalls identified changes in payment policy, not demands for increased wages, as the root cause of the strike. He noted that "the rice planters issued these checks instead of money . . . they are only redeemed in goods that must be purchased at exorbitant prices at the store of the planters." Furthermore, Smalls claimed that he "found no lawless disposition among the strikers . . . not one of them appeared upon the ground with any kind of weapon, except a club or a stick, saying that they knew it was against the law to bring their guns." By contrast, he found "forty to sixty white men, mounted and armed with Spencer rifles and sixteen shorts and double barreled shot guns; the presence of these armed white men did much to alarm and excite the strikers."

Overall, Smalls described a more orderly and quiet scene than the one Elliott painted for the congressional committee. Nevertheless, Smalls's sympathy was clearly with the strikers, and he believed that trial justice Fuller should "be removed" from the pending cases of strikers who had been arrested "as he is a large planter and one who issues checks to his laborers," a fact that provoked "dissatisfaction on the part of laborers when brought before him."[31] Labor strikes and the threat of interracial violence were only the tip of the iceberg; the violence that pervaded South Carolina weighed heavily on Smalls's mind as he returned to Congress. He would do his part to make sure that the travails of his people would gain national visibility.

Instances like the Combahee Riot would severely test African American leaders' commitment to gaining civil and political equality as well as their ability to govern effectively in an unfamiliar interracial political order. As black congressmen won elections following the establishment of Republican Reconstruction regimes across the South, the violence and instability that plagued early state politics increasingly threatened to undermine their authority and destroy all that they had worked so hard to build in the immediate aftermath of the Civil War.

The extent and impact of the electoral violence were chronicled by an editorial in the *Chicago Daily Inter Ocean* on November 2, 1876, that described events at a Mississippi political rally twelve days prior: "When [John Roy] Lynch arrived on the ground he was informed that he could not speak unless he made a Democratic speech, upon which, desiring to avoid a conflict, he dispersed the meeting. Lynch was obliged to leave town and seek refuge in the country." The local White League was targeting Lynch and the local deputy U.S. marshal. "On Saturday evening," the editorial continued, "the [White] League offered $10 to disclose the whereabouts of Congressman John R. Lynch, that they might 'give him a hemp necklace.' Deputy United States Marshal Sprott and Congressman Lynch were both fortunate enough to get away in time."[32] Such threats to Lynch's life and other challenges to black political participation informed his extensive testimony on the subject of Southern violence before the U.S. Senate.

Commenting on the acts of violence in Jefferson and Claiborne Counties, Lynch testified later, "In the first place, the democratic party in these two counties was an armed military organization, brought into existence for aggressive political purposes. They would allow no republican meeting to be held and no republican speeches to be made by anybody; I speak now of a few weeks preceding the election." Lynch explained that he had an appointment to speak at Port Gibson in Claiborne County, but when he arrived he found the town "filled with armed democrats, and I felt that there was a great deal of danger that that excitement would culminate in a riot if I should attempt to make a speech." He gathered blacks together and told them that he would speak only if the local sheriff "would guarantee a peaceable meeting." It soon became apparent to Lynch that neither the sheriff nor his aides would protect Lynch and his constituents. Furthermore, one of the aides remarked that "they did not intend to allow the democratic party or its candidates to be slandered, and if I made a speech which they felt called upon to object to I would be given the lie, and be liable for the consequences. I understood from that that I would not be allowed to talk without interruption."[33]

Lynch's testimony was backed by national newspapers such as the *New York Times,* which printed an article denouncing the intimidation tactics of Mississippi's Democratic Party. Describing an attempted Republican political meeting in Fayette (Jefferson County), Mississippi, the correspondent noted that African Americans left the meeting site after "a large number of armed members of the Democratic clubs had made their appearance on the ground and warned them to leave, as there would be bloodshed if the Independents and Republicans attempted to hold a meeting."[34]

Given such developments, Lynch's blunt description of the Democratic strategy in Mississippi was appropriate. He noted, "This terrorism was so intense, and especially in Claiborne, as in my judgment to make life, liberty, and happiness perfectly insecure except to democrats. I do not think there is any such thing as law in that society."[35]

Smalls Fights for Political (and Personal) Survival

Increasing violence and political instability in the South provided the backdrop for Smalls's speech of February 24, 1877, which, like several of his colleagues' speeches, was relegated to the back of the *Congressional Record.* By then South Carolina had two opposing state governments vying for legitimacy. Responding to the congressional investigation of these elections, Smalls attempted to undermine the Democratic majority's ruling against Republican claims to be the legitimate state government for South Carolina. But his message was directed not only at the House but to all Americans. Black congressmen in this period generally drew upon three themes in defending their political rights: they cited their own political integrity, demanded freedom in the realm of politics, and decried white intimidation and violence. The rhetorical strategy employed by Smalls relied on describing depredations against white supporters of the Republicans, rather than solely focusing on atrocities perpetrated against black voters. Along these lines, Smalls asserted, "The Democratic party pursued a policy calculated to drive from the State every white man who affiliated with the Republican party or who would refuse to join them in their attempts to deprive the Negro of the rights guaranteed to him by the Constitution of South Carolina and of the United States." This policy, he continued, intended to reduce blacks to political dependence on their former masters, placing blacks at the mercy of those who had degraded their manhood.[36]

Smalls acknowledged that "the white race of the South possesses intelligence and courage," but asserted that the "existence of the institution of slavery cemented their personal interests and compelled them to act in concert in political matters." He carefully avoided alleging any innate tendency toward racism or violence among white Southerners, emphasizing instead the deleterious effects of slavery as an institution on their character. That institution inculcated in whites (particularly the ruling class) "a domineering spirit, a disposition to ignore and trample down upon the rights of those they could not control."[37] It was for this reason, according to Smalls, that the United States had experienced both the Civil War and the unsettling strife and instability of Reconstruction.

Smalls declared, "The late slaveholding class will not submit peacefully to a government they cannot control, believing they are a superior race . . . they feel justified in resorting to any means of power to accomplish their end." He was merciless in his blunt depiction of the Southern mentality and the methods used by white Southerners to overthrow legitimate Republican governments in the Palmetto State. He outlined how the use of such unconscionable violence would stand as a bloody legacy tarring the whole country's reputation. The determination of ex-slaveholders to wield control over their former property "has prompted many scenes of cruelty that make the history of the new South one of blood and form the subject for one of the darkest pages in American history."[38] Smalls then offered detailed evidence and clear examples of the abuses rocking his native state.

In direct contrast to the skewed perceptions of corruption by both Southern opponents and suspicious Northerners, Smalls argued that Governor Daniel Chamberlain's administration was "one of marked reform, of a character to command the admiration of every citizen." Chamberlain had significantly curtailed abuses of "the pardoning power" and had reduced wasteful spending and corruption with respect to taxation. The "grand total" of savings under Chamberlain's guiding hand had been $1,719,488, and Smalls made a point of noting that all his evidence had been published by a major Democratic newspaper, the *Charleston News and Courier.*[39] Since there was no basis for criticizing South Carolina's Republican administration, the cries against rampant corruption were simply a ruse to justify violent opposition to Republican government in South Carolina.

Smalls boldly claimed that Chamberlain was still alive only because "it would not be good policy at this time, when [Wade] Hampton is seeking to win the confidence of northern people, to murder him."[40] He knew the realities of South Carolina politics, who was behind the violence and depredation, and who truly controlled the state of affairs—namely, ex-Confederates such as Hampton. Within this context, noting the contradictions in the opposition to Republican rule as well as the realities of racially motivated violence, Smalls gave concrete examples of the nature of violence in his state and how it influenced black voting, thereby contributing to electoral instability and uncertainty during the 1876 election. Smalls's list of intimidation tactics included "the killing of colored men; making threats of personal violence; sending threatening letters, coffins, bullets, etc.; by riding armed through the country, by day and by night; by firing into the houses of republicans; by breaking up republican mass meetings; by forming armed bodies, dressed in red shirts, called rifle clubs; by discharging employees who refused to promise to vote the democratic ticket, etc."

Smalls concluded that these measures formed part of an "organized system, a reign of terror among the Republicans of the State." Undoubtedly, he was speaking from personal experience; at the Edgefield rally of August 1876, Smalls had seen the full force of the Democratic "reign of terror" against Republicans. Yet he kept silent about his own experience at Edgefield (save for testimony regarding the treatment of Governor Chamberlain) and among striking black laborers while making his case against Democratic abuses.[41] Most likely Smalls chose not to emphasize his personal experience because he believed that the white Democrats in his audience would merely take pleasure in his humiliation and intimidation, and that calling attention to such moments would hinder rather than help his defense of his embattled constituents.

Despite (or perhaps because of) his spirited attempts to expose ruthless Democratic tactics, Smalls would soon face direct challenges to his office in the form of two contested election cases. The first case pitted him against George Dionysus Tillman, the older brother of future governor "Pitchfork Ben" Tillman. George Tillman challenged Smalls's victory in the 1876 election for the Fifth Congressional District (which consisted at that time of Edgefield, Aiken, Barnwell, Colleton, and Beaufort Counties). The majority ruling, published on June 8, 1878, found that neither candidate was entitled to take the seat and declared it vacant, whereas the minority report urged that Smalls be allowed to keep his seat.[42]

The language embraced by the majority report indicates the shifts already well under way that would undermine Reconstruction and illustrates the growing obstacles confronting qualified black leaders. George Tillman marshaled evidence of local forms of intimidation that impressively reflect the local black community's commitment to Smalls and the success of the Republican Party in the Fifth Congressional District. Two black witnesses spoke on behalf of Tillman and painted a picture of internal black coercion and intimidation. At times the testimony seemed to border on the ridiculous, but it also appeared to substantiate prevalent white myths surrounding black incompetence as voters.

Responding to a question regarding violence at the polls, forty-three-year-old John Bird, an African American from Parris Island, testified that black Republicans "sent in a lot of women after me, and they took hold of me and brought me out before the door, and said, 'Kill him; he is a Democrat man.'" At that point, Bird claimed, "A Republican got up and made a speech to them, and told them to keep quiet, or if not the poll would be thrown out; said . . . that he came there to give them advice not to vote for

Hampton; that if they voted for Hampton they would not go into slavery, but they would have been better in slavery, for they would be treated like a dog."[43]

This colorful testimony, despite its questionable veracity, may contain some interesting kernels of truth about the political consciousness of the black community, especially during the violent waning years of Reconstruction. According to Bird, Smalls traveled to Parris Island before the election and instructed black women to throw their husbands out of the house if they voted for the Democratic ticket. He then gave an example, explaining that Smalls had told the story of a black man named John who went to "Massa Hampton" pledging to vote for him. No sooner had he returned back home that his wife declared that "she would not give him any of that thing [sex] if you vote for Massa Hampton." John returned and said that he couldn't vote for Hampton "for woman is too sweet, and my wife says if I vote for you she won't give me any." Smalls allegedly concluded, "And, ladies, I think, if you all do that, we won't have a Democratic ticket polled on Parris Island."[44]

The significance of this testimony, and indeed the existence of black Democrats, has always been a source of tension and confusion for scholars of Reconstruction and the postwar period in general.[45] Irrespective of partisan bias inherent in local newspapers and in congressional testimony, there is general scholarly consensus that most of the violence and intimidation was a product of white opposition to black political participation.[46] Even so, most likely there were lesser instances of black electoral violence. No political community, no matter how oppressed, is ever a fully united or monolithic bloc. Indeed, as intraparty and intraracial factionalism throughout the South illustrated, African Americans were not immune to divisions even if they embraced broad agreement on fundamental goals such as civil rights and expanded educational opportunities. The presence of increased black militancy (particularly instances of black-on-black militancy), armed black rallies, and politically active black women (some of whom carried rifles) should only increase the presumption that there were a few black Democrats in the mix of post–Civil War political life. As the Republican establishment became moribund in most parts of the South by the close of the 1870s, many African Americans opted to engage in third-party agrarian movements or even fuse with Democrats in order to carve out niches in which some modicum of black political activism could persist. Undoubtedly, many African Americans voted for Democrats because of intimidation or bribery. But the strong possibility also exists that some blacks chose to side with the Democrats either for strategic reasons (to pressure recalcitrant white Republicans) or because they shared views held by the planter class. Just as blacks responded very differently to the destruction of slavery, some segments of the black community may have favored a less radical course of action and thus chose to support the Democratic Party.[47] While the overwhelming majority of newly freed men and women embraced the party of Lincoln, not all blacks unquestioningly supported the national Republican Party or the Republican candidates put up for local office.

Even though Bird's testimony may have been jaundiced, it contains certain points that cannot be ignored. First, the presence of politically active black women illuminates concretely the tangible connections between black politicians and the black community. Consider the testimony of another black man, John Mustifer, who had been involved in the tumultuous rice-field strikes that Smalls was asked to quell. When asked about further instances of intimidation at the polls, he stated: "The only thing I know about the practice of intimidation before I went to the polls, the last meeting we held in the camp-ground, Mr. Robert Smalls give us to understand any gentlemen courting the ladies to not marry them until we get through voting. If a gentleman vote the Democratic ticket, to don't marry them. [Those] what is married 'don't service to them in bed.'" Mustifer claimed that his own wife would "throw hot lead in his throat" while he was sleeping if he even spoke about voting for the Democrats. Smalls, he said, "wants every womens to follow her husband with her club in her hand, and dare him to vote any Democratic ticket, and all our mens that fail to vote the Republican ticket, and the women to make a row, and all colored mens [that] vote the Democratic ticket [are] selling their wives and children."[48]

When pressed further with a series of partisan and leading questions, Mustifer noted the presence of many women at the polls: "Women had sticks; no mens were to go to the polls unless their wives were right alongside of them; some had hickory sticks; some had nails—four nails drive in the shape of a cross—and dare their husbands to vote any other than the Republican ticket." Some of the women also had a "few pistols and razors." When asked if there were many women present, he claimed that there were more than one hundred.[49]

Mustifer affirmed that black women did not just threaten to withhold sex but used even more coercive means to secure their men's allegiance to the Republicans on Election Day: "My sister went with my brother-in-law to the polls, and swear to God if he voted the Democratic ticket she 'would kill him dead in his sleep.' I got a son to-day was to have been married in

December; on the cause of his voting the Democratic ticket the woman refused to marry him."[50] Such testimony both reveals the grassroots nature of black political mobilization and highlights the power, influence, and respect that a leader like Smalls commanded among his constituents. Both Bird and Mustifer alleged that Smalls had successfully encouraged aggressive campaign activities by black female constituents. Their testimony conformed conveniently to the well-worn stereotype of the angry black woman. Perhaps this was Tillman's intent. Nevertheless, even though they were testifying on behalf of Tillman, Bird's and Mustifer's observations suggested that politics had become a black community affair, and that the community (women as well as men) was deeply dedicated to ensuring its fellow black political leaders' success at the polls.

Two distinct perspectives emerge when considering this testimony. First, Smalls did not hew to traditional gender norms. In contrast to the tactics embraced by John Roy Lynch (who drew upon traditional gender roles during the debates over the Civil Rights Act), Smalls encouraged women to take an active role in politics. Indeed, if this testimony can be believed, he was telling them to use their power in the bedroom and during courtship to bring black men into the Republican fold on Election Day. For Smalls, women were not pure, passive ladies who needed to be defended by black men. Rather, they were active political actors capable of withholding sex, canceling weddings, and even taking violent action to rally the local black community behind Radical Reconstruction. Second, for Smalls's white Southern opponents, the presence of politically active black women signaled a world turned upside down. The testimony depicted the women firmly in the angry Sapphire stereotype (an assertive black woman who forcefully attempts to usurp a man's role) while impugning their claims to be on a par with their white counterparts. Ultimately, this second narrative—that of the angry black woman disrupting traditional white male patriarchy—would play a major role in buttressing the Democratic case against Smalls's claim to have won the election.[51]

These subtleties and nuances, however, were lacking in the majority report, which gave several intriguing reasons for contesting Smalls's victory. Two of the accusations, one dealing with the use of federal troops and the other with black intimidation of whites, demonstrate how Democratic tactics of intimidation could be reversed in order to cast blame on the victims. With respect to undue influence on the part of the federal government, the majority report asserted: "The Government of the United States, without cause other than to influence the result of said election in favor of the contestee [Smalls] and the Republican party, sent troops into every county in said district, and that the presence of said armed forces of the United States and their influence at the polls had the effect to greatly change, by intimidation, the result of said election in said several counties." The majority report also asserted that blacks engaged in violent intimidation and ostracism against their own people to prevent them from casting their ballots for the Democrats. Drawing upon the testimony of men like Bird and Mustifer, the report noted the presence of "armed and organized" blacks at the polls. It conveniently ignored the fact that black men and women typically walked to the polls in groups for protection, and that women often guarded stacked guns during political rallies. Left alone at home, blacks were easy prey for white Democrats, but while they were together, they were much harder to intimidate at the polls. The alleged threats directed against black Democrats by these rabble-rousers took the form of "social and religious ostracism, and persecution by colored Republican social and religious organizations" that "materially changed" the results of the election in favor of Smalls over Tillman.[52]

Ultimately, the majority committee agreed with Tillman's accusations and ruled that "the evidence in this case shows that troops were sent into this district for the sole purpose of influencing the election; that such influence is destructive to free government, and should be met by declaring the election void." With no sense of irony, it further declared that "the intimidation and terrorism which existed in this district at and before the election, owing to the presence of troops and other causes . . . were such as to destroy the election."[53] The report conveniently overlooked the true reason for the presence of U.S. troops in South Carolina. When Smalls countered Tillman's allegations by asserting that whites had been engaging in violent intimidation and not the other way around, the Democrat-led committee paid little heed and simply put forward a balanced-sounding conclusion that all parties were to blame and that therefore no one was entitled to the seat. Smalls won election to Congress again in 1878, but, as illustrated by the harrowing incident related in this book's introduction, he campaigned amid severe personal danger just as in 1876.

Black Opposition to the Compromise of 1877

In addition to drawn-out, contested elections (such as those faced by Smalls), black congressmen also forcefully confronted the prospect of a Democratic presidential victory in 1876, opposing the creation of a Federal Electoral

Commission to resolve the disputed Hayes-Tilden election. The fifteen-member commission, consisting of House members, U.S. senators, and U.S. Supreme Court justices, was ostensibly a bipartisan attempt to resolve the electoral crisis posed by election fraud and intimidation (which had occurred in both Southern and Northern states). Among the staunchest opponents of the commission was Lynch, who suspected that any compromise would result in the abandonment of black Southerners to the whims of their former masters. Unable to secure federal intervention to stop widespread violence in his home state, Lynch moved to prevent the presidential election from being hijacked by his white Democratic opponents.

The terrorism afflicting Mississippi and South Carolina almost certainly informed black congressional opposition to the appointment of the Federal Electoral Commission. Lynch, Smalls, and the other four remaining black congressmen were among the sixty-eight Republicans who voted against the bill that established the electoral commission. Lynch gave two reasons for his opposition. First, he "believed it was a bad and dangerous precedent to subject the presidency of the United States to a game or scheme of luck or chance as was contemplated by the bill then under consideration." Second, he suspected that the commission "was the outgrowth of an understanding or agreement which would result in the abandonment of Southern Republicans by the national administration."

Lynch sensed something suspicious after observing the behavior and rhetoric of his Democratic counterparts. For example, Mississippi's L. Q. C. Lamar "did not hesitate to declare that it was more important that the South should have local self-government than that the president should be a Democrat." Southern Democrats wanted to be left alone without any interference or oversight by the president or the national government, even if that "should result in a virtual nullification, in part at least, of the war amendments to the federal Constitution."[54]

Lynch believed that Southerners were willing to accept a Republican president, knowing what they would get in exchange for their support, and that they knew this early enough in order to lend their support to the creation of the Federal Electoral Commission. Lynch's suspicions were heightened by the fact that the main opposition to the commission came from Northern Democrats and not their Southern counterparts. The Mississippi congressman's fears were borne out once Hayes implemented his Southern Policy, removing all remaining troops from Southern states and allowing white Southerners to run their affairs without federal interference. Lynch wrote later, "The new administration had been in power only a short while before it became apparent to Southern Republicans that they had very little to expect or hope from this administration." It was clear that Hayes would appoint a Southern Democrat to his cabinet as a postmaster, and the appointment of such a person, "especially at that particular time, was a crushing blow to Southern Republicans."

Lynch further noted that even Mississippi senator James L. Alcorn, an ex-Confederate and former governor, understood just how damaging the unfolding series of events would be to the fate of Southern Republicanism and of Reconstruction in the South. According to Lynch, Alcorn stated, "It would have been far better . . . not only for the Republican party and the South, but for the country at large, to have allowed the Democrats to inaugurate Tilden to have taken charge of the government than to have purchased Republican victory at such a fearful cost." Alcorn explained the dilemma now faced by Southern whites who had rallied to the Republican banner: "What inducement can a Southern white man now have for becoming a Republican? Under the present state of things he will be hated at home and despised abroad. He will incur the odium and merit the displeasure and censure of his former friends, associates, and companions, with no compensating advantages for the sacrifices thus made."[55]

Alcorn's statements signaled another great shift occurring among the electorate in the South. White Southerners who cooperated with the Republicans and freedmen (long derisively labeled by their opponents as "scalawags") would now be hard-pressed to continue to stand by their Republican and black allies. Alcorn saw it as futile to continue to work for Republican successes when Reconstruction itself was untenable; according to Lynch, "he realized that it was time for Southern white men who have been acting with the Republican party . . . to stop and seriously consider the situation." Lynch concluded that the "announced Southern policy of the Hayes administration not only completed the destruction of what had been thus accomplished, but made any further progress . . . absolutely impossible."[56]

When the troops were at last removed and Hayes's Southern Policy was put into effect, Lynch expressed criticism of the administration to his close friend and Mississippi's black senator, Blanche Kelso Bruce. Writing on September 21, 1877, about an address that he had just prepared, Lynch stated, "I thought it best to give the country the real and truthful reasons why the Republican party in this state [Mississippi] can not maintain an organized existence. You will see that the document is not very sweet on the Southern Policy, still I am satisfied that there is nothing in it to which his Excellency [President Hayes] can take exception."[57]

The note of sarcasm in Lynch's letter reveals his true feelings. He was bitter at how Hayes had won the presidency and even more contemptuous of the new policies that Republicans had embraced. Here, in the privacy of a letter to a close friend, Lynch could vent his anger and frustration. Both his anger and his sense of Republican and black doom would only worsen. Writing to "Friend Bruce" a month later, on October 27, 1877, Lynch examined the changing partisan climate of the United States and offered his perspective on how espousing the Southern Policy was hurting Republicans. According to Lynch, the Republican conventions in Maine and Iowa did not endorse Hayes's policy and "the usual Republican Majorities were given." By contrast, the Republican convention in Ohio "strongly endorsed the Southern Policy and the result is a humiliating Republican defeat." Lynch thought that the policy was "a lamentable failure," and he believed that the Senate would fall to the Democrats for the next two years of Hayes's administration. He believed that the South would be united and the North would be divided in 1880, "which of course will result in a Democratic victory." He bitterly concluded, "We may as well therefore prepare for the worst."[58]

Lynch remained a loyal Republican, but he could not countenance the betrayal and foolishness of his party. Hayes's Southern Policy effectively barred white Southerners from working with blacks and Republicans, and it removed the one force that could guarantee some measure of equality to former slaves—the army. Despite clear signs of waning Northern interest in Republican Reconstruction, Lynch thought he saw some support for Reconstruction among the masses. He believed that there was a strong connection between voters and Republican opposition to Hayes's approach, and he attributed Republican successes and failures to how different state Republican organizations positioned themselves on this particular issue. Whatever lingering optimism Lynch might have felt regarding a potential resurgence in the active defense of Reconstruction, it was undeniable that sustained political violence and persistent instability had taken their toll on the black community. In spite of these difficulties, African Americans remained resilient and determined, even engaging in militant acts of resistance in defense of their elected representatives.

Practical Politics in an Age of Racial Violence

The long-standing challenges of intraparty factionalism, political instability, and rampant interracial violence that plagued black communities were not lost on the elected leaders who made their way to Washington. Their experiences in their home states and congressional districts played a substantial role in determining how they would approach policymaking at the national level. Black congressmen brought with them firsthand experiences of contested elections, white intransigence, and open violence against their constituents. Upon their arrival in the House, they were constrained by the inefficiency of the postwar Congress. Nevertheless, they adapted quickly to the culture of Congress and effectively represented the interests of their constituents while skillfully avoiding conflict with whites of both political parties.

The combination of resurgent violence and increasing Northern indifference marked a watershed in the politics and political culture of black America. The sense of endless possibility and optimism that characterized the age of emancipatory politics was over, to be replaced by tense biracial alliances and agrarian revolts that would take center stage in the age of fusion politics. Members of the first generation of black congressmen now faced an extremely difficult political environment, and they were further hampered by unfriendly judicial rulings and the policies of newly "Redeemed" Southern governments. Nevertheless, older black leaders persisted in their efforts and would soon be joined by a new generation, some of whom had not experienced the travails of the Civil War. Together, old and new national black politicians would draw on the sophisticated political philosophy developed during the 1870s in order to launch effective challenges to white racism and defend what remained of black civil and political equality.

Armed with their previous experiences and with a firm conviction of their race's capacity for moral and social progress, black leaders in the South broke loose from some of their traditional Republican roots. The new political environment did not guarantee success at the polls. Some, like Josiah Walls, would lose all influence after suffering crushing electoral defeats. Others, like James Rapier and John Mercer Langston, would carve out new spaces for their political activism by advocating the cause of black emigration.

Many black leaders would begin to experiment with fusion politics, joining with disgruntled Democrats, white farmers, and dissident third parties in order to influence the course of state and national affairs to their advantage. Though fusion politics became the preferred strategy, several nagging questions remained at the forefront of the black community, causing major divisions among black leaders and within the black electorate generally. Given the failure of Reconstruction, should blacks remain in the South? If they stayed, with whom should they join politically? Could they trust former white opponents who offered them a measure of political power and civil rights protections in exchange for their votes? As the 1870s gave way to the 1880s, these were the fundamental questions facing leaders like Langston, Rapier, Lynch, and Smalls. How they answered these questions would determine the course of black politics in the aftermath of Reconstruction and guide the strategies that they pursued in defense of the increasingly embattled rights of their constituents.

PART III

*The Changing of
the Guard*

6

The Politics of Uncertainty

*Emigration and Fusion
in the New South*

O N NOVEMBER 11, 1877, South Carolina congressman Robert
Smalls was convicted of accepting a $5,000 bribe while serving
as a state senator in January 1873. Josephus Woodruff, clerk of the
Senate and a member of the Republican Publishing Company, allegedly
offered Smalls the bribe in exchange for his support of a $325,000 appro-
priation for public printing that would have benefited Woodruff's company.
The conviction would forever tarnish his career.[1] Two other men—one
white Republican congressman, and fellow black officeholder and former
secretary of state Francis L. Cardozo—were found guilty of related charges.

The local South Carolina press jumped on the chance to impugn Smalls's
legitimacy as an officeholder. The *Keowee Courier* made fun of Smalls's petition for a change of venue (due to alleged prejudice on the part of the presiding judge), observing snidely that "in Radical ridden, negro governed South
Carolina, the colored race have enjoyed higher rights than the whites, while
the law secures them equal rights by the Constitution and the most stringent
legislation."[2] Northern responses to the affair were more measured, with
some outlets strongly defending Smalls and deriding the proceedings as a
farce. The *New York Times* stated, "The case of Robert Smalls, member of
Congress from the Fifth District of South Carolina, deserves a fair hearing
by the country, as well as in the courts. Indeed, it deserves a fairer hearing
by the country, as well as in the court that convicted him." Smalls issued
a statement in his own defense, arguing that the entire proceedings were
driven solely by the "special hatred" that Democrats felt for the "hero of
the Planter" and should not be viewed as conclusive evidence of guilt or
corruption on his part.[3]

Regardless of the veracity of the charges, such instances of apparent black corruption reflected negatively on blacks as political figures and buttressed the contention, put forward by white Southerners toward the end of Reconstruction, that blacks were a corrupting influence and should have never been granted the rights defended by well-meaning but ignorant Northerners. Even though Smalls did not lose his congressional seat and was later pardoned in exchange for dropping federal charges against whites accused of intimidation, the stain on his record would dog him through his final (contested) congressional campaign of 1886.[4]

Political corruption in the mid-to-late nineteenth century was not an unusual phenomenon; in fact, many saw patronage appointments and lucrative, shady railroad deals as part of business as usual. Southern whites always hinted that aggressive black males were after money and power rather than justice, but data rarely supported those charges. Nevertheless, as Smalls's experience indicates, corruption was viewed differently when black politicians (or their white Republican allies) were the accused. Such incidents provided a veneer of justification for the acts of intimidation and violence that, by the close of the 1870s, would cause blacks to consider fleeing the South en masse.

New Options for Black Politics in the
Post-Reconstruction South

In 1878, Alfred Brokenbrough Williams, the special correspondent for the *Charleston News and Courier,* published a small pamphlet, *The Liberian Exodus,* documenting the voyage of the vessel *Azor.* This ship had left Charleston carrying African Americans who had decided to leave the violent oppression of South Carolina in search of better opportunities in Liberia. The pamphlet told how the *Azor,* with its "experimental load," left Charleston amid shouts of "The Gospel ship is sailing" and "We'r boun' for the promise land."[5] It then detailed the travails, sickness, and death that the passengers experienced on their way to Monrovia, Liberia.

Having interviewed several of the emigrants, Williams expressed skepticism regarding the blacks' allegations of white violence and terrorism in South Carolina. He claimed that "groundless fears" among blacks had played a major role in encouraging their openness to emigration.[6] Nevertheless, his account showed why some African Americans were willing to risk their lives to escape unfavorable conditions in the American South. He explained that some fled because they believed they would have greater opportunities to "rise in the world" in a "generous and cheaply procured soil" complete with "perfect social equality." Others noted that their wages were depressed in the South, and "others could give [no] good reason for going, falling back on the old talk of the 'Ku-Klux,' 'Night Hawks' and 'political persecutions.'"[7]

The idea of helping blacks to exit the South—or to leave the United States completely—divided black leaders. As early as January 1877, former South Carolina congressman Richard H. Cain noted the "deep and growing interest taken by the Colored people . . . in the subject of Emigration." He wrote to the secretary of the American Colonization Society for more information regarding passage to Liberia. Movements seeking to organize migrations to Liberia sprang up in many South Carolina counties, including Edgefield, Charleston, and Robert Smalls's native Beaufort. These movements posed a major challenge to Smalls, who opposed emigration. In 1879, in fact, blacks were migrating *into* Beaufort County, a majority black area where freedmen could live in relative safety. Smalls's view (which he would develop further during South Carolina's 1895 constitutional convention) was that blacks should leave counties where their lives and property were unprotected and migrate to safe havens like Beaufort. According to the historian George Brown Tindall, Smalls "favored emigration only from communities where it was absolutely impossible for whites and Negroes to live together in peace, and then not out of the United States."[8] Lynch (who was initially supportive of some emigration) and Frederick Douglass opposed any kind of emigration away from the South. But Langston and Rapier disagreed, encouraging the Black Exodus to Kansas.[9]

As relentless white political pressure dismantled the gains of Reconstruction, two new strategies emerged among African Americans: emigration and participation in fusion voting. These two interrelated forces wrought decisive changes in black political culture following the "Redemption" of the South. Between the late 1870s and the mid-1890s, agrarian reformers and dissident Democrats formed new political alliances that, for a time, provided an alternative avenue for both black and white Southerners to participate in Southern politics. Some of the better-known movements and organizations providing new pathways of political engagement were the Farmers' Alliance, the Grange Movement, the Greenback Party, the Readjuster Party in Virginia, and the People's (Populist) Party, which was very powerful in the late 1880s and early 1890s.

The black community and its political leaders took advantage of alliances with dissident agrarian third parties to regain power in some states and, in other instances, to shift the balance of power between competing white factions. Divisions emerged between national black leaders as to which strategy, fusion or emigration, best served the needs of their black constituents. It was no accident that the two alternatives emerged almost simultaneously in the wake of Redemption, although other historians have tended to favor emigration and dismiss the significance of fusion political arrangements.[10] Those leaders who believed that blacks should stay in the South saw the potential viability of alliances with dissident Democrats; those who advocated that blacks should leave the South had lost hope in promised opportunities for redress within the American political system. But many leaders also embraced both strategies, changing their tactics as the situation on the ground demanded. Generally speaking, emigration would be deployed in areas or states where fusion voting was impossible or party competition was moribund. In areas where dissident third parties existed and the black vote could make a difference, emigration was not the favored strategy. Rather, it was used selectively and, in some cases (particularly as Jim Crow cast its dark shadow more decisively over the region), as a last-ditch effort to protect blacks from violence and economic depredation.

The debate among black leaders over emigration and fusion occasionally led to angry disagreements and the rupture of long-standing friendships. For example, while Langston believed that emigration might be necessary, Douglass dismissed the idea entirely. Also, whereas Douglass remained an unswervingly loyal Republican (opposing independent campaigns or fusion voting), Langston worked with the emergent Readjuster-Republican coalition in Virginia and then rebelled against the Republican establishment, running an independent (and ultimately successful) U.S. House campaign in Virginia's Fourth Congressional District. These ideological disagreements (in addition to Douglass's growing personal animus toward Langston) led to Douglass's decision to denounce Langston and support the white Republican candidate against him. Whatever friendship existed between the two during the Civil War and Reconstruction was thoroughly destroyed by the time Langston ran for office in 1888.

Thus, despite the possibilities and new political avenues offered by black emigration and fusion voting, the 1880s and 1890s witnessed an increasing fracturing of black political communities and growing signs of tension and disunity among black political leaders. Granted, divisions and disagreements were present in black communities even during the more optimistic period of Reconstruction.[11] But the relative ideological unity over matters of civil rights and policymaking that characterized black congressional leadership in the 1870s dwarfed these disagreements. This unity dissolved by the end of that decade, as black politicians and their constituents confronted a more coercive and more fluid political environment. In this new political world, African Americans could no longer count on the federal government to defend their rights, but dissident whites were willing to forge alliances with blacks in areas where segregation and disfranchisement had not yet taken root.

Division over the Black Exodus: The Nashville Conference of 1879

Former congressman John Roy Lynch of Mississippi presided over the National Conference of Colored Men at Nashville in May 1879. Those in attendance included former Alabama congressman Rapier, former South Carolina congressman Joseph Rainey, P. B. S. Pinchback, Mifflin Gibbs, and Pennsylvania abolitionist William Still. Local leaders and younger activists were also present, including James C. Napier of Tennessee (Langston's son-in-law), William A. Pledger of Georgia, and Ferdinand L. Barnett of Illinois (future husband of Ida B. Wells).[12]

The convention was planned before mass black emigration began, but newspapers covering the event captured connections between black political struggles and the emerging wave of departures. "Flying from Bull-Dozers," an article in the *New York Times* on April 3, 1879, discussed the "remarkable movement of colored people from the South to the West," which was "exciting much attention here, as well as considerable alarm in the South." The migration was attributed to two causes: African Americans were cheated out of their earnings, and they were denied "their right to a free ballot." Noting that emigration was taking hold most strongly in Mississippi, Louisiana, and South Carolina, the *Times* described many prominent black leaders, including several who were to meet in Nashville, as being "in sympathy with the immigration scheme."[13]

Not all African Americans accepted the legitimacy of the convention, nor did all blacks consider the activists who met there to be national leaders. For example, the *Nashville Weekly American* published an editorial titled "A Colored Man on the Race Problem" on April 3, 1879, stating that the Nashville convention had been planned by individuals who "style themselves the leading colored men." It specifically cited three men—Pinchback, former state treasurer Francis L. Cardozo of South Carolina, and Cardozo's brother, former Mississippi superintendent of public instruction Thomas W.

Cardozo. Pinchback had gained an unsavory reputation in Louisiana and was embroiled in two contested election cases; Francis Cardozo had been convicted of bribery along with Robert Smalls; Thomas Cardozo had also been charged with embezzlement and bribery related to his work as a circuit court judge. The Nashville convention, the writer concluded, "is only for all the defeated colored Congressmen and all other office seekers who are disappointed, to give vent and expression, as if they were the leaders of the colored people, and could control their votes."[14]

Although the editorial claimed to be by a "colored man," the *Weekly American* was a white newspaper. While some members of the black community also viewed black leaders with skepticism, it was hardly a coincidence that a negative assessment of black leaders appeared in a local white newspaper shortly before a convention of blacks met in the city. The choice to focus on three "corrupt" black leaders indicates that whoever wrote the editorial may have been attempting to divide the black community and undermine the legitimacy of the upcoming convention. Nevertheless, the views expressed in the editorial illustrated emerging divisions within the black community, ones that would play out as the delegates assembled in Nashville to discuss the topic of emigration.

In his opening remarks, Lynch stated that, several months earlier, a group of gentlemen had suggested that a conference of prominent black leaders should come together "not in the interest of any particular party . . . but as free, independent American citizens, for the purposes of presenting to the country the grievances of the colored people. There were some differences of opinion as to how best this could be done." Organizers had decided to call a large conference "for the purpose of conferring together on the solution, not to speak authoritatively except as our standing in the community will authorize and justify us in doing, but that we would meet and present to the country some of the reasons that agitated the public mind in regard to the colored people."[15] Lynch's opening remarks reflect a conscious decision to step back from broad-based programs for the defense of African Americans. Furthermore, in his capacity as president, Lynch was responsible for appointing delegates to specific committees, and he may have played a role in drafting the specific statement of policies put forward by the convention.

As in previous conventions, the delegates created a new national society, called The American Protective Society to Prevent Injustice to the Colored People, with the purpose of fighting for black rights to education, property holding, and civil and political participation.[16] But the decision to de-emphasize political considerations in favor of creating an activist and in-dependent black civil rights organization departed from the formal political involvement once favored by the black community. Lynch's remarks suggest that many participants were abandoning the formal politics of the 1870s and venturing into uncharted waters. He placed the emigration discussion within the context of blacks' civil and political uncertainty: "In considering this matter you should bear in mind the fact that the South being the home of the colored people . . . we should not advise them to leave there unless they have very good reason to do so. On the other hand, we should not advise them to remain where they are not well treated."

With an appreciative audience applauding, Lynch asserted that the con-vention should urge African Americans toward independent positions, so that they could "say to the country and to the people with whom they are surrounded, that 'if our labor is valuable, then it should command respect.'" If blacks received respect, if their rights were protected, if they were able to progress as a people—then blacks and whites should remain together. Lynch concluded, "If the colored man can receive that treatment, attention, consideration and respect he is entitled to under the law in the South, the South is the place for him. If not, they are justified in receiving it where they can."[17] Unlike some of his counterparts, Lynch was cautious with respect to emigration. In measured language, he argued that African Americans should leave only if the South became too oppressive.

Lynch's speech was tame compared to resolutions proffered by others. Consider these two resolutions: "*Resolved.* That the colored man of the South save his dollars and cents in order to emigrate." "*Resolved,* That we pay no heed to such men as Fred. Douglass and his accomplices, for the simple reason that they are well-to-do Northern men who will not travel out of their way to benefit the suffering Southern Negro, and who care not for the interests of their race." A more moderate resolution called for Congress to appropriate $350,000 "to aid the suffering freedmen in the West." Another delegate put forward a plan to encourage emigration and petition Congress for a $500,000 appropriation.[18] When the conference moved to propose that this medley of motions be considered for congressional appropriations, dis-sent broke out. Arkansas's Henderson B. Robinson, a wealthy mulatto and former assessor, questioned the direction of the assembly and the wisdom of rushing to encourage black migration. He took aim at several delegates, especially the confusing cacophony of opinions they expressed. One dele-gate claimed that blacks were "self-supporting and can go when and where they please"; another claimed that blacks could take care of themselves and engage in self-defense. "The next thing is a resolution asking Congress to donate $500,000 for the purpose of sending people to Kansas from this country. When the time comes that we cannot live in this country I am as much in favor of going to Kansas as anybody else. But let us be men; let us be like white men and see the impossibility of taking 4,000,000 people away and setting them suddenly down in a strange country."[19]

No sooner had Robinson finished than an unnamed "young delegate" questioned his motives, asking him, "Who paid you to come here?" Robinson replied, "I suppose the young man is just out of school, and don't suppose he ever hoed cotton in his life." The tension was broken when former congressman Rainey called for order and asserted that the conference "ought to permit a difference of opinion to be expressed on so important and vital a question." Rainey himself supported migration, but he wanted "to proceed intelligently." He allowed Robinson to continue. The situation was not as bad as some said, Robinson claimed. He interacted with poor blacks all the time, and he did not see them starving. When pressed by a delegate who asked why blacks would want to migrate if things were not so bad, Robinson acknowledged that white oppression was making them consider leaving. Nevertheless, Robinson opposed "encouraging wholesale migration, and having the poor colored man strewn along the banks of the Mississippi, there to die." It was difficult to expect poor blacks, who had little money to spare, to leave the South for an unfamiliar life in Kansas or the West.[20]

In spite of the cautious approach by Lynch and the opposition from local politicos like Robinson, many delegates voiced overwhelming support for emigration. On May 9, 1879, during the evening session on the last day of the conference, the Committee on Migration delivered its report to the assembled delegates. This committee included two former congressmen (Rapier and Rainey) and several local leaders and younger activists (Napier and Barnett). The report enumerated the causes for black migration, denied the presence of any political or sectional motive behind the movement, and then listed a series of resolutions supporting the work of an official Senate committee (chaired by Republican senator William Windom of Minnesota) on the subject, emphasizing that black emigration "should be encouraged and kept in motion" until black civil and political equality was guaranteed across the South. One final resolution recommended that the Windom Committee appoint three individuals to investigate conditions in the West. At 12:15 a.m., after three hours of debate and twenty-three speeches, the conference unanimously adopted the report on black migration.[21]

This support was further solidified by the adoption of the other major report of the conference, the "Report of the Committee on Address." This committee's report supported emigration and concluded (in language similar to Lynch's opening remarks) that if black laborers were not respected in the South, they had no other choice but to leave, even though the vast majority would prefer to stay. Furthermore, the committee affirmed that "the disposition to leave the communities in which they feel insecure, is an evidence of a healthy growth in manly independence."[22] Despite divisions, personal rivalries, and strategic arguments, the delegates reached a moderate compromise in support of emigration.

The 1879 conference appeared to end in consensus, but soon the divisions and disagreements cropped up again, as Lynch backed away from his initial support for emigration while Rapier continued to endorse it and appeared before a Senate committee investigating the causes of the exodus. While both were determined to fight for African Americans, they differed widely as to their understanding of blacks' political future.

Following the close of the Nashville conference in 1879, Senator William Windom appointed Gibbs and Rapier to the committee that would investigate conditions among African Americans settling in the West and in the territories.[23] The two men traveled to Kansas in August 1879, stopping in Topeka and various "colonies." According to Gibbs, Kansas had taken in about 7,000 or 8,000 black migrants. When they arrived in Topeka, they found nearly one hundred migrants at an immigrant camp where they obtained rations. Some of them were sick; others were looking for work. Many had settled on land or found jobs. Gibbs noted, "At Dunlop we found a colony of 300 families settled upon 20,000 acres of land. In Wabunsee County 230 families had settled on their land, while in Lawrence and other counties hundreds had found work. Mechanics receiving $2 to $2.25 per day and farm hands $13 to $15 per month and board. We found women in great demand for house servants from $6 to $8 per month."

Gibbs and Rapier spent twenty days in Kansas, but did not investigate conditions in Indiana or other states that received emigrants. The two men interviewed black settlers and described conditions that were difficult but less dire than the rumors of destitution and failure, reporting that "we found the list and nature of their grievances were the same to have impelled men in all ages to endeavor to better their condition. . . . There had been suffering and destitution in some localities during the past winter; that was to be expected, as many had come wholly unprepared and without that push and ready adaptation to the status of a new country."[24]

Rapier's experiences in Kansas made him an expert on black migrants, and in early April 1880 he was called to testify before the Select Committee of the United States Senate to Investigate the Causes of the Removal of the Negroes from the Southern States to the Northern States. The hearings gave him the opportunity to address members of the Senate's Democratic majority and to explain his support for black emigration.

In response to Windom's sympathetic questioning, Rapier described why blacks were leaving: "I advised these colored people to leave Alabama, because 32 per cent of the lands are so poor that they cannot make a living on them; and I think I have demonstrated that fact to them in figures. I think the colored people are leaving there in order to better their condition, and I think they can do it anywhere except in the Southern States."[25] Rapier emphasized his disillusionment with affairs in his own state and throughout the South. Though no longer serving in Congress, Rapier had been appointed as collector of internal revenue for the Second District of Alabama in 1878, and this position almost certainly helped him bolster some of his statistical and economic arguments as he testified before the committee.[26] He also feared for the mental development of black children in his state as a result of widespread discrimination and white racism, saying, "You cannot develop mentally and morally the colored children of the State, for at every spring branch and cross roads he will find something to remind him that he is a negro." In addition to the impact of racism, Rapier addressed the specific economic motivations of black migrants. Presenting statistics on black wages and expenses to demonstrate that black sharecroppers were severely cash-strapped in his home state, Rapier noted that "a man in the West can make as much as three men in Alabama."[27]

Though the former congressman laid out a convincing case for black emigration, the bulk of Rapier's testimony involved disputes with Senator Zebulon Vance of North Carolina, which began toward the end of the first day and occupied almost all of Rapier's second day on the witness stand. Vance's questioning sought to establish that Southern laws regarding sharecropping and penalties for larceny applied equally to both races and to undermine black support for the Republican Party. In addition, Vance tried to trip up Rapier on questions related to social equality. Vance asked him, "Do you suppose it would be any better in the country your people are going to?"[28]

"That depends upon where they go," Rapier replied.

"Is there any State in the North where you would be received on a social equality with the whites?"

Rapier refused to fall into Vance's trap: "That is not the question. But I will tell you what I do know; if I go to Atlanta . . . a thirsty man, I cannot get a glass of beer at the depot there, simply because I am a colored man. If my child sees that, and sees that I am not considered as good as a white man, that is bound to chill one's ambition and everything else. That is what I said."

Seeing that he was not going to lure Rapier into a public-relations gaffe on social equality, Vance turned his attention to politics, asking Rapier whether or not he could vote in the District of Columbia. Rapier replied — accurately at the time — that nobody could vote in Washington, D.C.

"But that would remind you of the promise of the Republican party to give you the right of suffrage, would it not?"

"No," Rapier replied. "It would remind me of this: that the black man is as good as the white man, so far as voting here is concerned."

Whatever expectations Vance had of undermining Rapier were disappointed by the former congressmen's deft responses. Just as he and his colleagues had done in their defense of the Civil Rights Act of 1875, Rapier carefully avoided linking social equality with political equality. In his opinion, they had nothing to do with each other, nor did they pertain to the subject of black emigration from the South.

Windom interjected a question, bluntly asking Rapier, "So you think that in Alabama there is no remedy for the exodus, even if your people received better treatment there?"[29]

"No; for even if they made the best kind of laws, we advise them to go." Rapier went on to explain the relationship between black progress and conditions in the South: "The colored people . . . have been slaves . . . [and] the majority of them have contracted superstitious habits and ideas that you cannot rid them of very readily. There are only two ways for me to learn; one is by books, and the other is by observation. As there will be no chance for the colored people to get rid of these old habits and ideas by books, because their children have only three months of the year to go to school in, I would advise that they had better scatter." Rapier concluded by directly linking the impulse for emigration with blacks' long-standing desire for economic autonomy, saying that "anywhere in the Western country where a colored man can get ten dollars a month for his labor" would be preferable than carrying on as landless workers on Southern plantations.[30]

Rapier believed that blacks should be "scattered from the Atlantic to the Pacific, and not huddled together. This has been our weakness." He saw blacks' concentration in the South as an economic and political liability, suggesting that perhaps, in smaller numbers, African Americans would not "excite the prejudices of the people" and might thus receive better treatment.[31]

Rapier's faith in emigration as the most viable path to success for his embattled constituents stood in stark contrast to the position of Lynch, who believed that the challenges they faced in America added to blacks' strength of character. If blacks ran away from adversity, Lynch contended, they would undermine all their accomplishments. He outlined his views at the Annual Douglass Banquet in Washington, D.C., on January 1, 1883: "The colored people of the South are in the line of progression and ascension. They have made and are making rapid and material progress in spite of many unfavorable surroundings. My prediction is that in the space of a very short period of time, the colored people of the Southern States will be the representatives of wealth and the intelligence of their respective commonwealths."

After honoring Lincoln, Grant, Sumner, and Douglass, Lynch explained his opposition to emigration, arguing that the challenges that blacks confronted in the South served as an "incentive for nobler and higher aspirations." If blacks went to another country where they encountered "no such opposition and resistance," then the probabilities were high "that we will find ourselves in the line of retrogression instead of progression. My judgment, therefore, is that we should work out our destiny here."[32]

Lynch framed the debate over whether blacks should leave or stay in terms of manhood and strength of character. To leave would mean forfeiting the gains made in the decades since emancipation; to stay would mean building on the progress of the race. Having worked out his own destiny first in Louisiana and then in the tumultuous arena of Mississippi, Lynch found it impossible to consider advising his constituents to leave. Even in the midst of violence in the late 1870s (including threats to his own life), he had not forsaken Mississippi or the South; rather, such experiences had only strengthened his resolve. This position would guide Lynch's subsequent embrace of alternative political alliances in his native state.[33] Though emigration (first the Liberian exodus and then the larger one to Kansas and the West) did have a large number of adherents, the majority of African Americans could not or chose not to leave.[34]

The violent overthrow of Reconstruction had forced the black community and its leaders to reexamine their political goals and their overall strategy. Initially emigration took center stage, influencing the debates and strategies at the Nashville conference in 1879. But the combination of black poverty and Southern coercion limited the appeal of black migration.

Ultimately, the political sentiments expressed by delegates at the 1876 Nash-ville convention won the ideological battle for dominance in black political culture.

The white South's Redemption was neither monolithic nor complete. The emergence of fractures within the Democratic fold provided the oppor-tunity for a new political program to complement the perspective of Lynch. Blacks, he proposed, should stay and fight because they could use their numbers to force political concessions from their erstwhile foes. Thus the downfall of Reconstruction and the failure of emigration paved the way for blacks to work with dissident Democrats and forge alliances with agrarian reformers so that, by the 1880s, the Southern political landscape would be rocked once more — this time by the powerful force of fusion voting.

The Pitfalls and Potentials of
Fusion and Third Parties: Mississippi

Black leaders and their constituents who chose to stay behind and work out their political future in the South faced a wide range of opportunities and electoral possibilities. The main cause of political fluidity across the South in the 1880s was the rise of dissenting white Democrats and agrarian reformers who occasionally allied with Southern Republicans and Afri-can Americans in order to achieve their political goals. But the emergence of fusion voting also coincided with the redrawing of Southern political districts that served to limit the power, scope, and influence of the black electorate. Fusion political alliances (especially those forged with the Demo-cratic establishment) were often intimately related to the creation of heavily black congressional districts, enabling what was left of the Southern wing of the Republican Party to remain competitive in certain areas of the South. Thus, at the same time as dissident Democrats and agrarian reformers were fusing with Republicans and black voters, the Democratic establishment unwittingly provided room for the continued survival of Republicans, en-abling several black congressmen to serve in Congress during the 1880s.[35] The possibilities of fusion were not lost on old-guard politicians like Lynch, who moved to capitalize on the emergence of dissident Democrats and the Greenback Party in order to fight for his constituents in Mississippi.

In the 1881 election, having noticed the rise of the Greenbackers (a na-tionwide political party that supported increasing the paper money supply in order to relieve the nation, particularly farmers, from America's eco-nomic depression) in his state during the late 1870s, Lynch moved to forge a

Republican-Greenback alliance in order to gain control of politics in Mississippi. While the suggestion of fusion between both groups "was favorably received," Lynch thought "that the ticket would be very much stronger if we could find a liberal and conservative Democrat who would be willing to accept the nomination for governor."[36] The man whom Lynch had in mind was Democratic state senator Benjamin King of Copiah County. After consulting with Republican and Greenback leaders, Lynch was "authorized to approach the senator upon the subject." King met with Lynch and was surprised by the black politician's proposal.

The fact that King did not immediately dismiss his suggestion gave Lynch hope. He pressed his case before King forcefully: "As a member of the state senate," Lynch said, "I recognize the fact that you are a representative of the Democratic party. . . . You are not asked to renounce your party allegiance or change your political affiliations. All that is asked and desired of you is to allow the people of your state, without regard to race or party differences, to avail themselves of the benefit of your right experience." King listened to Lynch's proposal and asked for a few days to consider the matter.

When Lynch called upon him again, King said he would run if "he should be nominated as an Independent Democrat, his candidacy endorsed by a regular delegate convention of both the Republican and Greenback parties, each to ratify the action of the other."[37] The two parties joined forces and nominated King for governor. Despite Democratic fraud and some acts of intimidation, King performed remarkably well, officially winning 40 percent of the statewide vote (Lynch and his Republican and Greenback allies believed that King actually won more than that). Though the fusion party had succeeded in raising a credible statewide threat, the Greenbackers "had practically no organization in any of the black counties, and King could not command a sufficient following among the whites in those counties to secure for the ticket a fair election and an honest count."[38] The loss did not dissuade Lynch from continuing to see the possibilities available through such alliances.

Not long after the failure of King's candidacy, Lynch was forced onto the defensive, fighting against a challenge to his congressional victory over former Confederate James R. Chalmers in the election of 1880.[39] On April 27, 1882, speaking in defense of his right to be seated in the Forty-Seventh Congress, Lynch described his contested election and the state of affairs across the "Solid South." After summarizing the vote counts and fraud committed by the Democrats and Chalmers, Lynch explained why he thought fraud and violence characterized the South: "I deny that race prejudice had anything to do with fraud and violence at elections in the Southern States. Colored men are not now persecuted in this section from which I come on account of their color, but Republicans, white and colored, are persecuted in many localities on account of their politics."[40]

Lynch articulated his view of Southern race relations in ways that appeared contrary to social and political realities across the South, but he may have been trying to cut through the racial veneer of the Southern Democratic establishment's electoral tactics. As the historian Michael Honey has argued, "The post–Civil War era . . . offered the possibility that transracial, class-based voting alliances could reconfigure Southern society to the benefit of people at the bottom." Democrats were using the banner of "white supremacy" to secure the economic and political dominance of the planter class, former slaveholders, and ex-Confederates.[41] Lynch's politics, on the other hand, threatened Bourbon Democrats' (a popular title for conservative Redeemers) control throughout the South.

Lynch claimed, "The southern bourbons are simply determined not to tolerate honest differences of opinion upon political questions. They make no distinction between those who have the courage, the manhood, and the independence to array themselves in opposition to bourbon methods and measures." In fact, Lynch argued that it did not matter in what form opposition parties came. They could be Republicans, Greenbackers, Independents, or Readjusters. They were all considered "enemies to the South" by the fact that they stood in opposition to the Bourbon Democrats. As a solution to this unjust Democratic governance, Lynch called for "inculcation of a just and liberal public sentiment" that could undermine "political proscription and intolerance," producing a "free ballot" and a "fair count."

Turning his attention to the origins and workings of the "solidly Democratic" South, Lynch made certain prescient observations. He wondered, "If it be true that the Democratic organization at the South is the exclusive representative of the wealth and intelligence of that section, why is it they do not establish by law an educational or a property qualification for electors?" Mississippi's black congressman thought he knew why Democrats had not taken that step: "It is because they know they cannot disfranchise the illiterate Republican voter without disfranchising at the same time and in the same way the illiterate Democratic voter."[42]

In response to criticism of Southern Republicans for not forcibly resisting fraud at the polls, Lynch underscored that such frauds "are always committed under some sort of color of law." Given these circumstances, "What lawful redress have Republicans. . . . You certainly cannot expect them to resort to mob law and brute force, or to use what may be milder language, inaugurate a revolution." He thought that Southern Republicans and African American voters should not embrace the tactics of their opponents. Those areas that engaged in electoral fraud "must be made to understand that there is patriotism enough in this country . . . to prevent any party from gaining the ascendancy in the government that relies upon a fraudulent ballot and a false return as the chief source of its support."[43]

Lynch then discussed the "bravery and fidelity of the colored people" in their struggle for equal rights. In spite of the challenges they faced, blacks affirmed their dignity as men: "You may deprive me . . . of the opportunity of making an honest living . . . you may close the schoolhouse door in the face of my children; yea, more, you may take that which no man can give, my life, but my manhood, my principles you cannot have!" African Americans remained faithful to the United States, making the same demands that they had claimed in the immediate post–Civil War period. Lynch said they were asking for "no special favors as a class, they ask no special protection as a race." Repeating the traditional theme of "democracy of the dead," he argued that blacks had secured their citizenship rights through their sacrifices on the field of battle — they had "watered the tree of liberty with the precious blood that flowed from their loyal veins."[44]

Lynch regretted that Southern Democrats were determined to "have a centralized government or no government at all." To achieve their goals they sought to destroy the "sanctity and the purity of the ballot," which Lynch saw as "the chief pillar in our governmental structure. Destroy that pillar, and the structure must necessarily fall." He asserted that he was not speaking as a member of any party, but as a patriot; he acknowledged that parties could differ on policies, but on matters concerning the stability of democratic government in the United States, they must be in agreement. Lynch was convinced that the systematic use of fraud at the polls needed to stop. Such practices were unworthy of the American experiment and "contrary to the spirit of the age in which we live and to the civilization of the nineteenth century."[45]

Lynch's arguments drew heavily from long-established threads in African American political discourse. Nevertheless, the nation and the Republican Party would not fulfill his lofty expectations. Perhaps this reality drove Lynch to continue to actively support fusion political arrangements, even if it meant working with the enemy — that is, the Democrats.

Addressing a crowd of Republicans and Democrats in Raymond,

Mississippi, on September 29, 1883, Lynch outlined his reasons for supporting fusion voting. He first stated his continuing commitment to the Grand Old Party, asserting that, if fair elections prevailed, a straight Republican ticket would be as certain of winning in Yazoo and Claiborne Counties as a straight Democratic ticket in New York City. The only reason why this result did not occur was that "Republicans in these, as in many other counties in the State are still groaning under the iron yolk of bourbon [Democratic] oppression — counties in which the Republican vote is lawlessly suppressed."[46]

Going well beyond the traditional confines of fusion voting, Lynch responded to opponents who "claim that [fusion] is nothing more than a bargain between the two parties, and therefore should not be ratified by the people." He had no problem acknowledging fusion for what it was — a bargain.[47] It was a bargain when Republicans joined forces with Greenbackers in 1881, and the same would hold true if Republicans and Democrats banded together. The bargain that Lynch wanted to see Democrats and Republicans make was simple — Republicans, though "numerically in the majority," would work for the Democratic ascendancy in the state, while Democrats would "openly and publicly declare and in good faith do all in their power to put an end to bulldozing and fraud in all elections."[48] Democrats did already permit a "fusion principle" that Lynch and others tepidly supported; this plan involved coordination between the local county Democratic executive committee and black Republican leadership to decide what county and legislative positions would go to black Republican candidates. Though the choice of black candidates was to be made by local blacks, the acceptance of particular candidates was decided by the Democratic committee. Lynch approved of fusion because it was the best deal African Americans could make given their tenuous situation. Such a position was not a sign of weakness, however. Lynch forcefully argued that blacks were not accepting the Democrats who had undermined them during Reconstruction; rather, blacks would vote alongside Democrats or anyone else who offered political concessions until Republicans could once again become a viable force in the state's political arena. Lynch did not just simply acquiesce to Democrats; rather, he offered to work with cooperative Democrats — and promised to fight those who refused to cooperate. He stated that Republicans "should not only do all in their power . . . to defeat these candidates, but they should . . . utilize such material and co-operate and combine with such elements outside the Democratic party and antagonistic thereto, as will contribute to this result."

Lynch drew the line as to where fusion stopped and partisanship began, declaring that "Republicans should not, under any circumstances, support the nominees of the Democratic or any other party outside of the Republican party, when they draw party lines and make straight nominations."[49] When Democrats and others were willing to cross party lines, Lynch was willing to work with them. But when they nominated a straight slate of candidates, the choice was clear: Republicans must oppose Democrats at the polls. No other choice was possible. In short, Lynch was willing to compromise as long as he was able to obtain something for his constituents. When he could not compromise, he would take the battle directly to the gates of the enemy with a clear conscience.

The *Civil Rights Cases* Push Langston Deeper into Politics

One of the most striking signs of changing political currents was the series of 1870s Supreme Court decisions that culminated in its October 1883 ruling in the *Civil Rights Cases*, which declared the Civil Rights Act of 1875 to be unconstitutional.[50] Shortly after this decision had been handed down, and ten years after his Oberlin speech on "Equality before the Law," Langston was serving as minister-in-residence to Haiti. He returned to Washington, D.C., in 1884 to speak to an audience on the "Civil Rights Law." Among the black political leaders in attendance were Douglass and Blanche Kelso Bruce, a former slave from Virginia and the second black senator in the nation's history.

"Out of slavery," Langston asserted, "we have passed . . . into American citizenship, a good deal like coming out of the land of Egypt into a promised land, one flowing with milk and honey." Langston thus presumed that American citizenship implied civil equality for black citizens. He continued, "The Civil Rights Law of April, 1866, was enacted to declare exactly to what we are entitled. Our citizenship is affirmed and made complete. So that whatever man, a citizen of the United States, can do, that the colored man, also a citizen can do." As his counterparts did in the 1870s, Langston stated clearly what specific rights blacks had gained: "In short; with freedom come those civil rights which are implied in and are essential to citizenship. No reference is made here to social equality. Social rights are not being considered; they will take care of themselves, with equal protection before the law assumed."[51]

Langston could not contain his anger at the foolishness of the Supreme Court. Whereas, in 1875, Langston could embrace a more optimistic position—laying out a strong legal case for Sumner's legislation and then putting forward an expansive vision of emancipatory diplomacy buttressed by strong civil rights protections at home — the situation had now turned bleak, and the opportunities available to blacks during Reconstruction were rapidly disappearing. Disgusted by the turn of events since 1875 and firmly rejecting the recent Supreme Court ruling on the Civil Rights Act of 1875, Langston employed his rhetorical abilities to attack what he considered a flagrant violation of the Reconstruction-era constitutional amendments, one that placed the enforcement of black civil rights in the hands of untrustworthy local authorities. "The Supreme Court would seem desirous of remanding us back to that old passed condition. It advises that we appeal to the legislatures of the States for protection and defense of our rights. But let us be patient. Wait a little while, some one counsels." Langston's frustration came through as he exclaimed, "My God! how long a time are we to wait! Think of it; an American citizen advised to wait for fair treatment on a railroad with a first-class ticket! We want to ride like other men — not like brutes. . . . How long must we wait for change of public opinion, and how long must we wait for State action to give us our rights in this regard?"[52]

The Court's ruling disappointed Langston, yet he remained hopeful for the future progress of African Americans: "My Colored Friends; let us not despair; let us advance with solid, earnest, manly tread, feeling that we are nothing other than American citizens. Colored we may be; our hair and our face may be dark; and our circumstances may not be quite so good as those of others in worldly goods as a rule; but above all let us not forget that we are American citizens, and can claim all the rights that any other American citizens can claim, while we are rich in ability to make their legal defence."[53]

Langston's response to the demise of the Civil Rights Act of 1875 signaled a profound shift in his political career; his disgust redoubled his determination. Having previously served largely as an outside political activist and in minor appointed positions, he moved decisively into the Southern political arena by the mid-1880s.

Walls's Last Stand in Florida, Smalls's Valiant Stand in Congress

As Langston made his way into the arena of post-Reconstruction politics, another old warhorse was on his last political legs. Having been ousted from his final term during the Forty-Fourth Congress in April 19, 1876, Josiah Walls found himself disillusioned with the Republicans and moved toward embracing alternative parties. By the early 1880s, he was despondent and bitter. On August 28, 1882, writing from Alachua County, Florida, to Rev. Joseph E. Lee (a lawyer who would eventually become the state's first black municipal judge), he expressed his belief that whites had betrayed their black neighbors and his fear of the increasing violence spreading through Florida: "See how many of our best men have been shot down, for their lasting fidelity to some man, who is safely looking on, from some northern city or some safe place in the State."[54] Where once there was optimism and a willingness to work across racial lines, now Walls saw the awful reality of increased violence and political impotence. Though he tried to continue as a political figure after Reconstruction (and indeed would serve again in the Florida State Senate in 1879), his career was virtually over by the early 1880s.

Increasingly dissatisfied with the state of affairs in the Republican Party and in his home state, Walls declared himself politically independent. Writing in the *New York Globe* on February 9, 1884, Walls explained how he had decided to resign from the Florida Republican District Committee and turn toward the "Independent movement" in Florida (this movement was the equivalent of the Greenbackers, Readjusters, and Populists in other Southern states; it included a biracial coalition of dissident whites and African Americans who sought to challenge the hegemony and economic policies of Bourbon Democratic regimes). After citing personal reasons, ranging from distrust of the Republican leadership in the state to unfair patronage appointments, Walls asserted: "I do not believe that it is to the best interest of the colored voters of the South, from past experience, to even dream of holding the Republican organization intact, and to urge it upon them as a duty, would be a crime against their manhood." Furthermore, Walls saw the continued violation of black civil rights, unfriendly Supreme Court decisions, and blacks being "shamefully ignored" by Republican leaders as signs that it was time for blacks to part ways with the party of Lincoln.[55]

In 1884, Walls ran for the seat held by white Republican congressman Horatio Bisbee Jr. When Bisbee challenged Walls to debate him during the campaign, promising him "courteous treatment and fair division of time," Walls accepted the challenge.[56] The candidates met during a rally on September 6, 1884, in Gainesville, Florida, with about 1,000 people in attendance. After listening to Bisbee speak for twenty minutes, Walls stood up and demanded to know whether he would have the chance to participate in the debate. Bisbee responded with a curt "By and by," at which point Walls jumped to his feet and shouted, "Will you do it, will you do it, will you do it? For, by God, I demand it."[57]

Bisbee declared that his opponent would have a chance to speak, but that several others from Bisbee's campaign would speak first. As the moderator stood up to introduce the next speaker, Walls quickly rose and reached the rostrum before Bisbee's supporter could open his mouth. The crowd broke out into a "stupendous uproar" and shouted out Walls's name. The correspondent for the *Florida Times-Union* described Walls's demeanor in vivid detail.

"Colonel Bisbee! Colonel Bisbee!! Colonel Bisbee!!! I demand my rights Colonel Bisbee, and, of you, my countrymen." Walls faced the audience, then "wheeling quickly around he extended his hand to Bisbee" all the while continuing to shout. "Colonel Bisbee! *Colonel* Bisbee!! COLONEL Bisbee!!!" Bisbee took Walls's hand. The former congressman began to speak, "Will you give me my rights?" After asking this question he faced the audience again and cried out, "By God, I'll have my rights or I'll die for it right here."[58]

Eventually Bisbee sat down and Walls addressed the crowd, which had begun to chant his name, but few could appreciate what he had to say. According to the correspondent, there was such a commotion and Walls was so excited in his delivery that it was hard for the crowd to understand his speech. Eventually the "crowd suppressed its effervescence," and, according to the reporter, Walls proceeded to attack his white Republican opponent viciously, specifically branding Bisbee a liar for claiming that Walls's newspaper (the *Farmer's Journal*) was supported by Democratic funds. The former congressman shouted loudly to the audience, "Intelligent people—you people before me—we know what he wants; he wants only to elect himself. . . . He cannot know whether a Democrat ever paid me a cent. We will fight him till the election night. . . . He has lied to me, and he has lied about me, and he talks to me, and he talks to you, as if we are fools. I know about these things. What are your interests? Are they not identical with the interests of the people among whom you live? Let Bisbee go to hell."[59]

Indeed, so alienated had Walls become from the Republican establishment that, at one point, he denounced white Northern allies "who have wound their coils around us until we must crush them or die." While the rally suggested that Walls retained significant personal popularity, he could no longer turn it into electoral success; in fact, he could not even win 1 percent of the vote. The Democratic candidate, Charles Dougherty, carried the race with 16,895 votes to Bisbee's 15,595, while Walls could claim only 215 votes (of which 149 came from his home county, Alachua).[60]

While Lynch and Langston castigated the federal government and

Southerners in general for their unwillingness to deal fairly with African Americans, and as Walls made his last stand in Florida, Robert Smalls took up the fight to protect his constituents' rights by preventing segregation in railroad transportation. Shortly after Walls's electoral debacle, on December 17, 1884, Smalls delivered a brief speech denouncing an amendment by Congressman Charles F. Crisp (D-Ga.), aimed at segregating transportation services, to an interstate commerce bill. Crisp had stated his belief "that before the law all men are equal" and contended that his amendment did "not seek to invade that right of the citizen," whereas opponents of segregated transportation were supporters of the unconstitutional "social-equality law" (that is, the Civil Rights Act of 1875).[61] Indeed, the 1883 Supreme Court ruling in the *Civil Rights Cases* significantly bolstered Democrats' efforts to create "Jim Crow" cars on railroads, as the Civil Rights Act of 1875 had barred racial discrimination in accommodations and transportation.

Smalls's response was not remarkable in terms of rhetorical flourishes, but it offers insight into his thinking seven years after the end of Radical Reconstruction.[62] Using somewhat sarcastic tones, he meant to hold Democrats accountable for their discriminatory practices. "Right-thinking Democrats of the House" should vote down the amendment, he said. These representatives "who are hallooing and crying out that there is no trouble about this matter . . . will do all that is best for the welfare of the colored people. I do not believe those men are going to say here now today the colored people shall have nothing but a 'Jim Crow' car in Georgia under the action of the railroad commissioners."[63] Smalls was sarcastic, but his challenge was serious; if indeed some Democrats wanted to claim concern for the interests of African Americans, then they would have to prove their sentiments through action. Otherwise, they would be engaging in the same duplicity that Smalls had regularly observed among Democrats in his home state, where some (such as Wade Hampton) spoke of moderation with respect to racial issues but did very little to protect the rights of blacks. However, Smalls's remarks did not move the Congress, which voted in favor of a substitute amendment permitting the railroads to do "as they deem best for the public comfort and safety, or to relate to transportation regarding to points wholly within the limits of one State." The amendment passed by 137 to 131, with 55 members not voting.[64]

The policy stances and rhetoric embraced by Lynch and Smalls in defense of black voting rights and in opposition to segregation served as a prelude to the last serious attempts by Republicans to address the "negro problem" in the early 1890s. As older black leaders tried to salvage what they could from the wreckage of Reconstruction through either emigration or fusion voting, a relatively young black man from North Carolina capitalized on agrarian discontent to win a seat in the U.S. Congress.

George Henry White and the
Rise of Fusion in North Carolina

Born on December 18, 1852, near Richland Branch, Bladen County, North Carolina, George Henry White was one of the youngest members of the emergent black political establishment. Like his counterpart from Virginia, Langston, White was of mixed ancestry—part black, part white, and part American Indian. His father, Wiley Franklin White, was a free mulatto, and his mother may have been a slave. The young White later lived with his black stepmother, Mary Anna Spaulding, who married his father on April 16, 1857. By all accounts, White considered Spaulding his natural mother. The course of his early education is a matter of speculation, since it is unclear whether he was born slave or free. White may have completed the equivalent of a middle-school education between 1869 and 1872, possibly attending local schools or classes offered at the newly established Freedmen's Bureau school nearby. He also graduated in 1872 from the Whitin School (a normal school), which trained White to be a teacher and exposed him to Latin.

On January 5, 1874, White entered Howard University, from which he graduated with a normal certificate in teaching in May 1877. Settling in New Bern, North Carolina, he served as principal for black public schools while studying law on the side. He eventually passed the bar and entered politics, winning election to the state House of Representatives in 1880. White unsuccessfully sought election for state solicitor, lost an election for state senate in 1882, but won election to the state senate in 1884. In 1886, White became the first black state solicitor in the nation, defeating his previous opponent, John Collins.[65]

White needed both persistence and patience in his endeavors to win election as solicitor and then to run for Congress. Coming politically of age long after the downfall of Reconstruction, White rose to power in the New South and capitalized on the advantages of the heavily black Second Congressional District in the northeast portion of his state. Beginning in 1872, the Democrats gerrymandered a black-majority district that would change slightly over the next quarter century but would remain a bastion for black

Congressman George Henry White of North Carolina.
(Library of Congress, Prints and Photographs Division,
LC-USZ62-44956)

politics and Southern Republicanism.[66] Democrats often gerrymandered most of the black population into a single district in order to dilute the strength of the black electorate across the remainder of the state. As of the 1900 census, the district's racial composition showed clearly why Republicans could still be successful there: the district had 53,923 black males and 47,352 white males.[67] But these encouraging figures hid uncomfortable intraracial and interracial tensions within North Carolina's Republican Party and among its black leaders. White and his predecessors were often involved in bitter power struggles among themselves and with the Republican establishment. This situation could (and occasionally did) lead to electoral defeats for blacks and Republicans even in a black-majority district. By the time White began to seriously consider running for Congress, other forces would conspire to make the already tense nature of black politics in the Second Congressional District even more difficult for an aspiring black politician.

Two major developments had a significant impact on White's political fortunes during the 1890s: the change in the composition of the district and the emergence of the Populist Party in North Carolina. Though blacks retained a majority in the Second District, that majority decreased somewhat by 1890, thanks to the efforts of the North Carolina General Assembly, which moved three black-majority counties (Jones, Vance, and Craven) out of the district. Vance County was home to the current black congressman from the Second District, Henry Plummer Cheatham (White's brother-in-law). Craven County contained the largest city in the former district, New Bern, where White lived. The shift of the district's boundaries led to a more equally divided electorate in the 1890s than in the 1880s, with blacks holding only a 400-vote majority over whites.[68] In addition, the emergence of the Populist Party in the state reshaped political calculations. In each congressional election from 1892 through 1898, the Populists fielded separate candidates from the Republicans, generally siphoning votes away from the Republican candidate.

Thus the situation confronting North Carolina's most concentrated black electorate by 1892 included a reduced congressional district, a divisive third party, and the continuation of long-standing internal and interracial squabbles within the Republican Party. The unwillingness of some within the Republican establishment to countenance a single, interracial slate of candidates proved disastrous in the 1892 elections. White opposed fusion with the Populists and attempted to ameliorate internal disputes within his own party, urging caution and strongly discouraging the practice of running separate Republican slates for statewide office. His advice went unheeded. The combined force of the redrawing of the Second Congressional District, the rise of the Populists, and factional disputes within the Republican Party concerning whether to support black candidates for statewide offices resulted in a terrible defeat at the polls. Black congressman Cheatham was defeated in a three-way race in which the Democratic candidate polled 13,925 votes, while Cheatham had 11,814 and the Populist candidate 5,457.[69]

Though factionalism, demographic changes, and shifting political currents damaged Republican chances in the election of 1892, the disappointing results opened the door to a brighter long-term future for both White and the state party. With Cheatham's political career effectively over (he would run again unsuccessfully in a three-way race in 1894, preventing White from earning the nomination), White saw a possible opening for his own political ambitions. Furthermore, the new Populist Party eventually forged a powerful coalition with North Carolina Republicans.

Redemption and Readjustment in Virginia

While fusion alliances produced mixed results in Mississippi and would not bear fruit until several years later in North Carolina, they rattled conventional politics in Virginia in the form of the Readjuster movement that took root by the early 1880s. The alliance forged by Virginia Republicans and dissident Democratic Readjusters made it feasible for Langston to seek elected office. By no means would fusion alliances and support for independent political movements be easy choices or sure guarantees of success, but through them the black community gained a much-needed respite from the coercive political machinations of white Democrats, and eventually one of their own would win a seat in the U.S. House of Representatives.

While the 1880s witnessed the potential power of fusion political alliances and dissident third parties, most of these movements were unable to overcome the significant obstacles of racism and intimidation in order to defeat white Democrats at the polls.[70] The exception was in Virginia, where the Readjuster movement was the single most effective challenge to Southern Democratic hegemony to emerge in the late 1870s and early 1880s. The restoration of Democratic control of the state upon its readmission into the Union in 1870 did not end the influence of African Americans in Virginia's political life. The state was unique in the South in that it never experienced the full force of Radical Reconstruction or saw Republican dominance of its government during its occupation by federal troops. This distinction is reflected in the moderate nature of the 1868 "Underwood" Constitution, which provided for universal male suffrage, granted amnesty to former Confederates, and included a vaguely defined provision for "a uniform system of free public schools" without mentioning issues of integration or the treatment of white and black pupils.[71] These developments transpired as Virginia's large debt presented a highly divisive challenge for the Conservatives (Democrats).

The question of whether to make paying off the debt a first priority split the Democrats into two factions: Funders and Readjusters. Funders wanted to focus the state's efforts on fully paying off its enormous prewar debt. Readjusters desired to lower or "readjust" the debt and use the remaining funds for much-needed domestic reforms, such as support for the state's school system. This division within Virginia's Democratic rank and file benefited African Americans, because it resulted in the emergence of the Readjusters as a reform-minded third party, thereby offering blacks an effective means to engage actively in the state's political life and to pursue their own community's civil and political goals.[72]

Virginia's Democrat-controlled state legislature had previously gerrymandered a large area of southern Virginia that became the Fourth Congressional District, containing eleven counties, including the major urban center of Petersburg. This district boasted a black-majority population of 102,064 in 1880. Over the next ten years the African American population would remain almost steady; it numbered 100,009 as of 1890. According to the 1890 census, 19,263 blacks were eligible to vote as opposed to 14,247 native-born and 453 foreign-born whites.[73]

The potential political strength of African Americans in the district was not lost on Langston. He wrote that the "people consist of two classes, white and colored. . . . The latter class with its descendants, largely predominates in numbers, so much so that the whole section of the district and adjoining counties are designated the 'Black Belt of Virginia.'" Nevertheless, Langston, especially with respect to Petersburg, had no political illusions. The city contained a population of 25,000, with blacks being "numerically superior" to whites, but "what the whites lack in numbers . . . they supplement in superior intelligence and power, using when it becomes necessary to that end, trick or fraud, intimidation, hindrance, and obstruction at the polls on election-day."[74] The dichotomy between the numerical superiority of blacks and the fraud and intimidation employed by whites was never far from Langston's mind. Both factors played roles in his turbulent congressional campaign of 1888. His own campaign, however, was not the first time that blacks in the Fourth Congressional District had impacted the tumultuous political arena of post-Reconstruction Virginia.

Well before the election of 1888, the district was a hotbed for Readjuster agitation.[75] Made up of a diverse coalition of African Americans, Republicans, and Democrats, the Readjusters capitalized on the Virginia electorate's dissatisfaction with the Conservative-dominated (that is, Bourbon Democrat) legislature's desire to pay off the state's antebellum debt and scored remarkable electoral victories as early as 1879. By 1881, the Readjuster movement had grown to such proportions that the party successfully elected William Cameron, a native of Petersburg, as governor.[76] The emergence of the Readjusters presented a viable political alternative for African Americans, and, unlike Virginia's moribund Republicans, white Readjusters proved that they could deliver on promises to their black supporters. Upon arriving in Richmond, the Readjusters abolished the poll tax and the whipping post, and they enabled African Americans to serve on juries and receive equal pay as teachers. In 1883, the Readjuster legislature established the Virginia Normal and Collegiate Institute to educate African Americans; Langston would become the school's president in 1885.[77] As a result of these reforms Readjusters gained valuable support from blacks, even those who remained Republicans. William Mahone, the white leader of the Readjuster-Republican machine, and William Cameron, the white Readjuster governor, both had their bases of power in the Fourth District; the political fortunes of both men were thus tied to the black-majority population in the district. Even if African Americans did not completely abandon their loyalty to the Republican Party, they willingly cooperated with the Readjusters in Virginia, and, as the historian James Tice Moore notes, the "Republican legislative bloc—which included fourteen Negroes—held the balance of power in the General Assembly. Indeed, blacks alone could tip the scales in the House of Delegates. Their influence was definitely on the rise."[78]

In addition, the church—one of the strongest pillars of the African American community—played an integral role in Langston's campaign. Black ministers threatened their congregants with expulsion if they voted against Langston.[79] The campaign also enjoyed support from members of local clubs such as the Langston Female Invincibles, who arranged festivities for political rallies and urged black men to vote for Langston. As the November 4, 1888, *New York Times* reported, "A remarkable feature of Langston's campaign has been the organization of women clubs in every town and county in the district. These clubs not only work, but they pray for Langston's success. Every political meeting held in Langston's interest is opened with prayer. The colored ministers are encouraging him, and every possible influence is exerted to elect him."[80]

It is notable that Langston's campaign organized women's clubs to spearhead political events and rallies. To a certain extent, this could be viewed as a break with the past. The latter half of the nineteenth century saw the birth of more "respectable" forms of female participation in the political arena. Perhaps Langston wanted to evade some of the pitfalls that had confronted Smalls's campaign activities in South Carolina and to insulate his campaign from charges that angry black women were stepping out of their "proper" sphere as ladies. Whatever the case, there was no mistaking the continued militancy of black women or the strong links that had developed between women's clubs and the black church.

This situation was not surprising. Black membership in churches exceeded that of whites by 31 percent, and ministers wielded great moral and practical influence in the daily lives of African Americans. Churches offered many useful services to the community. They schooled illiterate parishioners in reading and writing and offered social spaces for community gatherings. They were also the locus of debating organizations, where African Americans honed their oratorical abilities.[81] The black church's political mobilization was crucial to the effectiveness of Langston's 1888 campaign.

As Readjusterism faded in the wake of race baiting by Bourbon Democrats, the movement itself began to fuse with the Republican organization. Former Confederate general William "Billy" Mahone personified the bond between Readjusters and Republicans. He had fought at the Battle of the Crater in 1864, where his forces murdered black troops; now, ironically, he found himself working alongside African American leaders and politicians. Mahone led the Republican machine that dominated the Fourth Congressional District. Though he supported some Funder legislation, he became one of the major political figures in the Readjuster cause. Mahone's skillful negotiations with newly elected black Republicans enabled the Readjusters to secure a majority in the state legislature.[82] The fusion of predominantly white Readjusters with fourteen black Republicans was a crucial factor in Mahone's election to the U.S. Senate in 1881. Mahone's power and influence secured Langston his position as president of the Virginia Normal and Collegiate Institute, and Langston actively campaigned for the Readjusters in Virginia at Mahone's request in 1881 and 1882.[83] In 1888, the cooperation between Mahone and Langston ended when Mahone's Readjuster-Republican machine supported the candidacy of Judge Richard W. Arnold over Langston for the Republican nomination to Congress. The resulting division within Republican ranks, however, proved to be a mixed blessing for the party, for the Fourth District, and for Langston's ambitions to secure the congressional seat for himself.

Open rebellion against Mahone's control of the party was becoming increasingly evident by the mid-to-late 1880s. Mahone was the "only . . . dissatisfied man in the party in Virginia today. . . . He is a faction by himself. He is going down and out," said Republican gubernatorial hopeful John S. Wise, who placed the blame for the internal divisions within the Virginia Republican Party squarely on Mahone's shoulders. Lurid descriptions of intraparty divisions appeared on the front page of the *Petersburg Daily*

Index-Appeal. Wise stated confidently, "The republican party of Virginia is a party and not an army of political serfs subservient to Czar Mahone. A man who joins it will not feel as if he were an enlisted soldier, without voice and subject to military orders from a leader whose word was absolute law."[84] The reality, however, was far more complex. Mahone had led the Readjusters to victory in their earlier campaigns, and he continued to provide many benefits to the black community in the wake of that success.

With the election of Democrat Grover Cleveland to the White House in 1884, the Republican Party in Virginia faced one of its darkest hours. General Mahone, who finished his term in the U.S. Senate in March 1887, attempted to hold the party together in the face of a sequence of damaging developments from 1883 to 1885. These included the party's loss of its majority in the state legislature, the reduction of the state's number of Republican congressional representatives, and the accompanying loss of federal patronage. Combined with the "rebellion of discontented elements within the party," all these developments served to weaken Mahone's position as state Republican chairman in 1888 as he faced challenges from Readjuster governor William E. Cameron, gubernatorial hopeful John S. Wise, and congressional candidate John Mercer Langston.[85] "Czar Mahone," intent on granting power to no one but his supporters, would not give the nomination for the district's congressional seat to an upstart, educated black man like Langston. Meanwhile, African Americans in the district had long desired a politician of their own race to serve them in Congress, "feeling that their large share of the voters of their district earned them such representation."[86] Furthermore, Mahone's actions played a significant role in eroding what support the Readjuster-Republicans retained among the black electorate. At the 1884 Republican state convention, he ensured that Joseph Evans, a black candidate, did not receive the party's nomination to represent the Fourth District in Congress. The white contender, James Brady, secured the Republican nomination and won the election, with the Democratic candidate taking second place and Evans, running as an independent, finishing third.[87] Evans's defeat in the Fourth District prompted the black editor of the Petersburg *Lancet*, George F. Bragg Jr., to write, "It is no use for any colored man to make an attempt to go [to] Congress unless he has plenty of money to buy up the leaders, because as long as there are two white men in the party in this district one of them will want to go to Congress and his money will elect them."[88]

This background helps to explain why Langston's 1888 campaign was characterized by intense warfare that pitted Republicans against Republicans and blacks against blacks. It also became a national affair. The *Chicago Daily Inter Ocean* published a letter to the editor describing Langston as a "horse thief" who had been "handsomely provided for by the Republican party at the beginning of reconstruction, having held a high position under General Howard's management of the Freedmen's Bureau. . . . It is certainly in bad taste, to say nothing of his ingratitude, to fling mud in the eyes of those who so carefully guarded his fame and his purse."[89] Langston defended his right to the nomination in a letter sent to Republican national chairman Matthew Quay and distributed publicly. He said that he faced opposition "in a most positive and . . . violent manner by Gen. William Mahon[e]" and that he desired nothing more but the chance to win or lose an election "in orderly, regular, republican honorable methods."[90]

The national election also highlighted the personal and political differences between Langston and Frederick Douglass, who had become one of Langston's most outspoken critics. The two men represented distinct forms of activism within the national black community: Langston presented himself as a polished and well-educated man of means, while Douglass was a self-educated runaway slave (who also presented himself as one who had risen up in the world in ways very close to those used by Langston). Similarly, Langston's favorable recollection of his family, particularly his white father, contrasted sharply with Douglass's memories. Douglass wrote that he rarely saw his mother and "was not allowed to be present during her illness, at her death, or burial." He never knew who his white father was, and he remained disgusted by white planters who maintained dual relationships as both master and father to their slaves.[91]

The radically different upbringings of these two prominent former slaves did not, at first, bring them into conflict. William F. Cheek and Aimee Lee Cheek assert that the initial source of division was Douglass's unkind remarks in 1884 concerning Langston's youngest son, who had been accused of murder. The *New York Freeman* stated, "Mr. Douglass and Mr. Langston are at dagger's points, Mr. Langston believing that Mr. Douglass sought to prejudice the case of Mr. Langston's son Frank, who was charged (but acquitted) with murder a few years since. The two gentlemen met in the office of Mr. Wm. E. Matthews last week . . . when some very hot words passed between them. Mr. Douglass was disposed to explain but Mr. Langston refused to listen."[92]

In addition, the two diverged politically on the subject of black emigration from the South (which was a fraught and difficult subject given the prohibitive costs that impeded most blacks from heading north or out west).[93] Whatever the reasons, by 1888 they viewed each other as rivals, and when William Mahone requested that Douglass write a letter opposing Langston's candidacy, Douglass agreed to vilify his former colleague: "He was on the finance committee of the Freedmen's Bank when most of its bad loans were made. . . . He remained with Howard University so long as there was a chance to make himself its president. . . . No encouragement should be given to any man whose mad political ambition would imperil the success of the Republican Party." Impressively, Douglass's letter provoked outrage from the local black community and increased Langston's popular appeal in the Fourth District. Furthermore, his public opposition to Langston's candidacy drew criticism from black newspapers like the *Richmond Planet* and the *New York Age*.[94]

Langston recognized that, to ensure his election, he needed to create a well-organized and equally well-funded political campaign and to monitor the polls on Election Day. Running as an independent, he threw himself fully into the task of campaigning and drew upon his own financial resources. His personal fortune was somewhere between $50,000 and $100,000; Langston sold $10,000 worth of bonds and spent $15,000 of his own money to pay for his campaign. The results of the election, however, indicated that Langston had lost: 13,300 votes had been cast for Democratic candidate Edward C. Venable, 12,657 for Langston, and 3,207 for the Republican nominee, Judge Richard W. Arnold.

Langston refused to accept the legitimacy of the election. He knew that the district's majority black vote should have favored an African American candidate. The election was characterized, on all sides, by bribery and corruption. As one Mahone supporter stated, "While we were buying Langston votes, Langston and Venable were buying ours." Langston himself noted how Democrats, "fearing that [he] might become demoralized and abandon the contest, sought to reach him, and by promises and gifts of funds strengthen and sustain his purpose to wage to the last moment the fight in which he found himself engaged."[95] The Democrats were encouraging Langston's independent candidacy in the hope that it would divide the Republican vote and ensure a Democratic victory. Langston astonished the Democrats "when he not only looked with cold indifference upon their [proposition], refusing utterly to give it a moment's consideration," but declined "to put a dollar of Democratic funds in his canvass."[96]

Langston hired a number of well-educated and youthful activists to monitor the polls on Election Day, and their testimony supported Langston's claim against Venable.[97] M. N. Lewis, a thirty-year-old editor and lawyer from Petersburg, served as the secretary of Langston's campaign committee. He testified that Langston had sent out a letter instructing his surrogates to "remain at the polls all day" writing down the names of all men who cast their votes for Langston. After the polls closed, according to Langston's instructions, these men were to "witness the counting of the ballots" to make sure that all returns were "properly made out and signed by the judges and clerks of election according to the form on the poll books."[98]

One glaring example from Petersburg illustrates the outright fraud that took place during the election. In the city's Sixth Ward, where blacks outnumbered whites by three to one, local officials tampered with the election process by using a wooden barrier to segregate black voters from whites "in two lines . . . to receive the ballots from each side alternately, a white man's ballot, and then a negro's ballot; and so on throughout the day, unless some colored man who wished to vote the white men's tickets could get permission to fall in . . . the line of the whites." When the polls closed at sunset, 251 of 265 whites had been able to cast their ballots, but only 401 of 709 African Americans had voted; the rest were still in line when the polls closed.[99] Such acts were not confined to Petersburg, and Langston was able to present a detailed analysis of each ward and election district, documenting the irregularities and outright fraud at the polls.

Once again, Douglass lent his support to Langston's opponents in the form of a letter published in the *Lancet* in January 1889. Douglass wrote that Langston's "reason for taking himself outside of the Republican party and forming a colored Langston party was weak and worthless. It was that General Mahone had control of the Republican convention and prevent[ed] his nomination." Douglass asked pointedly, "Shall we have one law for the white and another for the mulatto, who, when it suits him, may avail himself of either?"[100]

For most of the period from 1874 through 1894, Democrats held a majority in the House of Representatives. The new Republican majority that took power in 1888, however, though not entirely willing to stake its political fortunes on the issue of seating a black congressman, eventually seated Langston along with South Carolina's Thomas Ezekiel Miller. House Republicans, according to the *Boston Journal*, were tired of the Democrats' efforts to delay congressional business and determined "not to permit any more time to be wasted in discussion of these contested election cases."[101]

When he finally secured his victory, Langston entered Petersburg in triumph and spoke to a crowd gathered at Langston Hall, his campaign's headquarters. "The state that first gave you slavery is now sending one of the old slave class to Congress," he declared, recalling the venom of his opponents who had said, "Don't seat that man because you'll put him where Daniel Webster used to stand, you'll put him where Henry Clay used to stand. It won't do." Concluding his speech, Langston embodied both his father and his mother as he described his true mission: "When I was elected I thought it was to represent this District, but since . . . I have been seated, I've found to an extent I represent the entire country. I have letters from all sections of it congratulating me. I have the most loyal men and the most loyal women in my District. My first endeavor is to make old Virginia the first state in the Union and the Fourth Congressional District the first in the Union."[102]

The Fluidity of Black Political Strategies: Impressive Creativity in Increasingly Desperate Times

Langston's battle for his seat illustrated new possibilities for African American politics in the New South, but it also demonstrated the increasing limitations on black political participation in the aftermath of Redemption. While some national black leaders would be able to continue their struggle in this unfamiliar landscape, others were unable to maintain their power in the face of white racism and intimidation.

Across the South by the mid-to-late 1880s, the upsurge in agrarian reform movements, political fusion, and independent third parties had been checked by renewed fraud, violence, and intimidation on the part of the white Democratic establishment. Even the formidable Readjuster-Republican coalition of Virginia proved no match for the tactics of Democrats, who, on their way to regaining power, often connected fusion alliances with white fears of a resurgent era of "Negro rule" and the threatening specter of "social equality."

Nevertheless, the period between 1877 and 1888 witnessed a profound shift in black political culture, one that influenced the strategies embraced by national black leaders. Though most blacks continued to support the Republican Party (even at the height of fusion initiatives), they would not do so with the same ideological fervor that they used in the immediate aftermath of the Civil War and during the heyday of Radical Reconstruction. National black political leaders increasingly drew upon a diverse range of interests that occasionally brought them into conflict with one another. Where once there had been substantial unity, now there was no uniform ideological position to bring all black politicians together.

In some respects, black participation in third parties and support for emigration were not entirely new. Prior to the Civil War, small numbers of blacks had participated in abolitionist third parties and entertained calls to leave the United States in favor of better treatment elsewhere.[103] But the differences in the postwar period were striking. This time the emergence of emigration and fusion as viable political alternatives was rooted firmly in the context of African American citizenship rights. Blacks considered leaving the South in order to protect their rights as American citizens. Most African Americans did not consider themselves a separate nation; rather, they saw themselves as citizens entitled to the same rights as other Americans. When those rights were threatened in the wake of the failure of Reconstruction, the black community and their leadership reacted immediately to the changing political tides, seeking alternative ways to affirm their equality as men and as Americans.

The fact that African Americans could still affirm their rights as citizens (albeit in more limited ways) and participate in the political life of the New South well after the violent overthrow of Reconstruction did not sit well with many white Democrats. Even though most fusion alliances were utter failures and those that did succeed (like the Readjuster alliance in Virginia) were unraveling by the mid-to-late 1880s, the very existence of such alternative and viable political opportunities threatened the fabric of race relations in the South. Indeed, African Americans were still able to secure the election of several black leaders to Congress. In some instances, blacks were able to hold the balance of power in counties or even play a substantial role at the state level by supporting dissident Democrats and agrarian reform movements. So long as this fluid and uncertain state of affairs persisted, African Americans could still have an impact in Southern politics. And that fact meant that it was possible, albeit unlikely, for African Americans to help in toppling Southern Redeemers.

At the same moment as national black politicians pursued alternate political avenues, whether through fusion or emigration, the white Democratic establishment moved to solidify its gains by codifying racial segregation and disfranchising the majority of blacks (along with large numbers of whites) in order to preclude a black or Republican resurgence in the South. By the beginning of the 1890s, national black political leaders who remained in Congress or who maintained powerful positions in local areas across the South were forced to respond to these efforts to disfranchise African American voters. Those members of the old guard who remained continued to champion economic modernization and private legislation, but they became increasingly more vocal about civil rights issues — especially voting rights and antilynching legislation.

The age of fusion politics may have witnessed the birth of more fluid political alliances and a willingness to part ways with the Republican Party, but such strategies would not be useful if the black electorate could not even vote. While pulmonary tuberculosis took the life of James Rapier in 1883 and Josiah Walls had met his political demise by the mid-1880s, John Roy Lynch, Robert Smalls, John Mercer Langston, and George Henry White capitalized on the changes wrought by emigration and political fusion. Their ideas helped to modernize the South and slow the campaigns of violence and voter disfranchisement that had begun to engulf the region.

Whether crafting civil rights legislation in Congress or participating in state constitutional conventions, national black political leaders confronted an uncertain political future. Increasingly, they faced challenges to their authority and an unforgiving environment. Despite these daunting obstacles, their determination and long-term vision never flagged, as vividly shown by an article on Rapier in the *Christian Recorder* a few weeks after his death. In describing his struggle to keep his job as tax collector several years earlier, the newspaper recalled that one of Rapier's adversaries had told him, "It is reported that you don't represent the colored race in your section," to which Rapier replied, "No sir; I do not, at present. I represent the possibilities of the colored race fifty years hence."[104] Despite these prescient observations about the gathering storm overtaking them, the black leaders who were left behind continued to fight for policies that would serve their black constituents and preserve their rights as free men and citizens.

7

The Last Hurrah

The Demise of Black Politics and the Rise of the New Order

T HE AIR IS FULL of politics, the woods are full of politicians. Some clever traps are being set, and some skillful moves are being made upon the political board. In North Carolina the Negro holds the balance of power, which he can use to the advantage of the race, state and nation, if he has the manhood to stand on principles, and contend for the rights of a man." So began a brief editorial published on September 28, 1895, on the front page of black journalist Alexander Manly's *Wilmington Daily Record*. This editorial came a year before the triumph of the Fusionists (an interracial alliance between Republicans and Populists) that inaugurated the "Second Reconstruction" of North Carolina between 1896 and 1898. The editorial is filled with cautious optimism, suggesting that blacks needed to tread cautiously and not rush behind any political banner, but also that they had to act firmly and continue to fight for their rights in the political arena. Manly continued, "Every step should be made after calm and mature deliberation. While all the views of the old leaders cannot be endorsed we would remind the young leaders to be sure you are right, otherwise it will be suicide to go ahead. While concocting a safe remedy for the people, death may be dropped in the pot." Though Manly was writing for a local audience, the editorial captured major shifts occurring within black policy circles. It concluded, "Some have already shown their hand, others are lying low, others are sleeping with one eye open. We will wait till the iron is hot, then grasp our sledge and strike at selfishness, corruption and every man who looks as if he wants to use the Negro vote to further personal ends."[1]

As Manly's editorial made clear, by 1895 the political situation confronting black political leaders was changing rapidly. No longer would the solutions or the stature of the old guard be enough to unite all segments of the black community behind their authority. New leaders had emerged to challenge the approach of Langston, Lynch, and White. Prominent black leaders of the new generation tended to be writers, journalists, and teachers rather than politicians; Ida B. Wells-Barnett, Timothy Thomas Fortune, W. E. B. Du Bois, and Booker T. Washington all fell into this category. This new generation would not forge a monolithic response to the needs of the black community. As a result, its leaders often clashed with older black politicians and, increasingly, with each other in ways that would change the course of black civil rights activism by the early twentieth century.

The Force Bill and the Limits of Practical Politics

Following his drawn-out, contested election, Congressman Langston was finally able to take his seat in the House of Representatives. He arrived too late to vote on Henry Cabot Lodge's Federal Elections Bill, which the House passed in July 1890. Born in 1850, scion of a prominent Massachusetts family, Lodge was one of the few Republicans who championed black civil rights in the late nineteenth century. He would eventually become a strong ally of Theodore Roosevelt and a supporter of American involvement in the Spanish-American War. His support for black civil rights was understandable. Lodge's father was a close friend of Charles Sumner, and the abolitionist senator visited the family estate often during summers, where he almost certainly exerted a powerful influence on what the young Lodge thought about civil rights. His bill sought to prevent intimidation and corruption at the polls in congressional races by ensuring oversight of local elections by national party officials and involving federal circuit courts in contested election cases.[2] The bill also stated that federal intervention could occur only if at least one hundred citizens of a congressional district signed their names to a petition charging irregularities in the election; such a petition would trigger circuit court review of the local electoral process.

Southerners reviled the bill as "that thing of evil names and memories, a force bill," believing it would "destroy the sovereign rights of the states . . . and bring strife, bloodshed, and dictatorship in its train."[3] However, as the historian Richard Welch asserts, the bill "embodied little coercion and was inspired as much by a wish to validate the principles of national citizenship and the Fifteenth Amendment as by a desire to undermine Bourbon control of southern politics and enhance the national position of the Republican

Party." The bill never made it out of the Senate, thus ending, for a period of more than sixty years, the federal government's attempts to protect the voting rights of black Americans. While stating that black leadership did not question the sincerity of the bill's Republican backers, Welch also observes that a minority of Southern Republicans (both black and white) doubted whether Lodge's Federal Elections Bill was the right path for blacks to take in their quest to regain their political rights.[4]

Among those holding this minority view was the newly elected black congressman from Virginia's Fourth Congressional District, whose opinions regarding the bill's merits were well known. Langston was squarely opposed to the so-called Force Bill because he believed that it had very little chance of success. He thought that it lacked a reliable method of enforcement, since it required Southerners to make a complaint before federal authorities could intervene. The alternative for him would have been a bill that did not rely on locals to enforce it. Langston stated candidly, in an interview with the *Richmond Leader*, that he was opposed to the Lodge bill, "as I would be to any other bill that sought an honest ballot and a fair count in the south, and yet depended, in any degree, upon the people of that locality to secure a compliance with the law." The proposed law was worthless when one considered the "temper of the people of the south." He wondered how many precincts existed in the South where it would be possible to obtain the necessary signatures required for federal intervention: "Do not you understand that an overt act like that would instantly bring upon the signer's head all the odium and opprobrium, all the ostracism and concentrated hatred which that people can feel as deeply perhaps as can any people on earth?"

Langston understood that fair elections were impossible to obtain under the auspices of white Southerners. He thus believed that any federal elections bill was worthless unless it had a mechanism to provide for election oversight not subject to the authority of local whites. Intimidation and fraud could easily prevent citizens from signing their names to a petition meant to enforce the fairness of local elections. Langston did not believe that either white Republicans or his fellow African Americans could enforce the bill; in his eyes, Republican "timidity and hesitation and doubt" reinforced black powerlessness, thereby rendering Lodge's bill useless. Langston stated, "The negro is dependent upon the white Democrat of the south to-day for his daily bread and butter. Do you expect him to sacrifice all his hopes . . . to secure a liberty that the white Republican himself would not take any risk to secure?" Langston believed that the only way to ensure Southern electoral fairness lay in the adoption of the secret ballot. His support for this mechanism presumed intervention by federal authorities rather than any reliance on local politicos to ensure enforcement.[5]

On January 16, 1891, however, Langston shifted his position, offering a speech on the House floor in support of Lodge's bill. Perhaps he was aware that the Senate would be meeting that very night to take up the bill. He may have decided that a faulty piece of legislation that offered some protection of voting rights was better than none at all.[6] Langston's misgivings about Lodge's bill led him to propose a constitutional amendment governing the use of literacy tests to prevent otherwise eligible citizens from voting. His amendment embodied the egalitarian spirit of Lodge's bill, but did not rely solely on local officials or a petition by local residents to enforce it.

In his speech in support of Lodge's bill, Langston reminded his fellow congressmen, on both sides of the aisle, of the sacrifices made to save the nation and emancipate the slaves: "How dark it was in 1861! How dark it was in 1850! Ah! compromises were made; the greater orators spoke; the great parties resolved; and the friends of freedom came well-nigh to despair." He linked the fortunes of the nation with those of the Hebrews of old: "The voice of the faithful and the truth was still heard; and finally in the thunder of great guns, in the midst of terrible smoke as of the Mountain of Sinai, and in the flashes of light that made every slave in the land glad, emancipation was declared and the country was saved."[7]

Having taken the moral high ground, Langston then went to the heart of the matter, drawing on his own experiences in the South and emphasizing that the issue was not a racial question: "When I stand here to-day speaking for the cause of the people of my State, of my native State, the State of Virginia, I am pleading for her people *both white and black*. I am speaking for white men as well as for negroes; for white men in my State are proscribed, and they are denied a free ballot, though their 'locks be flaxen and their eyes blue.'"[8] Langston's challenge to his fellow congressmen was unmistakable: "Now, oppress negroes if you must, but for God's sake stop oppressing white voters. Deny to the negro the ballot if you will, but for God's sake do not take the ballot from your own brothers with flaxen hair and blue eyes!"[9] Here he was clearly referring to the fraud that he had seen committed against both blacks and white Republicans.[10] Langston may also have been referencing earlier instances of white disfranchisement in his state; between 1876 and 1882, a quarter of all eligible white voters in Virginia were denied the right to vote because they could not pay the poll tax.[11]

In Langston's rhetoric one can see the ideological underpinnings of his national literacy test amendment. If literacy tests were to be the order of the day, Langston maintained that such tests should be implemented equally across all voters. Here was a classic example of how accommodation could be used cleverly for tactical purposes. Langston begged his colleagues not to take away the white man's vote. Why would a black man take such a stance? Because the programs needed to promote literacy (in order to equip citizens to vote) would benefit not only poor, illiterate whites but also downtrodden blacks. In fact, blacks would gain the greatest political advantage, especially in those areas where they were numerically superior. Langston's argument accommodated whites while also seeking to enhance black political strength.

In addition, Langston insulated himself against charges of racial favoritism by defending the voting rights of poor whites as well as blacks. Indeed, in an interview with E. L. Thornton of the *New York Age,* Langston highlighted his true intentions. As Thornton reported, Langston "argues that the Southern States . . . are rapidly passing laws the effect of which will be to disfranchise the Afro-American elements of our voters *en masse* and insists that his resolution embodies the fundamental principles of a National election law with an educational qualification. He thinks that the leading idea of his resolution ingrafted into a law will disarm the enemy and at the same time stimulate the great body of our people to prepare themselves for suffrage rights."[12]

Specific elements of Langston's proposed constitutional amendment reflect his strategic intentions. Langston ensured that the amendment would rely on the federal government and not local authorities to make the laws. For this reason, he made sure to include the sentence "under such laws as Congress shall enact," thereby providing a slap in the face to Southern theories of states' rights. Langston also cleverly stipulated that a state's number of representatives in Congress would be reduced "in the proportion which the number of those allowed to vote shall bear to the whole number of male citizens twenty-one years of age in such a State."[13] Though the language is tortuous, Langston clearly intended to reduce representation based on the number of adult males denied the right to vote due to their illiteracy. Thus, in those states with the highest illiteracy rates (many of which were in the South), congressional representation would be significantly decreased. Presumably, the South would be forced to invest a substantial amount of money into educating its citizens so that it would not lose congressional representation. Had Langston's proposed amendment passed and been ratified as the Sixteenth Amendment to the Constitution, it would have modified (and enforced) the provisions of the second section of the Fourteenth Amendment. Whereas, previously, only "participation in rebellion, or other crime" constituted a legal basis for disfranchisement, Langston's amendment would have legitimized disfranchisement of voters on the basis of literacy.[14]

Though the *Congressional Record* reveals only that Republicans applauded Langston's defense of Lodge's bill, the response among Democrats to his impassioned speech indicates the potential viability of his pragmatic approach. According to the *Cleveland Leader,* "When he began the Democrats showed a disposition to ignore him, but he compelled them to hear him, and before he had finished a dozen such Bourbons . . . were over on the Republican side listening intently to his every word. It is scarcely credible, but it is true that he caused the eyes of some of these case-hardened Democrats to moisten by his impassioned appeals for justice to the black man and to the white man of the South."[15] Despite the effectiveness of Langston's powerful rhetoric, however, the House never considered his proposed amendment.

Smalls and the Red Shirts, Redux

While Lodge, Langston, and other Republicans struggled in vain for federal protection of black voting rights, battle-hardened Robert Smalls, no longer a member of Congress, continued to fight the good fight in South Carolina. As the promises of Reconstruction gave way to the hardening of segregation, Smalls confronted a growing white supremacy tide led by what he called the "personification of red-shirt Democracy," Ben Tillman.[16]

In November 1890, Smalls published an essay in the *North American Review* titled "Election Methods in the South." Moved to action by Tillman's candidacy for governor, Smalls described instances of Democratic electoral fraud in his home state and made three major points. First, he argued in favor of Lodge's Federal Elections Bill. Second, he urged blacks to vote for the moderate Democratic candidate, rather than the Republican, in order to prevent Tillman's election as governor. Finally, he tapped into familiar themes of black manhood and valor to castigate the illegitimacy of Democratic victories at the polls and emphasized that blacks would not leave the South but would stay and fight.

In his argument for the Federal Elections Bill, Smalls described some of the means by which local officials prevented free and fair elections from taking place in South Carolina. If a Republican was "fortunate enough to obtain a certificate" to vote, Smalls said, "the Republican goes to the polls. . . . The hour for the opening of the polls comes and goes, and neither managers nor boxes make their appearance." Gradually, the number of Republican voters swells, and soon 400 to 500 voters arrive ready to cast their ballots: "Anxious inquiries are made for the managers. It is learned later that, of the managers, Colonel Jones had gone to town, Mr. Brown has gone hunting, and Mr. Smith says he does not intend to serve, as there is no pay in it. Four or five hundred Republicans are disfranchised by the neglect of the managers, and not even the letter or spirit of the law is violated by the poll not being opened."

Smalls went on to detail more overt methods of disfranchisement, stressing that they affected poor whites as well as blacks.[17] Smalls likely mentioned poor whites because of fears engendered in the white community by the new registration laws, which had contributed to depressing *white* turnout for Democratic gubernatorial nominees.[18] Such laws were repugnant, according to Smalls, because they imposed an "educational qualification upon voters contrary to the constitution of the State."

Smalls explained the use of the "eight-box" law, a strategy as simple as it was dishonest. Separate ballots and boxes were provided for eight specific political offices, making it highly likely that illiterate or relatively uneducated voters would place their ballots in the wrong boxes, causing their votes to be discarded. The election managers were required by law to read the names on the ballot boxes when requested, but Smalls noted that "managers have been caught lying so often when they pretended to read the names, the apparent protection is only a further abuse of a free ballot." In such a setting, Smalls argued, the only solution was federal supervision of elections.

In the wake of a split between more moderate "straight-out" Democrats and those who supported Tillman, Smalls urged African Americans to do the unthinkable—to cast their votes for Tillman's Democratic opponent, Alexander Haskell. He wrote, "While it is repugnant to my feelings as a Republican to advise my people to vote for any Democrat, yet in this emergency I must advise them to do anything that is legitimate to bring about the defeat of this arch-enemy of my race [Tillman]." Smalls believed that Haskell represented the "better element" of the Democratic Party in South Carolina. Haskell (and others like him), according to Smalls, would oppose fraudulent elections and counter the unfathomable evil that would be inaugurated under the regime of Tillman and his supporters.[19]

It is curious that a seasoned politician like Smalls would feel capable of trusting any Democrat to provide electoral fairness to South Carolina's black population. Indeed, as Stephen Kantrowitz argues, the differences between so-called moderates such as Wade Hampton or Alexander Haskell and their Red Shirt or Tillmanite opponents were more rhetorical than real. Though Democrats like Hampton and Haskell might make statements that indicated a desire to deal fairly with the black electorate, their actions suggested otherwise.[20] Perhaps this was Smalls's way of trying to forestall the inevitable. Perhaps a more moderate Democratic governor would not have moved as swiftly as Tillman to call for a constitutional convention to fully disfranchise what remained of the black electorate. If so, this strategy may explain Smalls's final point—his understanding of black citizenship and its connection to black military prowess and courage.

After urging blacks to vote for Haskell, Smalls emphasized that the Democrats had never legitimately won a majority of the state's votes. A vote for a Democrat by desperate blacks could still be an affirmation of Republican sentiments: "At any election in South Carolina, when the votes shall be counted as cast, it will be found that the negroes of the South are as true and as loyal to the principles of Republicanism as they were to the flag of this great country when treason sought to blot it out." Smalls emphasized the character and martial valor of blacks, even as he urged them to cast their votes for a candidate not of the party of Lincoln. He also emphasized, once again, his opposition to emigrationism, alluding to the desire among some in Congress who are "willing to vote . . . to have us sent out of the country."[21] Smalls referred to South Carolina Democratic senator and former Red Shirt Matthew C. Butler's 1890 Emigration Bill, which would appropriate $5 million per year to fund voluntary emigration from the South.[22]

Blacks, as men and citizens, had fought long and hard for their rights. So long as Democrats governed in Washington and they could get "false representation" in Congress, white Southerners opposed black emigration. But beginning in 1888, with the Republican majority bolstered by the presence of President Benjamin Harrison, whites cringed at the possibility that fair elections might be enforced and, according to Smalls, became receptive to the idea of blacks leaving the state lest whites lose their grip on power. Returning to his emphasis on valor, manhood, and citizenship, Smalls asserted, "These men forget that the negroes of the country gave 186,000 men who fought in 252 battles for the perpetuity of this great nation. We do not intend to go anywhere, but will remain right here and help make this the most powerful of all governments."[23]

Perhaps one reason why Smalls evoked the memory of blacks who had fought for their rights as citizens—and for their lives—was the rising tide of anti-black violence in the form of angry white mobs lynching black men.

Black Politicians Confront "Lynch-Law" in the New South

Lynching was not a new phenomenon. Sporadic violence against African Americans had occurred throughout the 1880s, including intimidation at the polls. In some cases, armed mobs of white men drove blacks from the polls or massacred them wholesale.[24] But by the late 1880s and early 1890s, white mobs were finding other outlets for their hatred of African Americans, turning to "lynch-law" to intimidate the black community. As political disfranchisement became the central focus of the Democratic establishment, white Southerners moved to consolidate their pervasive power through spectacles of mob violence.[25]

No part of the South was immune from these acts of brutality, as the black-owned *Richmond Planet* emphasized in an article titled "Twenty-Eight Colored Persons Lynched." Published on August 25, 1888, the article described unprovoked violence against blacks in Mississippi and Louisiana, identifying various sources of white violence and lauding blacks who defended themselves. In Utica, Mississippi, Bob Broom, a black man, refused to give way to a white man on the sidewalk. When the white man returned with friends to attack, Broom and his friends "were prepared for them and opened fire," killing one white and wounding two others. For this act of bravado Broom was promptly lynched. The *Planet* nevertheless viewed the clash positively: "It is this kind of dealing with southern Bourbons that will bring about a change. We must have martyrs and we place the name of the fearless Broom on that list."

The *Planet* urged all African Americans to "awaken to the necessity of protecting themselves when the law fails to protect them." The hypocrisy of the federal government's guarantees of protection was fully evident: "It is declared that the strong arm of the law shall protect the weak, but when it is called upon it mocks the distressed and sides with the strong. After this let every man resolve with us that *lynch-law must go!*"[26] .

The scale and brutality of lynching inspired a new generation of militant leaders to demand government protection and urge the black community to fight back against white depredations. Chief among this new generation of black leaders was the antilynching crusader Ida B. Wells of Memphis, Tennessee. But not all black leaders were so convinced of the need to combat the threat of lynching in so militant a fashion. The divisions between older and younger black leaders came to the fore when John Mercer Langston was quoted as disagreeing with Wells's approach.

On a visit to Memphis in June 1894, according to remarks published in a local newspaper, Langston voiced his antipathy to Wells's message: "I do not know Ida Wells personally, but I certainly don't uphold her views concerning the condition of our people in the South. It is no doubt true that in times past wrongs have been perpetrated upon the negro, but they have almost become a thing of the past, and such as still appear occasionally are being righted every day."[27]

Strangely, Langston's assertions concerning Southern race relations contrasted sharply with the body of evidence that he had in his possession. Among his preserved papers is a "lynch-list" documenting the cases of 640 blacks murdered between July 26, 1887, and December 26, 1889. For Langston to say that injustices against black Americans "have almost become a thing of the past" contradicts the recorded number of 207 lynchings that occurred in 1888, the year in which he waged his campaign for the House of Representatives.[28] It was a curious position for him to take, especially considering his long career of fighting for black constituents. How could a former congressman who had recruited soldiers for the Fifty-Fourth Massachusetts Colored Regiment during the Civil War, served as general inspector of schools in the Freedmen's Bureau, and established Howard University's law school downplay the daily atrocities that afflicted blacks throughout the South? Given how quickly the white Southern press newspapers jumped on the story, it is possible that Langston's words were misquoted or taken out of context to undermine Wells and sow division in the black community.

Perhaps Langston took issue with Wells because of his belief that black progress could be achieved only through compromise and a judicious use of rhetoric. In view of the diplomatic strategies that he embraced while in Congress, Langston may have believed that Wells's tactics, which included impugning the moral character of white women, unnecessarily incensed white Southerners. Indeed, Wells's statements to that effect in 1892 had led to the destruction of her newspaper's offices and her banishment from Memphis.[29] Such tactics were unacceptable to Langston because they exacerbated racial hatred and obviated the advances of blacks toward civil and political equality. He may also been challenging Wells's position as a black leader on gender-based grounds as well. Even if what she was saying was true, one could not attack white women. It could not have been far from Langston's mind that black slights against white women's virtue were often used as the basis for lynchings. Moreover, though Langston was happy to use black churchwomen in his rallies, they had a particular place to play in the political arena. Perhaps he viewed Wells's forthright activism as out of character for a respectable black woman. Considering all these factors, it should perhaps not be so surprising that Langston, in speaking to a white newspaper, downplayed violence against blacks. Irrespective of strategic differences over black civil rights activism, Langston's decision to deliver these remarks in Memphis, the city Wells once called home, was a slap in her face, and the newspaper appears to have seized on his words to undermine Wells's credibility.

Whatever Langston actually said, he quickly discovered the controversial nature of his published remarks. Within a few weeks, attacks started coming in. On June 16, the *Indianapolis Freeman* published an editorial by a black lawyer, G. W. Walker, on the front page of the newspaper next to a large picture of Langston. Writing from "Surrounded Hill," Arkansas, Walker asked Langston to clarify his "evasive" comments to the white press: "Do you differ as to Miss Well[s]'s statement regarding our condition civilly[,] financially, morally or religiously? Or do you mean all that Miss Wells has said in England is untrue? What past can you mean? Only think of the lynchings for this year." He also added an ominous admonition to the former congressman. "Be careful, Mr. Langston in your attempt to please an enemy at the expense of an honest friend. Miss Wells is only doing for us what we have needed ever since the first lie about us was sent or carried abroad; why not counteract or stop the effect of such lies as are told about us, by letting the truth be known?" The firmly pro-Douglass *Washington Bee* followed suit on June 23 with a scathing response to Langston's comments, adding: "Prof. Langston must have said what the dispatches have quoted him as having said. He has not denied it." The black newspaper defended Wells's efforts in "doing what others have failed to do, no matter what her motives are. Langston had a motive in coming to Congress and he played the race racket for all it was worth."[30]

Chastened by the criticism, Langston wrote a letter to the editor of the black-owned *Indianapolis Freeman* (published on June 30, 1894), flatly denying that he had said anything to undermine Wells or her mission. Langston provided testimony to refute the remarks that white newspapers claimed he had made.[31] The editors at the *Indianapolis Freeman* accepted Langston's account and stated that his letter and the accompanying documents "must at once put an end to vituperative arraignment of Mr. Langston, and at once reestablish him, where for so many years he had reigned unquestioned, in the hearts and confidence of his people." The *Freeman* hoped that those segments of the black press that had "been hasty in condemning will be just as hasty in making the only honorable amends."[32]

Langston's repudiation of his quoted remarks suggests that the conservative white Southern press might have been trying to divide the black community, but the fact that he waited to deny the charges indicates that he was testing whether he could challenge Wells's tactics in order to soften whites without alienating blacks. The fact that not all African Americans (including Wells herself) were convinced by his denials indicated how much times had changed since leaders like Langston commanded nearly universal respect within the black community.[33] Other prominent black leaders continued to support Wells; for example, Frederick Douglass regarded her almost as a daughter, helped her career in numerous ways, and even wrote material to be incorporated into her antilynching pamphlets.[34]

Robert Smalls and the Disfranchising Convention of 1895

While Langston tried to extricate himself from an uncomfortable public relations debacle, the situation in South Carolina had deteriorated further. Despite Robert Smalls's efforts, Tillman won the governorship and moved to call a state constitutional convention in 1895. Smalls attended the convention and, perhaps because he came from one of the most independent and heavily black areas of the state, did not hesitate to speak openly. One of only six black delegates elected to the constitutional convention, Smalls represented coastal South Carolina counties where (as late as the 1890 census) sharecropping was not as prevalent as in other parts of the South; instead, many local citizens, both white and black, cultivated their own lands as independent farmers. The knowledge that, at least in his section of the state, many blacks were property holders influenced Smalls's tactics at the convention, particularly how he presented and defended two amendments regarding suffrage and interracial marriage.

Smalls's forthright advocacy for black rights placed him in direct conflict with "Pitchfork Ben" Tillman, and he relished the chance to assail his longtime rival's white supremacist rhetoric, combining sound facts, humor, sarcasm, and disgust to frame his arguments against disfranchisement. Smalls presented his case by using records of property taxes and literacy based on the 1890 census. He stated that, according to the census, South Carolina's blacks paid taxes on $12,500,000 worth of property. In spite of this, Tillman and his allies rejected "a proposition for a simple property and educational qualification. What do you want? You tried the infamous eight-box and registration laws until they were worn to such a thinness that they could stand neither the test of the law nor of public opinion. In behalf of the 600,000 Negroes in the State and the 132,000 Negro voters all that I demand is that a fair and honest election law be passed."[35]

Smalls's willingness to accept some voting qualifications is not difficult to explain, as he was searching for a way to preserve some measure of civil and political rights for his embattled constituents. "We care not what the qualifications imposed are: all that we ask is that they be fair, honest and honorable, and with these provisos we will stand or fall by it." Combating undisguised attempts by others at the convention (including Tillman) to wipe out black voting entirely, Smalls was willing to accept a literacy test provided that it applied equally to whites and blacks. Taunting Tillman, Smalls added, "if you dare pass it." But he would not accept giving election officials latitude to assess whether a voter demonstrated sufficient understanding to be permitted to vote, because he believed that whites would receive more favorable assistance at the polls than blacks.

Smalls threatened economic repercussions against South Carolina if the convention voted to disfranchise black voters: "Some morning you may wake up to find that the bone and sinew of your country is gone. The Negro is needed in the cotton fields and in the low country rice fields, and if you impose too hard conditions upon the Negro in this State there will be nothing else for him to do but to leave." He asked his fellow delegates what they would do if thousands of blacks departed. Black labor was needed not only in the fields but also in other areas of South Carolina's economy, such as the phosphate mining industry. According to Smalls, only blacks could work at these mines, which paid the interest on the state's debt. Using this evidence, he emphasized that whites could not do without black labor. He did not believe that they wanted to "get rid of the Negro"; otherwise why would they impose a high tax on "immigration agents" who could enter South Carolina and entice African Americans to leave the state? Though opposed to black emigration, Smalls used the prospect of blacks leaving in large numbers as a possible threat to the stability and prosperity of the Southern economy.[36]

The language that Smalls used to define his opposition to Tillman and disfranchisement was clothed in the Republican ideology of free labor and emancipation. Smalls did not deny the existence of illiterate and ignorant blacks and granted that such people should not be allowed to vote, but he emphasized the economic strength of the black laborer and firmly opposed imposition of a double standard against blacks. By 1895, many Northerners were no longer willing to defend the rights of blacks because they had come to see the mass of the freedmen and their descendants as unworthy impediments to the progress of industrial capitalism and free labor.[37] But class anxieties alone were not solely responsible for the dramatic changes that had taken place. African Americans also confronted an increasingly racist North that was complicit in the segregation emerging in the late nineteenth-century South.[38] In this climate, not only was Smalls unlikely to succeed in altering the opinion of white supremacists led by Tillman, but he could not fall back upon a pro-black Republican majority in the North. Even his willingness to allow only the knowledgeable (and presumably the respectable and property-holding) elements of his race to vote could not hold back the march toward one-party white rule in South Carolina.

Smalls saved his most explosive statements for the convention's discussion of an amendment banning interracial marriage. Smalls proposed modifying this amendment to also bar any white man who had sexual relations with a black woman from holding public office in the state — a direct attack on white male Southerners' widespread practice, even while treating blacks as an inferior race, of taking black mistresses. Moreover, Smalls's proposed legislative language would have given the offspring of any such liaison the right "to inherit and acquire property the same as if they were legitimate."[39]

This challenge to the standard myths of Southern life, and to Southern assumptions about race, gender, and sexuality, caused quite a stir among the delegates.[40] Smalls wanted to highlight the hypocrisy of the proposed amendment by making sure that it would force white men to take legal responsibility for interracial offspring. The obvious double standard disturbed Smalls, who wondered aloud, "If your women are as pure as you stated, and I have reason to believe that they can be trusted; then why the necessity of this being placed in the Constitution? Can you not trust yourselves? When I say you, I mean the white men of the entire State." In taking this approach, Smalls was walking on a thin line. White Southerners often tied female purity to the evil of the black beast who should be lynched, while simultaneously denying black women the dignity accorded to white women.

It is unclear if Smalls was aware of the antilynching activities of Ida B. Wells. Certainly he framed his brief defense of his amendment to the interracial marriage ban in terms reminiscent of her approach. He outlined the fundamental hypocrisy in white opposition to interracial marriage: "If a Negro should improperly approach a white woman his body would be hanging on the nearest tree filled with air holes before daylight the next morning—and perhaps properly so. If the same rule were applied on the other side, and white men who insulted or debauched Negro women were treated likewise, this Convention would have to adjourn *sine die* for lack of a quorum." This statement surely made many white delegates uncomfortable. But Smalls then backed off from these more radical statements and, uncharacteristically, expressed agreement with Tillman and his supporters.

Smalls labeled both interracial marriages and cohabitation as "the root and branch of this evil" that needed to be stopped. Furthermore, he thought that, once it was rooted out, there would be no need for an amendment banning such practices. He then attempted to reach out across the aisle to Tillman, stating, "I oppose the intermarriage of races as strongly as you do, and I feel that I echo the sentiment of the respectable classes of both sides; because with few exceptions, we find these marriages are among the lower elements of both races, and therefore, they degrade and [do] not elevate either race." Smalls insisted that Tillman and his cronies could not "make a law to prevent lawful marriages and give full license to illicit marriages"— that is, one could not prohibit black men from marrying white women while refusing to see the illicit relationships between white men and black women.

To some extent, Smalls retreated from his earlier encouragement of black women's political activism, especially in his acceptance of the premise that interracial marriage was more prevalent among lower-class black women. Nor was Smalls alone in his views on the issue. Many black leaders opposed mixed marriages while attacking white depredations against black women. Black male views on this issue were also quite nuanced, as the historian Rosalyn Terborg-Penn makes clear. Some, like Timothy Thomas Fortune, came out against antimiscegenation laws. Black delegates at the State Convention of Colored Men in Texas urged the state government to amend its antimiscegenation law so that all acts of "carnal intercourse" between blacks and whites would be penalized. Likewise Calvin Chase, the editor of the *Washington Bee*, attacked the double standard when black women's words were questioned in court on the subject of white violence, noting that a black man would have been lynched simply on the word of a white woman. Smalls's position then must be viewed in the wider context of black male responses to white violence and the sexual exploitation of black women.[41]

Perhaps he had no choice given the environment that confronted him. Smalls had to play by the rules of white Southern gender politics, but within that framework the least he could do was to demand equality for both blacks and whites. To pursue that goal, he chose to draw a sharp distinction between the black and white upper classes and the presumably less moral, working-class whites and blacks. Smalls also appeared to ignore his own personal history—it could not have escaped him that he was the product of the very practice of interracial relationships that he was fighting to ban. Certainly he did not consider his slave-born mother to be an immoral woman, nor would he have been unaware of the sexual violence and rape typical of the white males who engaged in interracial relationships and illicit cohabitation. Indeed, as the historian Michele Mitchell has illustrated, Smalls and other leaders were operating in a "particularly fraught" environment when they dealt with issues of black sexuality. Black gender roles were sites of contestation from the very moment of emancipation (as Smalls knew well from his experience with contested elections in the 1870s). Mitchell sheds some light on some of the motivations that might have informed Smalls's approach to the subject of cohabitation: "Since slavery had purportedly engendered wanton sexual behavior and warped how black women and men interacted with each other, striving race members of the postemancipation period considered it critical that women radiate inviolable modesty, that men embody controlled manliness, that couples marry and establish patriarchal households." For these reasons, Smalls chose to frame the debate in traditional terms of class (black uplift and respectability) and Southern gender roles (pitting the pure nobility of both races against the supposedly immoral members of the lower class).[42]

In his conclusion, Smalls returned to his discourse of respectability, declaring that, by opposing both interracial marriage and cohabitation, "Then you will make your men as true as your women. And our race will be freed from a vice, that is as degrading as the system of slavery." Smalls effectively exposed white hypocrisy while also attempting to avoid alienating Tillman and his supporters. Whether or not Smalls actually believed what he was preaching remains an open question. According to Edward A. Miller's recent biography, Smalls sincerely wanted the practice of interracial cohabitation to cease, but he did not think a legal prohibition would have been sufficient because white men could not be trusted to fulfill their side of the bargain.[43] He believed that the desire for interracial cohabitation (and sexual abuse of women) was diminishing among blacks, but not among whites. But he did not entirely trust white men's ability to control their sexual appetites. It is less clear whether Smalls sincerely opposed social equality, as reflected by the right of white and black citizens to marry across racial lines. After all, African Americans fought the Civil War to secure full citizenship, which should logically mean equality with any other American citizen, including the right to marry whomever one chose regardless of race.

Regardless of his motives, Smalls was aware of the extent to which "miscegenation" was occurring, not only in South Carolina but across the South. Many African Americans (including Smalls himself) were products of interracial relationships. Like his black political contemporaries, Smalls attempted both during and after Reconstruction to gain a hearing with white opponents by appealing to their sensibilities through the rhetoric of elevating all races. By defining the problem of interracial cohabitation as one that was prevalent "among the lower elements of both races," Smalls appealed to shared values of class unity and self-improvement.[44]

It is unclear what possessed Smalls to excoriate the hypocrisy of white Tillmanites so unabashedly. His accusation that many of the white men around him were among those "who insulted or debauched Negro women" was quite forceful; according to one New York newspaper, the assembled delegates burst into laughter at this statement.[45] White Southerners were well aware of the long history of interracial relationships, but had always been loath to admit their existence openly. Furthermore, in the postwar period, whites often attributed interracial sexual depredations to black men, rather than to upright white male patriarchs.[46] By making such a forthright statement against white hypocrisy, Smalls was taking a calculated risk. Ultimately, the delegates rejected Smalls's proposed modifications of the ban on interracial marriage.

Interestingly, Smalls's rhetorical flourish received praise from both the Northern press and the major Democratic newspaper of Charleston, South Carolina. The *New York Press* viewed his comments as a brilliant slap in the face to white supremacists. Indeed, according to its editorial, the politically attuned Tillman "proceeded at once to save his record by espousing the Negro cause. He cut himself loose promptly from the majority in the course into which he knew its provincial ignorance would direct it. He went so far as roundly to berate his own chairman for the attempt to choke off the plea of the black men for the integrity of black women." The editorial stated that Smalls's "victory of black mind over white matter" proved that blacks were quite competent and should be entitled to voting rights. It concluded, "It is now made plain . . . that the fear of Negro domination is not born so much of a regard for the numbers as for the developed intellectual ability of the blacks. It is not Negro ignorance, but Negro intelligence, that is feared."[47]

The *Charleston News and Courier* also praised Smalls, but drew different conclusions. This newspaper believed that the "troublesome matter of mis-cegenation was settled" by the adoption of the original marriage ban. How-ever, "the provision would have been strengthened and improved by the adoption of Gen. Smalls's proposed addition to it . . . but the Convention rejected the addition by the largest vote recorded recently. Its action was a mistake. The addition was a proper corollary to the section adopted, and should have been extended to disqualify from voting, as well as holding office, the class of offenders at which it was aimed."

Arguing that interracial sex was wrong, the *News and Courier* noted that of "the two offences—miscegenation within the marriage bond and miscege-nation without it—the latter is the greater social evil. It should have been treated accordingly."[48] Here the leading Democratic newspaper of Charles-ton was agreeing to disfranchise white men who engaged in interracial sex, implicitly lauding Smalls's efforts to affirm equality before the law. While his efforts to preserve some measure of civil and political equality for his black constituents failed, he unexpectedly gained a measure of support from among the more racist forces within South Carolina's Democratic culture.

South Carolina was not the first state to embrace disfranchisement, nor would it be the last. Throughout the 1890s and into the 1900s, Southern states called constitutional conventions that disfranchised black voters and significant numbers of white voters as well. The South also moved to cod-ify a rigid system of legal segregation. Collectively, disfranchisement and segregation undermined the black community and national black political leaders, giving birth to the Jim Crow South.

Conservative Democrats strove so diligently to disfranchise large seg-ments of the electorate because they feared the potential impact of alliances between dissident whites and African Americans. They also encouraged the spread of lynching and mob violence as a means of destroying black political power and subjugating the black community.

Blacks Take Aim at Their Own

While Smalls received positive attention from both white and black media, John Roy Lynch, like Langston, faced bitter attacks from elements of the black press. One of the most virulent attacks was levied by the *Broad Ax*, published in Salt Lake City (and later in Chicago) by black Democratic editor Julius F. Taylor. On March 20, 1897, the paper castigated another local newspaper for devoting "one column of its worthless space last week to lauding the Hon. John R. Lynch to the skies." Taking issue with the other newspaper's belief that "Mr. Lynch towers head and shoulders above the late Frederick Douglass," Taylor stated that "we can never believe that this gentleman will ever live to see the day . . . that he will be able to command the respect or to exert the influence that Mr. Douglass did. It is our firm belief that Frederick Douglass was the greatest and the best leader that the race has ever had, and now that he has passed away, the next and the only true leader of the race is Prof. Booker T. Washington." To a certain extent the criticism levied against Lynch might have emanated from Taylor's desire to honor the recently deceased Douglass. Nevertheless, the criticism struck harshly against Lynch, especially on his legislative performance.

The *Broad Ax* justified its reasoning on several grounds, attacking Lynch for elitism, a mediocre legislative record, and a tendency to favor the company of whites over blacks. Taylor declared, "Mr. Washington and his estimable wife are doing more real and practical work for the upbuilding of the negro race than what Messrs. Lynch, Langston, Bruce or Pinchback ever did or ever can do." He proceeded to eviscerate Lynch's congressional record, claiming that Lynch "never introduced one bill or one measure which possessed the least bit of merit; neither did he ever raise his voice in behalf of the downtrodden race." He even attacked Lynch for holding two separate wedding receptions, one for his white friends and another for his black friends. Taylor concluded, "We always dislike to pass judgment upon any person but we have come to the conclusion that Mr. Lynch is very selfish and that he is as cold blooded as a rattlesnake."[49] Despite the article's partisan nature and its inaccurate portrayal of Lynch's congressional service, it represented some of the shifting currents in black policy and strategy that were taking root by the late nineteenth and early twentieth centuries.

These shifting currents emerged amid growing black voter disfranchisement and a rising tide of lynchings. All the promise that emigration, fusion, and biracial political alliances may have held for the black electorate now paled in comparison to the forces amassed against them. For some members of the black community, old solutions to long-standing political problems no longer sufficed. Nevertheless, as national black political leaders confronted challenges to their own legitimacy and came into conflict with a younger cadre of aspiring leaders, they continued their struggle for black civil rights by focusing on the most urgent issues confronting the black community—voter disfranchisement and lynching. Their strategies and solutions were not always perfect, nor did all blacks agree with them. But black leaders like Lynch, Smalls, Langston, and White attempted to hold the line against the forces of white supremacy and segregation that threatened black citizenship rights and the emancipationist legacy of the Civil War.

Fusion's High Tide in North Carolina
Sends George Henry White to Congress

While fusion voting had passed its peak in most Southern states by the 1890s, its heyday in North Carolina occurred in 1894. Struggling to make ends meet due to high prices, exorbitant railroad freight rates, and the general economic approach favored by the Democrats, thousands of North Carolina farmers began supporting the Populists in 1892. As a divided opposition would never have a chance of toppling Democratic hegemony at the statehouse, in 1894 white Populists merged with white and black Republicans to form the Fusionist movement that swept the November 1894 elections, winning control of both houses of the state legislature. "The result of yesterday's elections is anything but cheering, viewed from a Democratic standpoint. The party has been beaten, and very badly beaten. Two years ago it swept the country like a whirlwind. Yesterday, there was another whirlwind, but it was a Republican whirlwind," reported the *Wilmington Messenger.*[50]

The new majority in the statehouse proceeded to dismantle Democrats' pattern of appointing local government officials in favor of making all offices elective. The Fusionists also moved to liberalize the state's election and voter registration laws, making it easier for black North Carolinians to vote across the state. Aided by these changes, Fusionists increased their majority in the legislature in 1896 and elected Wilmington native Daniel L. Russell as the Republican governor of North Carolina; in addition, the "Black Second" District sent George Henry White to Congress for his first term.[51] Once tepid about supporting fusion voting arrangements between Populists and Republicans, White softened his position and rode the biracial political wave to victory in 1896, winning a seat in the U.S. House of Representatives.[52]

As in the success of the Readjuster movement in Virginia from 1879 to 1883, dissident whites cast their political fates with black Republicans and created a winning coalition capable of challenging conservative Bourbon Democrats. But the Fusionist victories in North Carolina would lead to a powerful backlash, in the form of the most destructive and violent campaign for white supremacy that the South had witnessed since Redemption swept away Reconstruction at the close of the 1870s. An ominous 1894 editorial in the *Wilmington Messenger* presaged what was ahead: "The election is over. It is a good time to do some plain talking. Henceforth it is the duty of the Democratic party to take care of itself and to make its next fight on the line of a White Man's Government. It is useless to try to conciliate or draw the negroes in by acts of kindness. . . . When elections come . . . the ungrateful negroes, through twenty years the recipients of the largest favors, turn against their friends. . . . It is time for the Democracy to take a decided, open, square stand for a white man's government in North Carolina."[53]

During his two terms as the last black congressman of his era, George Henry White continued his predecessors' tradition of exposing racism through colorful, revealing rhetoric. One of his best performances occurred during an 1897 debate on a tariff bill proposed by Republican Nelson Dingley Jr. of Maine. After expressing amusement regarding Democratic support for free trade, White observed that Democrats "have from time to time advocated 'free whisky' also; and in the last campaign their shibboleth was 'free silver.' In fact, the Southern element of the Democratic party has advocated 'free' everything except free ballots and free negroes." This last line received laughter and applause from the Republicans and in the galleries. But along with this satire, White tied national policy, internal improvements, and racial issues together more clearly than previous black congressmen, as seen by his reasoning for support of the Dingley Tariff, which he argued would directly benefit and protect the bulk of his black constituents who were laborers. In making this argument, he presented himself explicitly as a voice for African Americans across the nation: "I am here to speak, and I do speak, as the sole representative on this floor of 9,000,000 of the population of these United States, 90 per cent of whom are laborers. Under this bill they are protected; they are given an opportunity to earn their living. Bread and butter are what we want, not finespun Democratic campaign theory. We want an honest dollar. We want pay for an honest day's work. We believe that by this bill these things may be brought about or that such may largely be the effect." White's speech, which received prolonged applause from Republicans in the House, effectively exposed the hypocrisy of Southern Democrats who claimed to represent the interests of their citizens while supporting arrangements under which the overwhelming majority of black males were unable to vote.[54]

White would make similarly race-based appeals as the issue of emancipatory diplomacy emerged, for the first time since the Cuban independence debates of the 1870s, due to hostilities with Spain that culminated in the Spanish-American War of 1898. As the United States ousted Spain from

Cuba, Puerto Rico, and the Philippines, it acquired new lands with large majorities of nonwhite peoples. White (like Langston and Walls) supported the liberation of colonies held by the Spanish and even called for annexation of some of these territories (going well beyond the policies of earlier black congressmen). However, he tempered his support for acquiring new territories by calling attention to the hypocrisy of U.S. policy at home and abroad. Taking over these territories, White contended, obligated American leaders to provide equal treatment to racial minorities at home and to provide the same measure of constitutional equality to Cubans, Puerto Ricans, and Filipinos abroad. He thus used foreign policy considerations as a platform to attack American racial inequality throughout the South. Tragically, 1898 would see racial violence, not racial equality, ravage the Carolinas.

From High to Low:
The Wilmington Riot of 1898

On February 21, 1898, a white mob of about 300 or 400 met at the home of black Republican postmaster Frazier B. Baker, whom President William McKinley had recently appointed as postmaster of Lake City, South Carolina. The mob set fire to Baker's house and shot his family as they tried to escape. Baker himself was killed, and his body remained in his home as it burned to the ground.

The savage murder disgusted Congressman White, who moved to secure compensation for Baker's widow and her family. However, his actions did not impress Ida B. Wells, who spent five weeks in Washington trying to convince White to "withdraw a bill he had already presented in which he asked one thousand dollars indemnity for the widow and children of the burned Negro postmaster." White told her that he reduced the bill from $50,000 to $1,000 "because he thought the southern congressmen would not object to that sum." Wells declared in her scathing summary of the conversation that White "did not know the South as well as I had hoped for; if he did, he would know that they would object to the compensation of five dollars not because of the amount, but because of the principle of the thing."[55]

Wells thought that more compensation should have been demanded, but the two leaders were confronted with vastly different realities. Like Frederick Douglass before her, Ida B. Wells was an activist whose approach, by her own admission, often burned bridges and prevented her from forging lasting relationships with other leaders.[56] White remained a politician and understood the necessity of compromise. Perhaps Wells felt slighted for reasons of gender too, as a black male politician confronted a black female activist. Nevertheless, the disagreement between the two mattered little. With the Spanish-American War dominating national life, White was unable to secure any compensation for Baker's family.

Baker's murder and the McKinley administration's lack of response sent a powerful signal to whites across the region that the federal government would not interfere in the internal affairs of the South. Encouraged by this turn of events, white Democrats in North Carolina embarked on a massive struggle for racial supremacy, centered on the majority-black city of Wilmington.[57]

In many respects, what occurred at Wilmington mirrored the Meridian Riot of March 1871 in Mississippi. In both cases, conspiring whites sought to overthrow blacks and Republicans from power. Both incidents involved whites burning down black houses and killing multiple victims. Local Republican leaders were forced to resign in both cities as Democrats placed the blame for these disturbances squarely on the victims of the violence. But one major difference separated Wilmington from Meridian. The Meridian Riot inspired the passage of the Ku Klux Klan Act in April 1871, prompted the dispatching of federal troops, and resulted in massive indictments and convictions of some of the perpetrators. By contrast, Wilmington twenty-seven years later confirmed the federal government's unwillingness to defend the rights of blacks and established a precedent by which white supremacy and Jim Crow would be established not only in North Carolina but throughout the New South.

Across North Carolina, during the 1898 electoral campaign, Democrats engaged in intimidation, fraud, and naked appeals to whites of all political stripes to abandon their association with black voters. In conjunction with these tactics, the local white press took every opportunity to portray blacks, in North Carolina and across the country, in a negative light and to raise fears of race riots and "Negro rule."[58] Through their systematic campaign, Democrats wiped out Fusion gains, but they were unable to defeat White, who won his second term in Congress. Moreover, the Fusionists were still in control of Wilmington's municipal government, where the terms of the mayor and other officeholders were not set to expire until 1899. This situation remained unacceptable to local whites. Victory at the polls throughout the state was not enough; white Democrats needed to send a clear message to blacks across the South. They did so within days after the 1898 election.

According to later recollections by the Democratic editor of the *Wilmington*

Messenger, Thomas W. Clawson, "For a period of six to twelve months prior to November 10, 1898, the white citizens of Wilmington prepared quietly but effectively for the day when action would be necessary."[59] In reality, those citizens consisted of a handful of leading white men in the city. Clawson was very clear about the real motives behind the riot: "The Revolution or 'race riot,' in Wilmington . . . was purely and solely a movement on the part of the Democratic citizenry to overthrow the political domination and control of the negro." But white Democrats would need an instigating event to put their plans in motion. They found it in a "defamatory and disgusting editorial in a paper published by negroes in Wilmington" that brought "the situation to a climax."[60] That editorial was published by the black editor of the *Wilmington Daily Record,* Alexander Manly.

Unlike the caution that Manly had previously expressed (in the editorial quoted at the outset of this chapter) when discussing emergent black political strength in North Carolina, his comments in August 1898 hued closely to the arguments made by Ida B. Wells in her 1892 editorial that got her exiled from the South. Manly was responding to statements made by Rebecca Latimer Felton of Georgia (who would go on to become the first female U.S. senator), who maintained that "if it needs lynching to protect a woman's dearest possession from the ravening human beasts—then I say lynch; a thousand times a week if necessary."[61] Manly tore into these arguments: "We suggest that whites guard their women more closely, thus giving no opportunity for the human fiend, be he white or black. You leave your goods out of doors and then complain because they are taken away." Discussing the consensual nature of interracial relationships, Manly pushed his provocative line of argument still further, stating that white women were no different from white men when it came to "clandestine meetings" with black lovers. These relationships between white women and black men could go on for a while "until the woman's infatuation or the man's boldness brings attention to them and the man is lynched." Manly concluded, "Every Negro lynched is called 'a big, burly, black brute,' when in fact many of those who have thus been dealt with had white men for their fathers, and were not only not black and burly but were sufficiently attractive for white girls of culture and refinement to fall in love with them as is well known to all."[62] This explosive editorial was repeatedly printed and reprinted for weeks on end until the riot took place. Not surprisingly, among the first casualties of the riot were the offices and printing press of the *Wilmington Daily Record.*

More than a week after the riot, on November 19, 1898, the *Richmond Planet* published a shocking editorial on its front page: "Horrible Butcheries at Wilmington." Unlike almost every other local or national publication, the *Planet* told what had actually happened: "Twenty-five colored persons were killed and as many more wounded at Wilmington, N.C., Thursday, Nov. 10, 1898. The cause of this butchery was the result of a concerted conspiracy which has been under way for several weeks. It was decided to secure the reins of the city government by treasonable practices. The leaders of the murderous band had openly threatened that unless the Republicans declined to put up a legislative ticket the streets of Wilmington would be run with blood."[63]

This was the terrible price of black disfranchisement and segregation. It was a price that national black politicians like Robert Smalls tried bravely to avert during disfranchisement conventions early in the decade. Now George Henry White, the last black member of Congress, was witnessing full-scale violence against blacks in his own state. His terse but poignant comment two years later summarized the plight of African Americans: "I cannot live in North Carolina and be treated as a man."[64] In the aftermath of the violent electoral campaign of 1898, White understood that he would not be able to seek reelection in the Jim Crow South. He would use the remainder of his term in office to speak out against such atrocities and voice the concerns, fears, and aspirations of African Americans across the country.

The Last Black Congressman Gives Up on the South

On January 3, 1899, White was honored at a dinner in Washington, D.C., and his extemporaneous remarks on the future of the race were reported by the *Colored American*. After speaking on the legacy of the Civil War and the abolitionist movement, White contrasted public sentiment during the Civil War era with blacks' present-day struggles. On one hand, the public had caused the destruction of slavery almost forty years earlier. On the other hand, "We are now without one of the great levers we formally had—the press. . . . The crimes of the Negro are exaggerated, his virtues minimized, and there is no one to contradict the lies that are told." Citing the Wilmington Riot as evidence of the severity of the situation, White said that "the problem . . . will not be solved by emigration, for we will not emigrate, except where as individuals we find we can do the most good. Amalgamation will not solve the difficulty, for it weakens both races, and the black man should feel proud of the dark feature and the kinky hair." Perhaps mirroring Smalls's arguments at the 1895 constitutional convention, White added that "amalgamation" needed to stop or African Americans would put a stop to the practice themselves. After praising blacks' progress since their emancipation, he concluded, "All the sensible Negro clamors for is a man's chance in the battle of life, and then if he fails, the fault lies with no one but himself."[65] Though he offered a largely reassuring assessment of the progress of African Americans, White may have been concealing his own support for emigration. With the destruction of the Fusionists in North Carolina and disfranchisement a fact of life, no option seemed viable other than to flee the South for places where blacks might be able to live without the fear of lynching or economic depredations.

In contrast to White's own public remarks, the white North Carolina press emphasized his support for emigration. White called together a Council of Colored Men of the State to meet to discuss the future direction of black politics. On January 18, 1899, the *Raleigh News and Observer* claimed that "Congressman White is the author of the meeting and its moving spirit. One of the advertised purposes of the meeting is to encourage the negro to emigrate."[66] A day later, the *Charlotte Daily Observer* described "an effort . . . made by White and some others to have a resolution adopted advising the negroes to emigrate in case the Democrats made their stay in North Carolina intolerable, and agreeing that each would aid the others in so emigrating."[67] The paper reported that these resolutions, though supported by White, were not adopted by the assembled delegates. Regardless of the motives of the white newspaper editors who published these reports, White's own views were apparently shifting toward an endorsement of emigration.

Not long after his meeting with local blacks to discuss emigration, on January 26, 1899, White delivered remarks in Congress during debate on the army reorganization bill (H.R. 11022). He began by expressing support for U.S. annexation of the territories gained as a result of the Spanish-American War but then, with apologies for the digression, shifted to other concerns, stating that he felt compelled to speak on behalf of all African Americans. It was difficult, White said, to sit patiently while hearing his race "referred to in terms anything else than dignified and complimentary" with little regard for "their better qualities, their better manhood, or their developed American citizenship."[68]

Although White did not mention the speech directly, it is clear from his references to Mississippi that comments by Democratic congressman John Sharp Williams of Mississippi (ten days after the signing of the Treaty of

Paris had ended hostilities between the United States and Spain) provoked him. Williams commented in explicitly white-supremacist terms about the undesirability of annexing territories, like the Philippines, with populations that were not of "a character easily assimilable." He stated, "With each acquisition made by the United States, up to the time of the purchase of Alaska, it will be found that the territory acquired was contiguous, the population was of our race, or else there was virtually no population at all." Boldly evidencing his nostalgia for the pre–Civil War Constitution, he claimed that the Philippines could have been ruled well "before reconstruction, because we could have given the rule of the country to its white population. . . . We could, prior to the passage of the fifteenth amendment, have ruled the Philippine Islands either as a comparatively self-governing Territory or as a State in the American Union, because we could have conferred by law the suffrage only upon such male inhabitants as were 'free, white, and 21 years of age.'"[69]

White found such rhetoric intolerable. He listened to Williams wax eloquently about "white supremacy" and was openly disgusted: "Just permit me to say that I have no respect for a 'supremacy,' white or black, which has been obtained through fraud, intimidation, carnage, and death—'white supremacy' in the great State of Mississippi; about the Anglo-Saxon ruling this country. I did not know that it required any specific reference of this kind for the world to know the fact that the Anglo-Saxon will rule the United States."[70]

White then refuted the insinuation that blacks were innately inferior. By "force of circumstances, we are your inferiors," he declared. "We are inferior. We regret it. But if you will only allow us an opportunity we will amend our ways, we will increase our usefulness, we will become more and more intelligent, more and more useful to the nation. It is a chance in the race of life that we crave." He directly reached back to the immediate aftermath of the Civil War for his next image, focusing on the unfulfilled promise of the Union cause: "We do not expect any special legislation. We do not expect the mythical '40 acres and a mule.' The mule died long ago of old age, and the land grabbers have obtained the 40 acres. But we have a right to expect a man's chance and opportunity to carve out our own destiny."[71]

White went on to address the frequent allegation that the drafters of the Declaration of Independence "did not mean what they said in that declaration, for the reason that at the very time it was promulgated they owned slaves, and therefore when they spoke of all men being free and equal they did not mean the black population." In response he argued that the

Declaration of Independence did not have the broad reach of the Constitution, which he saw as "a very elastic instrument." Yet this broad conception of constitutional powers was not applied to the cause of African Americans. Instead, Americans refused to see fraudulent elections and widespread efforts to legally disfranchise black voters.[72]

To illustrate the injustice of his race's plight, White told of a judge who instructed his law students as follows: "My dear boys, whenever you have a case in regard to which the law is in your favor and the facts against you, you must lean hard on the law; but if the law is against you and the facts in your favor, then lean hard on the facts." According to White's story, one precocious student asked, "Well, Judge, suppose both the law and the facts are against us, then what must we do?" The instructor replied, "Ah, my boys . . . then you must beat about the bush." White then made his application clear: "Every time a construction of the Constitution or an interpretation of the law is made with reference to the humble race with which I am identified, the principle of that old judge's instruction is brought into play. . . . If the negro happens to have both the law and the facts on his side, all the decisions touching his rights seem to be beating around the bush."[73]

Producing substantive evidence of electoral fraud in recent elections in Mississippi and South Carolina, White contended that, if the Southern states insisted on maintaining white supremacy in this way, their congressional representation should be diminished in proportion to the number of voters (including both poor blacks and whites) being disfranchised.[74] He concluded with a scathing attack on the hypocrisy of annexing foreign territories while leaving domestic racial problems unresolved: "Recognize your citizens at home, recognize those at your door, give them the encouragement, give them the rights that they are justly entitled to," and only then could Americans begin to incorporate Cuba, the Philippines, and Puerto Rico as part of the United States. If Americans did this, they would be better able to "let the Christian civilization go out and magnify and make happy those poor, half-civilized people; and then the black man, the white man—yes, all the riff-raff of the earth that are coming to our shores—will rejoice with you in that we have done God's service and done that which will elevate us in the eyes of the world."[75] While White lauded Americans' desire to liberate and uplift colonial peoples, he had a more urgent message: America must first treat blacks as equals at home before attempting to work out the affairs of nonwhite colonial subjects in the Philippines, or else the presence of racist forces at work in the South would blight American expansion overseas.

Blacks' "Temporary Farewell" to the Halls of Congress

In the opening months of 1900, White embraced a multifaceted approach to the cause of racial equality. First he supported a bill, introduced by Indiana Republican Edgar D. Crumpacker, that sought to reduce congressional representation in the Southern states that had already instituted disfranchisement (South Carolina, Louisiana, Mississippi, and North Carolina) through some combination of poll taxes, literacy tests, and grandfather clauses. Then he called for antilynching legislation. Finally, he challenged racism and the myth of the black rapist openly before the House of Representatives. While he pursued these strategies, White was also coming to accept the reality that blacks would be unable to obtain justice through the federal government, and he openly embraced emigration from the South. Meanwhile, during the last year and a half of his second term in Congress, White drew on twenty years of black political culture in his attempt to stave off disfranchisement and the solidification of a violent Jim Crow segregationist order throughout the South.

On January 18, 1900, White wrote a rebuttal to Mississippi Democratic senator Hernando De Soto Money, who argued that disfranchisement was predicated not on race but rather on illiteracy. Money cited the recent U.S. Supreme Court ruling in *Williams v. Mississippi* (1898), which stated that no discrimination existed when a state implemented poll taxes or literacy tests if they were applied equally to all voters, to bolster his case against Crumpacker's pending bill. White countered Money's arguments by highlighting naked instances of voter fraud and ballot-box stuffing. He urged support for Crumpacker's bill, arguing, "I do not believe that anybody should be permitted to thrive by his own dishonesty and rascality. These frauds in the South while terribly unjust to the colored man will certainly react upon the white people."[76] Crumpacker's bill was eventually set aside in 1901 by a vote of 136 to 94.[77]

After failing to gain a measure of protection for black voters, White turned to the primary effort that would dominate the remainder of his term: seeking to secure meaningful antilynching legislation. On January 20, 1900, White presented "a petition of 2,413 names of citizens of the United States, asking for national legislation against the crime of lynching and mob violence." He moved to have the heading of the petition read, and that it should accompany a bill he had drafted to "be referred to the Committee on the Judiciary." Democrat James D. Richardson of Tennessee promptly objected. Engaging in a delaying tactic, Richardson argued that White's motion "ought to take the regular course of all other petitions and memorials."[78] But White raised the subject again ten days later. Interjecting himself into a debate between Romulus Z. Linney (R-N.C.) and Robert E. Burke (D-Tex.) after Burke asserted that "in almost every instance the lynching occurs in consequence of the assaults of colored men upon the virtue of white women," White defended his race against such aspersions: "I have examined that question and I am prepared to state that not more than 15 per cent of the lynchings are traceable to that crime, and there are many more outrages against colored women by white men than there are by colored men against white women."[79]

By 1900, White grew increasingly frustrated at the repeated and unsubstantiated charges leveled against his race as justification for disfranchisement, segregation, and murder. His anger boiled over following the publication of a scathing editorial in the conservative *Raleigh News and Observer*. The editor of the paper, Josephus Daniels (who would later serve as secretary of the navy under President Woodrow Wilson), was a white supremacist who had fanned the flames that led to the Wilmington Riot. On February 5, 1900, White had the clerk of the House read Daniels's incendiary editorial, which included these words: "It is bad enough that North Carolina should have the only nigger Congressman. It is sufficiently humiliating to the white people of the Second district. . . . What shall be said when that nigger Congressman gives utterance to the following on the floor of the House?"

Daniels then proceeded to misquote White's earlier statements regarding lynching. He continued, with a not-so-subtle reference to the circumstances of the Wilmington Riot, arguing that the "Manleyism [*sic*] of 1898" was showing its head again in 1900. In the same way that Manly slandered white women in the pages of his newspaper, "WHITE justifies assaults by negroes on white women by slandering white men in a speech in the Congress of the United States. We are told that 'the public galleries contained many colored people who applauded this utterance vigorously.'"[80]

Daniels claimed that White's statements could be easily discounted. In the same breath, he warned that White's alleged statements should be viewed "as a fresh manifestation of negroism" and of the true attitude that blacks held toward white men. Nor should the significance of that attitude be discounted. Daniels scoffed at the notion that there could ever be an "inoffensive negro official." White "was typical of his kind." He was venomous and a slanderer of whites, "appealing to the worst passions of his own race." More ominously, Daniels noted that White's example "emphasizes anew the need of making an end of him and his kind." Whites had "more than enough of Negro Congressman WHITE. He must be made an impossibility in the future, and will be."[81]

White had the entire article read on the House floor so "that the world may see what the poor colored man in the Southland has to undergo from a certain class." Daniels misquoted his statements, he said. Whoever participated in the crime of rape, be he white or black, "ought to be hung—hung by the neck till dead. But it ought to be done by the courts, not by an infuriated mob such as the writer of this article would incite."[82] White described Daniels's article as "evidence of what we have got to contend with." The nation and the world were put on notice "that those whom the Constitution of these United States . . . has enfranchised are to be reduced once more to the condition of goods and chattels, if such men as the one who edits the *News and Observer* can have the control of affairs in North Carolina."[83]

Understanding fully the desperate times that confronted all African Americans, White prepared a speech on behalf of his antilynching legislation. While ostensibly participating in a discussion on the subject of Puerto Rico, on February 23, 1900, White explained why Congress must pass his proposed bill. Declaring that charity should "first begin at home," he decried the hypocrisy that he saw in his country. The United States proposed to civilize and Christianize the darker-skinned peoples of the Philippines, Puerto Rico, and Cuba when, at the same time, "fully 50,000 of my race have been ignominiously murdered by mobs, not 1 per cent of whom have been made to pay for their crimes in the courts." White denounced Congressman James M. Griggs of Georgia for highlighting the case of Sam Hose, a black Georgian lynched for killing his employer and allegedly raping his wife. White thought that Griggs "might have depicted also, if he had been so inclined, the miserable butchery of men, women, and children in Wilmington, N.C., in November, 1898, who had committed no crime, nor were they even charged with a crime."[84] White showed that lynching had little to do with the crime of rape by listing sixty-three individuals who had been lynched between April 24 and October 20, 1899. Out of this group, only two were lynched on grounds related to dishonoring a woman (one for putting a hand on a white woman while another had "entered a lady's room drunk"). The sixty-three victims included one Italian, one Cuban, four white men, and fifty-seven blacks.[85]

White then explained the provisions of his bill, under which participants in mob violence "aiding and abetting in such murder and lynching shall be guilty of treason against the Government of the United States, and shall be tried for that offense in the United States courts."[86] White adduced

constitutional arguments and the letter of a prominent Massachusetts lawyer to bolster his claims regarding the bill's constitutionality, but for him the
key constitutional support was contained in the clause relating to national
citizenship in the second section of the Fourteenth Amendment.[87] White
denied that he was trying to stir up tension between the races. Rather, he
brought the issue up against what he saw as one of the most "dangerous
evils" confronting the United States on behalf "of a people who have no
one else to speak for them here from a racial point of view."[88] There is no
evidence that Congress took any action on White's bill.

By 1900, White understood that he had no political future in the Jim
Crow South. Men like Josephus Daniels and Ben Tillman had, through
a mix of coercion and mob violence, robbed African Americans of their
voting rights and enforced a rigid system of segregation that permeated
every aspect of black life. In this environment, White saw no path to victory. He announced that he would not seek reelection and would leave the
South. Before he left, White delivered one of the most powerfully prophetic
speeches of his time.

On January 29, 1901, White inserted himself into a debate on an agri-
culture bill. As he had done before, he used the issue being debated at the
moment as a platform to call attention to the condition of his race. We have
no information on how White expressed his emotions as he delivered his
final remarks, but he was certainly cognizant of his status as the official political voice for African Americans, and as the outgoing last black member
of Congress. He reflected: "This, Mr. Chairman, is perhaps the negroes'
temporary farewell to the American Congress; but let me say, Phoenix-like
he will rise up some day and come again. These parting words are in behalf of an outraged, heart-broken, bruised, and bleeding, but God-fearing
people—rising people—full of potential force." Even here, at the end of
his political career, White was uncompromising. He made no apologies for
his honesty, save for the fact that he was "pleading for the life, the liberty,
the future happiness, and manhood suffrage for one-eighth of the entire
population of the United States." According to the *Congressional Record,* the
House resounded with loud applause.[89]

Although his term would not end until March 1901, this was White's
last major speech before the House. But the last black congressman of the
nineteenth century had not finished serving his constituents. In August
1901, White, through the Afro-American Equitable Association, purchased
land in Cape May County, New Jersey, to create an all-black town, which
would be named Whitesboro in his honor. The North Carolina blacks who

migrated there, including some refugees from the Wilmington Riot, represented a prelude of things to come as blacks began leaving the South in droves, reshaping the Northern political landscape in the twentieth century. If White could not protect the rights of black people or secure antilynching legislation, he would do something more concrete for them—he would buy land for a town where they could live free from the fear of the violent segregationist order overtaking Dixie.[90]

CONCLUSION

O N SEPTEMBER 27, 2009, President Barack Obama began his speech at the Congressional Black Caucus Foundation's Annual Phoenix Awards Dinner by remembering North Carolina's George Henry White, the "lone African American" serving in Congress at the opening of the twentieth century.[1] The president noted that White "was the last of that first generation of African Americans elected to Congress in the aftermath of Appomattox. But at the end of the 1800s, with a segregationist Supreme Court handing down 'separate but equal,' with African Americans being purged from the voter rolls, with strange fruit growing on the poplar trees, White decided against seeking reelection—meaning that once again, neither the House nor the Senate would be occupied by a single African American member."[2]

Reviewing the rise and fall of black America's political fortunes, Obama emphasized that his own presence on that stage, surrounded by a wide range of black officeholders, indicated just how far the nation had come since White left Congress in 1901. The president's speech provided a reminder that the modern history of black politics is grounded in the careers of nineteenth-century black politicians, such as White, who blazed the path so that other blacks might have "an even chance in the race of life."[3] But before African Americans could rise up "Phoenix-like," as White had prophesied, came decades of racial discrimination and marginalization as the Jim Crow era took firm hold in the South.

The Torch Passes to the Next Generation

Even before White's dramatic departure from elected office, a changing of the guard was taking place among national black leadership. As an editorial in the April 1898 issue of the *A.M.E. Church Review* stated: "The death of Hon. N[orris]. W[right]. Cuney, of Texas [an alderman in Galveston, a union activist, and the former chairman of the Texas Republican Party], followed so soon by that of Hon. B. K. [former U.S. senator Blanche Kelso]

Bruce, emphasizes what the deaths of Messrs. Douglass and Langston suggested, that in a few years those who made Negro ability respected and Negro leadership confessed will all be gone."[4] As of 1898, not all of the old guard were gone; Smalls, Lynch, and Pinchback were still alive, and White was still serving in the U.S. House of Representatives. But the passing of so many powerful activists and national black political leaders reverberated within the black community. The *A.M.E. Church Review* wondered what sort of leadership would emerge: "What then? Why, simply that the new times will produce new leaders. They will not . . . be men who will tower so colossally above all their race fellows as to suggest that there are no others as able. They may be less aggressive, but will be more persuasive; less picturesque, but fully as potent; less considered as individuals, but more consulted as forces." For the *Church Review*, leadership was a matter of contingency, not an artificial creation foisted upon the black community. Rather, black leaders emerged as the circumstances dictated.[5]

Nor was the *Church Review* alone in its assessment of black leadership. On April 30, 1898, the *Colored American* reported on remarks delivered by ex-governor P. B. S. Pinchback to a special meeting of the Bethel Literary and Historical Association honoring the late John Mercer Langston. After discussing the outlines of Langston's career, Pinchback addressed the future of the race and commented on the model of leadership that Langston had provided. He bemoaned the injustices that would eventually drive people like George Henry White out of public life and that limited black opportunities to respond: "It seems to be the purpose of our so-called white friends to repress anything that approaches manly independence and courageous action in defense of their own by colored men. It matters not how just the complaint, how grievous the wrong, how shocking and horrible the outrages perpetrated upon the race . . . colored men must not complain and cry out against the wrong, or even protest against the diabolical deeds."[6]

Pinchback saw the "superserviceable friends and their newspaper allies who are endeavoring to manufacture leaders for the colored people" as "doing more harm than we are prepared to admit. Neither doubting friends nor insidious foes should deter us from performing our duty as nobly and as heroically as [Langston] performed his." The former governor also believed that African Americans had "reached a critical stage" in the "transition from slavery to freedom and citizenship." No longer could they rely upon the aid or kindness of other races. Rather, they "are now entering upon a man to man struggle for an honorable place in the citizenship of the country, with no safe reliance but their own resources and captains. No outside influences, however seductive or influential, should be permitted to select such captains." Pinchback believed that the "extraordinary condition" confronting African Americans made their need for "manly and fearless leadership as apparent and pressing today as at any period in their history."[7]

The *Colored American* also summarized the remarks of John Roy Lynch at the same April 1898 event. It stated that Lynch had referred to "the speech by Mr. Langston at Natchez, Miss., which sowed in his youthful breast the seeds of ambition that made him what he is." Lynch urged the "rising generation" of leaders to "acquire and develop the character and noble qualities necessary to true leadership, as the members of the 'Old Guard' are rapidly passing from the scene of action, and newer hands must take up the burden where they are being compelled to lay it down." He concluded that "the older leaders had done their best, and their only ambition now is that their successors shall bring to the cause their life's best energies and unselfish devotion."[8]

Pinchback and Lynch celebrated Langston's achievements and their own, glossing over imperfections, mistakes, and outright failures, as well as clashing egos and broken friendships. Such was the nature of politics. Nevertheless, the collective reflections on the passing of the old guard and the future of American race relations transcended uncritical celebrations of past accomplishments. Langston and Lynch, Smalls and White, Rapier and Walls—they had indeed done their best. Their best was not enough to preserve the rights of their constituents through the last decade of the nineteenth century. Nor did it prevent repeated acts of political and racial violence against the black community in the South. But national black political leaders had articulated the aspirations of their constituents and gave voice to the hopes of those who had been enslaved for well over two centuries.

The first generation of Southern black leaders came of age politically in the Civil War era and gained preeminence in the 1870s. The twin legacies of the Civil War and emancipation dominated African American political thought for the remainder of the nineteenth century, guiding the emancipatory generation of leaders in their fight to secure passage of the Civil Rights Act of 1875. Likewise, the manly ideal of citizenship rights as earned on the battlefields of the Civil War shaped national black responses to emigration and the possibilities of fusion voting that emerged by the opening of the 1880s. These dominant themes—the components of the "democracy of the dead" rhetoric that formed the bedrock of black politics—continued to inform both old-guard and younger black leaders who attained elective office in the 1890s. But white Americans had long since lost interest in the "negro problem." The shift began in earnest by the mid-1870s and continued as new issues replaced the "bloody shirt." Americans were concerned with the economy, civil service reform, and imperial and colonial projects of their own. Though blacks had a few allies in the North during the 1890s, most white Northerners were content to let the South manage African Americans without federal interference. The move toward Yankee imperialism and the emergence of a shared discourse of racism transcended sectional lines, quickening the pace by which the North and the Republican Party turned their backs on African Americans.[9]

Against these odds, national black political leaders did not abandon their constituents. They challenged American society to live up to its ideals and deal fairly with newly enfranchised black citizens. These leaders were not perfect. They made mistakes, misjudged political currents, allowed their egos to get in the way of unified action at times, and occasionally leveled unfair charges at each other and other black leaders. Nevertheless, they were sources of pride for the black community. Whenever whites spoke of black inferiority, African Americans could point to towering, articulate, and well-educated leaders to prove otherwise. These leaders' brave, resourceful efforts to secure and defend black civil and political equality helped to pave the way for later generations who would eventually topple the edifice of disfranchisement and segregation that their predecessors had opposed with such determination.

The Barber, the Historian, and the Congressman

The full flowering of the Jim Crow South recast the terms of African Americans' struggle against white supremacy. As disfranchisement had firmly closed the doors of formal political activism, blacks turned their attention to a mix of legal activism and direct protests. Nevertheless, the legacy of earlier black political leaders would not be easily forgotten. Though the methods of activism embraced by African Americans had to change, the recollection of what had transpired in the immediate aftermath of emancipation did not. As Southern white historians sought to rewrite the story of Reconstruction and black disfranchisement to align with white supremacy, one of the last remaining black politicians from that era would once again raise his voice in defense of his conduct and that of all African Americans. Just as he had had the gall, at age twenty-eight, to challenge President Ulysses Grant's courage, John Roy Lynch, incensed by reading accounts of Reconstruction that he knew to be factually inaccurate, challenged the emerging historical consensus by debating one of the foremost historians of this period, James Ford Rhodes.

The struggle over the historical memory of Reconstruction was not simply a rhetorical exercise. Rhodes and others like him (most notably William Archibald Dunning and John W. Burgess) sought to justify the Solid South and its system of Jim Crow segregation by highlighting the incompetence of black political leadership during Reconstruction. In the process, they silenced the counternarrative of black progress and formal politics embodied by the careers of men such as Lynch.[10]

The correspondence between Rhodes and Lynch, which took place through an unusual intermediary—the influential African American barber George A. Myers—was most likely the only (albeit private) exchange between a prominent white historian and a black activist from the Reconstruction period. Rhodes published the Reconstruction volume of his *History of the United States from the Compromise of 1850 to the Final Restoration of Home Rule at the South in 1877* in 1906.[11] Lynch did not read it until after he had published his own history on the period of Reconstruction, *The Facts of Reconstruction* (1913). Myers brought Rhodes's book to Lynch's attention and then sent Rhodes a copy of Lynch's bold defense of Reconstruction.[12] Rhodes replied on March 29, 1914, expressing appreciation for the book and saying that he had been "reading it here and there and I have been much interested in it," but that he did not plan to write further on Reconstruction anyhow.[13] Rhodes was clearly not interested in engaging with the challenges posed by Lynch's account. Perhaps the matter would have ended there had Myers not shown Rhodes's book to Lynch.

Lynch recalled his initial reaction to the book in an article in the *Journal of Negro History* in October 1917: "In glancing over one of the volumes, I came across the chapters giving information about what took place in the State of Mississippi during the period of Reconstruction. I detected so many statements and representations which to my own knowledge were absolutely groundless that I decided to read carefully the entire work. I regret to say that, so far as the Reconstruction period is concerned, it is not only inaccurate and unreliable but it is the most biased, partisan and prejudiced historical work I have ever read."[14]

Rhodes's description of the performance of black congressmen during Reconstruction must have been particularly offensive to Lynch. The esteemed historian wrote: "From the Republican policy came no real good to the negroes. Most of them developed no political capacity, and the few who raised themselves above the mass did not reach a high order of intelligence.

At different periods two served in the United States Senate; thirteen in the House; they left no mark on the legislation of their time; none of them, in comparison to their white associates, attained the least distinction."[15]

Through Myers, Lynch wrote a response to Rhodes's work. Rhodes replied to Myers on April 19, 1916: "It does not surprise me that [Lynch] thinks I am inaccurate, unjust and unfair for he was a severely partisan actor at the time while I, an earnest seeker after truth, am trying to hold a judicial balance and to tell the story without fear, favor or prejudice. Why does not Mr. Lynch write a magazine article and show up my mistakes and inaccuracies and injustice?"[16]

Though Rhodes claimed to be an objective "seeker of the truth," the tone of his response was clearly dismissive. Lynch, nevertheless, took up the challenge. He wrote to Myers on April 2, 1917, indicating that he was "putting the finishing touches upon the article" and asking Myers to forward it to Rhodes for review, "before any step is taken looking to its publication, with a view to allowing him to prepare an answer to it, should he desire to do so."[17]

Rhodes responded almost immediately upon receipt of Myers's communication, on April 5, 1917. He thanked Lynch for "showing a politeness and candor that some of my assailants have not shown. But I do not care to see the [manuscript] of his article as I shall not answer it. It is my rule never to indulge in controversies; such indulgence is the rock on which some historians have split. But I always correct errors of fact."[18] Nevertheless, Rhodes eventually did read the article, writing to Myers on November 22 that he had finally been able to "give Mr. Lynch's article a thorough investigation and sifting."[19] Rhodes used the services of an "expert" to write a rejoinder, and much of this debate would eventually see publication in 1922 as a book compiled by Lynch and titled *Some Historical Errors of James Ford Rhodes*.

There is no indication that Rhodes ever revised his volume concerning Reconstruction. He merely stated, "The difference between Mr. Lynch and me is the point of view. It is the old story of two warriors fighting about the shield—one saying it was golden, the other silvern because they looked at it from two different sides. The discussion will probably go on to the crack of doom."[20]

More than discrimination was undoubtedly on Lynch's mind as he engaged in this debate. The white South had achieved what Rhodes called "home rule" through violence and intimidation. There was neither heroism nor honor in the "Redemption" of the South. The fact that Rhodes would not consult living participants and would uncritically accept white perspectives on a man like Lynch merely confirmed the general amnesia and increasing racism prevalent among white Americans. Whatever hope Lynch had seen in the masses of Northern Republicans in the immediate aftermath of Hayes's Southern Policy had been extinguished by the 1900s. The ultimate significance of Lynch's feisty debate over how to remember and record the history of Reconstruction lay in the nation's failure to fulfill its promises to black Americans.

In his youth, Lynch had challenged Ulysses S. Grant's inaction; in his old age, he found himself fighting against those who sought to distort the legacy of black political participation in American life. For Lynch, Rhodes's errors opened up old wounds. They also awakened the youthful spirit of a bold fighter who never let violence, intimidation, or a U.S. president stand in the way of his struggle to serve his black constituents. Lynch would not allow anyone to impugn the brave efforts of the political generation of African Americans who came of age immediately following the war. Unfortunately, the perspective embodied by Rhodes and Dunning would not be success-fully challenged until the 1960s and early 1970s when, once again, the na-tion was forced to deal with black demands for civil and political equality.

Barrier Breakers

From the very beginning of formal black politics in the mid-1860s, this diverse set of leaders, which included black abolitionists like John Mercer Langston and Union veterans like Josiah Walls and Robert Smalls, spoke to the desires of their newly freed constituents. Modern scholarship on this period emphasizes that, at the grassroots level, freedmen and women desired economic autonomy, full citizenship rights, and access to educa-tion.[21] Newly elected black congressmen fought determinedly to gain these rights for blacks, whether by speaking out in favor of the Civil Rights Act of 1875, attempting to secure expanded educational opportunities for their home states, or directly intervening in local labor difficulties in their home districts. Undoubtedly, black politicians behaved in elitist ways at times and bickered with each other, or with others in the black community who disagreed with their strategies. Nevertheless, many of their white contem-poraries viewed them as capable leaders, and many segments of the black electorate, both in the black press and at the grassroots level, admired them and took pride in their example.

Black congressmen were far more than symbolic leaders of their race. From the defenders of the Civil Rights Act, to Rapier's testimony on emigration, to White's last speech in the House, they functioned as national spokesmen for all African Americans. Not only did they battle tenaciously for constituents in their districts, but they consistently emphasized events outside their own states, repeatedly speaking on behalf of the rights and interests of all African Americans. Of course they made mistakes, some were corrupt, and others may have engaged in the same fraudulent campaign strategies that white Northerners used in ethnic urban enclaves. Several were elitist and patronizing. But none of these realities should obscure the fact that they did their jobs well. They articulated the aspirations of the black community in a national arena and participated powerfully in some of the most important policy debates of their day.[22]

Indeed, a wide range of white Northerners, local Southern Republicans, and even some Democratic opponents respected the abilities of black congressmen. White Republicans as varied as James A. Garfield, Alabama congressman Charles Hays, and Speaker of the House James G. Blaine supported black politicians like Langston and Rapier. For their part, black politicians quickly learned to forge relationships with white politicians while not fully entrusting themselves to any single group or faction. During Reconstruction, blacks embraced a strategy of magnanimity in an attempt to coax white colleagues to support stronger civil rights guarantees. But black congressmen also recognized the limits of these approaches. The skills that they acquired by working with and against whites of various political stripes served them well as they entered the era of fusion politics. Thus John Roy Lynch could convince a white Democrat to join forces with him and run as the fusion candidate for governor in Mississippi.

Beyond navigating relationships with white politicians, black congressmen also relied heavily on alliances and relationships with informal political activists and black newspapers. The existence of the black press enabled black congressmen to communicate their message and policy agendas to a broader audience, as John Mercer Langston did when he granted a lengthy interview on his proposed national literacy test amendment to a correspondent for Timothy Thomas Fortune's *New York Age*. Key strategy meetings often brought black congressmen into contact with activists like Frederick Douglass and George T. Downing, as well as with members of the black press. These engagements provide a more complete understanding of black high politics, one that places black congressional policy and rhetoric in the context of developments at the ground level and the desires of both white and black constituents.

Long after this heroic group of black congressmen left the scene, their memory was treasured by another great black American: John Mercer Langston's great-grandnephew, the famed Harlem Renaissance poet Langston Hughes. Late in his career, Hughes recalled hearing about how "several of the Reconstruction congressmen of color drove from their Washington mansions to the Capitol in the handsomest rigs money could buy behind the finest horses available."[23] With pride he related an account that conveyed the multiple worlds in which John Mercer Langston lived and how he coped with the realities of race relations surrounding him: "Congressman John M. Langston possessed a sleek black rubber-tired carriage, drawn by two snow-white horses with a coachman at the reins. He lived in LeDroit Park near Howard University, whose Law School he founded. To get home he had to pass through a well-to-do white neighborhood whose inhabitants did not relish seeing a Negro ride in such style. Some of them put up a wooden barrier across the street to keep him from passing."

Warming to his conclusion, using the vivid imagery that he brought to his poetry, Hughes continued: "Mr. Langston did not believe in barriers so one day on the way home from the Halls of Congress he stopped at a hardware shop on Pennsylvania Avenue and bought himself an axe." When Langston's carriage reached the wooden barrier, "he got out, took his axe and chopped it down while the coachman held his gloves. From then on, without hindrance, he rode behind his snow-white horses through the streets of Washington, the ebony spokes of his highly lacquered carriage wheels gleaming—such wheels being the nearest thing in those days to the contemporary elegance of white-walled tires."[24]

Langston could have demanded immediate removal of the barrier. He could have openly denounced the existence of such barriers in the local newspapers or even in a speech before Congress. Or he could have accommodated white prejudices by avoiding the barrier altogether. Instead, Langston chose to affirm his dignity as a man and as an American citizen by personally destroying the barrier erected before his carriage. In so doing, he epitomized the legacy of black congressmen in the post–Civil War South, as they eloquently affirmed the dignity of black citizens and respectfully yet forcefully pursued an America without racial barriers.

NOTES

Introduction

1. Towne, *Letters and Diary*, 288–89 (entry of 29 October 1878); Dray, *Capitol Men*, 307–8.

2. Towne, *Letters and Diary*, 289–90 (entry of 6 November 1878).

3. Ibid., 290.

4. Ibid., 290–91.

5. For Langston's views on Christianity and freemasonry, see Cheek and Cheek, *John Mercer Langston*, 221–22; Caffey, "Lodge History." For White, see Justesen, *George Henry White*, 52–53; "George H. White (George Henry), 1852–1918," in "Documenting the American South." For Smalls, see State Historic Preservation Office, "African American Historic Places in South Carolina" (June 2009), 4–5; Denslow, *10,000 Famous Freemasons*, 146; Muraskin, *Middle Class Blacks*, 52–53. For Lynch, see his *Reminiscences of an Active Life*, 23–25; Muraskin, *Middle Class Blacks*, 52–53. There is considerably less information for Josiah Walls and James Rapier.

6. In this regard I have been most influenced by Keller, *Affairs of State*; Woodward, *Origins of the New South*; Ayers, *Promise of the New South*; Freehling, *The South vs. the South*; Vorenberg, *Final Freedom*; Benedict, *Preserving the Constitution*; and Oakes, *The Radical and the Republican*.

7. For an excellent overview of how blacks understood freedom with respect to these issues, see Foner, *Reconstruction*, 77–123. A more recent discussion of the struggle of blacks to obtain education in the era of emancipation is Williams, *Self-Taught*.

8. Friend, *Southern Masculinity*, x–xii.

9. For the significance of Brer Rabbit as a symbol of black farce and manipulation, see Levine, *Black Culture and Black Consciousness*, 108. For more recent examinations, focusing on the Jim Crow period, that discuss the use of lying and manipulation, see Kelley, "'We Are Not What We Seem,'" 76, 80–81. The best study that illuminates the nature, aims, and tactics embraced by Northern black reformers and which informs my study of Southern blacks may be found in Kantrowitz, *More Than Freedom*; for the bisectional exchange of ideas, see especially 356–57, 373. My understanding of the violent nature of Reconstruction has been informed by several works, including Rable, *But There Was No Peace*; Lemann, *Redemption*; Rosen, *Terror in the Heart of Freedom*; and Egerton, *Wars of Reconstruction*.

10. A brief but insightful discussion of the "lessons" that previous examples of emancipation held is Foner, *Nothing But Freedom*, 39–45. There is a rich and expanding scholarly literature on comparative history that I have found most useful. In addition to Foner's small book, see Hahn, "Class and State in Postemancipation Societies," 75–98; Holt, *Problem of Freedom*; Scott, *Degrees of Freedom*; Mark M. Smith, "The Past as a Foreign Country: Reconstruction, Inside and Out," in Brown, *Reconstructions*, 117–40; and Kolchin, "Comparative Perspectives on Emancipation," 203–32.

11. My work here draws on the rich scholarly literature from within the field of speech and communications. See especially Mann, "Black Leaders in National Politics"; Logue, "Rhetorical Ridicule of Reconstruction Blacks," 400–409; Haskins, "Rhetoric of Black Congressmen"; Haskins, "Rhetorical Vision of Equality," 116–22; and Haskins, "Rhetorical Perspectivism of Black Congressmen." See also Ferguson, "Race and the Rhetoric of Resistance," 4–32.

12. Their behavior has much in common with what Darlene Clark Hine labels "the culture of dissemblance" among black women who faced similar obstacles when speaking about sexual exploitation and abuse. Perhaps these black men believed that it was better to forgo discussions of personal experiences of discrimination that might reinforce prevailing stereotypes of their race as a whole. See Hine, "Rape and the Inner Lives of Black Women," 912–20. A fantastic discussion of black male political dissemblance and pragmatism (that provides an excellent counterpoint to the example of black congressmen) may be found in Robert J. Norell's excellent revisionist history, *Up From History.*

13. Richardson, *Death of Reconstruction,* 89; see Richardson's larger portrayal on 83–121.

14. On social rights, see John Roy Lynch, "The Civil Rights Bill" (3 February 1875), in Middleton, *Black Congressmen during Reconstruction,* 154–58. For more on questions of social equality that have informed my approach, see Rosen, *Terror in the Heart of Freedom;* Kantrowitz, *More Than Freedom,* 382–89. On creative ways to combat the imposition of literacy tests, see Dinnella-Borrego, "From the Ashes of the Old Dominion," 236–39, citing Langston, *Congressional Record,* 51st Cong., 2nd Sess. (16 January 1891): H. 1481–82. My approach to the ways in which blacks positioned themselves with respect to their white audience has also been informed by Bell, "*Brown v. Board of Education* and the Interest-Convergence Dilemma," 518–33. Though Bell deals with the reasons why white jurists and certain white political leaders began to support school integration in the 1950s and 1960s, the idea of "interest-convergence" may also be germane for understanding the motivations behind policy agendas embraced by black congressmen in the postbellum era.

15. This distinction between articulation and implementation is fundamental, as it is much more nuanced than the few pieces of scholarship that treat black congressmen in a historiographical context. I am specifically countering Hosmer and Fineman, "Black Congressmen in Reconstruction Historiography," 97–107.

16. Meier, *Negro Thought in America;* Holt, *Black over White;* Painter, *Exodusters;* Toll, *Resurgence of Race;* Hahn, *Nation under Our Feet.*

17. Hahn draws a sharp distinction between what he labels as liberal-integrationist scholarship (the work of Eric Foner) and his own work. See his *Nation under Our Feet,* 6, 9. Two other sources have influenced my approach: Du Bois, *Black Reconstruction in America,* and Litwack, *Been in the Storm So Long.*

18. For these perspectives, see Kantrowitz, *More Than Freedom,* and McCarthy and Stauffer, *Prophets of Protest.* For an example of similar human rights struggles against slavery in the Revolutionary and early Republican period (with due attention paid

to developments in the North as distinguished from the way things played out in the South), see Nash, *Forgotten Fifth*, and Egerton, *Death or Liberty*. A compelling case can be made that blacks moved away from their largely integrationist position (by embracing emigrationism) only when Southern racism and violence made it virtually impossible for them to have a voice over their affairs. See Lichtenstein, "Roots of Black Nationalism?," 261–69. See also Hahn, *Political Worlds of Slavery and Freedom*, 112–13.

19. Schweninger, *James T. Rapier*, 147.

20. Prather, *We Have Taken a City*, 98.

21. Dinnella-Borrego, "From the Ashes of the Old Dominion," 219. My views on balancing strategies relate intimately with concepts of "cultural hegemony" as discussed by Lears, "Concept of Cultural Hegemony," 567–93. See Genovese, *Roll, Jordan, Roll*, 658–60; Genovese, *From Rebellion to Revolution;* and Hale, *Making Whiteness*. My understanding of black politics has also been influenced and inspired by Kelley, "'We Are Not What We Seem,'" 75–112, and Jordan, "'Damnable Dilemma,'" 1562–83. Thomas J. Sugrue has made similar arguments regarding twentieth-century black politics. See especially Sugrue, *Not Even Past*.

22. My understanding of history, narrative, and memory has been influenced by Trouillot, *Silencing the Past*, 22, 25; Schama, *Dead Certainties*, 319; and Blight, *Race and Reunion*, 31. My understanding of the possibilities of narrative history has been influenced by Goodman, "For the Love of Stories," 255–74.

23. Brown, "Negotiating and Transforming the Public Sphere," 107–46; Hunter, *To 'Joy My Freedom;* Edwards, *Gendered Strife and Confusion;* Dailey, *Before Jim Crow;* Ortiz, *Emancipation Betrayed*.

1. Democracy of the Dead

1. Miller, *Gullah Statesman*, 9.

2. My biographical sketch of Smalls draws heavily on Miller, *Gullah Statesman*, as well as on Foner, *Freedom's Lawmakers*. For a solid description of Hunter's actions and how they motivated Smalls, see Egerton, *Wars of Reconstruction*, 29.

3. Gooding, *On the Altar of Freedom*, 84.

4. Billingsley, *Yearning to Breathe Free*, 84–86; for a newspaper summary with a slightly different account of this heroic episode, see "A Brave Colored Man. Congressman Smalls, of South Carolina—The Man Who Defeated Sunset Cox—His Eventful History," *New York Times*, 30 July 1876.

5. Klingman, *Josiah Walls*, 6. For more on Walls, see Luis-Alejandro Dinnella-Borrego, "Manhood and Freedom in the Sunshine: State Josiah Thomas Walls and Reconstruction Florida," in Lynch, *Before Obama*, vol. 1, 47–68. In addition to Klingman's biography, I have relied heavily on Foner, *Freedom's Lawmakers*, 222–23; Brown, *Florida's Black Public Officials*, 135–36; and Middleton, *Black Congressmen during Reconstruction*, 357–89.

6. Langston, *Virginia Plantation*, 12.

7. Ibid., 18.

8. Cheek and Cheek, *John Mercer Langston*, 254. Other works useful for biographical information on Langston include Middleton, *Black Congressmen during Reconstruction*, 125–39, and U.S. Congress, House of Representatives, "John Mercer Langston 1829–1897," *Black Americans in Congress*, 206–13.

9. Cheek and Cheek, *John Mercer Langston*, 9, 116, 410–11; Cheek, "John Mercer Langston," 115.

10. Cheek and Cheek, *John Mercer Langston*, 437–38. I was unable to find the newspaper that the Cheeks cite for this event, as they apparently cited the wrong date for the *Anglo-African Magazine*. Based on the evidence that they provide in the chapter, it is possible that this meeting took place on 27 November 1864.

11. Savage, *Standing Soldiers, Kneeling Slaves*, 97. The link between manhood and black military exploits is also made by Edwards, *Gendered Strife and Confusion*, 195–96. An excellent accounting of white understandings of manhood as opposed to those of blacks may be found in Kantrowitz, *Ben Tillman*. Black understandings of citizenship, as tied to military service during the Civil War and emancipation, have been the subject of many fine works. In addition to Savage, I rely on Glatthaar, *Forged in Battle;* Blight, *Race and Reunion;* and Samito, *Becoming American under Fire*. A more broadly conceived study focusing on the legacy of the final battle of the Civil War may be found in Varon, *Appomattox*, 93–101, 249–55 (which includes her discussion of black understandings of military service).

12. Gilmore, *Gender and Jim Crow*, 78–82. In this respect, Gilmore affirms Robert A. Nye's observation that "political rights were at least latent in the body of the male conscript or volunteer, whose actual or potential sacrifice would then earn him his nation's gratitude." See Nye, "Western Masculinities," 418.

13. Douglass, *Narrative*, 69.

14. Cheek, "Forgotten Prophet," 41, 43–44; Langston, *Virginia Plantation*, 165–67.

15. The title of this chapter is drawn from Chesterton, *Orthodoxy*, 74. Writing about the crucial role played by tradition in the life of human societies, Chesterton noted, "Tradition may be defined as an extension of the franchise. Tradition means giving votes to the most obscure of our classes, our ancestors. It is the democracy of the dead. Tradition refuses to submit to the small and arrogant oligarchy of those who merely happen to be walking about. All democrats object to men being disqualified by the accident of birth; tradition objects to their being disqualified by the accident of death." Chesterton's insight powerfully captures some of the essential features of black politics that emerged after the Civil War.

16. Gallagher makes this salient point in *Union War*, 4.

17. For an influential older study, see Genovese, *Roll, Jordan, Roll*. For folk thought and the role played by stories, see Levine, *Black Culture and Black Consciousness*. For a broad generational approach, see Berlin, *Many Thousands Gone*. For an astute examination of the experience and significance of the antebellum slave market, see Johnson, *Soul By Soul*. For the experiences of black women, see White, *A'rn't I a Woman?*, and Brown, "Uncle Ned's Children." For the connections between collective experiences ("pre-political" activities) and the political culture that emerged among African Americans after the Civil War, see Hahn, *Nation under Our Feet* and *Political Worlds of Slavery and Freedom*.

18. "To Our Oppressed Countrymen," *North Star,* 3 December 1847. See Kersh, *Dreams of a More Perfect Union,* 157.

19. For the Freedmen's Bureau, see Cimbala, *Under the Guardianship of the Nation.* For the Union League, see Fitzgerald, *Union League Movement in the Deep South.*

20. "Citizens' Meeting in Bethel A.M.E. Church," *Christian Recorder,* 3 December 1864. My biographical sketch of Langston draws heavily from Dinnella-Borrego, "From the Ashes of the Old Dominion," 214–49.

21. For a penetrating analysis of antislavery politics and federal policy (which touches upon some aspects of what I view as emergent black political culture), see Oakes, *The Radical and the Republican.* An excellent source that highlights the shifting currents of the Lincoln administration and captures the sense of excitement and possibilities opened up by his embrace of emancipation is Foner, *Fiery Trial.*

22. Litwack, *Been in the Storm So Long,* 502–56; Foner, *Reconstruction,* 77–123.

23. Langston, "Colored People Before the Ohio Senate," *Anti-Slavery Bugle,* 8 April 1854.

24. Langston, "From the Anglo African Extracts from a Lecture delivered by J. Mercer Langston, at Cooper Institute, New York," *Elevator,* 12 May 1865.

25. Jones, *All Bound Up Together,* 124–25.

26. J. A. Garfield to Hon. E. M. Stanton, 28 March 1865, enclosing John M. Langston to Hon. E. M. Stanton, 20 March 1865; A. A. Genl. C. W. Foster to John M. Langston, 17 May 1865, all filed with W-276 1865, Letters Received, ser. 360, Colored Troops Division, RG 94 (B-158). Reprinted in Berlin et al., *Freedom,* Series 2, 346.

27. Berlin et al., *Freedom,* Series 2, 347. As the editors of the series made clear in an earlier essay, "Moreover, at precisely the time that it approved their commissions [those of Major Martin R. Delaney and Captain O. S. B. Wall], the War Department delayed considering the application of black Ohio recruiter, John M. Langston, for appointment as a colonel of a black regiment. After the fighting stopped, the department informed Langston that it had no vacancies for black officers. Even as it took the first meaningful steps toward admitting blacks to commissioned offices, the War Department hedged its actions to prevent blacks from attaining significant authority and responsibility" (311).

28. Langston, *Virginia Plantation,* 232, 234, 236–37.

29. Hannah Rosen makes this point quite clearly in *Terror in the Heart of Freedom;* see, for example, 40–41, 55–60, 125–26.

30. Gilmore, *Gender and Jim Crow,* 116.

31. Langston, *Virginia Plantation,* 267; Cheek and Cheek, *John Mercer Langston,* 9–11. Cheek and Cheek, "John Mercer Langston," 116. The Cheeks are citing Langston's own words, although the Litwack and Meier volume does not provide citations for any of the essays contained in it.

32. Cheek and Cheek, *John Mercer Langston,* 390–411; Certificate of Appointment as General Inspector of Schools of Freedmen's Bureau, 17 June 1867, Box 3, Folder 12, Langston Papers.

33. Langston to Oliver Otis Howard, 30 July 1867, Records of the Education Division of the Bureau of Refugees, Freedmen, and Abandoned Lands, 1865–1867, Letters

Received, Microfilm No. 803, Roll 6, Slide 040 (hereafter cited as Freedmen's Bureau Ed. Div. Microfilm).

34. Cheek, "Forgotten Prophet," 93.

35. Langston to Howard, 3 August 1867, Freedman's Bureau Ed. Div. Microfilm, Roll 7, Slide 0667.

36. Ibid., Roll 7, Slide 0671.

37. Ibid., Roll 7, Slide 0681.

38. Harper, *Are We Not Men?*, 68; Friend, *Southern Masculinity*, xiv.

39. Foner, *Reconstruction*, 77–123; Williams, *Self-Taught;* Span, *From Cotton Field to Schoolhouse.*

40. Excerpts from [Chaplain James A. Hawley] to Col. Samuel Thomas, 4 July 1865, H-42 1865, Registered Letters Received, ser. 2052, MS Asst. Comr., RG 105 [A-9045], reprinted in Hahn et al., *Freedom,* Series 3, 110.

41. Hahn et al., *Freedom,* Series 3, 110.

42. Ibid., 110, 116.

43. Ibid., 126.

44. This biographical sketch is based on John Hope Franklin's introduction to Lynch, *Reminiscences of an Active Life,* ix–xxxix; Stephen Middleton's brief sketch in *Black Congressmen during Reconstruction,* 145–47 (which is followed by a compilation of most of Lynch's major speeches on 147–225); and Eric Foner's entry for Lynch in *Freedom's Lawmakers,* 138–39.

45. Lynch, *Reminiscences of an Active Life,* x (Franklin's introduction), 41, 42.

46. Lynch, *Reminiscences of an Active Life,* 42.

47. Ibid., 42–43, 54–55.

48. Ibid., 55–56

49. The general outlines presented here are drawn from Egerton, *Wars of Reconstruction;* Rosen, *Terror in the Heart of Freedom* (which provides an excellent examination of the Memphis Riot of 1866); and Varon, *Appomattox* (which explores the contrasting meanings the war had for white Northerners, white Southerners, and African Americans).

50. Klingman, *Neither Dies Nor Surrenders,* 18.

51. Ibid.

52. Ibid., 19.

53. Brown, *Florida's Black Public Officials,* 7.

54. Ibid., 7–8.

55. Ossian Bingley Hart presents an interesting example of Unionists (Scalawags) in Florida. For more on his remarkable career, see Brown, *Ossian Bingley Hart.* Brown notes that Hart attended a meeting in Philadelphia of the National Union Convention (3 September 1866), where Frederick Douglass was present as a delegate for the North. It was at this meeting that Hart stood out very early in favor of black suffrage. See ibid., 181–82.

56. Ibid., 173.

57. Brown, *Florida's Black Public Officials,* 10.

58. Ibid.

59. Ibid.

60. Ibid., 10–11.

61. Schweninger, *James T. Rapier,* 16–18, 20–21, 30–36.

62. Ibid., 30–31.

63. Ibid., 37–39.

64. "The Outrage at Tuskegee," *Mobile Daily Republican,* 20 October 1870. Elaine Frantz Parsons covers in excellent fashion the nature of Northern and Democratic ambiguities regarding the Klan in "Klan Skepticism and Denial," 68–76. Unfortunately, availability of Alabama newspapers for this period (1868–72) is spotty at best. For example, the 18 October coverage of the "Outrage at Tuskegee" did not survive in the microfilm available at the Alabama Department of Archives and History. For coverage of the *Tribune,* see Ellison, *History and Bibliography,* 124–25.

65. R. Starkweather to General Crawford, Stevenson, Alabama, 1 March 1870, Telegram, Administrative Files, Alabama, Governor (1868–1870: Smith), Ku Klux Klan, SG023109, Folder 020, in Alabama Department of Archives and History, Montgomery.

66. Rapier to Chester A. Arthur, Montgomery, Alabama, 31 May 1882, Rapier Papers: letters regarding Rapier's position as U.S. Tax Collector, 1881–1882, LPR 59 Eugene Feldman Papers, 1856–1978, Box 2, Container 2, Folder 2, Alabama Department of Archives and History, Montgomery. For more on Rapier's career in the Treasury Department as an assessor of internal revenue in the early 1870s, consult the envelope titled "James T. Rapier Assessor of Internal Revenue–ALA–2nd Dist.," Applications for Positions as Internal Revenue Collectors and Assessors, 1863–1910, ALA 1st–2nd District to CAL 1st–5th, RG 65: General Records of the Department of the Treasury, Entry 258, Box 1, HM 2005, National Archives and Records Administration, College Park, Md.. For more on his activities as a tax collector (between 1878 and 1882), see Correspondence of the Office of the Secretary of the Treasury, Letters Received from Collectors of Internal Revenue, 1864–1908, Ariz. 1st Ark. 2nd and 3rd, RG 65: General Records of the Department of the Treasury, Entry 166, Box 1, National Archives and Records Administration, College Park, Md..

67. Schweninger, *James T. Rapier,* 68–69.

68. U.S. Senate, *Removal of the Negroes, Part II,* 471.

69. Kolchin, *First Freedom,* 4–8; see also the maps and tables documenting migration in the state on 10–20.

70. Charles Hays to Hon. George S. Boutwell, Secretary of the Treasury, 14 March 1871, in Internal Revenue Papers, RG 65: General Records of the Department of the Treasury, Entry 258, Box 1, HM 2005.

71. U.S. Senate, *Testimony Taken by the Joint Select Committee . . . Alabama,* vol. 2, 42nd Cong., 2nd sess., Report No. 41, part 9 (Washington, D.C.: Government Printing Office, 1872), 1088–89.

72. "Difficulty between Negroes and Mean White Men. Negroes Kill a White Man in Disguise," unidentified newspaper clipping, 11 August 1870, in Administrative Files, Alabama. Governor (1868–1870: Smith), 1870–November General Correspondence, SG023108, Folder 029, in Alabama Department of Archives and History, Montgomery.

73. "In Memory of Langston," *Colored American,* 30 April 1898.

2. Ballots, Bullets, and Blood

1. PAX, "Letter from Alabama," *New Era,* 26 May 1870.

2. "The Fifteenth Amendment. The Grand Celebration in Baltimore on the 19th. A Day of Jubilee. Immense and Brilliant Procession. A Most Magnificent Display. Crowded Streets and Sidewalks. The Outburst of Enthusiasm. Displays in the Line of March. The Ratification Mass Meeting. Eloquent Speeches—Welcome Sentiments," *New Era,* 26 May 1870 (reprinting a 20 May article from the *Baltimore American*). The Baltimore celebration also featured rousing speeches by Frederick Douglass and William Lloyd Garrison.

3. Ibid.

4. For a fascinating discussion on interconnections between gender, race, and class in the context of black masculinity, see Summers, *Manliness and Its Discontents,* 26–65.

5. "Fifteenth Amendment." My reading here is influenced by the spectacle of voting in mid-nineteenth-century America. See especially Bensel, *American Ballot Box,* x, and Neely, *Boundaries of American Political Culture,* 9, 14. My understanding of visual culture from the black perspective also draws on Marzio, *Democratic Art,* which discusses Frederick Douglass's impressions of a portrait of the first black senator, Hiram Rhodes Revels. Douglass's words are revealing: "Pictures come not with slavery and oppression and destitution, but with liberty, fair play, leisure, and refinement. These conditions are now possible to colored American citizens, and I think the walls of their houses will soon begin to bear evidence of their altered relations to the people about them" (104).

6. For the emergence of women's suffrage in the nineteenth century, see Du Bois, *Feminism and Suffrage.* For an excellent account of the ways in which black women negotiated their place in African American public life, see Jones, *All Bound Up Together.* For a more recent examination of the clash between women's rights and black rights in the period of Reconstruction (which has influenced my perspective), see Dudden, *Fighting Chance.* For the five petitions put forward by Robert Smalls and Richard Harvey Cain, see *Congressional Record,* 45th Cong., 2nd Sess. (14 January 1878), 322–23.

7. Harris, *Day of the Carpetbagger,* 371.

8. For partisan Democratic newspaper coverage of the riot, see "The Meridian Riot Latest Particulars. One White Man and Eight Or Ten Negroes Killed!! J. Aaron Moore, Negro Member of the Legislature, Said To Be Shot, His House Burned! Sturgis, Carpet-Bag Mayor, Gone where the Woodbine Twineth!!" and "Fire and Riot!! Terrible State of Affairs in Meridian. Four Men Killed, Several Wounded— Seventy-Five Thousand Dollars Worth of Property Destroyed," *Weekly Clarion,* 9 March 1871, along with more detailed coverage in "The Meridian Riot," *Weekly Clarion,* 16 March 1871. Several letters were written to Governor James Lusk Alcorn on the subject. See especially B. F. Moore, Circuit-Clerk, to J. L. Alcorn, Meridian, Mississippi, 11 March 1871; Albert Snowden to Jas. L. Alcorn, Lauderdale County, Mississippi, 19 March 1871; and J. S. Hamm to Alcorn, Meridian, Mississippi, 27 March 1871, all in State Government Records, Correspondence and Papers, 1869–1871, Mississippi Governor (1870–1871: Alcorn), Series 786, Box 972, Mississippi Department of Archives and History, Jackson (hereafter cited as Alcorn Papers). For later memoirs recalling the

riot, see Warren, *Reminiscences,* esp. 58–62. My outline of the basic information concerning the Meridian Riot is based on Rable, *But There Was No Peace,* 97. The nature of the Ku Klux Klan and its role in Mississippi (with a focus on events in Meridian) is covered exhaustively in McNeilly, "Enforcement Act of 1871," 109–71. McNeilly's lengthy article is rich in detail but is written firmly in the tradition of the Dunning school, making many of his interpretations untenable. A more balanced analysis of the Klan as a whole, with a focus on the Klan's ambiguity, may be found in Parsons, "Klan Skepticism," 53–90.

9. B. F. Moore, Circuit-Clerk, to J. L. Alcorn, Meridian, Mississippi, 11 March 1871, Alcorn Papers.

10. "Fire and Riot!!" *Weekly Clarion,* 9 March 1871. The *Clarion* was crediting a correspondent from the *Vicksburg Herald* as the author of the piece.

11. Warren, *Reminiscences,* 58.

12. Fitzgerald, *Union League Movement,* 50, 207–13, 60.

13. Hanes Walton Jr. provided me with the electoral vote totals, which he draws from the *Congressional Quarterly's Guide to U.S. Elections,* 945–1070. Ortiz, *Emancipation Betrayed,* 19; see also the University of Virginia Geospatial and Statistical Data Center's *Historical Census Data Browser.*

14. Klingman, *Josiah Walls,* 3.

15. *Historical Census Data Browser.*

16. There were other conventions before this one, including the National Convention of Colored Men (Syracuse, N.Y., 4–7 October 1864); the first meeting of the National Equal Rights League (Cleveland, 19–21 October 1865), which was a direct outgrowth of the 1864 convention; and the Colored National Labor Convention (Washington, D.C., 6–10 December 1870). Three earlier articles have influenced my observations on black political consciousness and the postbellum convention movements: Lewis, "Political Mind of the Negro," 189–202; Foner, "Languages of Change," 273–88; and Timothy Patrick McCarthy, "'To Plead Our Own Cause,'" in McCarthy and Stauffer, *Prophets of Protest,* 114–44. Lewis's article must be used with caution as it is dated, and some of his observations—regarding the ignorance of the black electorate and the narrow focus of black leaders (who he says were only concerned with racial issues and completely uninterested in national issues outside of race and civil rights)—need to be taken with a grain of salt. For more on the National Equal Rights League and earlier conventions, see Davis, *"We Will Be Satisfied with Nothing Less."*

17. "Address," Convention of Colored People of Southern States, 21 October 1871, Pinkney Benton Stewart Pinchback Papers, Folder 20, Box 81-1, Moorland-Spingarn Research Center, Founders Library, Howard University, Washington, D.C.; for another copy of this address, see the microfilmed *Proceedings of the Southern States Convention of Colored Men,* 46.

18. *Proceedings of the Southern States Convention of Colored Men,* 47.

19. Richardson, *Death of Reconstruction,* 89; for her larger portrayal, see 83–121.

20. *Proceedings of the Southern States Convention of Colored Men,* 48–49.

21. Ibid., 49–50.

22. Ibid., 48–50, 18–19, 23, 25. Rapier's endorsement of Grant is on page 18; Walls's

resolution supporting the Republican Party and endorsing Northern Republicans is on page 19; Walls's argument in favor of adopting a pro-Republican amendment appears on pages 23–24; and his statement in support is on page 25.

23. For a more human perspective on Grant, emphasizing his psychology and examining his failure during Reconstruction, see McFeely, *Grant,* 356–79. For a more sympathetic view of Grant in this period, see Smith, *Grant,* 542–72.

24. Gillette, *Retreat from Reconstruction,* 166–67.

25. *Proceedings of the Southern States Convention of Colored Men,* 51, 58–60; the text of the resolution is on page 60.

26. Ibid., 63; Klingman, *Josiah Walls,* 102. For newspaper accounts of the proceedings of this convention, including references to Walls, see "The Colored People. Address of the Southern States Convention in Columbia to the People of the United States," *New York Times,* 26 October 1871; "Southern States Convention," *Morning Republican,* 28 October 1871. For examples of African American dissidence (including this account of Walls's actions), see also Klingman and Geithman, "Negro Dissidence," 172–82.

27. Lynch, *Reminiscences,* 101.

28. Ibid., 101–2.

29. Ibid., 103. The sixteen counties that made up the district between 1872 and 1877 were Adams, Amite, Claiborne, Copiah, Franklin, Greene, Hancock, Harrison, Jackson, Jefferson, Lincoln, Marion, Pearl, Perry, Pike, and Wilkinson. Much has been written on the Yazoo-Mississippi Delta during the period of Reconstruction; especially helpful to me were Willis, *Forgotten Time,* and Bercaw, *Gendered Freedoms.* My discussion of Mississippi during and after Reconstruction has been guided by Wharton, *The Negro in Mississippi;* Harris, *Day of the Carpetbagger;* and Fitzgerald, *Union League Movement.* Excellent studies of Reconstruction violence that focus on Mississippi include Rable, *But There Was No Peace,* esp. 142–64, and Lemann, *Redemption.*

30. These numbers rely heavily on the *Historical Census Data Browser* and on the U.S. Census Bureau's digitization of the original 1870 Census of Population and Housing (http://www.census.gov/prod/www/decennial.html). Pearl County was created in 1872 and dissolved in 1878, its territory being reincorporated into Hancock and Marion Counties. The statistics from the census of 1870 thus reflect the composition of the fifteen counties that existed prior to the creation of Pearl County. A useful study examining the place of education among black Mississippians is Span, *From Cotton Field to Schoolhouse.* As Willis notes, "Most of Mississippi's adult freed people in the last third of the nineteenth century were unable to read or write. Much of this can be attributed to slavery's legacy of denying education to bondsmen" (*Forgotten Time,* 62).

31. My discussion of Alabama in the postbellum period draws on several crucial state studies and examinations of black officeholders. Most useful for me have been Kolchin, *First Freedom;* Schweninger, *James T. Rapier;* Fitzgerald, *Union League Movement;* Bailey, *Neither Carpetbaggers Nor Scalawags;* and Fitzgerald, *Urban Emancipation.* The numbers that I present are drawn from the *Historical Census Data Browser.*

3. Dark Days

1. My views on race and white racism have been informed by Frederickson, *Black Image in the White Mind;* Horsman, *Race and Manifest Destiny;* Fields, "Ideology and Race in American History," 143–77; Fields, "Slavery, Race and Ideology in America," 95–118; Freehling, *Road to Disunion*, vol. 1; Roediger, *Wages of Whiteness;* Bay, *White Image in the Black Mind;* Kantrowitz, *Ben Tillman;* Kolchin, "Whiteness Studies," 154–73; and Fabian, *Skull Collectors.*

2. Keller, *Affairs of State*, 108. My subsequent discussion of the culture of Congress and policymaking in the mid-to-late nineteenth century also draws from Seip, *The South Returns to Congress;* Thompson, *"Spider Web";* Bensel, *Political Economy of American Industrialization;* and Summers, *Party Games.*

3. Keller, *Affairs of State*, 108–10.

4. Foner, *Fiery Trial*, 171–72.

5. Keller, *Affairs of State*, 108.

6. My subsequent discussion of corruption comes from the following sources: "The Patronage Business," *Daily Cleveland Herald*, 10 November 1870; "Congress and Corruption," *Daily Rocky Mountain News*, 4 March 1873; *Natchez Courier*, 1 February, 1871; "Congress Yesterday. Blaine Makes Another Personal Explanation—Charges of Corruption Indignantly Denied," *Daily Evening Bulletin*, 2 May 1876; and Amos Tuck, "The Uses of Patronage for Political Purposes," *Boston Daily Advertiser*, 19 November 1877.

7. Thompson, *"Spider Web,"* 73.

8. "Patronage Business"; "Congress and Corruption"; Thompson, *"Spider Web,"* 73, 98–99, 102–6. See Thompson's larger portrayal of this subject on 71–115.

9. U.S. Congress, House of Representatives, *Black Americans in Congress*, 3.

10. For more detailed tabulations and discussions of black legislative policy (including a series of charts) that explore these different policy interests, see Dinnella-Borrego, "'That Our Government May Stand,'" 105–20, 180–88. An excellent older account of all the careers and policymaking of black congressmen may also be found in Taylor, "Negro Congressmen a Generation After," 127–71. As far as I can tell, this is the only work of scholarship (outside of certain sections in Du Bois's *Black Reconstruction in America*) that seriously examines black congressional policy in the postbellum period.

11. *Congressional Globe*, 42nd Cong., 2nd Sess. (29 January 1872): H. 683.

12. *Congressional Record*, 43rd Cong., 1st Sess. (26 January 1874): H. 927–28.

13. *Congressional Record*, 43rd Cong., 2nd Sess. (23 December 1874): H. 228.

14. *Congressional Globe*, 42nd Cong., 1st Sess. (13 March 1871): H. 79.

15. Republicans, prior to the Civil War, embraced an ideology centered on individual initiative and rooted in the ideal of free labor. The best source for understanding labor republicanism and its connection to Republican ideology is Foner, *Free Soil, Free Labor, Free Men.* An understanding of how free labor functioned in the postbellum period, with an emphasis on the gendered formulations of this ideology, may be found in Stanley, *From Bondage to Contract.* For a class analysis of free labor ideology and Reconstruction, consult Richardson, *Death of Reconstruction.*

16. A comparative examination of emancipation that emphasizes the sensibilities

and autonomy of black rice workers in the South (particularly focusing on a series of strikes in the South Carolina Low Country in 1876) appears in Foner, *Nothing But Freedom*, 74–110. For later permutations of this strain of thought, particularly through the Knights of Labor, agrarian insurgency, and its appeal to black laborers, consult Hahn, *Nation under Our Feet*, 412–64, and Edwards, *Gendered Strife and Confusion*, esp. 218–254.

17. *Congressional Globe*, 41st Cong., 2nd Sess. (1 March 1870): S. 1607 (opposing the franking privilege); 41st Cong., 3rd Sess. (19 January 1871): S. 593 (reporting on the status of a bill incorporating a savings bank in Washington, D.C.); 42nd Cong., 3rd Sess. (6 January 1873): H. 351 (on funding the steamship company); *Congressional Record*, 43rd Cong., 1st Sess. (22 April 1874): H. 3296; 43rd Cong., 1st Sess. (12 December 1873, 10 April 1874, 11 April 1874, 19 June 1874): H. 178, 3005–6, 3015, 5202 (covering currency debates, taxes, and congressional procedures), in "A Century of American Lawmaking."

18. *Congressional Record*, 43rd Cong., 1st Sess. (15 December 1873): H. 206; Josiah Thomas Walls, "Cuban Belligerency. Speech of Hon. Josiah T. Walls, of Florida, in the House of Representatives, 24 January 1874, on the Joint Resolution Declaring the Right of the Cuban Republic to Recognition as a Belligerent," *Appendix to the Congressional Record*, 43rd Cong., 1st Sess. (24 January 1874): H. 27–29, in "A Century of American Lawmaking."

19. *Congressional Record*, 43rd Cong., 1st Sess. (5 January 1874): H. 382. Rosalyn Terborg-Penn deals with these varied perspectives (including the support of black South Carolina congressmen, of Frederick Douglass, and of John Mercer Langston on the issue of women's rights) in her perceptive essay, "Black Male Perspectives on the Nineteenth-Century Woman," 28–42 (see esp. 35–38).

20. Frederick Douglass, *"The Anti-Slavery Movement. A Lecture by Frederick Douglass. Before the Rochester Ladies' A.S. Society,"* *Frederick Douglass' Paper*, 23 May 1855; Jones, *All Bound Up Together*, 101–2.

21. Dudden, *Fighting Chance*, 80–82, 84–87, 96.

22. Brief surveys of Walls's legislative activity and political motivations may be found in Richardson, *African Americans in the Reconstruction of Florida*, 177–83, and Klingman, *Josiah Walls*, 71–87.

23. "How the Colored Members of Congress Look," *Christian Recorder*, 25 May 1872.

24. *Congressional Globe*, 42nd Cong., 2nd Sess. (28 May 1872): H. 3939 (postal routes and water communication); (18 December 1871): H. 198 (custom houses, postal offices, courthouses, and other federal buildings); (7 June 1872): H. 4331 (on granting lands and the right-of-way for a railroad company and accompanying telegraphs); and 42nd Cong., 3rd Sess. (16 December 1872): H. 198 (appropriations for improvement of local harbors and granting substantial acreage of public lands for a theological institute).

25. For examples of the class and racial tensions that coexisted with, and characterized, state Republican factionalism at the local level, see Holt, *Black over White;* Anderson, *Race and Politics in North Carolina;* Bailey, *Neither Carpetbaggers Nor Scalawags;* Brown, *Florida's Black Public Officials;* and Fitzgerald, *Urban Emancipation.*

26. Specialized studies of black aspirations for economic autonomy and land include Fitzgerald, *Union League Movement;* Saville, *Work of Reconstruction;* Bercaw, *Gendered Free-*

doms; Ortiz, *Emancipation Betrayed;* and O'Donovan, *Becoming Free in the Cotton South.* For the perspective of white Southerners, see Seip, *The South Returns to Congress.*

27. Seip, *The South Returns to Congress,* 273.

28. The experiences of Southern Republicans and Democrats, respectively, are detailed by Thompson, *"Spider Web,"* 71–115, and Seip, *The South Returns to Congress,* esp. 114–18.

29. Bell, *"Brown v. Board of Education* and the Interest-Convergence Dilemma," 518–33.

4. The Emancipatory Vision of Civil Rights in America

1. U.S. Congress, Senate, *Joint Select Committee Florida,* 42nd Cong., 2nd sess., Report No. 41, part 13 (Washington, D.C.: Government Printing Office, 1872), 159. Myers also provided a pamphlet outlining the constitution of the Young Men's Democratic Club (see 157–58).

2. Klingman, *Josiah Walls,* 31; Ortiz, *Emancipation Betrayed,* 24; U.S. Congress, House of Representatives, *Niblack vs. J . T. Walls* (16 January 1872), House Miscellaneous Document No. 34, 42nd Congress, 2nd Sess., 57–58.

3. U.S. Congress, Senate, *Joint Select Committee Florida,* 61, 63. Hannah Rosen deals with the experience of Samuel and Hannah Tutson more fully in *Terror in the Heart of Freedom,* 214–16. Both Samuel and Hannah Tutson delivered their testimony on 10 November 1871.

4. "The Ku-Klux in Florida. They Won't Allow 'D—d Niggers to Live on Land of Their Own.' Colored Men, Women, and Children Whipped!" *Tallahassee Sentinel,* 19 October 1872; U.S. Congress, Senate, *Joint Select Committee Florida,* 279; U.S. Congress, House of Representatives, *Black Americans in Congress,* 88–93; Klingman, *Josiah Walls,* 37.

5. U.S. Congress, House of Representatives, *Finley vs. Walls* (24 January 1876), 44th Congress, 1st Sess., House Miscellaneous Document No. 58.

6. Rable, *But There Was No Peace,* 81.

7. *Congressional Globe,* 42nd Cong., 1st Sess. (7 April 1871): H. 522; (19 April 1871): H. 808. The subsequent vote on whether to agree to the conference committee report regarding this bill occurred on 19 April 1871, with the House concurring by 93 to 74 (four black congressmen voting yea, while De Large did not vote).

8. Seip, *The South Returns to Congress,* 126–27.

9. *Congressional Globe,* 42nd Cong., 2nd Sess. (13 March 1872): H. 3382. Eric Foner writes that General William T. Sherman estimated that between 10,000 to 15,000 white Confederates had been disfranchised by the Reconstruction Acts (Foner, *Reconstruction,* 276). Older historians, like James A. Rawley, largely accepted inflated totals (one figure numbering to 150,000); see Rawley, "General Amnesty Act of 1872," 480–84.

10. *Congressional Globe,* 41st Cong., 3rd Sess. (1 February 1871): H. 881–82.

11. *Congressional Globe,* 42nd Cong., 2nd Sess. (13 March 1872): H. 3383.

12. Ibid. (18 December 1871): H. 198; Klingman and Geithman, "Negro Dissidence," 177.

13. Klingman, *Josiah Walls,* 79.

14. *New National Era,* 21 December 1871; Klingman, *Josiah Walls,* 78–79; Klingman and Geithman, "Negro Dissidence," 177.

15. Unfortunately, we do not have any correspondence from Walls on these issues. But considering that Walls himself had been a target of violence, barely avoiding an assassin's bullet at a campaign event, the palpable link between politics and the culture of violence would have been unmistakable. *Congressional Globe,* 42nd Cong., 2nd Sess. (13 March 1872): H. 3383. Walls subsequently admitted his involvement in a quid pro quo exchange between amnesty and civil rights in a short speech that he delivered when Sumner's Civil Rights Bill returned to the floor during the 43rd Congress.

16. Seip, *The South Returns to Congress,* 132.

17. *Congressional Globe,* 42nd Cong., 2nd Sess. (13 March 1872): H. 3383.

18. Blaine, *Twenty Years of Congress,* vol. 2, 515; Lynch, "Introduction," in Lynch, *Before Obama,* vol. 1, xxii–xxiii.

19. Foner, *Reconstruction,* 96.

20. Ibid., 96–97.

21. *Congressional Globe,* 42nd Cong., 2nd Sess. (15 January 1872): H. 396.

22. *Congressional Globe,* 42nd Cong., 2nd Sess. (2 February 1872): H. 801.

23. Ibid.

24. *Congressional Globe,* 42nd Cong., 2nd Sess. (3 February 1872): H. 808–9; Josiah Walls, "The National Education Fund" (3 February 1872), in Middleton, *Black Congressmen during Reconstruction,* 359.

25. *Congressional Globe,* 42nd Cong., 2nd Sess. (3 February 1872): H. 809; Walls, "National Education Fund," 359–61.

26. *Congressional Globe* 42nd Cong., 2nd Sess. (8 February 1872): H. 902–3.

27. Loyal, "Letter from Mississippi," *New National Era,* 14 March 1872. The dockets with case information for the indictments concerning the Meridian Riot may be found in RG 21, U.S. District Court, Southern District of Jackson, Mississippi, Criminal Cases, 1872, Case #1290–1392, Box 19; and the verdicts and additional summaries concerning the specific cases may be found in RG 21, U.S. District Court, Southern District of Mississippi, Jackson Division, General Minutes, Minute Book No. 1 (June 1866–January 1874), Retrieval No. 2, Shelf Order 10, at National Archives and Records Administration–Southeast Region (Atlanta). The summaries and verdicts in this minute book span from Friday, 1 September 1871 (400–409) and from Friday, 9 February 1872, through 2 July 1872 (438–509). Out of the twenty-seven cases that I sampled from the minute book, there were sixteen guilty verdicts, eight not-guilty verdicts, and three cases where the district attorney did not "further present the said indictment in this charge" and the defendant was released. I did not undertake an exhaustive examination of all cases related to the Meridian Riot listed in the minute book, nor did I look at all motions and indictments available in the dockets. These numbers therefore should not be used to make generalizations about Ku Klux Klan prosecutions in this period, but they nevertheless reveal that not all perpetrators of violence escaped punishment for their crimes. Four cases (from among a large number of rulings delivered on 1 July 1872) in particular provide a nice sampling of the differing results that could occur in these sorts of prosecutions. Not-guilty verdicts were reached in *U.S. v. Robert J. Moseley,*

case 1302, and *U.S. v. Lorenzo D. Belk*, case 1332 (Moseley was the sheriff in Meridian, and Belk was his deputy). By contrast, guilty verdicts were reached in *U.S. v. Hugh W. Wilson*, case 1308, and *U.S. v. Thomas Lilly*, case 1320 (Wilson and Lilly were found guilty of injuring black state legislator J. Aaron Moore). See General Minutes, Minute Book No. 1, esp. 491–95, which presents many verdicts concerning a large number of participants in the Meridian Riot.

28. Loyal, "Letter from Mississippi."

29. *Congressional Globe*, 41st Cong., 2nd Sess. (8 March, 18 March, 25 March, 1870): S. 1752, 2051, 2210 (Hiram Revels); 42nd Cong., 2nd Sess. (26 February, 6 May 1872): H. 1211, 3083 (Benjamin Turner), in "A Century of American Lawmaking"; *Congressional Record*, 43rd Cong., 1st Sess. (2 February, 2 March 1874): H. 1121 (Lynch), 1901 (Rapier); 43rd Cong., 2nd Sess. (20 January, 3 February 1875): H. 610, 938–41 (Lynch, the latter citation is part of the debate over the Civil Rights Bill and touches upon circuit courts, though Lynch was only able to get one line in this part of the debate); and 44th Cong., 1st Sess. (14 December 1875): H. 206 (Lynch).

30. Schweninger, *James T. Rapier*, 116–20; the other black congressmen were Joseph Rainey, Robert Elliott, Richard Cain, and Alonzo Ransier, all from South Carolina; Josiah Thomas Walls from Florida; and John Roy Lynch from Mississippi.

31. *Congressional Record*, 43rd Cong., 1st Sess. (2 December 1873): H. 2.

32. Most recently, Hugh Davis makes this assertion in *"We Will Be Satisfied with Nothing Less,"* 103. Multiple pieces of evidence highlight Langston's likely role in Sumner's Civil Rights Bill. Langston actively petitioned Congress to pass this legislation beginning in the early 1870s. He wrote an editorial expounding on his beliefs regarding the bill, "A Letter from Prof. Langston. The Civil Rights Bill, &c.," *New National Era*, 28 December 1871. Sumner himself presented petitions from an address by a convention of colored men (at which Langston had presided); see *Congressional Globe*, 42nd Cong., 2nd Sess. (8 January 1872): S. 294. In the wake of the U.S. Supreme Court's ruling in the *Civil Rights Cases* (1883), which struck down the Civil Rights Act of 1875, several news outlets mentioned Langston's participation in drafting Sumner's original bill; see especially "The Civil Rights Decision Still an Absorbing Subject of Discussion—A Sensible Colored Man's Views—Langston's, Sumner's and Butler's Bills," *Daily Arkansas Gazette*, 20 October 1883, and D. A. Str[a]ker, "Civil Rights. The Causes and Effects of the Decision of the Supreme Court Analyzed—Minister Langston on Charles Sumner," *New York Globe*, 3 November 1883. However, neither in his memoir, his public speeches, nor in any editorial does Langston mention his involvement in helping Sumner draft the bill.

33. S. 916, *Congressional Globe*, 41st Cong., 2nd Sess. (13 May 1870): S. 3434. For a later version of the bill, see *Congressional Record*, 43rd Cong., 1st Sess. (29 April 1874): S. 3451. Indeed, the phrasing in this section may have also come from Langston, who often denounced color-based discrimination in various speeches throughout the decade. See "Citizenship and the Ballot" (25 October 1866); "Eulogy on Charles Sumner" (24 April 1874); and "Equality before the Law" (17 May 1874), all in Langston, *Freedom and Citizenship*, 99–122, 141–61, 162–79. Language related to the use of the word "white" also features heavily in Langston's lengthy response to the Supreme Court's overturning of

the 1875 Civil Rights Act, "The Civil Rights Law. Hon. John Mercer Langston Defines Citizenship and the Rights Attached to It," *New York Globe*, 27 October 1883.

34. Schweninger, *James T. Rapier*, 121.

35. U.S. Congress, *Civil Rights*, 43rd Cong., 1st Sess., House Miscellaneous Document No. 44 (18 December 1873), 1–4.

36. *Congressional Record*, 43rd Cong. 1st Sess. (18 December 1873): H. 310.

37. U.S. Congress, *Civil Rights*, 2.

38. Ibid.

39. Ibid.

40. For more on Elliott, see Lamson, *Glorious Failure*.

41. *Congressional Record*, 43rd Cong., 2nd Sess. (6 January 1874): H. 410.

42. Lamson, *Glorious Failure*, esp. 174–81.

43. *Congressional Record*, 43rd Cong., 2nd Sess. (6 January 1874): H. 408.

44. Robert A. Johnson, "Interesting from Cleveland, Ohio. Speech of John M. Langston, Esq.," *Christian Recorder*, 25 August 1866; Litwack, *Been in the Storm So Long*, 539.

45. Rosen, *Terror in the Heart of Freedom*, 137–44.

46. *Congressional Record*, 43rd Cong., 1st Sess. (6 January 1874): H. 416.

47. For a penetrating analysis of the series of Cuban independence movements, grounded in racial terms, see Ferrer, *Insurgent Cuba*. There is a rich literature of comparative and transnational studies of emancipation focusing on the Caribbean; some of the most influential studies are Foner, *Nothing But Freedom*, which deals with Haiti and with a comparison with the example of British emancipation in the West Indies; Holt, *Problem of Freedom;* and Scott, *Degrees of Freedom*. Mark M. Smith rightly notes the absence of a discussion of foreign and diplomatic developments in the immediate post–Civil War period; I have benefited from his analysis in "The Past as a Foreign Country," 117–40. For a gendered analysis of late nineteenth-century American foreign policy, see Hoganson, *Fighting for American Manhood*. A discussion of the relationship between Florida Reconstruction and the Cuban independence movements may be found in Poyo, "Cuban Revolutionaries," 407–22, and Poyo, "Key West and the Cuban Ten Years War," 289–307.

48. Ferrer, *Insurgent Cuba*, 15.

49. Keller, *Affairs of State*, 88.

50. Shofner, *Nor Is It Over Yet*, 268. It is surprising that Smith omits discussion of the *Virginius* affair in his otherwise perceptive essay "The Past as a Foreign Country."

51. Walls, "Cuban Belligerency," *Appendix to the Congressional Record*, 43rd Cong., 1st Sess. (24 January 1874): H. 27–29; see also the edited version, "Cuban Belligerency," 24 January 1874, in Middleton, *Black Congressmen during Reconstruction*, 377–78 (emphasis added). Note that the speech appeared in the *Appendix;* there was tendency to relegate certain speeches to the back, meaning that they might not have been heard at all on the floor of Congress.

52. Bederman, *Manliness & Civilization*, 5.

53. Ibid., 36.

54. Hoganson, *Fighting for American Manhood*, 26.

55. Ibid.

56. Ibid., 26–27.

57. LaFeber, *New Empire,* esp. 62–101. LaFeber's approach goes far beyond a purely economic-centered understanding of American expansion as he deals with questions of civilization, Christianity, and the fate of American democracy, as well as the desire for open markets.

58. Love, *Race Over Empire,* 43–45.

59. Ibid., 48.

60. Ibid., 65–66.

61. Walls, "Cuban Belligerency," 378.

62. Langston, *Freedom and Citizenship,* 142.

63. Hannah Rosen's succinct description of this theme comes to mind here, as she discusses it within the context of racial and sexual violence on the part of whites: "Thus those who gained their freedom in this period believed that to be free was not only not to be enslaved but also to be a citizen, that is, to be an equal member of a political community represented by a state that bestowed the same rights and obligations upon all its (adult male) members" (*Terror in the Heart of Freedom,* 2).

64. Langston, *Freedom and Citizenship,* 142–43, 145, 147–48; Wirt, *Rights of Virginia Free Negroes,* 506–9; Legare, *Pre-Emption Rights of Colored Person,* 147–48; Bates, *Citizenship,* 382–413. See also Rosen, *Terror in the Heart of Freedom,* 11–16, especially her discussion of Bates's position (13–14), and Foner, *Fiery Trial,* 235–36. The *New York Times* commented on the significance of Bates's opinion: "Attorney-General Bates on the Dred Scott Decision," *New York Times,* 17 December 1862.

65. Langston, *Freedom and Citizenship,* 151, 153, 154–55, 159–60. The phrase "the dread arbitrament of war" was in common use throughout the Civil War. As early as 15 April 1861, a Cleveland newspaper used this phrase, referring directly to the course of action necessary to take against the seceded states of the Confederacy. "The Dread Arbitrament of War," *Daily Cleveland Herald,* 15 April 1861.

66. Rapier, "Civil Rights," *Congressional Record,* 43rd Cong., 1st Sess. (9 June 1874): H. 4782, in "A Century of American Lawmaking"; see also Middleton's edited version in *Black Congressmen during Reconstruction,* 312–18.

67. Rapier, "Civil Rights," H. 4782; Middleton, *Black Congressmen during Reconstruction,* 312–18.

68. Rapier, "Civil Rights," H. 4784. For more on comparative history in this period, see Hahn, "Class and State in Postemancipation Societies," 75–98, which compares Southern planters and German *Junkers,* and Kolchin, "Comparative Perspectives on Emancipation," 203–32.

69. Rapier, "Civil Rights," H. 4784.

70. Ibid.

71. The full text of their declaration is not extant; many different newspapers noted the meeting and published its outcome. I rely on the following sources: "A Timely Address. Representative Colored Men Give Their Views on the Condition of the South and Appeal to Congress for the passage of Certain Measures," *Boston Daily Advertiser,* 2 February 1875; "Washington. Recruits for the Regular Army—Address of the Newly

En[fran]chised—Public Debt," *Daily Arkansas Gazette,* 2 February 1875; "Political. An Appeal from Pinchb[a]ck, Fred Douglass and Others, 'Considering' the Civil Rights Bill," *Daily Rocky Mountain News,* 2 February 1875; "Washington. Meeting of Southern Colored Men," *Milwaukee Daily Sentinel,* 2 February 1875; "Domestic News. Washington. The Colored Men's Address," *Bangor Daily Whig and Courier,* 2 February 1875; "The Impending Danger. An Address to the Country at Large and to Congress," *Chicago Daily Inter Ocean,* 2 February 1875; "Colored Men in Council," *North American and United States Gazette,* 2 February 1875; also Schweninger, *James T. Rapier,* 147. Philip Joseph had served as president of the Union League in Mobile, and George Price was a Union naval veteran and local state politician. Dr. Charles Burleigh Purvis, son of the famed black abolitionist Robert Purvis, was instrumental in forming the medical department at Howard University, where he taught for almost thirty years. The newspapers also mention that other individuals were present, including a Professor Sampson, Dr. Augusta, J. A. Emerson from Arkansas, "and others." I have been unable to identify any of these individuals.

72. "Colored Men in Council," *North American and United States Gazette,* 2 February 1875.

73. Schweninger, *James T. Rapier,* 147–48.

74. *Congressional Record,* 43rd Cong., 2nd Sess. (3 February 1875): H. 943. See John Roy Lynch, "The Civil Rights Bill" (3 February 1875), in Middleton, *Black Congressmen during Reconstruction,* 151–64; McLaughlin, "John R. Lynch," 42–47.

75. *Congressional Record,* 43rd Cong., 2nd Sess. (3 February 1875): H. 944. Kenneth Eugene Mann's "Black Leaders in National Politics" presents a brief and overly simplistic analysis of Lynch's legislative efforts. Examinations of black elitism may be found in Gatewood, *Aristocrats of Color;* Gaines, *Uplifting the Race;* and Gilmore, *Gender and Jim Crow.*

76. *Congressional Record,* 43rd Cong., 2nd Sess. (3 February 1875): H. 944.

77. Ibid., H. 944–45. For a superb analysis of the origins of this discourse and its implications for later developments, see Scott, "Public Rights, Social Equality," 777–804.

78. Harper, *Are We Not Men?;* Karen Taylor, "Reconstructing Men in Savannah, Georgia, 1865–1876," in Friend, *Southern Masculinity,* 1–24.

79. *Congressional Record,* 43rd Cong., 2nd Sess. (3 February 1875): H. 945.

80. Ibid.

81. Ibid.

82. "The Civil-Rights Bill and Our Public-School System," *Jackson Clarion,* quoted in ibid., H. 945; Span, *From Cotton Field to Schoolhouse,* 125–26.

83. *Congressional Record,* 43rd Cong., 2nd Sess. (3 February 1875): H. 945; Lynch asserted that citizens in his own state were making this choice. Whether or not Lynch saw any problems with this assertion, it is hard to gauge to what extent his black constituents were truly making a voluntary choice. As of 1870, the opportunities available for public schooling in Lynch's own congressional district were intimately tied to race. Of the 7,296 individuals attending school in Mississippi's Sixth Congressional District, 6,038 (82.8 percent) were white, and only 1,258 were black. See *Historical Census Data Browser* and Martis, *Historical Atlas of U.S. Congressional Districts,* 242.

84. *Congressional Record,* 43rd Cong., 2nd Sess. (4 December 1875): H. 1011; William P. Kladky, "Joseph Hayne Rainey and the Beginnings of Black Political Authority," in Lynch, *Before Obama,* vol. 2, 143.

85. McAfee, *Religion, Race, and Reconstruction,* 6, 159. McAfee's observations are prescient but must be applied with caution. He questions the wisdom of African Americans' increased militancy and specifically cites what he considers the damaging replacement of white Republican Legrand Perce in favor of the less experienced Lynch.

86. See Kersh, *Dreams of a More Perfect Union,* esp. 153–97.

5. "Color-Line Politics" and the Coming of Redemption

1. *Congressional Record,* 43rd Cong., 2nd Sess. (2 March 1875): H. 2110; Josiah Walls, "Condition of Affairs in the South. Speech of Hon. Josiah T. Walls, of Florida, March 2, 1875, on the Report of the Committee of Affairs in Arkansas and the Condition of the South Generally," *Appendix to the Congressional Record,* 43rd Cong., 2nd Sess. (2 March 1875): H. 166; Josiah Walls, "Condition of Affairs in the South" (2 March 1875), in Middleton, *Black Congressmen during Reconstruction,* 383. This time one of Walls's colleagues intervened in the debate so that Walls could "have leave to print in the RECORD a speech on the subject" (H. 2110). Once again this illustrated what could happen to the forceful arguments of black congressmen, which could be relegated to the confines of the back pages of the *Congressional Record.*

2. Walls, "Condition of Affairs in the South," H. 166–67; Middleton, *Black Congressmen during Reconstruction,* 384.

3. Walls, "Condition of Affairs in the South," H. 167; Middleton, *Black Congressmen during Reconstruction,* 384. For a useful discussion of the process by which the Thirteenth Amendment was ratified and the conflicted legacy of this amendment, see Vorenberg, *Final Freedom.*

4. Walls, "Condition of Affairs in the South," H. 167; Middleton, *Black Congressmen during Reconstruction,* 385.

5. Bay, *White Image in the Black Mind,* 38–74.

6. Walls, "Condition of Affairs in the South," H. 167; Middleton, *Black Congressmen during Reconstruction,* 385–86.

7. Walls, "Condition of Affairs in the South," H. 167; Middleton, *Black Congressmen during Reconstruction,* 387–88.

8. Langston, "Future of the Colored American. His Civil Rights and Equal Privileges—Mental and Physical Qualities—Adaptation to Skilled Labor," in Langston, *Freedom and Citizenship,* 278.

9. Ibid., 280.

10. Ibid., 286.

11. Lynch, *Reminiscences,* 174–75; Lemann, *Redemption,* 135–69.

12. Lynch, *Reminiscences,* 174–75; Lemann, *Redemption,* 136. It is uncertain whether Lynch accurately remembered the exact wording of the conversation, but the twenty-eight-year-old congressman's approach was consistent with his long political career; he was a fighter, but he knew when to pick his fights.

13. Lynch, *Reminiscences,* 167.

14. Unfortunately, the published proceedings of this convention are not extant. My discussion draws on the following sources: Gibbs, *Shadow and Light,* 122–24; "Colored National Convention," *Boston Daily Advertiser,* 6 April 1876; "National Colored Convention," *Daily Arkansas Gazette,* 7 April 1876; "Preliminaries of the Colored National Convention—Pinchback to Take Advanced Political Ground," *Newark Advocate,* 7 April 1876; "True to Their Friends. The Colored Men, in National Convention, Reaffirm Their Devotion and Adherence to the National Republican Party and Its Principles," *Chicago Daily Inter Ocean,* 8 April 1876; "National Colored Convention. Large Attendance—The Democratic Party Charged with Outrages and Oppression—Resolutions Indorsing the Republican Party and Principles," *New York Times,* 8 April 1876; untitled news clipping taken from the *New York Sun* in *Daily Arkansas Gazette,* 14 April 1876; and "A New Departure. The Colored National Convention at Nashville, Tenn., April 6th," *Frank Leslie's Illustrated Newspaper,* 6 May 1876, 147.

15. Gibbs, *Shadow and Light,* 123–24.

16. Foner, *Reconstruction,* 412–25.

17. "National Colored Convention. Large Attendance."

18. Ibid.

19. "National Colored Convention."

20. "New Departure," 147.

21. For more on Pinchback's electoral contests, see Haskins, *Pinckney Benton Stewart Pinchback,* 196–222; Nicholas Patler, "The Startling Career of P. B. S. Pinchback: A Whirlwind Crusade to Bring Equality to Reconstructed Louisiana," in Lynch, *Before Obama,* vol. 1, 211–33.

22. The wide divide between whites and blacks in South Carolina is striking. In 1870, there were 415,814 blacks (59 percent) and 289,667 whites in the state. In the Fifth Congressional District (which elected Smalls), there were 35,808 male citizens twenty-one years of age and older. In that same district, 20,870 black males twenty-one years of age and older and 1,837 whites could not write. My analysis of South Carolina in the postbellum period draws upon a wide range of secondary sources, including Tindall, *South Carolina Negroes, 1877–1900;* Holt, *Black over White;* Zuczek, *State of Rebellion;* Saville, *Work of Reconstruction;* and Kantrowitz, *Ben Tillman.*

23. Saville, *Work of Reconstruction,* esp. 72–101.

24. Miller, *Gullah Statesman,* 93.

25. U.S. Congress, House of Representatives, *South Carolina Testimony,* House Miscellaneous Document No. 31, Part III, 44th Cong., 2nd Sess., 198–99. The disruptive rally is vividly described in Dray, Capitol Men, 256–57.

26. *South Carolina Testimony,* Part III, 199.

27. For accounts of similar meetings after the disruptive August 1876 rally, see Smalls's testimony in *South Carolina Testimony,* Part III, 199–200; H. C., "The Rifle Clubs 'Dividing Time.' Gen. Butler's Forces at a Republican Meeting—What They Did and What the Meeting Proved—The Power of United States Troops—The Men Who Shout for Tilden and Reform," *New York Times,* 20 October 1876.

28. My summary of the main developments related to the strike is based on Foner, *Nothing But Freedom*, 95–102. George C. Rable places this episode in the context of the widespread violence across South Carolina. See Rable, *But There Was No Peace*, 163–76; his brief treatment of the rice strikes and Smalls's role in calming them down is on 170–71.

29. *South Carolina Testimony*, Part III, 78–79.

30. Ibid., 79.

31. Robert Smalls to Governor Daniel H. Chamberlain, 24 August 1876, 1, 3, 5, in Governor Daniel H. Chamberlain Letters Received, S518004 Box 14, Folder 9, South Carolina Department of Archives and History, Columbia; Foner, *Nothing But Freedom*, 97–98.

32. "Mississippi. How the 'Reformers' Are Working the Campaign," *Chicago Daily Inter Ocean*, 2 November 1876.

33. U.S. Congress, Senate, Senate Misc. Doc. 45 109–10.

34. "Free Speech in the South. Mob Violence in Mississippi. Republicans Persecuted for their Opinions—The Democratic Plan of Conducting Political Campaigns—Radical Speeches Not Permitted—How Bloodshed Was Avoided," *New York Times*, 18 September 1877. Lynch describes this affair in his testimony; see Senate Misc. Doc. 45, 112–14.

35. Senate Misc. Doc. 45, 114.

36. Haskins, "Rhetoric of Black Congressmen," 205. Here I am relying on Haskins's discussion of a "Rhetorical Strategy of Anti-Violence." With respect to the connection between these strategies and Smalls's 1877 speech, see ibid., 229–32; Robert Smalls, "'An Honest Ballot Is the Safeguard of the Republic.' Speech of Hon. Robert Smalls, of South Carolina, in the House of Representatives, February 24, 1877, On the Electoral Vote of South Carolina," *Appendix to the Congressional Record*, 44th Cong., 2nd Sess. (24 February 1877): H. 123; Robert Smalls, "An Honest Ballot Is the Safeguard of the Republic" (24 February 1877), in Middleton, *Black Congressmen during Reconstruction*, 335–42. Once again, it is possible that the speech might not have been delivered at all given the fact that it was placed in the back of the *Congressional Record* (recall that two of Walls's speeches, including one mentioned at the outset of this chapter, faced a similar fate).

37. Smalls, "Honest Ballot," H. 123.

38. Ibid.

39. Ibid., H. 124.

40. Ibid.

41. Ibid., H. 125, 133–36.

42. I focus only on the first challenge by George D. Tillman. See U.S. Congress, House of Representatives, *Tillman vs. Smalls* (1877), and U.S. Congress, House of Representatives, *Tillman vs. Smalls* (1878).

43. *Tillman vs. Smalls* (1877), 26–27. Dorothy Sterling quotes excerpts of these testimonies, which directed me back to the contested election reports, in Sterling, *We Are Your Sisters*, esp. 370.

44. Tillman vs. Smalls (1877), 26–27.

45. Rable correctly points out the pitfalls of relying too heavily on either newspapers or congressional testimony due to the biases, the partisan squabbles, and the presence of exaggeration on both sides (see his bibliographical note in *But There Was No Peace,* 248–49). Future research should be undertaken to examine more thoroughly the presence and motivations of black Democrats in the postbellum South.

46. However, the work of Elsa Barkley Brown and Steven Hahn illuminates the presence of politically active women and a more violent and militant black community. See Brown, "Negotiating and Transforming the Public Sphere," 107–46, and Hahn, *Nation under Our Feet,* 302–13 (which focuses specifically on South Carolina).

47. See Litwack, *Been in the Storm So Long,* 212–20.

48. *Tillman vs. Smalls* (1877), 193.

49. Ibid., 193–94.

50. Ibid., 195.

51. For a solid discussion of this stereotype (among other prevalent ones), see White, *A'rn't I a Woman?,* 176. The Sapphire stereotype, as White notes, was explicitly defined in the twentieth century but had crystallized in the minds of white Southerners long before it was given a name. See Rosalyn Terborg-Penn's discussion of the defense of black men against the "wench" description of black women in "Black Male Perspectives on the Nineteenth-Century Woman," 41–42.

52. *Tillman vs. Smalls* (1878), 2. The 1878 document was a second report on the same contested election case.

53. Ibid., 42.

54. Lynch, *Reminiscences,* 195. The four other black congressmen voting against the Federal Electoral Commission's establishment were Jeremiah Haralson (Alabama), John Adams Hyman (North Carolina), Charles Edmund Nash (Louisiana), and Joseph Hayne Rainey (South Carolina). An accounting of the vote totals may be found in the *Congressional Record,* 44th Cong., 2nd Sess. (26 January 1877): H. 1050. For his private comments to black Senator Blanche Kelso Bruce, see Lynch's relevant letters, Blanche Kelso Bruce Papers, Box 9–2, Folder 58, General Correspondence, Lynch, J. R., Howard University, Washington, D.C. (hereafter cited as B. K. Bruce Papers). For the text of his speech, see the *Congressional Record,* 44th Cong., 2nd Sess. (26 January 1877): H. 1025–26. For background and a detailed description of the 1876 presidential election, I rely heavily on Holt, *By One Vote.*

55. Lynch, *Reminiscences,* 199–200.

56. Ibid., 195–201.

57. John R. Lynch to Blanche Kelso Bruce, Natchez, Mississippi, 21 September 1877, in B. K. Bruce Papers. This is one of the clearest indications of Lynch's opposition to Hayes's Southern policy.

58. John R. Lynch to Blanche Kelso Bruce, 27 October 1877, in B. K. Bruce Papers. Stanley Matthews had been involved in negotiations with Southern representatives concerning the Hayes-Tilden election.

6. The Politics of Uncertainty

1. My discussion here draws from several newspaper accounts: "A Congressman Convicted. The Hon. Robert Smalls, Colored, Found Guilty of Accepting a Bribe," *Chicago Daily Inter Ocean*, 15 November 1877, and "Robert Smalls' Trial. A Sample of Southern Justice. Statement In Behalf of the South Carolina Congressman—Convicted on the Unsupported Testimony of a Confessed Criminal—Something of the Defendant's Case," *Bangor Daily Whig and Courier* (reprinted from the *New York Times*), 22 December 1877. Local Southern accounts may be found in "Congressman Smalls," *Keowee Courier*, 15 November 1877, and "Sentence of the Ex-Officials," *Orangeburg Times*, 1 December 1877, in "Chronicling America."

2. "Congressman Smalls," *Keowee Courier*, 15 November 1877, in "Chronicling America."

3. "Robert Smalls' Trial."

4. U.S. Congress, House of Representatives, *Arrest and Imprisonment of Hon. Robert Smalls*, 45th Cong., 2nd Sess. (25 January 1878), House Report No. 100, 11; ibid., *Robert Smalls vs. William Elliott*, 50th Cong., 2nd Sess. (7 December 1888), House Report No. 3536, 39–43. Whether or not Smalls was guilty of these charges has been the subject of some debate. Michael W. Fitzgerald argues that Edward A. Miller's biography produces "strong evidence" that Smalls took bribes but that Miller "refrains from saying so clearly" (Fitzgerald, "Reconstruction Politics and the Politics of Reconstruction," in Brown, *Reconstructions*, 111). He cites Miller, *Gullah Statesman*, 245–50. Nevertheless, given the politicized nature of such charges, it stands to reason that Smalls might have been innocent of all charges.

5. Alfred Brockenbrough Williams, "The Liberian Exodus. An Account of the Voyage of the First Emigrants in the Bark *Azor*, and Their Reception at Monrovia, with a Description of Liberia—Its Customs and Civilization, Romances and Prospects" (Charleston: News and Courier Book Presses, 1878), 1, in Frederick Douglass Papers, 1841–1867, Manuscript Division, Library of Congress, Washington, D.C., Box 12, Reel 18 (hereafter cited as Douglass Papers). The Douglass Papers have also been digitized. See "American Memory—The Frederick Douglass Papers at the Library of Congress," http://memory.loc.gov/ammem/doughtml/doughome.html. A more complete electronic version of Williams's pamphlet is available at the University of North Carolina's "Documenting the American South" project, http://docsouth.unc.edu/church/williams/williams.html.

6. Williams, "Liberian Exodus," 1, Douglass Papers.

7. Ibid., 11. For more on Liberia, see Painter, *Exodusters*, 137–45. Steven Hahn also presents an extended argument on the political meanings of emigration in *Nation under Our Feet*, esp. 317–63, which discusses the "Kansas Fever" and the emigrationist project to Liberia.

8. Tindall, *South Carolina Negroes*, 154–55, 179, 182.

9. As I discuss later in this chapter, Rapier became heavily involved in the emigration movement to Kansas. Langston's important support for emigration began at a relatively early point; he accepted an invitation to address the Emigrant Aid Society

of Washington, D.C., on 7 October 1879. See John Mercer Langston, "The Exodus. The Causes Which Led the Colored People of the South to Leave their Homes—The Lesson of the Exodus," in Langston, *Freedom and Citizenship*, 232–58.

10. See, for example, Painter, *Exodusters*, 26–29, and Hahn, *Nation under Our Feet*, 387. For a contrast to their perspective, Kevin K. Gaines argues that fusion political arrangements were very beneficial to blacks in spite of their brief existence, in *Uplifting the Race*, 23–24. Other excellent studies explore the possibilities of fusion politics and agrarian third parties, taking black participation in fusion seriously but not discussing the connections between emigration and fusion. My approach is guided by Anderson, *Race and Politics in North Carolina;* Cresswell, *Multiparty Politics in Mississippi;* Dailey, *Before Jim Crow;* and Ali, *In The Lion's Mouth*.

11. Michael W. Fitzgerald makes this important point in *Urban Emancipation* and argues that tensions within the black community actually began to abate after the downfall of Reconstruction, as blacks rallied together in the face of limiting opportunities. I agree that some sources of internal tension (for example, between mulattos and blacks or between more privileged and less privileged African Americans) may have dissipated following the end of Reconstruction, but the new political environment also brought other ideological divisions and tensions to the fore in ways not seen in policymaking during Reconstruction.

12. *Proceedings of the National Conference*, 5–6.

13. "Flying From Bull-Dozers. The Blacks Seeking New Homes. Remarkable Spread of the Movement—The Colored People Flocking in Large Numbers to the West—Louisiana and Other Southern States Reaping the Fruits of Cruelty and Political Ostracism," *New York Times*, 3 April 1879.

14. "A Colored Man on the Race Problem," *Nashville Weekly American*, 3 April 1879. The issue of black corruption has been examined extensively. For the case of Thomas Cardozo, see Brock, "Thomas W. Cardozo," 183–206. For a general discussion of modern scholarship and skepticism regarding black leaders, see Fitzgerald, "Reconstruction Politics and the Politics of Reconstruction," 111–14.

15. *Proceedings of the National Conference*, 4.

16. Ibid., 67–70 (Appendix F, "Report of the Committee on a Permanent Form of Organization").

17. Ibid., 4–5.

18. Ibid., 25–26, 30.

19. Ibid., 32–33. Robinson had served as assessor of Phillips County, Arkansas, between 1868 and 1872. According to the 1870 census, he owned $2,000 in real estate and $500 in personal property. According to his own testimony at the 1879 conference, he owned "five hundred acres in Mississippi" (33). A small biographical entry for him may be found in Foner, *Freedom's Lawmakers*, 185.

20. *Proceedings of the National Conference*, 33; *Daily Arkansas Gazette*, 11 May 1879. The conference adopted resolutions regarding congressional appropriations, prompting the *Daily Arkansas Gazette* to excoriate the delegates and praise Robinson's opposition as "sensible." The newspaper reported that Robinson "was cried down by the majority, who had certain political ends to attain without the least regard for the minor con-

sideration of whether the interests of the colored people would be benefited or not." Though the newspaper had its own ax to grind, the scale of the disunity among delegates highlighted by Robinson's opposition to asking for congressional appropriations was worrisome.

21. *Proceedings of the National Conference*, 105, 40–41.

22. Lynch, Reminiscences, xxx–xxxi (Franklin's introduction); *Proceedings of the National Conference*, 95.

23. A copy of Windom's letter appointing Gibbs and Rapier to this committee is reprinted in Gibbs, *Shadow and Light*, 180–82. Note that the date of Windom's letter (10 January 1879) is incorrect, as the National Conference took place in May 1879.

24. Gibbs, *Shadow and Light*, 183–84.

25. U.S. Congress, Senate, *Removal of the Negroes, Part II*, 476.

26. See Correspondence of the Office of the Secretary of the Treasury, Letters Received from Collectors of Internal Revenue, 1864–1908, Ariz. 1st Ark. 2nd and 3rd, RG 65: General Records of the Department of the Treasury, Entry 166, Box 1, National Archives and Records. Nor did the black press ignore his achievements; see the notice of his appointment to the post in the *Christian Recorder*, 20 June 1878.

27. U.S. Senate, *Removal of the Negroes, Part II*, 472.

28. The exchange that follows is drawn from ibid., 476.

29. Ibid., 481.

30. Ibid., 481–82.

31. Ibid., 472, 476, 481–82.

32. "The Colored Men of the South. Remarks of Hon. John R. Lynch at the Douglass Banquet, January 1," *New York Globe*, 10 March 1883. Lynch's manner of framing the debate with black emigrationists is instructive. As Michele Mitchell noted, "Emigrationists were no hopeless lot of people, but they were less optimistic about their chances for mobility and equality in the United States than were the majority of aspiring race women and men." See Mitchell, *Righteous Propagation*, 41.

33. Riser, *Defying Disfranchisement*, 46–61. By the 1890s, Lynch became a "quadrennial" visitor to the state (he spent most of his time outside of Mississippi) and engaged in a bitter feud with another black officeholder (his former ally), James Hill. The result of this feud, according to Riser, was detrimental to local efforts to rally against the forces of white disfranchisement.

34. Although most African Americans did not leave the South, the collective weight of migrations must not be understated, especially when one considers the existence of earlier waves of migration as well, including some 26,000 African Americans who settled in Kansas between 1870 and 1880. During the decade prior to the exodus of 1879, the "sustained migration of some 9,500 Blacks from Tennessee and Kentucky to Kansas . . . far exceeded the much publicized migration of 1879, which netted no more than about 4,000 people from Mississippi and Louisiana. It is important to keep these relative figures in mind, since the Kansas Fever Exodus attracted attention completely out of proportion to its actual numbers" (Painter, *Exodusters*, 146–47). Nevertheless, Painter notes that between March and May 1879, "some six thousand Blacks from Louisiana, Mississippi, and Texas" moved to Kansas (184–85). Painter concludes that

the Kansas Exodus did not end because of disillusionment or suffering among the settlers; nor did white intimidation, threats of murder, or the opposition of black leaders stave off emigration. Rather, "only the physical impossibility of keeping body and soul together during the long wait broke the back of the Kansas Fever Exodus" (200).

35. Ayers, *Promise of the New South*, 38. Michael F. Holt strongly asserts that there was much "political flux and uncertainty" during the era of the Civil War and Reconstruction. In the South, he observes, "the Civil War and Reconstruction was characterized by considerable political plasticity." Jane Dailey emphasizes that this carries through into the period of the 1880s and 1890s, stating that, "far from being solid . . . southern politics in the post–Civil War era was exceptionally fluid. To scratch the surface of the 'solid South' in the late nineteenth century was to discover multiple competing interest groups divided by region, race, ideology, and class." Michael F. Holt, "The Civil War and Reconstruction" (lecture, University of Virginia, Charlottesville, 19 February 2008); Holt, "Elusive Synthesis," 126, 128; Dailey, *Before Jim Crow*, 4; Woodward, *Strange Career of Jim Crow*, 32, 65.

36. Lynch, *Reminiscences of an Active Life*, 255–56. Stephen Cresswell examines the origins of the Greenbackers in *Multiparty Politics in Mississippi*, 22–57; the paraphrase on defining the party is taken from page 24.

37. Lynch, *Reminiscences*, 256–58.

38. Cresswell, *Multiparty Politics in Mississippi*, 65; Lynch, *Reminiscences*, 260.

39. Besides the relevant discussion of the Lynch-Chalmers rivalry in Cresswell, *Multiparty Politics in Mississippi*, see Halsell, "Republican Factionalism in Mississippi," 84–101, and Halsell, "James R. Chalmers," 37–58.

40. *Congressional Record*, 47th Cong., 1st Sess. (27 April 1882): H. 3385. See also Lynch, "Election Contest" (27 April 1882), in Middleton, *Black Congressmen during Reconstruction*, 211–19.

41. Michael Honey, "Class, Race, and Power in the New South: Racial Violence and the Delusions of White Supremacy," in Cecelski and Tyson, *Democracy Betrayed*, 166–67.

42. *Congressional Record*, 47th Cong., 1st Sess. (27 April 1882): H. 3385.

43. Ibid., H. 3386.

44. Ibid.

45. Ibid.

46. "Speech of Hon. John R. Lynch. At the Grand Ratification Barbecue in Raymond on Saturday, September 29th," *Raymond Gazette*, 13 October 1883; "Fusion in the South. Congressman John R. Lynch's View of It. The Duty of the Republicans in the Interest of Good Government—Attitude of the Administration," *New York Globe*, 20 October 1883.

47. For a discussion of fusion voting in Mississippi, see Cresswell, *Multiparty Politics in Mississippi*, 58–99; "Speech of Hon. John R. Lynch"; "Fusion in the South."

48. "Speech of Hon. John R. Lynch"; "Fusion in the South."

49. Wharton, *The Negro in Mississippi*, 202–3; "Speech of Hon. John R. Lynch."

50. *Civil Rights Cases*, 109 U.S. 3 (1883). For a fascinating discussion of the divergent ways of interpreting constitutional law in this period, see Michael Vorenberg, "Reconstruction as a Constitutional Crisis," in Brown, *Reconstructions*, 141–71.

51. Langston, *Civil Rights Law,* 20; John Mercer Langston [Microform]: Personal Papers, Manuscript Division, Library of Congress (hereafter cited as Langston Microfilm).

52. Ibid., 26.

53. Ibid., 30.

54. Ortiz, *Emancipation Betrayed,* 40–41.

55. "Gen. Walls on Fusion His Reason for Resigning from the Committee—Letter from Senator Greely," *New York Globe,* 9 February 1884.

56. "Bisbee Challenges Walls," *New York Times,* 18 August 1884; "Gen. Walls Accepts," *New York Times,* 19 August 1884.

57. My account of this rally is drawn from "Greek Meets Greek. A Pen Picture of Politics in Old Alachua," *Florida Times-Union,* 10 September 1884, and Klingman, *Josiah Walls,* 136–38 (which relies on the same article).

58. "Greek Meets Greek."

59. Ibid.

60. Ibid.; Klingman, *Josiah Walls,* 139–40; "Democracy Victorious All Along the Line!," *Weekly Floridian,* 11 November 1884; "Official Certificate of the Board of State Canvassers of the General Election Held on the Fourth Day of November, A.D. 1884," *Weekly Floridian,* 9 December 1884. One might be tempted to draw the conclusion from Walls's pitiful vote total that considerable intimidation was present, but by this time Walls had lost his once-potent political base.

61. *Congressional Record,* 48th Cong., 2nd Sess. (17 December 1884): H. 316.

62. Ibid. Smalls's speech is on the same page as Crisp's remarks. See also Robert Smalls, "Civil Rights" (17 December 1885), in Middleton, *Black Congressmen during Reconstruction,* 344–45. There is a mistake in Middleton's dating of the speech, as it should read 1884. Both the *Congressional Record* and Smalls's biographer affirm that the remarks were delivered in that year. See Miller, *Gullah Statesman,* 153. For the entire debates and the resulting vote totals, see *Congressional Record,* 48th Cong., 2nd Sess. (17 December 1884): H. 315–22.

63. *Congressional Record,* 48th Cong., 2nd Sess. (17 December 1884): H. 316.

64. Ibid., H. 320–21; Miller, *Gullah Statesman,* 153.

65. Justesen, *George Henry White,* 1–2, 9, 18–19, 25–34, 90–106, 119–24.

66. Anderson, *Race and Politics in North Carolina,* remains the definitive study of this entire district. For the origins of this district, see chapter 1 of Anderson's book, "The Shape of the Second District" (3–33), which has provided a valuable model for my discussions of congressional districts throughout this work.

67. The 1900 census discusses three different categories of white males. My figure combines native-born white males of native parentage, native-born white males of foreign parentage, and foreign-born white males. There was a separate category for colored males, which I did not incorporate as it seems to be repetitious. See *Historical Census Data Browser.*

68. Justesen, *George Henry White,* 166–67.

69. Justesen describes this infighting and complex political scenario effectively in ibid., 151–78; for the vote totals, see Anderson, *Race and Politics in North Carolina,* 348.

70. An earlier version of this section was published in Dinnella-Borrego, "From the Ashes of the Old Dominion," 219–31.

71. Dailey, *Before Jim Crow*, 15–25 (quotation on 24).

72. My understanding of the Readjusters has been influenced by Dailey, *Before Jim Crow*, as well as by Moore, "Black Militancy in Readjuster Virginia," 167–86; Henderson, *Gilded Age City;* and Hartzell, "Exploration of Freedom," 134–56.

73. The numbers that I provide are drawn from the University of Virginia Geospatial and Statistical Data Center's *Historical Census Data Browser;* U.S. Bureau of Census, *Statistics of the Population of the United States at the Tenth Census,* and U.S. Bureau of Census, *Report on the Population of the United States at the Eleventh Census: 1890. Part I.* Particularly useful were U.S. Bureau of Census, *Report on the Social Statistics of Cities, Part II. The Southern and Western States;* U.S. Bureau of Census, *Population of the United States Eleventh Census of the United States by Minor Civil Divisions;* and Martis, *Historical Atlas of American Political Parties.* For a discussion of the number of blacks in Petersburg in the 1880s and a brief study of gerrymandering, see Cheek, "A Negro Runs for Congress," 16. For more on Petersburg, see Hartzell, "Black Life in Petersburg, Virginia," and Henderson, *Gilded Age City.*

74. Langston, *Virginia Plantation,* 451.

75. Toll, "Free Men, Freedmen, and Race," 574.

76. *Lancet,* 9 September 1882, and 28 October 1882; Hartzell, "Exploration of Freedom," 140.

77. Hartzell, "Exploration of Freedom," 140.

78. Moore, "Black Militancy in Readjuster Virginia," 171.

79. Cheek, "A Negro Runs for Congress," 28. The black editor of the Petersburg, Virginia, *Lancet,* George F. Bragg Jr., presented a mixed view of the Readjusters: "We desire to state that we do not endorse the rascality and meanness in the Readjuster party no more than we endorse the hide-bound meanness and proscriptive policy of the Bourbons. . . . The Readjuster party, just like the Republican party, has shown a disposition to ignore the negro in the distribution of its patronage; yet we can say in all truthfulness that the party has approximated nearer the principles of right than even the Republican party. . . . [Blacks] are not such fools as to vote against their own interests, and put men in office who give no evidence of their honest intentions" (*Lancet,* 9 September 1882, and 28 October 1882; Hartzell, "Exploration of Freedom," 147).

80. See Cheek, "A Negro Runs for Congress," 26, 28; "Virginia for Cleveland. Republicans Losing Colored Votes by Mahone's Obstinacy," *New York Times,* 4 November 1888.

81. Henderson, *Gilded Age City,* 313.

82. Dailey, *Before Jim Crow,* 40; Moore, "Black Militancy in Readjuster Virginia," 171–72.

83. Moore, "Black Militancy in Readjuster Virginia," 172; Cheek, "A Negro Runs for Congress," 16.

84. "They Mean To Win. Virginia Republicans Do Not Intend to Allow Either Mahone, Brady, Wise or Any One Else to Stand in the Way of Success," *Petersburg Daily Index-Appeal,* 16 July 1888.

85. Henderson, *Gilded Age City,* 188.

86. Hartzell, "Exploration of Freedom," 144.

87. Ibid., 143.

88. Ibid.; Henderson, *Gilded Age City*, 177–86.

89. H. C. Carter, "John M. Langston," *Chicago Daily Inter Ocean*, 11 September 1887.

90. Cheek, "A Negro Runs for Congress," 20.

91. Douglass, *Narrative of the Life of Frederick Douglass*, 18. See also the larger discussion that Douglass presents on 3–40.

92. *New York Freeman*, 30 January 1886; Cheek and Cheek, "John Mercer Langston," 119.

93. The Cheeks may have overlooked the real ideological differences that divided Douglass and Langston. For more on these ideological divisions, specifically with respect to black emigration from the South, see Toll, "Free Men, Freedmen, and Race," 576–77.

94. Cheek, "A Negro Runs for Congress," 21–22; "Mr. Douglass' Letter," *Richmond Planet*, 25 August 1888; "Douglass and Langston," *New York Age*, 1 September 1888.

95. Cheek, "A Negro Runs for Congress," 26–27, 30. Cheek notes that "Langston's wealth, based on a rich legacy from his father, had been increased through investments in Ohio real estate" (27, n. 43).

96. Langston, *Virginia Plantation*, 466. Though certainly one must consider Langston's reflections with caution, his earlier actions suggest that he was not the kind of man who would have accepted campaign funds from the Democrats.

97. Cheek, "A Negro Runs for Congress," 25; Cheek and Cheek, "John Mercer Langston," 123.

98. U.S. Congress, House of Representatives, *Digest of Contested-Election Cases*, 444–45.

99. Cheek, "A Negro Runs for Congress," 30; *Digest of Contested-Election Cases*, 452.

100. U.S. Congress, House of Representatives, *Langston vs. Venable*, 19, 50.

101. "The Struggle Ended. A Republican Quorum in the House Finally Secured on Tuesday. Two Republicans, Langston and Miller, Given Seats. Incidents of the Closing Minutes of the Struggle. Serious Disagreements by the Tariff Conference," *Boston Journal*, 24 September 1890, in Langston Scrapbooks 1–4, Boxes 60-1 and 60-2.

102. *Richmond Planet*, 11 October 1890, Langston Scrapbooks 1–4, Boxes 60-1 and 60-2; Cheek, "A Negro Runs for Congress," 18; Langston, *Virginia Plantation*, 501–2.

103. For more on abolitionism and discussions of the place of emigration in the antebellum black community, see Sandra Sandiford Young, "John Brown Russwurm's Dilemma: Citizenship or Emigration?," in McCarthy and Stauffer *Prophets of Protest*, 90–113. For discussions of the political context of abolitionism and black support of alternative parties, see Oakes, *The Radical and the Republican*.

104. "Personal," *Christian Recorder*, 12 July 1883.

7. The Last Hurrah

1. *Wilmington Daily Record*, 28 September 1895.

2. Welch, "Federal Elections Bill of 1890," 514. For more on the Force Bill, see Upchurch, *Legislating Racism*.

3. Welch, "Federal Elections Bill of 1890," 514.

4. Ibid., 511, 522.

5. "John M. Langston. His Reasons for Placing No Confidence in the Lodge Bill. Some Very Plain Talk From a Man of Experience and One Who Has Probed the Question of Elections in the South to the Bottom," *Richmond Leader*, 15 August 1890, Langston Scrapbooks 1–4, Boxes 60-1 and 60-2; Kousser, *Shaping of Southern Politics*, 47–56. Kousser makes a very compelling argument that Southerners (and even Northerners) used the secret ballot for the purpose of disfranchising illiterate voters. Indeed, many white Southerners, by the early to mid-1890s, had appropriated the secret ballot in this way. I am distinguishing the intentions of white elites (whom Kousser examines) from Langston's sincere intentions with respect to the secret ballot (particularly his emphasis on federal supervision of Southern electoral politics). For a broad synthesis that examines politics and race in the New South, see Ayers, *Promise of the New South*, esp. 34–54, 132–59. More support for Kousser's arguments (specifically concerning Southern interest in using the secret ballot to disfranchise blacks as well as a fair number of white voters) may be found in Perman, *Struggle for Mastery*, esp. 321–28.

6. Upchurch, *Legislating Racism*, 157.

7. *Congressional Record*, 51st Cong., 2nd Sess. (16 January 1891): H. 1481. See John M. Langston, "The Election Bill" (16 January 1891), in Middleton, *Black Congressmen during Reconstruction*, 127–35.

8. *Congressional Record*, 51st Cong., 2nd Sess. (16 January 1891): H. 1481 (emphasis added).

9. Langston drew upon almost the exact arguments he had used in "Citizenship and the Ballot" in October 1865 in Indianapolis: "Shall those who are natives to the soil, who fight the battles of this country, who pledge to its cause their property, and their sacred honor be denied the exercise of the ballot?" Ibid., H. 1482; John M. Langston, "Citizenship and the Ballot. The Relations of the Colored American to the Government and Its Duty to Him—A Colored American the First Hero of the Revolutionary War," in Langston, *Freedom and Citizenship*, 107–8, 115.

10. Langston, *Virginia Plantation*, 515. In his memoir Langston cites the following article: "Langston Eloquent. The Colored Virginia Congressman Makes a Memorable Speech in the House. He Brings Moisture to the Eyes of Hardened Old Bourbon Members," *Cleveland Leader*, 17 January 1891.

11. Kousser, *Shaping of Southern Politics*, 71. Both Kousser and Jane Dailey examine the most severe effects of disfranchisement (many of which took place between the late 1890s and early 1900s). See ibid., 45–62, and Dailey, *Before Jim Crow*, 160–65.

12. E. L. Thornton, "In the Halls of Congress. Mr. Langston Explains His Suffrage Resolution," *New York Age*, 14 February 1891. There is some evidence that his tactic may have been successful in reaching out to conservative whites. See the favorable white newspaper coverage in "Langston's Amendment," *St. Paul Daily News*, 22 January 1891.

13. Langston, *Virginia Plantation*, 511.

14. U.S. Constitution. Art. XIV, Sec. 2. Langston's proposed amendment would have rephrased the Fourteenth Amendment. The second section of his proposed amendment asserted that "when the right to vote at any election for President and Vice President . . . Representatives in Congress, the executive and judicial officers of a State,

or the members of the legislature thereof, is denied to any of the male inhabitants of such State . . . or in any way abridged . . . the basis of representation therein shall be reduced in the proportion which the number of such male citizens shall bear to the whole number of male citizens twenty-one years age in such State."

15. Langston, *Virginia Plantation*, 515; "Mr. Langston on the Suffrage. A Splendid Effort Which Republican and Democratic Congressmen Applauded," *New York Age*, 31 January 1891.

16. Smalls, "Election Methods in the South," 599.

17. Ibid., 596, 598.

18. Kantrowitz, *Ben Tillman*, 97–98.

19. Smalls, "Election Methods in the South," 598–99. The eight-box law is described in Kantrowitz, *Ben Tillman*, 97.

20. Kantrowitz, *Ben Tillman*, 78–79. He discusses this theme further in chapter 5, "The Mob and the State" (156–97).

21. Smalls, "Election Methods in the South," 600; see also George Brown Tindall's discussion of some earlier comments that Smalls made in February 1890 in Tindall, *South Carolina Negroes*, 182.

22. Upchurch, *Legislating Racism*, 23–45, esp. 23–27. Smalls may have also denounced Butler's proposed legislation because of the latter's role as a Red Shirt who had placed Smalls's life in jeopardy at a Republican rally in Edgefield, South Carolina, in 1876 (as described in chapter 5).

23. Smalls, "Election Methods in the South," 600.

24. For the tactics used by whites to destroy the Readjuster-Republican government in Virginia in 1883, see Dailey, *Before Jim Crow*.

25. My approach to this subject has been guided by Bederman, *Manliness & Civilization*; Oshinsky, *"Worse Than Slavery"*; Blackmon, *Slavery by Another Name*; and Feimster, *Southern Horrors*.

26. "Twenty-Eight Colored Persons Lynched," *Richmond Planet*, 25 August 1888.

27. "He Has No Sympathy with Her. Ex-Congressman Langston Speaks Concerning Ida Wells," *Memphis Appeal-Avalanche*, 4 June 1894, Langston Scrapbooks 1–4, Boxes 60-1 and 60-2. Other white newspapers picked up on this story. See "No Sympathy with Her. Ex-Congressman Langston Talks of Ida Wells," *New Orleans Daily Picayune*, 4 June 1894, and "Langston on the Negro," *Galveston Daily News*, 4 June 1894. Both papers noted that "Mr. Langston expressed himself freely as having no sympathy with Ida Wells' English agitation, intimating that her efforts to arouse the sympathy of the English population of the south had less of the patriotism in it than a desire for notoriety and revenue." There may have been some creative license in this summary, which (coming from the white Democratic press) would not have been surprising. William Francis Cheek's dissertation on Langston does not examine this episode. Though I am not entirely satisfied with some of his conclusions, Cheek's comments on Langston's status as a black leader may shed light on some of the congressman's motivations. See Cheek, "Forgotten Prophet," 356–85.

28. "Lynch-List as Published in the *Richmond Planet*," *Richmond Planet*, 21 July 1888, Box 5, Folder 24, Langston Papers.

29. Ida B. Wells, "Lynch Law in All Its Phases," *Our Day* (May 1893), 333–37, in Foner and Branham, *Lift Every Voice*, 746, 752–53. On Wells's experience with lynching and her place in black leadership circles, see Bay, *To Tell the Truth Freely*, esp. 82–108, 271–73.

30. G. W. Walker, "Stand Up Mr. Langston! Was Your Interview in the Memphis Appeal-Avalanche the Result of Personal Pique, Ignorance or Pure Cussedness?—Lawyer Walker is Respectfully but Firmly After You," *Indianapolis Freeman*, 16 June 1894; "Hypocracy," *Washington Bee*, 23 June 1894, in "Chronicling America."

31. "Mr. Langston Speaks Out," *Indianapolis Freeman*, 30 June 1894.

32. "Langston's Manly Denial," *Indianapolis Freeman*, 30 June 1894.

33. For a discussion of these events (expressing the belief that Langston actually said what was reported by the white press), see Giddings, *Ida*, 308, 311–12. In contrast to Giddings's perspective, Patricia Ann Schecter (citing the coverage I have relied upon by the *Indianapolis Freeman*) believes that "enterprising white southerners" fabricated Langston's interview in order to "squelch the spirit of protest and discredit Wells among southern blacks"; see Schecter, *Ida B. Wells-Barnett*, 279–80, n. 143.

34. Bay, *To Tell the Truth Freely*, for example, 111, 122, 154.

35. Smalls, *Speeches at the Constitutional Convention*, 8.

36. No stenographers were used at the convention. As such, the only record of the speeches is what appeared in the newspapers. Smalls's daughter, Sarah, took it upon herself to compile relevant materials and major speeches that her father delivered and had them published in 1896, the year after the disfranchising convention had accomplished its work. Smalls, *Speeches at the Constitutional Convention*, 8–9. For more on the subject of black emigration and the economic threat this posed, see Tindall, *South Carolina Negroes*, 182.

37. Richardson, *Death of Reconstruction*, 183–224.

38. Upchurch, *Legislating Racism*, emphasizes the existence of high levels of racism even among champions of black rights in this period (as well as the simultaneous existence of anti–Native American and anti-Asian prejudice).

39. Smalls, *Speeches at the Constitutional Convention*, 16.

40. My understanding of gender during the postbellum period, and of the long and complex history of interracial relations in the South, has been influenced by Hodes, *White Women, Black Men;* Edwards, *Gendered Strife and Confusion;* and Hunter, *To 'Joy My Freedom.*

41. Terborg-Penn, "Black Male Perspectives on the Nineteenth-Century Woman," 40–42.

42. Mitchell, *Righteous Propagation*, 11.

43. Smalls, *Speeches at the Constitutional Convention*, 18–19; Miller, *Gullah Statesman*, 207.

44. Indeed, Gatewood, in *Aristocrats of Color*, emphasizes the attempts by upper-class blacks to disassociate themselves from lower-class blacks and find common ground with their white counterparts.

45. Smalls, *Speeches at the Constitutional Convention*, 18; "Editorial from the (N.Y.) Press, October 5, 1895," in ibid., 22.

46. Martha Hodes, in *White Women, Black Men*, argues that this change in white

views on the subject took place following the Civil War (see specifically the second half of her study, 125–208).

47. "Editorial from the (N.Y.) Press, October 5, 1895," 21–22.

48. "Editorial from the *News and Courier,* the Leading Democratic Paper of Charleston, S.C., November 23, 1895," in Smalls, *Speeches at the Constitutional Convention,* 22–23.

49. "John R. Lynch," *Broad Ax* (Salt Lake City), 20 March 1897. Nor was the *Broad Ax* alone in its commentary on Lynch's wedding. For a discussion of what other black news outlets (like the *Washington Bee*) and the black community thought about Lynch's marriage, see Gatewood, *Aristocrats of Color,* 166–70.

50. "The Republican Year in Politics," *Wilmington Messenger,* 8 November 1894 (from the *Baltimore Sun*). A separate article reported that the Republican-Populist Fusion ticket won control of both houses of North Carolina's state legislature. "The Election. The Republican Majority in New Hanover—The Democrats Beaten Not Only in the City But at Every Country Precinct—The Vote in Neighboring Counties," *Wilmington Messenger,* 8 November 1894, in 1898 Wilmington Reports File Box no. 1, Folder: 1870s–1890s.

51. Prather, *We Have Taken a City;* H. Leon Prather, "We Have Taken a City: A Centennial Essay," in Cecelski and Tyson, *Democracy Betrayed,* 18–19.

52. Justesen, *George Henry White,* 418.

53. "Plain Talk," *Wilmington Messenger,* 7 November 1894, in 1898 Wilmington Reports File, Box no. 1, Folder: 1870s–1890s.

54. *Congressional Record,* U.S. House, 55th Cong., 1st Sess. (31 March 1897): H. 550, 557.

55. Wells-Barnett, *Crusade for Justice,* 253. For the black community's efforts to provide funds for Baker's widow and her children, see "To Aid the Lake City Sufferers," *Colored American,* 19 March 1898.

56. Mia Bay points out this difficulty in *To Tell the Truth Freely,* 9.

57. My discussion of the "Wilmington Riot" is grounded in Prather, *We Have Taken a City,* and Cecelski and Tyson, *Democracy Betrayed.* I thank LeRae Umfleet for making available to me the draft of her exhaustive three-year study, *1898 Wilmington Race Riot Report,* which was the fruit of the North Carolina General Assembly's 2000 legislation calling for a commission to formally investigate the riot. Umfleet also granted me access to her extensive notes and research. For the final report, see North Carolina Office of Archives & History, "1898 Wilmington Race Riot Commission," http://www.history.ncdcr.gov/1898-wrrc/.

58. Indeed, this had been the pattern in North Carolina, and especially in Wilmington's white press, throughout the 1890s. See especially "The Bishopville (S.C.) Riot," *Weekly Star,* 28 November 1890; "Race Troubles. Between Striking White Miners and Negroes," *Weekly Star,* 3 July 1891 (focusing on racial conflicts in Washington State); "Negro Rioters," *Weekly Star,* 8 July 1892 (highlighting disturbances in Jacksonville, Florida); "Militia Ordered Out to Suppress a Riot in Beaufort County, N.C.," *Morning Star,* 23 April 1895; "Riot in Winston. It Came Near Being a Very Serious Affair," *Morning Star,* 13 August 1895; and "Looks Like Old Reconstruction Days in Wilmington," *Wilmington Messenger* (quoting from the *Charlotte News*), 12 February 1896 (which

focuses on black police in Wilmington and their "unprovoked" assault on a local merchant) in 1898 Wilmington Reports File, Box no. 1, Folder: 1870s–1890s.

59. Thomas W. Clawson, "The Wilmington Race Riot in 1898. Recollections and Memories, by the Late Thomas W. Clawson (At the time City Editor of the Wilmington Messenger, and Later, Editor of the Wilmington Morning Star)," Miscellaneous, Louis T. Moore Collection, P.C. 777.1, North Carolina Department of Archives and History, Raleigh (hereafter cited as Clawson, "Recollections").

60. Ibid.

61. "Mrs. Felton Speaks She Makes a Sensational Speech Before Agricultural Society. Believes Lynching Should Prevail as Long as Defenseless Women Is [*sic*] Not Better Protected," *Morning Star*, 18 August 1898. See also "Plain Speech by a Georgia Lady," *Wilmington Messenger*, 18 August 1897 (which was the date when the speech was originally delivered) in 1898 Wilmington Reports File, Box no. 1, Folder: 1870s–1890s. For a comparative analysis of Felton and Ida B. Wells, see Feimster, *Southern Horrors*. For an excellent introduction to the gendered component of racialized violence during the Wilmington Riot, see LeeAnn Whites, "Love, Hate, Rape, Lynching: Rebecca Latimer Felton and the Gender Politics of Racial Violence," in Cecelski and Tyson, *Democracy Betrayed*, 143–62. LeRae Umfleet's transcriptions of Felton's speech and Manly's controversial editorial are contained in her *1898 Wilmington Race Riot Report* (Draft, 15 December 2005), 99–100. An insightful, albeit brief, study that gave me insight and access to copies of the *Daily Record* may be found in Hodgson, "For the *Record*."

62. Clawson, "Recollections." My transcription here draws on the reprint of Manly's editorial in the *Colored American* (which has minor changes to the text compared with Clawson's version). See "An Editorial Bathed in Blood," *Colored American*, 19 November 1898.

63. "Horrible Butcheries at Wilmington. The Turks Out Done. Innocent and Unarmed Colored Men Shot Down. Hundred Run to the Woods. The Mob Captures the Town. — White Ministers Aiders and Abettors of Murder. The Governor Powerless and the President of the United States Silent. God's Aid Implored. The Cries of Defenseless. — Anarchy Rules," *Richmond Planet*, 19 November 1898. The number of black casualties will never be known with certainty; estimates range from 17 to 300 killed. The coverage and numbers of dead and wounded published by the *Richmond Planet* are very accurate in light of the recent exhaustive research by LeRae Sikes Umfleet. According to her count based on newspapers, tax returns, and other sources, twenty-two blacks died, with nine others listed as "Wounded, fate unknown." See Umfleet, *Day of Blood*, especially her list of "African Americans Killed or Wounded" on 117–19 (which also includes white versions of the list of the dead).

64. "Southern Negro's Plaint Congressman G. H. White Forced to Leave North Carolina. Will Not Re-Enter Congress Wife a Physical Wreck Owing to Attacks — Advises Negroes to Migrate West," *New York Times*, 26 August 1900. The article also appears in Justesen, *In His Own Words*, 1, 83.

65. "Homage to a Race Leader the Banquet to Hon. George H. White a Striking Evidence of Race Unity. A Congressman Representing a Constituency of Ten Million People — A Gathering Possible Only in the Nation's Capital — Mr. White's Ringing

Speech—The Affair in Detail," *Colored American,* 14 January 1899. See also "Account of Remarks to Appreciation Dinner at Delmo-Koonce Restaurant," Washington, D.C., 3 January 1899, in Justesen, *In His Own Words,* 95–96.

66. "Negroes Meet To-Day Convention Called to Memorialize the Legislature. There Was a Caucus He[l]d Last Night. Dr. Scruggs Refused To Be Bound by Resolutions He Had Not Seen," *Raleigh News and Observer,* 18 January 1899.

67. "Booker Pays the Penalty," *Charlotte Daily Observer,* 19 January 1899, in Justesen, *In His Own Words,* 97–98.

68. *Congressional Record,* 55th Cong., 3rd Sess. (26 January 1899): H. 1124. White was not speaking in isolation on this issue. The black press had a wide diversity of opinions regarding the prospect of territorial acquisitions (including opposition to annexation). For this perspective, see Kramer, *Blood of Government,* 119–22. Some excellent examples may be found in an untitled article in *Washington Bee,* 11 February 1899, and "The White Man's Burden," *Washington Bee,* 11 March 1899, both in "Chronicling America."

69. *Congressional Record,* 55th Cong., 3rd Sess. (20 December 1898): H. 339, 341 (the entire speech can be found on 338–46).

70. *Congressional Record,* 55th Cong., 3rd Sess. (26 January 1899): H. 1124.

71. Ibid.

72. Ibid.

73. Ibid.

74. Ibid., H. 1124–25. White provided statistics and voting results at the district level in both Mississippi and South Carolina to support his argument.

75. Ibid., H. 1126.

76. Hon. H. D. Money, "Shall Illiteracy Rule?," 174–75, and Hon. George H. White, "The Injustice to the Colored Voter," 176–77, both in *Independent,* 18 January 1900. The quotation from White's article is on 177. For a thorough discussion of the meaning of the *Williams v. Mississippi* ruling, see Riser, *Defying Disfranchisement,* 45–73.

77. An excellent discussion of the Crumpacker bill, with a discussion of its historical context and the vote totals, may be found in Perman, *Struggle for Mastery,* 224–31.

78. *Congressional Record,* 56th Cong., 1st Sess. (20 January 1900): H. 1017.

79. *Congressional Record,* 56th Cong., 1st Sess. (31 January 1900): H. 1365.

80. "The Colored Member," *Raleigh News and Observer,* in *Congressional Record,* 56th Cong., 1st Sess. (5 February 1900): H. 1507.

81. Ibid.

82. Ibid.

83. Ibid.

84. *Congressional Record,* 56th Cong., 1st Sess. (23 February 1900): H. 2151.

85. Ibid., H. 2152.

86. Ibid., H. 2153.

87. Ibid.

88. Ibid., H. 2154.

89. Ibid., H. 1638.

90. Umfleet, *Day of Blood,* 152–53. In 1880, there were only 306 nonwhite residents who had born in North Carolina living in the state of New Jersey (accounting for 52

percent of the black population of that state). By 1900, that number had soared to 3,586 (77 percent). For more on Whitesboro, see Justesen, *George Henry White*, 356–84.

Conclusion

1. Office of the Press Secretary, "Remarks by the President."

2. Ibid.

3. This concluding sentence is borrowed from the subtitle of Justesen's biography of White, *George Henry White*.

4. "Mr. Cuney and Mr. Bruce—A Comparison," *A.M.E. Church Review* (April 1898): 464.

5. Ibid.

6. "What Leadership Means. Ex-Governor P. B. S. Pinchback Pays an Eloquent Tribute to the Late J. M. Langston," *Colored American*, 30 April 1898.

7. Ibid.

8. "In Memory of Langston," *Colored American*, 30 April 1898.

9. This point is emphasized by Upchurch, *Legislating Racism*, 186–209. See also Riser, "Burdens of Being White," 243–72, and Kramer, "Empires, Exceptions, and Anglo-Saxons," 1315–53.

10. See Trouillot, *Silencing the Past*, 22, 25.

11. The Lynch-Myers-Rhodes episode is drawn from two tantalizing sources: Garraty, *The Barber and the Historian*, and the George A. Myers Papers held by the Ohio History Connection, which are cataglogued online at http://memory.loc.gov/award /ohiaee/myers12.html. For more on George Myers's fascinating life, see Ruth Martin, "Defending the Reconstruction: George A. Myers, Racism, Patronage, and Corruption in Ohio, 1879–1930," in Lynch, *Before Obama*, vol. 1, 187–209. For recent popular and scholarly examinations of the debate between Rhodes and Lynch, see Dray, *Capitol Men*, 367–68, and Lynch, "The Lynch-Rhodes Debate: Reconstruction on Trial," in Lynch, *Before Obama*, vol. 1, 235–65.

12. Lynch, *Reminiscences*, xxxiii (Franklin's introduction).

13. James Ford Rhodes to George A. Myers, 29 March 1914, in Garraty, *The Barber and the Historian*, 29–30.

14. John Roy Lynch, "Some Historical Errors of James Ford Rhodes," *Journal of Negro History* 2, no. 4 (October 1917): 345; Franklin, "Introduction," xxxiii.

15. Rhodes, *History of the United States from the Compromise of 1850*, vol. 7, 169. W. E. B. Du Bois would later explicitly challenge these ideas about black congressmen in *Black Reconstruction in America*, esp. 627–30.

16. Rhodes to Myers, 19 March 1916, in Garraty, *The Barber and the Historian*, 42–43.

17. MIC 82 George A. Myers Papers [microform], letter from John R. Lynch, 2 April 1917, Ohio History Connection.

18. Rhodes to Myers, 5 April 1917, in Garraty, *The Barber and the Historian*, 64.

19. Rhodes to Myers, 4 August 1917, MSS 70 George A. Myers Papers, 1890–1929, Box 17, Folder 3, Ohio History Connection; Rhodes to Myers, 22 November 1917, in Garraty, *The Barber and the Historian*, 76.

20. Rhodes to Myers, 22 November 1917, in Garraty, *The Barber and the Historian*, 77.

21. See Fitzgerald, "Reconstruction Politics and the Politics of Reconstruction," 111–12.

22. Here I am following the lead of Middleton, *Black Congressmen during Reconstruction*, xix–xx.

23. Hughes, "Bright Chariots," 59–62, in De Santis, *Collected Works of Langston Hughes*, vol. 9, 324. William Cheek and Aimee Lee Cheek paraphrase this story, in their conclusion, in emphasizing the need to recapture Langston's "legacy." See Cheek and Cheek, "John Mercer Langston," 126.

24. Hughes, "Bright Chariots."

BIBLIOGRAPHY

Manuscript Collections

Alabama Department of Archives and History, Montgomery
  Eugene Feldman Papers, 1856–1978
  Governor Ridgley Smith (1868–1870) Administrative Files

Alderman Library, University of Virginia, Charlottesville
  Records of the Education Division of the Bureau of Refugees, Freedmen,
    and Abandoned Lands, 1865–1867, Letters Received (microfilm)

Library of Congress, Manuscripts Division, Washington, D.C.
  Frederick Douglass Papers (microfilm/online)
  John Mercer Langston Papers (microfilm)

Mississippi Department of Archives and History, Jackson
  Governor James Lusk Alcorn Correspondence and Papers, 1869–1871

Moorland-Spingarn Research Center, Howard University, Washington, D.C.
  Blanche Kelso Bruce Papers, 1870–1891
  John Mercer Langston Collection (Scrapbooks), 1870–1891
  P. B. S. Pinchback Papers, 1867–1873
  Rapier Family Papers, 1836–1883

National Archives and Records Administration (Archives II), College Park,
  Maryland
  Record Group 65: General Records of the Department of the Treasury
    Applications for Positions as Internal Revenue Collectors and Assessors,
      1863–1910
    Correspondence of the Office of the Secretary of the Treasury, Letters
      Received from Collectors of Internal Revenue, 1864–1908

National Archives and Records Administration, Southeast Region, Atlanta
  Record Group 21: U.S. District Court, South District of Mississippi, Jackson
    Criminal Cases, 1872, Cases 1290–1392
    General Minutes, Minute Book No. 1, June 1866–January 1874

North Carolina Department of Archives and History, Raleigh
  Governors' Papers, Daniel L. Russell (1897–1901)
  Louis T. Moore Collection

Ohio History Connection, Ohio History Center, Columbus
  George A. Myers Papers, 1890–1929

South Carolina Department of Archives and History, Charleston
  Governor Daniel H. Chamberlain (1874–1877), Letters Received

Special Collections and Archives, Fisk University, Nashville, Tennessee
  John Mercer Langston Papers, 1846–1930

State Archives of Florida, Tallahassee
  Correspondence of the Governor, 1857–1888
  Governor's Office Letterbooks, 1836–1909
  Secretary of the Territory and Secretary of State incoming correspondence,
    1831–1917

State Records Center, Government Records Branch of North Carolina, Raleigh
  13977 Historical Research Reports File, Wilmington Race Riot of 1898
    (May 2003–June 2006)

Government Documents and Publications

Bates, Edward. *Citizenship.* 10 *Op. Att'y Gen.* 382 (29 November 1862).

Congressional Globe.

Congressional Quarterly. *Congressional Quarterly's Guide to U.S. Elections 4th Edition.* Washington, D.C.: Congressional Quarterly Press, 2001.

Congressional Record.

Legare, Hugh S. *Pre-Emption Rights of Colored Persons.* 4 *Op. Att'y Gen.* 147 (15 March 1843).

North Carolina Office of Archives and History. "1898 Wilmington Race Riot Commission." http://www.history.ncdcr.gov/1898-wrrc/.

U.S. Bureau of Census. "Census of Population and Housing." http://www.census.gov/prod/www/decennial.html.

———. *Population of the United States Eleventh Census of the United States by Minor Civil Divisions.* Washington, D.C.: Government Printing Office, 1891.

———. *Report on the Population of the United States at the Eleventh Census: 1890. Part I.* Washington, D.C.: Government Printing Office, 1895.

———. *Report on the Social Statistics of Cities, Part II. The Southern and Western States.* Washington, D.C.: Government Printing Office, 1887.

———. *Statistics of the Population of the United States at the Tenth Census.* Washington, D.C.: Government Printing Office, 1880.

U.S. Congress, House of Representatives. Office of History and Preservation, Office of the Clerk. *Black Americans in Congress, 1870–2007.* Washington, D.C.: U.S. Government Printing Office, 2008.

———. *Civil Rights. Memorial of National Convention of Colored Persons, Praying to Be Protected in Their Civil Rights.* 43rd Congress, 1st Sess., House Miscellaneous Document No. 44 (18 December 1873).

———. *Contested-Election Case of John M. Langston vs. E. C. Venable, From the Fourth Congressional District of Virginia.* Washington, D.C.: Government Printing Office, 1889.

———. *Digest of Contested-Election Cases in the Fifty-First Congress.* 51st Congress, 2nd

Sess., House Miscellaneous Document No. 137. Washington, D.C.: Government Printing Office, 1891.

———. *Finley vs. Walls. Papers in the Case of Jesse J. Finley vs. Josiah T. Walls, Second Congressional District of Florida.* 44th Congress, 1st Sess., House Miscellaneous Document No. 58 (24 January 1876).

———. *Recent Election in South Carolina. Testimony Taken by the Select Committee on the Recent Election in South Carolina.* 44th Congress, 2nd Sess., House Miscellaneous Document No. 31, Part III (12 January 1877).

———. *S. L. Niblack vs. J. T. Walls. Papers in the Case of S. L. Niblack vs. J. T. Walls, of Florida.* 42nd Congress, 2nd Sess., House Miscellaneous Document No. 34 (16 January 1872).

———. *Tillman vs. Smalls, Fifth Congressional District of South Carolina.* 45th Congress, 2nd Sess., House Report No. 916 (8 June 1878).

———. *Tillman vs. Smalls. Papers in the Case of Tillman vs. Smalls, Fifth District South Carolina.* 45th Congress, 1st Sess., House Miscellaneous Document No. 11 (9 November 1877).

U.S. Congress, Senate. *Mississippi. Testimony as to the Denial of Elective Franchise in Mississippi at the Elections of 1875 and 1876, Taken under the Resolution of the Senate of December 5, 1876.* 44th Congress, 2nd Sess., Senate Miscellaneous Document No. 45. Washington, D.C.: Government Printing Office, 1877.

———. *Report and Testimony of the Select Committee of the United States Senate to Investigate the Causes of the Removal of the Negroes from the Southern States to the Northern States. In Three Parts. Part II.* 46th Congress, 2nd Sess., Report No. 693, part 2. Washington, D.C.: Government Printing Office, 1880.

———. *Testimony Taken by the Joint Select Committee to Inquire into the Condition of Affairs in the Late Insurrectionary States. Alabama.* Vol. 2. 42nd Congress, 2nd Sess., Report No. 41, part 9. Washington, D.C.: Government Printing Office, 1872.

———. *Testimony Taken by the Joint Select Committee to Inquire into the Condition of Affairs in the Late Insurrectionary States. Florida.* 42nd Congress, 2d Sess., Report No. 41, part 13. Washington, D.C.: Government Printing Office, 1872.

Wirt, William. *Rights of Virginia Free Negroes.* 1 *Op. Att'y Gen.* 506 (7 November 1821).

Court Cases

U.S. v. Robert J. Moseley, case 1302 (1872)

U.S. v. Hugh W. Wilson, case 1308 (1872)

U.S. v. Thomas Lilly, case 1320 (1872)

U.S. v. Lorenzo D. Belk, case 1332 (1872)

Slaughter-House Cases, 83 U.S. 36 (1873)

United States v. Cruikshank et al., 92 U.S. 542 (1875)

United States v. Reese et al., 92 U.S. 214 (1875)

Civil Rights Cases, 109 U.S. 3 (1883)

Newspapers and Contemporary Periodicals

A.M.E. Church Review (Nashville, Tenn.)
Anti-Slavery Bugle (New Lisbon, Ohio)
Bangor Daily Whig & Courier (Me.)
Boston Daily Advertiser
Boston Journal
Broad Ax (Salt Lake City)
Charleston News and Courier (S.C.)
Charlotte Daily Observer (N.C.)
Chicago Daily Inter Ocean
Christian Recorder (Philadelphia)
Cleveland Leader
Colored American: A National Negro Newspaper (Washington, D.C.)
Daily Arkansas Gazette (Little Rock)
Daily Cleveland Herald
Daily Evening Bulletin (San Francisco)
Daily Rocky Mountain News (Denver)
Elevator (San Francisco)
Florida Times Union (Tallahassee)
Frank Leslie's Illustrated Newspaper (New York)
Frederick Douglass' Paper (Rochester, N.Y.)
Galveston Daily News (Tex.)
Harper's Weekly (New York)
The Independent (New York)
Indianapolis Freeman (Ind.)
Keowee Courier (Pickens Court House, S.C.)
Memphis Appeal-Avalanche (Tenn.)
Milwaukee Daily Sentinel (Wis.)
Mobile Daily Republican (Ala.)
Morning Republican (Little Rock, Ark.)
Morning Star (Wilmington, N.C.)
Nashville Weekly American (Tenn.)
Natchez Courier (Miss.)
Newark Advocate (Ohio)
New Era. A National Journal (Washington, D.C.)
New National Era (Washington, D.C.)
New Orleans Daily Picayune
New York Age
New York Freeman
New York Globe
New York Press
New York Times
North American and United States Gazette (Philadelphia)

North American Review (Boston)
North Star (Rochester, N.Y.)
Oberlin Weekly News (Ohio)
Orangeburg Times (Orangeburg Court House, S.C.)
Petersburg Daily Index-Appeal (Va.)
Lancet (Petersburg, Va.)
Raleigh News and Observer (N.C.)
Raymond Gazette (Miss.)
Richmond Leader (Va.)
Richmond Planet (Va.)
Southwestern Christian Advocate (New Orleans)
St. Paul Daily News (Minn.)
Tallahassee Sentinel (Fla.)
Washington Bee (Washington, D.C.)
Weekly Clarion (Jackson, Miss.)
Weekly Floridian (Tallahassee, Fla.)
Weekly Star (Wilmington, N.C.)
Wilmington Daily Record (N.C.)
Wilmington Messenger (N.C.)

Other Primary Sources

Berlin, Ira, Joseph P. Reidy, and Leslie S. Rowland, eds. *Freedom: A Documentary History of Emancipation, 1861–1867.* Series 2, *The Black Military Experience.* Cambridge: Cambridge University Press, 1982.

Blaine, James G. *Twenty Years of Congress: From Lincoln to Garfield.* Vol. 2. Norwich, Conn.: Henry Bill Publishing, 1886.

"Documenting the American South." University Library, University of North Carolina at Chapel Hill. http://docsouth.unc.edu/.

Douglass, Frederick. *Narrative of the Life of Frederick Douglass, an American Slave.* 1845. Reprint, New York: Barnes & Noble Classics, 2003.

Garraty, John A., ed. *The Barber and the Historian: The Correspondence of George A. Myers and James Ford Rhodes, 1910–1923.* Columbus: Ohio Historical Society, 1956.

Gibbs, Mifflin Wistar. *Shadow and Light: An Autobiography with Reminiscences of the Last and Present Century.* 1902. Reprint, Lincoln: University of Nebraska Press, 1995.

Gooding, Corporal James Henry. *On the Altar of Freedom: A Black Soldier's Civil War Letters from the Front,* edited by Virginia M. Adams. Amherst: University of Massachusetts Press, 1991.

Hahn, Steven, Steven F. Miller, Susan E. O'Donovan, John C. Rodrigue, and Leslie S. Rowland, eds. *Freedom: A Documentary History of Emancipation, 1861–1867.* Series 3, Vol. 1, *Land and Labor, 1865.* Chapel Hill: University of North Carolina Press, 2008.

Historical Census Data Browser. University of Virginia Geospatial and Statistical Data Center. http://www.mapserver.lib.virginia.edu/.

Hughes, Langston. "Bright Chariots." *Negro Digest* 9 (1951). In Christopher C. De Santis, ed., *The Collected Works of Langston Hughes.* Vol. 9, *Essays on Art, Race, Politics, and World Affairs,* 59–62. Columbia: University of Missouri Press, 2002.

Justesen, Benjamin R., ed. *In His Own Words: The Writings, Speeches, and Letters of George Henry White.* Lincoln, Neb.: iUniverse, 2004.

Langston, John Mercer. *Freedom and Citizenship. Selected Lectures and Addresses of the Hon. John Mercer Langston, LL.D., U.S. Minister Resident at Haiti. With an Introductory Sketch by Rev. J. E. Rankin, D.D., of Washington.* 1883. Reprint, Whiteface, Mont.: Kessinger Publishing, 2007.

———. *From the Virginia Plantation to the National Capitol or The First and Only Negro Representative in Congress from the Old Dominion.* 1894. Reprint, New York: Arno Press, 1969.

Lynch, John Roy. *Reminiscences of an Active Life: The Autobiography of John Roy Lynch.* Edited by John Hope Franklin. Chicago: University of Chicago Press, 1970.

———. "Some Historical Errors of James Ford Rhodes." *Journal of Negro History* 2, no. 4 (October 1917): 345–68.

Middleton, Stephen, ed. *Black Congressmen during Reconstruction: A Documentary Sourcebook.* Westport, Conn.: Greenwood, 2002.

Office of the Press Secretary, The White House. "Remarks by the President at the Congressional Black Caucus Foundation's Annual Phoenix Awards Dinner," 27 September 2009. http://www.whitehouse.gov/the_press_office/Remarks-By-The-President-At-The-Congressional-Black-Caucus-Foundations-Annual-Phoenix-Award-Dinner.

Proceedings of the National Conference of Colored Men of the United States, Held in the State Capitol of Nashville, Tenn., May 6, 7, 8, and 9, 1879. Washington, D.C.: Rufus H. Darby, Steam Power Printer, 1879.

Proceedings of the Southern States Convention of Colored Men, Held in Columbia, S.C., Commencing October 18, Ending October 25, 1871. Columbia, S.C.: Carolina Printing Company, 1871.

Smalls, Sarah V., comp. *Speeches at the Constitutional Convention, by Gen. Robt. Smalls. With the Right of Suffrage Passed by the Constitutional Convention.* Charleston, S.C.: Enquirer Print, 1896.

Sterling, Dorothy, ed. *We Are Your Sisters: Black Women in the Nineteenth Century.* New York: W. W. Norton, 1984.

Towne, Laura M. *Letters and Diary of Laura M. Towne Written from the Sea Islands of South Carolina 1862–1884.* Edited by Rupert Sargent Holland. 1912. Reprint, LaVergne, Tenn.: Kessinger Publishing, 2011.

Warren, Henry W. *Reminiscences of a Mississippi Carpet-Bagger.* Holden, Mass.: n.p., 1914.

Wells-Barnett, Ida B. *Crusade for Justice: The Autobiography of Ida B. Wells.* Edited by Alfreda M. Duster. 1970. Reprint, Chicago: University of Chicago Press, 1991.

Secondary Sources

Ali, Omar H. *In The Lion's Mouth: Black Populism in the New South, 1886–1900.* Jackson: University Press of Mississippi, 2010.

Anderson, Eric. *Race and Politics in North Carolina, 1872–1901: The Black Second.* Baton Rouge: Louisiana State University Press, 1981.

Ayers, Edward L. *The Promise of the New South: Life after Reconstruction.* New York: Oxford University Press, 1992.

Bailey, Richard. *Neither Carpetbaggers Nor Scalawags: Black Officeholders during the Reconstruction of Alabama, 1867–1878.* 3rd ed. 1991. Reprint, Montgomery, Ala.: Richard Bailey Publishers, 1995.

Bay, Mia. *To Tell the Truth Freely: The Life of Ida B. Wells.* New York: Hill and Wang, 2009.

———. *The White Image in the Black Mind: African-American Ideas about White People, 1830–1925.* Oxford: Oxford University Press, 2000.

Bederman, Gail. *Manliness and Civilization: A Cultural History of Gender and Race in the United States, 1880–1917.* Chicago: University of Chicago Press, 1995.

Bell, Derrick A., Jr. "*Brown v. Board of Education* and the Interest-Convergence Dilemma." *Harvard Law Review* 93, no. 518 (January 1980): 518–33.

Benedict, Michael Les. *Preserving the Constitution: Essays on Politics and the Constitution in the Reconstruction Era.* New York: Fordham University Press, 2006.

Bensel, Richard Franklin. *The American Ballot Box in the Mid-Nineteenth Century.* Cambridge: Cambridge University Press, 2004.

———. *The Political Economy of American Industrialization, 1877–1900.* Cambridge: Cambridge University Press, 2000.

Bercaw, Nancy D. *Gendered Freedoms: Race, Rights, and the Politics of the Household in the Delta, 1861–1875.* Gainesville: University Press of Florida, 2003.

Berlin, Ira. *Many Thousands Gone: The First Two Centuries of Slavery in North America.* Cambridge, Mass.: Harvard University Press, 1998.

Billingsley, Andrew. *Yearning to Breathe Free: Robert Smalls of South Carolina and His Families.* Columbia: University of South Carolina Press, 2007.

Blackmon, Douglas A. *Slavery by Another Name: The Re-Enslavement of Black Americans from the Civil War to World War II.* 2008. Reprint, New York: Anchor Books, 2009.

Blight, David W. *Race and Reunion: The Civil War in American Memory.* Cambridge, Mass.: Belknap Press of Harvard University Press, 2001.

Brock, Euline. "Thomas W. Cardozo: Fallible Black Reconstruction Leader." *Journal of Southern History* 47, no. 2 (May 1981): 183–206.

Brown, Canter, Jr. *Florida's Black Public Officials, 1867–1924.* Tuscaloosa: University of Alabama Press, 1998.

———. *Ossian Bingley Hart: Florida's Loyalist Reconstruction Governor.* Baton Rouge: Louisiana State University Press, 1997.

Brown, Elsa Barkley. "Negotiating and Transforming the Public Sphere: African

American Political Life in the Transition from Slavery to Freedom." *Public Culture* 7, no. 1 (Fall 1994): 107–46.

———. "Uncle Ned's Children: Negotiating Community and Freedom in Post-emancipation Richmond, Virginia." Ph.D. diss., Kent State University, 1994.

Brown, Thomas J., ed. *Reconstructions: New Perspectives on the Postbellum United States.* Oxford: Oxford University Press, 2006.

Caffey, Antonio O. "Lodge History." http://www.stmarks7.org/lodgehistory.html.

Cecelski, David S., and Timothy B. Tyson, eds. *Democracy Betrayed: The Wilmington Race Riot of 1898 and Its Legacy.* Chapel Hill: University of North Carolina Press, 1998.

Cheek, William F. "John Mercer Langston: Black Protest Leader and Abolitionist." *Civil War History* 16, no. 2 (June 1970): 101–20.

———. "A Negro Runs for Congress: John Mercer Langston and the Virginia Campaign of 1888." *Journal of Negro History* 52, no. 1 (January 1967): 14–34.

Cheek, William, and Aimee Lee Cheek. "John Mercer Langston: Principle and Politics." In Leon F. Litwack and August Meier, eds., *Black Leaders of the Nineteenth Century,* 103–26. 1988. Reprint, Urbana: University of Illinois Press, 1991.

———. *John Mercer Langston and the Fight for Black Freedom, 1829–65.* Urbana: University of Illinois Press, 1989.

Cheek, William Francis, III. "Forgotten Prophet: The Life of John Mercer Langston." Ph.D. diss., University of Virginia, 1961.

Chesterton, G. K. *Orthodoxy.* 1908. Reprint, Chicago: Moody, 2009.

Cimbala, Paul A. *Under the Guardianship of the Nation: The Freedmen's Bureau and the Reconstruction of Georgia, 1865–1870.* 1997. Reprint, Athens: University of Georgia Press, 2003.

Cox, Joseph Mason Andrew. *Great Black Men of Masonry.* 1982. Reprint, Lincoln, Neb.: iUniverse, 2002.

Cresswell, Stephen. *Multiparty Politics in Mississippi, 1877–1902.* Jackson: University Press of Mississippi, 1995.

Dailey, Jane. *Before Jim Crow: The Politics of Race in Postemancipation Virginia.* Chapel Hill: University of North Carolina Press, 2000.

Davis, Hugh. *"We Will Be Satisfied with Nothing Less": The African American Struggle for Equal Rights in the North during Reconstruction.* Ithaca, N.Y.: Cornell University Press, 2011.

Denslow, William R. *10,000 Famous Freemasons.* Vol. 4, *Q–Z.* 1957. Reprint, New Orleans: Cornerstone Book Publishers, 2007.

Dinnella-Borrego, Luis-Alejandro. "From the Ashes of the Old Dominion: Accommodation, Immediacy, and Progressive Pragmatism in John Mercer Langston's Virginia." *Virginia Magazine of History and Biography* 117, no. 3 (2009): 215–49.

———. "'That Our Government May Stand': African American Politics in the Postbellum South, 1865–1901." Ph.D. diss., Rutgers University, 2013.

Dray, Philip. *Capitol Men: The Epic Story of Reconstruction through the Lives of the First Black Congressmen.* Boston: Mariner Books, 2008.

Du Bois, Ellen Carol. *Feminism and Suffrage: The Emergence of an Independent Women's*

Movement in America, 1848–1869. 1978. Reprint, Ithaca, N.Y.: Cornell University Press, 1999.

Du Bois, W. E. B. *Black Reconstruction in America, 1860–1880*. 1935. Reprint, New York: Free Press, 1998.

Dudden, Faye E. *Fighting Chance: The Struggle for Woman's Suffrage and Black Suffrage in Reconstruction America*. New York: Oxford University Press, 2011.

Edwards, Laura F. *Gendered Strife and Confusion: The Political Culture of Reconstruction*. Urbana: University of Illinois Press, 1997.

Egerton, Douglas R. *Death or Liberty: African Americans and Revolutionary America*. Oxford: Oxford University Press, 2009.

———. *The Wars of Reconstruction: The Brief, Violent History of America's Most Progressive Era*. New York: Bloomsbury Press, 2014.

Ellison, Rhoda Coleman. *History and Bibliography of Alabama Newspapers in the Nineteenth Century*. Tuscaloosa: University of Alabama Press, 1954.

Fabian, Ann. *The Skull Collectors: Race, Science, and America's Unburied Dead*. Chicago: University of Chicago Press, 2010.

Feimster, Crystal N. *Southern Horrors: Women and the Politics of Rape and Lynching*. Cambridge, Mass.: Harvard University Press, 2009.

Ferguson, Jeffrey. "Race and the Rhetoric of Resistance." *Raritan: A Quarterly Review* 27, no. 1 (Summer 2008): 4–32.

Ferrer, Ada. *Insurgent Cuba: Race, Nation, and Revolution, 1868–1898*. Chapel Hill: University of North Carolina Press, 1999.

Fields, Barbara J. "Ideology and Race in American History." In J. Morgan Kousser and James M. McPherson, eds., *Region, Race, and Reconstruction: Essays in Honor of C. Vann Woodward*, 143–77. New York: Oxford University Press, 1982.

———. "Slavery, Race and Ideology in America." *New Left Review* 1, no. 181 (May–June 1990): 95–118.

Fitzgerald, Michael W. *The Union League Movement in the Deep South: Politics and Agricultural Change during Reconstruction*. 1989. Reprint, Baton Rouge: Louisiana State University Press, 2000.

———. *Urban Emancipation: Popular Politics in Reconstruction Mobile, 1860–1890*. Baton Rouge: Louisiana State University Press, 2002.

Foner, Eric. *The Fiery Trial: Abraham Lincoln and American Slavery*. New York: W. W. Norton, 2010.

———. *Freedom's Lawmakers: A Directory of Black Officeholders during Reconstruction*. 1993. Reprint, Baton Rouge: Louisiana State University Press, 1996.

———. *Free Soil, Free Labor, Free Men: The Ideology of the Republican Party before the Civil War*. 1970. Reprint, Oxford: Oxford University Press, 1995.

———. "Languages of Change: Sources of Black Ideology during the Civil War and Reconstruction." *Quaderno* 2 (1988): 273–88.

———. *Nothing But Freedom: Emancipation and Its Legacy*. Baton Rouge: Louisiana State University Press, 1983.

———. *Reconstruction: America's Unfinished Revolution, 1863–1877*. 1988. Reprint, New York: Perennial Classics, 2002.

Frederickson, George M. *The Black Image in the White Mind: The Debate on Afro-American Character and Destiny, 1817–1914.* 1971. Reprint, Hanover, N.H.: Wesleyan University Press, 1987.

Freehling, William W. *The Road to Disunion.* Vol. 1, *Secessionists at Bay, 1776–1854.* New York: Oxford University Press, 1990.

———. *The Road to Disunion.* Vol. 2, *Secessionists Triumphant, 1854–1861.* New York: Oxford University Press, 2007.

———. *The South vs. the South: How Anti-Confederate Southerners Shaped the Course of the Civil War.* New York: Oxford University Press, 2001.

Friend, Craig Thompson, ed. *Southern Masculinity: Perspectives on Manhood in the South since Reconstruction.* Athens: University of Georgia Press, 2009.

Gaines, Kevin K. *Uplifting the Race: Black Leadership, Politics, and Culture in the Twentieth Century.* Chapel Hill: University of North Carolina Press, 1996.

Gallagher, Gary W. *The Union War.* Cambridge, Mass.: Harvard University Press, 2011.

Gatewood, Willard B. *Aristocrats of Color: The Black Elite, 1880–1920.* 1991. Reprint, Fayetteville: University of Arkansas Press, 2000.

Genovese, Eugene D. *From Rebellion to Revolution: Afro-American Slave Revolts in the Making of the Modern World.* Baton Rouge: Louisiana State University Press, 1979.

———. *Roll, Jordan, Roll: The World the Slaves Made.* 1974. Reprint, New York: Vintage Books, 1976.

Giddings, Paula J. *Ida: A Sword among Lions.* New York: Amistad, 2008.

Gillette, William. *Retreat from Reconstruction, 1869–1879.* Baton Rouge: Louisiana State University Press, 1979.

Gilmore, Glenda Elizabeth. *Gender and Jim Crow: Women and the Politics of White Supremacy in North Carolina, 1896–1920.* Chapel Hill: University of North Carolina Press, 1996.

Glatthaar, Joseph T. *Forged in Battle: The Civil War Alliance of Black Soldiers and White Officers.* 1990. Reprint, Baton Rouge: Louisiana State University Press, 2000.

Goodman, James E. "For Love of Stories." *Reviews in American History* 26, no. 1 (March 1998): 255–74.

Hahn, Steven. "Class and State in Postemancipation Societies: Southern Planters in Comparative Perspective." *American Historical Review* 95, no. 1 (February 1990): 75–98.

———. *A Nation under Our Feet: Black Political Struggles in the Rural South from Slavery to the Great Migration.* Cambridge, Mass.: Belknap Press of Harvard University Press, 2003.

———. *The Political Worlds of Slavery and Freedom.* Cambridge, Mass.: Harvard University Press, 2009.

Hale, Grace Elizabeth. *Making Whiteness: The Culture of Segregation in the South, 1890–1940.* 1998. Reprint, New York: Vintage Books, 1999.

Halsell, Willie D. "James R. Chalmers and 'Mahoneism' in Mississippi." *Journal of Southern History* 10, no. 1 (February 1944): 37–58.

————. "Republican Factionalism in Mississippi, 1882–1884." *Journal of Southern History* 7, no. 1 (February 1941): 84–101.

Harper, Phillip Brian. *Are We Not Men? Masculine Anxiety and the Problem of African-American Identity.* New York: Oxford University Press, 1996.

Harris, William C. *The Day of the Carpetbagger: Republican Reconstruction in Mississippi.* Baton Rouge: Louisiana State University Press, 1979.

Hartzell, Lawrence L. "Black Life in Petersburg, Virginia, 1870–1902." M.A. thesis, University of Virginia, 1985.

————. "The Exploration of Freedom in Black Petersburg, Virginia, 1865–1902." In Edward L. Ayers and John C. Willis, eds., *The Edge of the South: Life in Nineteenth Century Virginia,* 134–56. Charlottesville: University Press of Virginia, 1991.

Haskins, James. *Pinckney Benton Stewart Pinchback.* New York: Macmillan, 1973.

Haskins, William A. "Rhetorical Perspectivism of Black Congressmen upon the 1875 Civil Rights Bill." Paper presented at the 70th Annual Meeting of the Speech Communication Association, Chicago, November 1–4, 1984.

————. "Rhetorical Vision of Equality: Analysis of the Rhetoric of the Southern Black Press during Reconstruction." *Communication Quarterly* 29, no. 2 (Spring 1981): 116–22.

————. "The Rhetoric of Black Congressmen, 1870–1877: An Analysis of the Rhetorical Strategies Used to Discuss Congressional Issues." Ph.D. diss., University of Oregon, 1977.

Henderson, William D. *Gilded Age City: Politics, Life and Labor in Petersburg, Virginia, 1874–1889.* Lanham, Md.: University Press of America, 1980.

Hine, Darlene Clark. "Rape and the Inner Lives of Black Women in the Middle West: Preliminary Thoughts on the Culture of Dissemblance." *Signs: Journal of Women in Culture and Society* 14, no. 4 (Summer 1989): 912–20.

Hodes, Martha. *White Women, Black Men: Illicit Sex in the 19th-Century South.* New Haven, Conn.: Yale University Press, 1997.

Hodgson, Margaret M. "For the *Record:* Revisiting and Revising Past and Present 1898 Wilmington Race Riot Narratives." M.A. thesis, University of North Carolina, Wilmington, 2010.

Hoganson, Kristin L. *Fighting for American Manhood: How Gender Politics Provoked the Spanish-American and Philippine-American Wars.* New Haven, Conn.: Yale University Press, 1998.

Holt, Michael F. *By One Vote: The Disputed Presidential Election of 1876.* Lawrence: University Press of Kansas, 2008.

————. "The Civil War and Reconstruction." Lecture, University of Virginia, Charlottesville, 19 February 2008.

————. "An Elusive Synthesis: Northern Politics during the Civil War." In James M. McPherson and William J. Cooper, eds., *Writing the Civil War: The Quest to Understand,* 112–34. 1998. Reprint, Columbia: University of South Carolina Press, 2000.

Holt, Thomas C. *Black over White: Negro Political Leaders in South Carolina during Reconstruction.* Urbana: University of Illinois Press, 1977.

————. *The Problem of Freedom: Race, Labor, and Politics in Jamaica and Britain, 1832–1938.* Baltimore: Johns Hopkins University Press, 1992.

Horsman, Reginald. *Race and Manifest Destiny: The Origins of American Racial Anglo-Saxonism.* Cambridge, Mass.: Harvard University Press, 1981.

Hosmer, John, and Joseph Fineman. "Black Congressmen in Reconstruction Historiography." *Phylon: The Atlanta University Review of Race and Culture* 39, no. 2 (2nd Quarter 1978): 97–107.

Hunter, Tera W. *To 'Joy My Freedom: Southern Black Women's Labors after the Civil War.* 1997. Reprint, Cambridge, Mass.: Harvard University Press, 1998.

Johnson, Walter. *Soul by Soul: Life Inside the Antebellum Slave Market.* Cambridge, Mass.: Harvard University Press, 1999.

Jones, Martha S. *All Bound Up Together: The Woman Question in African American Public Culture, 1830–1900.* Chapel Hill: University of North Carolina Press, 2007.

Jordan, William. "'The Damnable Dilemma': African-American Accommodation and Protest during World War I." *Journal of American History* 81, no. 4 (March 1995): 1562–83.

Justesen, Benjamin R. *George Henry White: An Even Chance in the Race of Life.* Baton Rouge: Louisiana State University Press, 2001.

Kantrowitz, Stephen. *Ben Tillman and the Reconstruction of White Supremacy.* Chapel Hill: University of North Carolina Press, 2000.

————. *More Than Freedom: Fighting for Black Citizenship in a White Republic, 1829–1889.* New York: Penguin Press, 2012.

Keller, Morton. *Affairs of State: Public Life in Nineteenth Century America.* 1977. Reprint, Union, N.J.: Lawbook Exchange, 2000.

Kelley, Robin D. G. "'We Are Not What We Seem': Rethinking Black Working-Class Opposition in the Jim Crow South." *Journal of American History* 80, no. 1 (June 1993): 75–112.

Kersh, Rogan. *Dreams of a More Perfect Union.* Ithaca, N.Y.: Cornell University Press, 2001.

Klingman, Peter D. *Josiah Walls: Florida's Black Congressman of Reconstruction.* Gainesville: University Presses of Florida, 1976.

————. *Neither Dies Nor Surrenders: A History of the Republican Party in Florida, 1867–1970.* Gainesville: University Presses of Florida, 1984.

Klingman, Peter D., and David T. Geithman. "Negro Dissidence and the Republican Party, 1864–1872." *Phylon: The Atlanta University Review of Race and Culture* 40, no. 2 (2nd Quarter 1979): 172–82.

Kolchin, Peter. "Comparative Perspectives on Emancipation in the U.S. South: Reconstruction, Radicalism, and Russia." *Journal of the Civil War Era* 2, no. 2 (June 2012): 203–32.

————. *First Freedom: The Responses of Alabama's Blacks to Emancipation and Reconstruction.* 1972. Reprint, Tuscaloosa: University of Alabama Press, 2008.

————. "Whiteness Studies: The New History of Race in America." *Journal of American History* 89, no. 1 (June 2002): 154–73.

Kousser, J. Morgan. *The Shaping of Southern Politics: Suffrage Restriction and the Estab-*

lishment of the One-Party South, 1880–1910. 1974. Reprint, New Haven, Conn.: Yale University Press, 1975.

Kramer, Paul A. *The Blood of Government: Race, Empire, the United States, and the Philippines.* Chapel Hill: University of North Carolina Press, 2006.

———. "Empires, Exceptions, and Anglo-Saxons: Race and Rule between the British and United States Empires, 1880–1910." *Journal of American History* 88, no. 4 (March 2002): 1315–53.

LaFeber, Walter. *The New Empire: An Interpretation of American Expansion, 1860–1898.* 1963. Reprint, Ithaca N.Y.: Cornell University Press, 1998.

Lamson, Peggy. *The Glorious Failure: Black Congressman Robert Brown Elliott and the Reconstruction in South Carolina.* New York: W. W. Norton, 1973.

Lears, T. J. Jackson. "The Concept of Cultural Hegemony: Problems and Possibilities." *American Historical Review* 90, no. 3 (June 1985): 567–93.

Lemann, Nicholas. *Redemption: The Last Battle of the Civil War.* New York: Farrar, Straus and Giroux, 2006.

Levine, Lawrence W. *Black Culture and Black Consciousness: Afro-American Folk Thought from Slavery to Freedom.* 1977. Reprint, New York: Oxford University Press, 2007.

Lewis, Elsie M. "The Political Mind of the Negro, 1865–1900." *Journal of Southern History* 21, no. 2 (May 1955): 189–202.

Lichtenstein, Alex. "The Roots of Black Nationalism?" *American Quarterly* 57, no. 1 (March 2005): 261–69.

Litwack, Leon F. *Been in the Storm So Long: The Aftermath of Slavery.* 1979. Reprint, New York: Vintage Books, 1980.

Logue, Cal M. "Rhetorical Ridicule of Reconstruction Blacks." *Quarterly Journal of Speech* 62, no. 4 (December 1976): 400–409.

Love, Eric T. L. *Race Over Empire: Racism & U.S. Imperialism, 1865–1900.* Chapel Hill: University of North Carolina Press, 2004.

Lynch, Matthew, ed. *Before Obama: A Reappraisal of Black Reconstruction Era Politicians.* Vol. 1, *Legacies Lost: The Life and Times of John Roy Lynch and His Political Contemporaries.* Santa Barbara, Calif.: Praeger, 2012.

———, ed. *Before Obama: A Reappraisal of Black Reconstruction Era Politicians.* Vol. 2, *Black Reconstruction Era Politicians: The Fifteenth Amendment in Flesh and Blood.* Santa Barbara, Calif.: Praeger, 2012.

Mann, Kenneth Eugene. "Black Leaders in National Politics, 1873–1943: A Study of Legislative Persuasion." Ph.D. diss., Indiana University, 1971.

Martis, Kenneth C. *The Historical Atlas of American Political Parties in the United States Congress, 1789–1989.* New York: Macmillan, 1989.

———. *The Historical Atlas of U.S. Congressional Districts, 1789–1982.* New York: Free Press, 1982.

Marzio, Peter C. *The Democratic Art, Pictures for a 19th-Century America: Chromolithography, 1840–1900.* Boston: David R. Godine, in association with the Amon Carter Museum of Western Art, Fort Worth, Tex., 1979.

McAfee, Ward M. *Religion, Race, and Reconstruction: The Public School in the Politics of the 1870s.* Albany: State University of New York Press, 1998.

McCarthy, Timothy Patrick, and John Stauffer, eds. *Prophets of Protest: Reconsidering the History of American Abolitionism.* New York: New Press, 2006.

McFeely, William S. *Grant: A Biography.* New York: W. W. Norton, 1981.

McLaughlin, James Harold. "John R. Lynch the Reconstruction Politician: A Historical Perspective." Ph.D. diss., Ball State University, 1981.

McNeilly, J. S. "The Enforcement Act of 1871 and the Ku Klux Klan in Mississippi." In Franklin L. Riley, ed., *Publications of the Mississippi Historical Society* 9 (1906): 109–71.

Meier, August. *Negro Thought in America, 1880–1915: Racial Ideologies in the Age of Booker T. Washington.* 1963. Reprint, Ann Arbor: University of Michigan Press, 1988.

Miller, Edward A., Jr. *Gullah Statesman: Robert Smalls from Slavery to Congress, 1839–1915.* 1995. Reprint, Columbia: University of South Carolina Press, 2008.

Mitchell, Michele. *Righteous Propagation: African Americans and the Politics of Racial Destiny after Reconstruction.* Chapel Hill: University of North Carolina Press, 2004.

Moore, James T. "Black Militancy in Readjuster Virginia, 1879–1883." *Journal of Southern History* 41, no. 2 (May 1975): 167–86.

Muraskin, William A. *Middle Class Blacks in a White Society: Prince Hall Freemasonry in America.* Berkeley: University of California Press, 1975.

Nash, Gary B. *The Forgotten Fifth: African Americans in the Age of Revolution.* Cambridge, Mass.: Harvard University Press, 2006.

Neely, Mark E., Jr. *The Boundaries of American Political Culture in the Civil War Era.* Chapel Hill: University of North Carolina Press, 2005.

Norell, Robert J. *Up From History: The Life of Booker T. Washington.* Cambridge, Mass.: Harvard University Press, 2009.

Nye, Robert A. *"Review Essay:* Western Masculinities in War and Peace." *American Historical Review* 112, no. 3 (April 2007): 417–38.

Oakes, James. *The Radical and the Republican: Frederick Douglass, Abraham Lincoln, and the Triumph of Antislavery Politics.* New York: W. W. Norton, 2007.

O'Donovan, Susan Eva. *Becoming Free in the Cotton South.* Cambridge, Mass.: Harvard University Press, 2007.

Ortiz, Paul. *Emancipation Betrayed: The Hidden History of Black Organizing and White Violence in Florida from Reconstruction to the Bloody Election of 1920.* Berkeley: University of California Press, 2005.

Oshinsky, David M. *"Worse Than Slavery": Parchman Farm and the Ordeal of Jim Crow Justice.* 1996. Reprint, New York: Free Press Paperbacks, 1997.

Painter, Nell Irvin. *Exodusters: Black Migration to Kansas after Reconstruction.* 1977. Reprint, New York: W. W. Norton, 1992.

Parsons, Elaine Frantz. "Klan Skepticism and Denial in Reconstruction-Era Public Discourse." *Journal of Southern History* 77, no. 1 (February 2011): 53–90.

Perman, Michael. *Struggle for Mastery: Disfranchisement in the South, 1888–1908.* Chapel Hill: University of North Carolina Press, 2001.

Poyo, Gerald E. "Cuban Revolutionaries and Monroe County Reconstruction Politics, 1868–1876." *Florida Historical Quarterly* 55, no. 4 (April 1977): 407–22.

————. "Key West and the Cuban Ten Years War." *Florida Historical Quarterly* 57, no. 3 (January 1979): 289–307.

Prather, H. Leon. *We Have Taken a City: The Wilmington Racial Massacre and Coup of 1898*. 1984. Reprint, Wilmington, N.C.: Dram Tree Books, 2006.

Rable, George C. *But There Was No Peace: The Role of Violence in the Politics of Reconstruction*. 1984. Reprint, Athens: University of Georgia Press, 2007.

Rawley, James A. "The General Amnesty Act of 1872: A Note." *Mississippi Valley Historical Review* 47, no. 3 (December 1960): 480–84.

Rhodes, James Ford. *History of the United States from the Compromise of 1850 to the Final Restoration of Home Rule at the South 1877*. Vol. 7, *1872–1877*. New York: Macmillan, 1909.

Richardson, Heather Cox. *The Death of Reconstruction: Race, Labor, and Politics in the Post–Civil War North, 1865–1901*. Cambridge, Mass.: Harvard University Press, 2001.

Richardson, Joe M. *African Americans in the Reconstruction of Florida, 1865–1877*. 1965. Reprint, Tuscaloosa: University of Alabama Press, 2008.

Riser, R. Volney. "The Burdens of Being White: Empire and Disfranchisement." *Alabama Law Review* 53, no. 1 (Fall 2001): 243–72.

————. *Defying Disfranchisement: Black Voting Rights Activism in the Jim Crow South, 1890–1908*. Baton Rouge: Louisiana State University Press, 2010.

Roediger, David R. *The Wages of Whiteness: Race and the Making of the American Working Class*. 1991. Reprint, London: Verso, 2007.

Rosen, Hannah. *Terror in the Heart of Freedom: Citizenship, Sexual Violence, and the Meaning of Race in the Postemancipation South*. Chapel Hill: University of North Carolina Press, 2009.

Samito, Christian G. *Becoming American under Fire: Irish Americans, African Americans, and the Politics of Citizenship during the Civil War Era*. Ithaca, N.Y.: Cornell University Press, 2009.

Savage, Kirk. *Standing Soldiers, Kneeling Slaves: Race, War, and Monument in Nineteenth-Century America*. Princeton, N.J.: Princeton University Press, 1997.

Saville, Julie. *The Work of Reconstruction: From Slave to Wage Laborer in South Carolina, 1860–1870*. Cambridge: Cambridge University Press, 1994.

Schama, Simon. *Dead Certainties (Unwarranted Speculations)*. 1991. Reprint, New York: Vintage Books, 1992.

Schecter, Patricia Ann. *Ida B. Wells-Barnett and American Reform, 1880–1930*. Chapel Hill: University of North Carolina Press, 2001.

Schweninger, Loren. *James T. Rapier and Reconstruction*. Chicago: University of Chicago Press, 1978.

Scott, Rebecca J. *Degrees of Freedom: Louisiana and Cuba after Slavery*. Cambridge, Mass.: Harvard University Press, 2005.

————. "Public Rights, Social Equality, and the Conceptual Roots of the *Plessy* Challenge." *Michigan Law Review* 106, no. 5 (March 2008): 777–804.

Seip, Terry L. *The South Returns to Congress: Men, Economic Measures, and Intersectional Relationships, 1868–1879*. Baton Rouge: Louisiana State University Press, 1983.

Shofner, Jerrell H. *Nor Is It Over Yet: Florida in the Era of Reconstruction, 1863–1877.*
　　Gainesville: University Presses of Florida, 1974.

Smith, Jean Edward. *Grant.* New York: Simon and Schuster, 2001.

Span, Christopher M. *From Cotton Field to Schoolhouse: African American Education in*
　　Mississippi, 1862–1875. Chapel Hill: University of North Carolina Press, 2009.

Stanley, Amy Dru. *From Bondage to Contract: Wage Labor, Marriage, and the Market in*
　　the Age of Slave Emancipation. Cambridge: Cambridge University Press, 1998.

State Historic Preservation Office, South Carolina Department of Archives and His-
　　tory. "African American Historic Places in South Carolina" (June 2009): 4–5.

Sugrue, Thomas J. *Not Even Past: Barack Obama and the Burden of Race.* Princeton,
　　N.J.: Princeton University Press, 2010.

Summers, Mark Wahlgren. *Party Games: Getting, Keeping, and Using Power in Gilded*
　　Age Politics. Chapel Hill: University of North Carolina Press, 2004.

Summers, Martin. *Manliness and Its Discontents: The Black Middle Class and the Trans-*
　　formation of Masculinity, 1900–1930. Chapel Hill: University of North Carolina
　　Press, 2004.

Taylor, Alrutheus A. "Negro Congressmen a Generation After." *Journal of Negro His-*
　　tory 7, no. 2 (April 1922): 127–71.

Terborg-Penn, Rosalyn. "Black Male Perspectives on the Nineteenth-Century
　　Woman." In Sharon Harley and Rosalyn Terborg-Penn, eds., *The Afro-American*
　　Woman: Struggles and Images, 28–42. Port Washington, N.Y.: Kennikat Press, 1978.

Thompson, Margaret Susan. *The "Spider Web": Congress and Lobbying in the Age of*
　　Grant. Ithaca, N.Y.: Cornell University Press, 1986.

Tindall, George Brown. *South Carolina Negroes, 1877–1900.* 1952. Reprint, Columbia:
　　University of South Carolina Press, 2003.

Toll, William. "Free Men, Freedmen, and Race: Black Social Theory in the Gilded
　　Age." *Journal of Southern History* 44, no. 4 (November 1978): 571–96.

———. *The Resurgence of Race: Black Social Theory from Reconstruction to the Pan-*
　　African Conferences. Philadelphia: Temple University Press, 1979.

Trouillot, Michel-Rolph. *Silencing the Past: Power and the Production of History.* Boston:
　　Beacon Press, 1995.

Umfleet, LeRae Sikes. *A Day of Blood: The 1898 Wilmington Race Riot.* Raleigh:
　　North Carolina Office of Archives and History, 2009.

———. "1898 Wilmington Race Riot Report Draft." Raleigh: Research Branch,
　　Office of Archives and History, North Carolina Department of Archives and His-
　　tory, 2005.

Upchurch, Thomas Adams. *Legislating Racism: The Billion Dollar Congress and the*
　　Birth of Jim Crow. Lexington: University Press of Kentucky, 2004.

Vorenberg, Michael. *Final Freedom: The Civil War, the Abolition of Slavery, and the*
　　Thirteenth Amendment. Cambridge: Cambridge University Press, 2001.

Welch, Richard E., Jr. "The Federal Elections Bill of 1890: Postscripts and Prelude."
　　Journal of American History 52, no. 3 (December 1965): 511–26.

Wharton, Vernon Lane. *The Negro in Mississippi, 1865–1890.* 1947. Reprint, West-
　　port, Conn.: Greenwood Publishers, 1965.

White, Deborah Gray. *A'rn't I a Woman? Female Slaves in the Plantation South*. 1985. Reprint, New York: W. W. Norton, 1999.

Williams, Andrea Heather. *Self-Taught: African American Education in Slavery and Freedom*. Chapel Hill: University of North Carolina Press, 2005.

Willis, John C. *Forgotten Time: The Yazoo-Mississippi Delta after the Civil War*. Charlottesville: University Press of Virginia, 2000.

Woodward, C. Vann. *Origins of the New South, 1877–1913*. 1951. Reprint, Baton Rouge, Louisiana State University Press, 2006.

———. *The Strange Career of Jim Crow*. 1955. Reprint, New York: Oxford University Press, 2002.

Zuczek, Richard. *State of Rebellion: Reconstruction in South Carolina*. Columbia: University of South Carolina Press, 1996.

INDEX

Page numbers in italic refer to illustrations.

abolitionism, 4, 10, 19, 25, 90

African Methodist Episcopal Church, 24, 35, 36; *A.M.E. Church Review,* 209–10

Akerman, Amos T., 56–57, 82

Alabama, 28–20, 30, 37–42, 43, 48, 49–50, 59–60, 68, 69, 70, 113, 148–49

Alcorn, James L., 47–48, 133

American Protective Society to Prevent Injustice to the Colored People, 144

Ames, Adelbert, 33

Amnesty Act, 12, 82–85

Anthony, Susan B., 72

Arkansas, 113, 115

Arnold, Richard W., 167, 170

Arthur, Chester A., 39

Attucks, Crispus, 25

Baker, Frazier B., 196

Barnett, Ferdinand L., 143, 146

Bates, Edward, 102

Bay, Mia, 114

Beck, James, 105

Bederman, Gail, 98

Billings, Liberty, 36

Bird, John, 127–30

Bisbee, Horatio, Jr., 158–59

black churches, 166–67

black citizenship, 4, 21, 22, 25–26, 28, 34, 56, 60, 95–96, 102–4, 182, 191, 235n63

Black Codes, 34, 54

Black Convention Movement, 24, 52

black manhood, 4, 21–22, 27, 29–30, 47, 56, 60, 98–99, 106, 109, 150, 154, 180, 182

black nationalism, 4, 7, 94, 96

black military service, 11, 17–26, 47, 56, 93, 99, 101, 182–83, 191; Massachusetts Colored Regiments, 18, 20, 21, 184; Ohio Colored Regiment, 20; United States Colored Troops, 19

black resistance and militancy, 24, 41–42, 49–50, 69, 107, 120, 122, 134, 183–84; black-on-black militancy, 128, 131; slave rebellions, 114

black women: political activism, 128–30, 166, 185, 189; Sapphire stereotype, 130, 166, 240n51; virtue and, 27, 109, 190

Blaine, James G., 84–85, 216

Brady, James, 168

Bragg, George F., Jr., 168, 246n79

Bright, John Morgan, 105

Broom, Bob, 183

Brown, John, *45, 46*

Bruce, Blanche Kelso, 120, 133–34, 156, 209–10

Burgess, John W., 213

Burke, Robert E., 204

Butler, Benjamin, 82

Butler, J. M., 38–39

Butler, Matthew C., 120, 182

Buxton (utopian community), 37

Cain, Richard Harvey, 47, 52, 71, 141

Cameron, William E., 165, 166, 168

Cardozo, Francis L., 139, 143–44

Cardozo, Thomas W., 143–44

Céspedes, Carlos Manuel de, 96

Chalmers, James R., 152

Chamberlain, Daniel, 120–21, 123, 126, 127

Chase, Calvin, 189

Cheatham, Henry Plummer, 163

Cheek, William F. and Aimee Lee, 169, 247n93
Chesterton, G. K., 222n15
Christian Recorder, 24, 74, 174
Civil Rights Act (1866), 34, 83, 89, 95, 156
Civil Rights Act (1875), 4, 10, 71, 89–91, 96, 101–13, 130, 149, 160, 215; declared unconstitutional, 156–57
Civil Rights Cases, 156–57, 160
Civil War, motivations for, 23, 60–61, 114
Clawson, Thomas W., 198
Cleveland, Grover, 168
Collins, John, 161
Colored American, 199, 210–11
Colored National Labor Union, 90
compromises and conciliation, 8, 14, 84, 95, 178, 184, 216. *See also* fusion voting
Crisp, Charles F., 160
Crumpacker, Edgar D., 203
Cuba, 5, 69, 71, 94, 96–101, 104, 195–96, 202; *Virginius* incident, 97, *98*
Cuney, Norris Wright, 209

Dailey, Jane, 244n35
Daniels, Josephus, 204–6
Declaration of Independence, 201–2
Delaney, Martin, *45*
De Large, Robert Carlos, 52, 71, 83, 84, 87
Dingley, Nelson, Jr., 195
District of Columbia, 53, 66, 70, 149
Dockery, Oliver, 84
Dominican Republic, 100–101
Dougherty, Charles, 159
Douglass, Frederick, 8, 9–10, 23, 43, *45,* 46, 57, 90, 107, 156, 193, 210, 216; background, 21, 169; emigration opposition, 141–42, 145, 169; Fourth of July speech, 106; Langston rivalry, 6, 169–70, 171, 247n93; on portraits, 226n5; Wells and, 186; women's rights and, 72

Downing, George Thomas, 10, 90, 107, 216
Dray, Philip, 3
Dred Scott decision, 102
Du Bois, W. E. B., 9, 176, 254n15
Dudden, Faye E., 72
Dunning, William Archibald, 213, 215
DuPont, Samuel, 19

education, 29, 32–33, 42, 45, 52, 54, 85–87, 89, 91, 149, 164, 179, 236n83; segregated schools, 4, 103–4, 110–11; vocational, 115–16
Egerton, Douglas R., 3
Elliott, H. D., 122–23
Elliot, Robert Brown, 52–53, 71, 83, 84, 87; Civil Rights Bill and, 90, 91–94, *92,* 95
emancipation movement, 11, 21, 23–25
Emancipation Proclamation, 24, 31
emancipatory diplomacy, 96–101, 104–5, 195–96, 202, 205
emigration, 8, 10, 12–13, 96, 100, 140–51, 173, 182, 187, 199–200, 206–7, 221n18, 243n34
Enforcement Acts, 82
Evans, Joseph, 168

Farmers' Alliance, 141
Federal Elections Bill (Force Bill), 176–78, 180
Federal Electoral Commission, 12, 131–32
Felton, Rebecca Latimer, 198
Fifteenth Amendment, 11, 43–47, 82, 176, 201; lithographs celebrating, *45–46*
Fish, Hamilton, 97
Fitzgerald, Michael W., 242n11
Florida, 17, 19, 35–37, 50–52, 55, 68, 69, 73–74, 113; Cuban population, 97; violence in, 79–81, 84, 113, 158
Foner, Eric, 7
Forster, C. W., 26

Fortune, Timothy Thomas, 8, 9, 176, 189, 216
Fourteenth Amendment, 34–35, 83, 92–93, 180, 206, 248n14
Franklin, John Hope, 32
fraternal orders, 45, 46
Freedmen's Bureau, 1, 10, 24, 27, 30, 35, 49, 169
Friend, Craig Thompson, 4
Fuller, Henry H., 122, 123
Fusionist movement, 175, 194, 197, 200
fusion voting, 8, 12–13, 135, 141–42, 151–56, 164, 172–74, 194, 216, 242n10

Garfield, James A., 26, 216
Garrison, William Lloyd, 43
Gary, Martin W., 120–21
Georgia, 17, 57, 69, 86–87
gerrymandering, 161–62, 165
Gibbs, Jonathan Clarkson, 35–37, 80
Gibbs, Mifflin Wistar, 10, 107, 117–18, 143, 147
Gilmore, Glenda, 28
Gleaves, Robert, 122
Gooding, James Henry, 18
Gordon, John Brown, 113
Grange Movement, 131
Grant, Ulysses S., 39, *45*, 49, 56–58, 65, 82, 83–84, 88, 100–101, 113; Lynch meeting, 116–17
Greenback Party, 8, 141, 151–52, 153, 155
Griggs, James M., 205

Hahn, Steven, 7, 220n17
Hampton, Wade, 121, 126, 128, 160, 182
Haralson, Jeremiah, 70, 120
Harper, Frances Ellen Watkins, 72
Harper, Phillip Brian, 29, 109
Harrison, Benjamin, 182
Hart, Ossian Bingley, 35, 36, 224n55
Haskell, Alexander, 181–82
Hawley, James A., 30–31
Hayes, Rutherford B., 132–34, 215

Hays, Charles, 40, 216
Hill, Robert A., 88
Hine, Darlene Clark, 220n12
Hoganson, Kristin L., 99
Holt, Michael F., 244
Honey, Michael, 153, 244n35
Hose, Sam, 205
Howard, Oliver Otis, 28, 169
Hughes, Langston, vii, 13, 217
Hunter, David, 17
Hyman, John Adams, 120

Independent movement, 158
Indiana, 147
interracial relationships, 186, 188–92, 198

Jacobson, E. P., 88
Jim Crow laws, 7, 142, 160, 192, 197
Johnson, Andrew, 32, 33–34, 66
Johnson, John H., 56
Jones, Martha S., 26, 72
Joseph, Philip, 10, 107, 236n71

Kansas, 141, 146, 147–48, 150, 243n34
Kantrowitz, Stephen, 4, 182
Keller, Morton, 65, 97
Kentucky, 27, 109
King, Benjamin, 152
King, William, 37
Kousser, J. Morgan, 248n5
Ku Klux Klan, 38–41, 48–50, 57, 79–81, 82, 87, 88–89, 120, 141
Ku Klux Klan Act, 12, 49, 70, 82, 88–89, 197

Lamar, L. Q. C., 58, 132
Langston, John Mercer, 4, 5–6, 9–10, 13, 24–28, 42, 43–44, 47, 57, 96, *103*, 117–18, 164–70, 174, 210–11, 216–17, 247n96; abolitionism and, 10, 20, 21; background, 3, 19–22, 102, 184, 223n27; on black citizenship, 100–105,

Langston, John Mercer (*continued*)
156; *Civil Rights Cases* and, 156–57;
college presidency, 166, 167; congressional activities, 89, 94, 107, 176–78,
233nn32–33; on education, 115–16,
179; election of 1888, campaign, 6,
165, 168–72, 184; elitism, 29–30; emigrationism, 135, 141–42, 169, 241n9;
"Equality before the Law" speech, 24,
102–5, 156; religious beliefs, 27–28, 29;
Union Leagues and, 10, 28, 49–50; on
voting procedures, 177–80, 248n14;
Wells opposition, 184–86, 249n27;
women's rights and, 25–26, 71–72
Lee, Joseph E., 158
Legare, Hugh S., 102
Lewis, Elsie M., 227n16
Lewis, M. N., 170–71
Liberia, 140–41, 150
Lincoln, Abraham, 24–25, *45, 46,* 65–66
Lincoln Brotherhood, 35, 36
Linney, Romulus Z., 204
literacy, 52, 59, 179; literacy tests, 5–6,
178–79, 186–87, 203
Lodge, Henry Cabot, 176, 180
Long, Jefferson Franklin, 52, 74, 83
"Lost Cause" ideology, 95
Louisiana, 51, 113, 143–44, 183, 203
Love, Eric T. L., 100
Loyal League of America (Mule Team),
35–36
Lynch, John Roy, 3, 9, 13, 37, 50, 58,
60, 91, 143–45, 211, 212–16, 237n12,
243n33; background, 31–33, 42;
congressional activities, 69, 70, 85,
89–90, 94, 107–11, 120, 123–25, 130,
151–56, 174, 193; criticism of, 192–93;
on emigration, 141, 145, 147, 150–51;
Grant meeting, 116–17, 212, 215; Hayes
opposition, 132–33; Rhodes criticism,
213–15
lynching, 10, 13, 174, 183–86, 188–89,
192, 198, 203–5

MacIntyre, Archibald Thompson,
86–87, 90
Mahan, Alfred Thayer, 100
Mahone, William, 166, 167–71
Manly, Alexander, 10, 175, 198, 204
Martí, José, 96
Masons, 3, 44–45
McAfee, Ward M., 111, 237n85
McCrea, George, 80
McKee, John K., 17
McKinley, William, 196
McNeilly, J. S., 227n8
Meridian Riot, 12, 48–49, 70, 88, 197,
232n27
Micow, J. M., 68
migration. *See* emigration
Miller, Edward A., 190, 241n4
Miller, Thomas Ezekiel, 171
miscegenation. *See* interracial marriage
Mississippi, 25, 29–30, 32, 42, 58–59,
69, 143, 164, 203, 213; violence in, 12,
47–50, 70, 79, 88, 113, 116, 123–25, 132,
150, 183; voter fraud in, 202
Missouri, 57
Mitchell, Michelle, 190, 243n32
Money, Hernando De Soto, 203
Monroe Doctrine, 98
Moore, B. F., 48
Moore, James Tice, 166
Mustifer, John, 129–30
Myers, Frank, 79
Myers, George A., 213–14

Napier, James C., 143, 146
Nash, Charles, 120
National Convention of Colored Men,
12, 117–19, 143–47, 150–51
New York Age, 9, 170, 179, 216
Nickerson, James, 18–19
North Carolina, 13, 57, 161–64, 175,
194–200, 203
Nye, Robert A., 222n12

Obama, Barack, 2, 13, 209
Osborn, Thomas W., 35, 36–37

Perce, Legrande Winfield, 58, 86–87
Phillips, Wendell, 72
Pinchback, P. B. S., 10, 57–58, 107, 117–19, 143–44, 210–11
Pledger, William A., 143
Populist (People's) Party, 8, 141, 163, 194
presidential election of 1876, 12, 111, 131–32
presidential office, 65–66
Price, George W., Jr., 10, 107, 236n71
Purvis, Charles Burleigh, 107, 236n71
Purvis, Robert, 107, 236n71

Quarles, Ralph, 19–20
Quay, Matthew, 169

Rable, George C., 82, 240n45
racial uplift, 28, 45–47, 93, 99, 101, 190
racism, 7, 22, 26, 31, 95–96, 100–101, 104–6, 125–26, 148, 164, 212, 215, 250n38; in Congress, 67; in War Department, 223n27
Rainey, Joseph Hayne, 52, 71, 83, 84, 87, 90, 95, 120, 143, 146
Ransier, Alonzo Jacob, 47, 52, 71, 90, 111
Rapier, James Thomas, 4–5, 9–10, *38*, 39–41, 43, 50, 52, 59–60, 143; background, 3, 37–38, 42; congressional activities, 68, 70, 85, 89–90, 94, 101, 105–7, 111; death, 174; emigration and, 13, 135, 141, 146–50, 215–16, 241n9; Grant and, 56
Readjuster Party, 8, 141, 142, 153, 164–68, 173, 246n79; vs. Funders, 164
Reconstruction Acts, 35, 38, 103
Red Shirts, 1–2, 120, 180, 182
Reed, Harrison, 35, 37
Revels, Hiram Rhodes, *45*, 46, 70, 83
Rhodes, James Ford, 13, 213–15
Richards, Daniel, 36

Richardson, Heather Cox, 5
Richardson, James D., 203–4
Richmond Planet, 170, 183, 199
riots: Combahee, 121–23; Memphis, 34, 88; Meridian, 12, 48–49, 70, 88, 197, 232n27; New Orleans, 34; Wilmington, 13, 197–99, 204, 252n63
Robinson, Henderson B., 145–46, 242nn19–20
Roosevelt, Theodore, 100, 176
Rosen, Hannah, 34, 94, 235n63
Rountree, Doc, 81
Russell, Daniel L., 194

Saunders, William U., 36
Savage, Kirk, 21, 99
Schama, Simon, 14
Seip, Terry L., 84
Shellabarger, Samuel, 82
Slaughter-House Cases, 92–93
slavery, 6, 17–19, 21, 23–25, 30–32, 42, 44, 61, 72, 90–92, 114, 125, 178, 190
Smalls, Robert, 13, 73, *121;* background, 17, 190; bribery scandal, 139–40, 144; in Civil War, 3, 10, 17–19, 20–21, 42; congressional activities, 69, 119–23, 125–27, 132, 160, 174; education issues, 85; election campaigns, 1–2, 6, 127–31, 140, 166; emigration opposition, 141, 187; female suffrage and, 47, 71; later political career, 180–83, 186–92, 199, 200
Smalls, Sarah, 250n36
South Carolina, 5, 12, 17–19, 21, 23, 52, 57, 69, 125, 139, 180, 186–92, 203, 238n22; emigration from, 140–41, 143; violence in, 1–2, 120–23, 126–28, 131, 132, 140, 196; voter fraud in, 180–81, 187, 202
Southern States Convention of Colored Men, 52–58, 60–61
Spanish-American War, 99, 176, 195–96, 197, 200–201

Stanton, Elizabeth Cady, 72
states' rights theory, 86, 90–91, 132, 176, 179
Stephens, Alexander H., *91*
Stevens, Thaddeus, *45*
Still, William, 143
Stone, William, 122
strikes, 32, 69, 121–23, 129
suffrage, 34–35, 43, 47, 72–73, 104, 174, 177–78, 186, 192, 201–2, 248n5
Sumner, Charles, 4, 10, 12, 84, 89–90, 100–101, 176. *See also* Civil Rights Act (1875)

Taylor, Julius F., 192–93
Tennessee, 37, 57, 109, 117
Tennessee Negro Suffrage Convention, 37
Ten Years' War, 5, 71, 96–97, 100
Terborg-Penn, Rosalyn, 189
Texas, 189
Thirteenth Amendment, 11, 24–25, 34, 56
Thompson, Margaret, 66
Thornton, E. L., 179
Tilden, Samuel J., 132, 133
Tillman, Ben, 127, 180–82, 186–91, 206
Tillman, George Dionysius, 127, 130, 131
Tindall, George Brown, 141
Towne, Laura M., 1–2
tradition, Chesterton on, 222n15
Truth, Sojourner, 72–73
Turner, Benjamin S., 70, 83, 84, 87
Turner, Nat, 114
Tuskegee Outrage, 38–39, 70
Tutson, Samuel and Hannah, 80

Umfleet, LeRae Sikes, 251n57, 252n63
Union League, 10, 24, 28, 49–50, 69
Union-Republican Club, 35, 36
United States Congress, 12, 65–78, 81–84, 89–90, 94, 105, 107–8, 111–12, 113,
120, 135, 171, 176, 206, 209; corruption, 65, 66, 70, 140; patronage system, 65, 66, 68, 140

Vance, Zebulon, 148–49
Varon, Elizabeth, 34
Venable, Edward C., 170
violence and intimidation, 1–2, 6, 11–12, 34, 37, 38–40, 47–50, 70, 79–82, 87–90, 111–12, 113, 116–17, 120–24, 140–41, 153, 183, 192, 205–6, 214; rape, 94–95. *See also* individual states; lynching
Virginia, 13, 19–20, 23, 28, 57, 164–72, 178

Walker, David, 114
Walker, G. W., 185
Walls, Josiah Thomas, 5, 13, *51*, 79–80, 135; in Civil War, 3, 19, 21, 42, 85; congressional activities, 68, 69, 71, 73–74, 78, 81, 83–87, 89–90, 94–96, 103, 111, 113–15, 120, 232n15; early political career, 36–37, 50–58; emancipatory diplomacy, 96–101, 104, 196; later political career, 157–59, 174, 245n60
Ward, John M., 41
Warren, Henry W., 49
Washington, Booker T., 9–10, 176, 193
Welch, Richard, 176–77
Wells, Ida B., 8, 9–10, 143, 176, 184–86, 188, 196–98
West Virginia, 57
White, George Henry, 9–10, 13, 161–63, *162*, 174; background, 3, 161; congressional career, 194–97, 199–207, 216; praised by Obama, 209; Whitesboro and, 206–7
White League, 124
white supremacism, 94, 99–101, 153, 180, 186, 188, 191, 193–95, 197, 201–2, 212
Williams, Alfred Brokenbrough, 140
Williams, John Sharp, 200–201

Williams v. Mississippi, 303
Windom, William, 146–49
Wirt, William, 102
Wise, John S., 167, 168
women's rights, 25–26, 47, 71–73

Woodruff, Josephus, 139
World's Columbian Exposition, 98–99

Young Men's Democratic Club, 79

THE AMERICAN SOUTH SERIES

Anne Goodwyn Jones and
Susan V. Donaldson, editors
*Haunted Bodies:
Gender and Southern Texts*

M. M. Manring
*Slave in a Box:
The Strange Career of Aunt Jemima*

Stephen Cushman
*Bloody Promenade:
Reflections on a Civil War Battle*

John C. Willis
*Forgotten Time:
The Yazoo-Mississippi Delta
after the Civil War*

Charlene M. Boyer Lewis
*Ladies and Gentlemen on Display:
Planter Society at the Virginia Springs,
1790–1860*

Christopher Metress, editor
*The Lynching of Emmett Till:
A Documentary Narrative*

Dianne Swann-Wright
*A Way out of No Way:
Claiming Family and Freedom
in the New South*

James David Miller
*South by Southwest:
Planter Emigration and Identity
in the Slave South*

Richard F. Hamm
*Murder, Honor, and Law:
Four Virginia Homicides from
Reconstruction to the Great Depression*

Andrew H. Myers
*Black, White, and Olive Drab:
Racial Integration at Fort Jackson, South
Carolina, and the Civil Rights Movement*

Bruce E. Baker
*What Reconstruction Meant:
Historical Memory in the American South*

Stephen A. West
*From Yeoman to Redneck in the South
Carolina Upcountry, 1850–1915*

Randolph Ferguson Scully
*Religion and the Making of Nat Turner's
Virginia: Baptist Community and
Conflict, 1740–1840*

Deborah Beckel
*Radical Reform: Interracial Politics in
Post-Emancipation North Carolina*

Terence Finnegan
*A Deed So Accursed:
Lynching in Mississippi and
South Carolina, 1881–1940*

Reiko Hillyer
*Designing Dixie:
Tourism, Memory, and
Urban Space in the New South*

Luis-Alejandro Dinnella-Borrego
*The Risen Phoenix: Black Politics
in the Post–Civil War South*